Fodor's
SICILY

Welcome to Sicily

A visit to the island of Sicily will put you face-to-face with an abundance of history and a collection of stunning landscapes. Some of the world's best-preserved Byzantine mosaics stand adjacent to magnificent Greek temples and Roman amphitheaters. Add the spectacular sight of Mt. Etna plus Sicily's unique cuisine—mingling Arab and Greek spices and Spanish and French techniques—and you understand why visitors continue to be drawn here. As you plan your upcoming travels to Sicily, please confirm that places are still open and let us know when we need to make updates by writing to us at editors@fodors.com.

TOP REASONS TO GO

★ **Beaches:** Resorts like Taormina are as close to perfection as a panorama can get.

★ **Food:** One of the oldest cuisines in existence, Sicilian food reflects the island's unique cultural mix, with delicious results.

★ **Architecture:** Virtually every great European empire ruled Sicily at some point, and it shows most of all in the diverse architecture, from Roman to Byzantine to Arab-Norman.

★ **Temples:** From Agrigento to Selinunte, not even in Athens will you find ancient Greek temples this finely preserved.

Contents

Chapter 1

EXPERIENCE SICILY

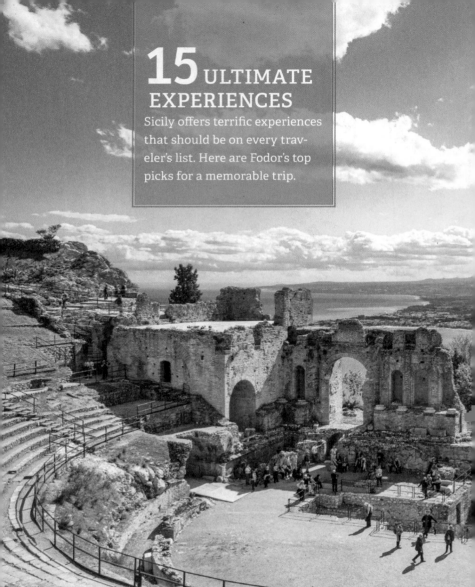

15 ULTIMATE EXPERIENCES

Sicily offers terrific experiences that should be on every traveler's list. Here are Fodor's top picks for a memorable trip.

1 Taormina

Luxurious glamour, seductive boutiques, archaeological appeal, and riveting scenery, all infused with a sophisticated exuberance, make the resort town of Taormina an unmissable stop. *(Ch. 6)*

2 Siracusa and Ortigia Island

Sicily's earliest Greek settlers picked a perfect site for their new city, which became one of the island's most powerful states and continues to fascinate. *(Ch. 7)*

3 Mount Etna

Sicily's eastern seaboard is dominated by the looming giant of Etna, a constant presence that is snow-capped for much of the year, emitting delicate wisps of vapor. *(Ch. 6)*

4 The Aeolian Islands

Visitors to this chain of volcanoes off Sicily's north coast can expect to find lively ports and resorts, sheltered coves, and remote wildernesses. *(Ch. 5)*

5 Palermo's Architecture

Sicily's hectic capital contains a rich smorgasbord of diverse architectural styles, from the exquisite intricacies of Norman-Arab to the swirling flamboyance of the Baroque. *(Ch. 3)*

6 Selinunte Temples

Hardly changed since it fell victim to a Carthaginian attack in the 5th century BC, the site of ancient Selinus is one of Italy's most extensive archaeological sites, well worth a wander. *(Ch. 8)*

7 Sicilian Markets

Boisterous street markets are the heart and soul of every Sicilian town and village, good for snacking on hot fried goodies or picking up armfuls of the freshest fruits and vegetables. *(Ch. 3–8)*

8 Wine

Once derided as only good for blending with superior varieties, Sicilian wines have undergone a revolution in recent years and the island's viniculture is now highly respected by the wine world. *(Ch. 3–8)*

9 Marsala Salt Pans

Although Sicily is full of visual surprises, it still comes as quite a shock to stumble across this flat area of dazzling white salt pans on the coast between Marsala and Trapani. *(Ch. 3)*

10 Seafood

Foodies can't get enough of the products of the seas that surround Sicily, whether proffered at street stalls, chalked on the walls of trattorias, or inscribed on the menus of refined restaurants. *(Ch. 3–8)*

11 Valley of the Temples

Often described as the greatest ensemble of classical architecture outside Greece, the Valley of the Temples presents a stunning vista outside the south-coast city of Agrigento. *(Ch. 8)*

12 Villa Romana del Casale

The evocative mosaics of the Villa Romana del Casale, outside Piazza Armerina, offer fascinating, instructive, and entertaining insights into the daily life and culture of the Roman aristocracy. *(Ch. 8)*

13 Cefalù

Sheltered beneath a rocky spur on the northern coast, Cefalù comprises a maze of medieval lanes that stretches between one of Italy's grandest Norman cathedrals and a pretty curve of beach. *(Ch. 4)*

14 Beaches

Sicily's three coasts and its offshore isles provide a rich selection of beaches, ranging from the black sands of Stromboli to the white strand of San Vito Lo Capo. *(Ch. 3, 4, 5, 8)*

15 Monreale Cathedral

Located outside Palermo, Sicily's finest cathedral is a dazzling example of the achievements of the Greek, Arab, and Jewish artisans who collaborated on it. *(Ch. 3)*

WHAT'S WHERE

1 Palermo and Western Sicily. The frenetic grandeur of Sicily's capital is in marked contrast to the rolling landscapes to its west, dotted with archaeological sites and lofty hilltowns and fringed by fishing ports and golden beaches.

2 The Tyrrhenian Coast. Cefalù is the jewel and most compelling town on Sicily's northern coastline, but wander away from the water to discover an equally entrancing inland world, including the scenic beauty of Piano Battaglia and the Parco Regionale dei Nebrodi and ultra-traditional villages like Castelbuono, Caccamo, Petralia Soprana, and Petralla Sottana.

3 The Aeolian Islands. Island-hopping between this archipelago of seven islands can become addictive, as each island reveals a distinctive character and mood. Lipari, the hub of the transport system, is the name of both the main island and the main town and in summer thrums with life, while in winter the Aeolians can be very quiet indeed.

4 Mount Etna and Eastern Sicily. Formidable Mount Etna is

Sicily's most striking physical feature and will lure you up its lava-strewn slopes. The volcano is easily visible from Sicily's glitziest resort, Taormina, and its black volcanic stone has gone into the buildings that make up the teeming streets of Catania, whose lively markets keep the region's restaurants well stocked.

5 Siracusa and the Southeast. Ancient Syracuse—now Siracusa—is replete with historic remains but is not short on cafés and good restaurants either. The dominant architectural style here is Baroque, which finds its full apotheosis in such inland towns of Noto, Ragusa, and Modica.

6 Central Sicily and the Mediterranean Coast. Sicily's under-populated interior is well worth investigating for Caltagirone's celebrated ceramics and the beautiful Roman mosaics of the Villa Romana del Casale, outside Piazza Armerina. A short drive away, the chief attraction on Sicily's south coast is Agrigento's Valle dei Templi, a stunning set of Greek ruins set amid almond groves.

Sicily Today

Sicily has beckoned seafaring wanderers since the trials of Odysseus were first sung in Homer's Odyssey—an epic that is sometimes called the world's first travel guide. Strategically poised between Europe and Africa, this mystical land of three corners and a fiery volcano once hosted two of the most enlightened capitals of the West: Siracusa and Palermo. And it has been a melting pot of every great civilization on the Mediterranean—Greek and Roman, then Arab and Norman, and finally French, Spanish, and Italian. Luckily for visitors, this means that the Sicily of today is just as complicated, fascinating, and diverse as it always has been.

THE NATURAL WORLD

For decades, Sicily had a dire record in relation to its natural environment, and was notorious for its illegal building, unregulated waste disposal, marine pollution, and destruction of wildlife habitats. Recent years, though, have seen a complete change of attitude. Protected areas have been established, and the island now boasts one national park, five regional parks, and dozens of nature and marine reserves, adding up to more than 10% of the Sicilian territory. The regional parks include mighty Mount Etna, the densely wooded Nebrodi Mountains in the northeast of the island, the high peaks and deep valleys of the Madonie Mountains south of Cefalù, and the Alcantara Gorge north of Catania; in all of these, new building has been severely curtailed and measures have been taken to preserve the wildlife. Nature reserves include the two coastal stretches of Vendicari on the east side and Lo Zingaro in the northwest, both left in a state of carefully curated abandon and only accessible on foot.

The island of Pantelleria was the most recent National Park to be instituted in Italy, and the first in Sicily. Three more have been planned: the Egadi Islands and nearby coastline around Trapani, the Aeoiian Islands, and the Iblei Mountains. The island of Ustica, north of Palermo, already has a marine reserve in place to restrict fishing activities and destructive water sports.

In the cities, the well-being and health of residents and visitors alike have been improved by the pedestrianization of large areas. In Palermo, for example, Via Maqueda and Via Vittorio Emanuele, once car-clogged thoroughfares that made walking an unpleasant and even menacing experience, have been barred to traffic and are now essential venues of the nightly *passeggiata*. Similar restrictions exist in Catania as well as in smaller towns like Trapani and Marsala, while most of the island's older centers have been designated as ZTLs (*zone di traffico limitato*), where drivers face steep fines for entering without a permit. All of this has greatly improved the pedestrian experience as well as having a marked impact on air pollution. There's still a long way to go, as lapses and abuses persist, but a corner has been turned.

MIGRATION

Since 2016, Sicily has seen a marked fall in the number of asylum seekers and economic migrants from Africa, Asia, and the Middle East. The island has been one of the front lines for illegal entry into European Union countries and, as in most other European countries, the issue has generated much heated discussion and a gamut of responses, from hardline crackdowns to more sympathetic approaches.

It is a complex emotional issue for islanders, not least because historically the movement was in the opposite direction. From the last decades of the 19th century through to the 1950s, Sicilians sought a better life outside the island, particularly in North America, the northern Italian cities, and northern Europe. Displacement, in other words, has been a familiar phenomenon for generations of Sicilians.

Visitors to the island will see very little evidence of the many *extracomunitari*, or non-Europeans, who have made their way here in dinghies and rafts, mostly because the authorities have been careful to confine them to detention centers on the island of Lampedusa, where they are processed and, in most cases, dispersed to other parts of Italy, with many moving on to other European countries.

Some immigrants, though, have chosen to remain on the island. In fact, the modern face of Sicily, whose cities are now a mix of different cultures and complexions, harks back to the distant Arab-Norman era of the island's history, when this was a richly cosmopolitan place and, for a relatively brief period, a showcase for how different communities could coexist and prosper, giving rise to the artistic splendors that today tourists flock to admire.

EARTHQUAKES AND ERUPTIONS

Dominating Sicily's eastern seaboard, the smoking and smoldering cone of Mount Etna is a constant reminder of the awesome power of this mighty volcano, and a quick tour of its lava-strewn slopes should remove any lingering doubt. Less visible is the devastation inflicted by the earthquakes that have periodically laid waste to large areas of the island. The evidence is there, however. Go to

Gibellina, in western Sicily, to see the damage caused by a relatively recent quake in the Belice Valley in 1968, where ruins have been left as symbols of the terrible destruction. A vast mantle of concrete artwork there, the Cretto di Burri, commemorates the disaster.

Better known are the effects of the Val di Noto earthquake of 1693, which extended over an area of about 5,600 square kilometers (2,200 square miles) in southeastern Sicily and caused the deaths of some 60,000 people. This, though, is a rare example of something good coming out of a major catastrophe, namely the graceful new towns that arose in the wake of the disaster, including Ragusa, Modica, and, most famously, Noto—all of which benefited from judicious town planning combined with the inspired work of a handful of exceptional architects.

The present appearance of Messina, too, is largely the result of seismic destruction, in this case wreaked by the earthquake of 1908, which killed 50,000–80,000 people on either side of the Strait of Messina and has been called the most lethal earthquake ever recorded in Europe. Almost everything of great historical note was reduced to rubble—and the buildings that survived or were rebuilt, including its 12th-century Duomo, were then razed again during World War II.

It should be added that serious earthquakes in Sicily are extremely rare events, occurring at most once or twice a century and in very localized areas. Equally, tectonic movements are closely monitored by scientists, and visitors to Sicily have no cause to worry about falling victim to eruptions from any of the island's volcanoes.

What to Eat and Drink in Sicily

SWORDFISH

Most of Sicily's *feluche* (traditional swordfish boats) have been replaced with modern vessels, but giant swordfish continue to find their way into markets and on dinner menus, perhaps in the form of stuffed roulades or simply fried in breadcrumbs and served with a wedge of lemon.

ARANCINI

You know you're in Sicily when you see fresh *arancini* (or *arancine* in the Western region) for sale in markets and snack shops. These deep-fried rice balls are the classic Sicilian fast food, either *rosso* (filled with a rich meat sauce) or *bianco* (with a mozzarella and ham white sauce).

GRANITA

These crushed ice drinks are the perfect thirst quencher, especially in their lemon or peach versions. The original Sicilian *granita* was made from lemons, almonds, or black mulberries, but it works well in a range of other versions.

CASSATA

Generally thought to have been introduced into Sicily by the Arabs, the *cassata* has since become part of the island's identity. The rich, impossibly sweet concoction is made from ricotta layered with sponge cake soaked in liqueur, covered in green almond paste, and decorated with candied fruit.

CITRUS FRUIT

Citrus fruits are among Sicily's greatest exports, and one of the greatest benefits of being on the island during the winter months, when they come into season. Mountains of giant blood oranges are a staple of markets, while lemons are an essential ingredient in juices, sauces, sorbets, and cocktails as well as being the most ubiquitous motif to appear on the island's colorful ceramics.

MARSALA WINE

Named after the town on Sicily's western tip, Marsala wine, a fortified wine, started life when John Woodhouse, an English merchant on a chance visit to Sicily in 1770, saw a commercial opportunity after sampling the strong local wine. By adding alcohol, he was able to both increase the wine's potency and ensure its preservation during long sea voyages to potential markets, rather like port. Other merchants followed, Marsala wine was soon carried on all naval vessels, and an industry was born.

Cassata

FRUTTA MARTORANA
Said to have been invented by enterprising nuns at the Martorana convent in Palermo, where they were hung on trees to amuse a visiting bigwig, these marzipan confections crafted to resemble fruit and vegetables can now be seen in *pasticcerie* and bars throughout the island.

CAPONATA
Either served as an antipasto or as a side dish, this eggplant salad is one of the simple glories of Sicilian cuisine. There are many variations, but the main ingredients should include red wine vinegar, diced tomatoes, capers, onion, and garlic.

PASTA
One of the pleasures of traveling around Sicily is in sampling its local pasta. In the far West, you'll find *busiate* (thick tendrils of pasta) on every menu, while Siracusa is known for *spaghettini* and Palermo is associated with *anelleti* (small rings), often going into a *timballo*, or pasta bake. Ridged *penne* or *rigatoni* are normally used in Catania's *pasta alla Norma*, while spaghetti is the favored pasta to accompany seafood island-wide.

SARDINES
Inexpensive and common around Sicily's coasts, sardines are most often found in dishes in Palermo and the West. Traditional and well-loved dishes include *pasta con le sarde*, an unmissable delight in the island's capital, and *sarde a beccafico* (stuffed sardines). Both are prepared with pine nuts and raisins.

WINE
With its warm, dry climate, Sicily has been producing wine for millennia, but the island's wineries were long associated with bulk yields used for boosting thinner varieties. With a recent resurgence of Sicily's viniculture, today the island turns out some of the most exciting labels in Italy.

What to Buy in Sicily

CALTAGIRONE POTTERY

Sicilian pottery has a bold, brash style, using exuberant colors and folky designs. Arguably the finest are in Caltagirone, home to over a hundred ceramics studios. Among the most popular wares for sale are pharmacy jars, decorative tiles, and plates with religious and mythological scenes.

COPPOLA HATS

Casually elegant, the coppola flat cap dates back to the 18th century and has traditionally been worn by farmers and aristocrats alike. These days, it's hand-printed in a variety of shades and designs and has become something of a style accessory. The choice of material has also evolved, from jute and tweed to wool, velvet, denim, and even leather, but if you're looking for something cooler for the summer, pure linen or cotton are ideal. Palermo is the home of the coppola.

MARTORANA FRUIT

Sicily is famed for its ultrasweet pastries and cakes, but none are more artistic than *frutta martorana*—marzipan fashioned into the shapes of fruits and vegetables. Said to have originated in the Martorana church and convent in Palermo, the confections are traditionally made in the weeks running up to the Day of the Dead, November 2, but nowadays they are available year-round. They look amazingly authentic and, because they are well preserved with sugar, travel well.

CARRETTINI SICILIANI

Ornately decorated in yellow and red, Sicilian carts (*carretti*) are no longer used on farms but, as enduring symbols of Sicily's rural culture, can often be seen displayed in museums or rustic-style restaurants. You'll see the miniature versions, *carrettini siciliani*, for sale in every town, meticulously crafted in wood and small enough to be packed away in a suitcase.

WINE

Sicily's profile as a wine-growing region has increased exponentially in recent years, and a bottle or a crate of its finest would be a wonderful way to celebrate the island. Wines to look out for include aromatic Zibibbo wine from Pantelleria, fortified wine from Marsala, anything from the Mount Etna region, and, from the southeast of the island, Cerasuolo di Vittoria, Sicily's only wine to have the DOCG designation.

MODICA CHOCOLATE

The crumbly texture, strong flavor, and unusual form (it comes in "ingots") of Modica chocolate is not to everyone's taste, but it's a unique product of Sicily, and especially evocative of the island's Baroque southeastern wedge where the town of Modica is located. Cold-processed and with no cocoa butter added, it is supposed to retain all the beneficial properties of cocoa. It's a

great accompaniment to an espresso, and also delicious with ice cream. There are specialist retailers in Modica itself, of course, but also it's sold in larger towns throughout the island.

PISTACHIO PRODUCTS

It's only when you arrive in Bronte, the town in the foothills of Mount Etna that is the Sicilian center of pistachio nut production, that you become aware of the many different forms pistachios can take. Products for sale here include pistachio pesto, nougat, chocolate, cream, and flour, or you might come away with a jar of *granella di pistacchio*, the crunchy grains that are used to make cannoli and are scattered over ice cream.

MARSALA SALT

The salt harvested from the salt pans of Marsala is prized by foodies for its natural properties, with a higher concentration of potassium and magnesium than common salt and lower levels of sodium chloride. It is particularly suitable for fish dishes. You'll find bags of the coarse grains in shops at the salt pans themselves and in Marsala and Palermo.

LAVA STONE ITEMS

Mount Etna is the most famous of Sicily's volcanoes, but by no means the only one. Most of the islands around Sicily are volcanic in origin (some still volcanically active), and in all of these places you'll find a variety of objects made from lava on sale, from natural lava bracelets and necklaces to tables and baking plates made from lava stone.

MARIONETTES

Sicilian puppetry is a venerable but living tradition, and you can still find puppet performances in Palermo, Catania, Siracusa, and some smaller towns. Wherever there are performances, there are also *laboratori* (workshops) where the marionettes are made and repaired. Here you'll find all the familiar characters from the stock stories: Orlando, Rinaldo, Angelica, and others. Just keep in mind that if the marionettes are authentic, they're not cheap nor are they small and compact enough to fit comfortably in a suitcase.

Best Historical Sites in Sicily

PARCO ARCHEOLOGICO DELLA NEAPOLIS, SIRACUSA

Siracusa's archaeological zone has a rich concentration of ancient sights, including the *latomie* (huge pits) where Athenian soldiers were imprisoned following their failed attack on the city. But the highlight is undoubtedly the awe-inspiring Greek theater, where performances of classical drama are still enacted.

GREEK TEMPLE RUINS, SELINUNTE

The ancient Greek city of Selinus was devastated by a Carthaginian army in the 5th century BC, and earthquakes later toppled most of what was still left standing. Despite its ruined state, this vast site still grabs your attention for its sheer scale.

MONREALE CATHEDRAL, MONREALE

Perhaps the greatest legacy of the Norman regime that ruled over Sicily in the Middle Ages is the imposing, densely decorated cathedrals that were designed and built by the finest Greek, Arab, Norman, and Jewish artisans. On a height above Palermo, Monreale's cathedral is a stunning example of this collective effort, the entire interior coated with a dazzling array of perfectly preserved mosaics.

VALLE DEI TEMPLI, AGRIGENTO

The Greek temples that make up Agrigento's Valley of the Temples constitute one of Italy's most significant and spectacular archaeological sites. Spread over a hillside between the city and the sea, the setting alone makes this an unmissable attraction.

NOTO'S ARCHITECTURE

The fruit of pioneering town planning in the 18th century, the town of Noto replaced a previous settlement that was razed in the earthquake that devastated this part of Sicily in 1693. The harmonious, honey-toned buildings are perfectly preserved and display the best of Sicilian Baroque.

ORTIGIA'S DUOMO

At Ortigia Island's Duomo, a pagan Greek temple has been incorporated into the city's principal church. Add to that traces of Sicily's early Siculi people who previously worshipped here, a Norman fort, Arabesque mosaics, and a majestic Baroque facade, and you have Sicilian history in a nutshell.

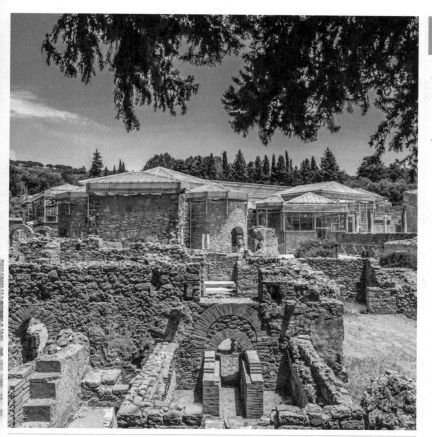

TEATRO GRECO, TAORMINA

Not the most important of Sicily's classical sites, perhaps, but surely one of its most striking, mainly for the inspired setting of this Greek and Roman theater, high above the sea with the massive silhouette of Etna to the south. Performances and screenings are still held here, providing one of the most memorable experiences that Sicily can offer.

VILLA ROMANA DEL CASALE, PIAZZA ARMERINA

Imagination has been allowed to run rampant in this entrancing series of Roman mosaics in what was once a hunting lodge in the center of the island. The images of wild animals, chariot racing, hunting and fishing parties, and women performing gymnastics have provided historians with a mass of historical data, and nonhistorians will find the scenes equally vivid and eye-opening.

TEMPIO DORICO, SEGESTA

The drama and impact of this skeletal but beautifully preserved temple isolated in the middle of the hilly Sicilian countryside exerts a powerful hold on all who view it. The incomplete and unadorned Doric temple stands proud on its romantic site, redolent of what once existed here and what could have been. A short distance away, Segesta's Greek theater is also full of echoes of this era of island history.

The Cosa Nostra in Sicily

The loose association of criminal groups that we know as the Mafia is in Sicily simply known as Cosa Nostra, translated to "our thing." Originating in the 19th century as a shadowy mutual support network set up in opposition to the often corrupt agents of the central government, the organization grew into a *piovra* ("octopus") whose reach extended to such activities as racketeering, drug trafficking, extortion, illegal gambling, money laundering, fraud, kidnapping, and robbery.

HISTORY

From its bases in Palermo and its hinterland, *capi* like Luciano Leggi, Salvatore Riina, and Bernardo Provenzano led Cosa Nostra in a relentless war against both the state and rival groups. The tide was only turned through the determined efforts of two prominent anti-Mafia magistrates, Giovanni Falcone and Paolo Borsellino, and thanks to the testimony of Tommaso Buscetta and other informants who followed his example. At a series of high-profile "maxi trials" held in a purpose-built bunker-courthouse in Palermo in 1986–87, 475 mafiosi were put on trial and 338 convicted. The shocking retaliatory assassinations of Falcone and Borsellino in 1992 only stirred up a further wave of revulsion against the criminals, and a street-level anti-Mafia movement took hold in Palermo and then across Sicily, vowing to resist payment by businesses of *pizzo*, or protection money.

THE MAFIA TODAY

Since those dark days, the focus of Mafia activity has moved from Sicily's Cosa Nostra to the Neapolitan Camorra and the Calabrian 'Ndrangheta, and visitors to Sicily will see no more signs of criminality than exist in most other places in Italy. Such Palermo neighborhoods as Capo and La Kalsa, once menacing and best avoided after dark, are now abuzz with lively bars and chic restaurants.

Although times have moved on since Sicily was automatically identified with organized crime, the deadly activities of Cosa Nostra should not be forgotten, if only for the sake of its many victims. Today, you can wise up on its history and background in the town of Corleone, one of the organization's former heartlands south of Palermo, where the C.I.D.M.A. Mafia and Anti-Mafia museum does a good job of chronicling its rise and fall.

What to Watch and Read

THE GODFATHER PART I AND II

Francis Ford Coppola's first two *Godfather* films in the 1970s broke new ground for modern day gangster movies and were compulsive viewing for modern day gangsters. The themes and storylines are Shakespearean in scope, the acting and production inspired, and the Corleone family's Sicilian background convincingly drawn. Best of all, you don't need to be a fan of gangster movies to enjoy them. Sicilian locations used in the films are mainly stand-ins for the town of Corleone, and include Sant'Alessio Siculo, Forza d'Agro, and Savoca, whose bar and church prominently feature.

DIVORCE ITALIAN STYLE

Starring the great Marcello Mastroianni and with music by Donizetti, this satire generated a whole genre of Italian comedy films. The movie's theme is the dead weight of the male-dominated conservative culture of 1950s Sicily, and it uses the oppressive heat of the climate to evoke its suffocating inertia. Mastroianni's performance as an impoverished and unscrupulous aristocrat is masterly.

STROMBOLI

Roberto Rossellini's film set on the eponymous Aeolian island is a neorealist classic. The rigors of a poor fishing community and the bleakness of the setting, overshadowed by Stromboli's menacing volcano, make it a grim watch, but it is redeemed by the compelling performance of Ingrid Bergman in the lead role as a displaced refugee after World War II. Only three members of the film's cast were professional actors, adding brutal authenticity to the famous tuna fishing scene.

CINEMA PARADISO

Sentimentality and nostalgia have always been strong elements in Italian cinema, and this visually ravishing movie has both in spades. Nonetheless, as a work of art and entertainment, it has achieved classic status through its warmth and integrity. Seen through a young boy's eyes, it's a love letter to both cinema and childhood itself, and is set and filmed in Bagheria, the town outside Palermo where writer and director Giuseppe Tornatore grew up.

INSPECTOR MONTALBANO

Based on the novels of Andrea Camilleri, the chronicles of Inspector Montalbano's career on the trail of assorted crooks and miscreants have been a huge TV hit all over the world. The plots are convoluted and frequently incomprehensible, the pace might drag, and the element of suspense is often completely absent, but the locations in the Baroque towns of southeastern Sicily are irresistible, as are the scenes of Montalbano's early morning swims and his regular slap-up lunches.

THE LEOPARD (IL GATTOPARDO) BY GIUSEPPE TOMASI DI LAMPEDUSA

Melancholy and elegiac yet also amazingly prescient, the Leopard is the quintessential novel of Sicily, mostly set during the time of the Risorgimento and revolving around the wise and tragic figure of Don Fabrizio, Prince of Salina. One of the book's main themes is the tension between the forces of tradition and change, encapsulated in the novel's most famous line: "For everything to stay the same, everything must change."

THE SILENT DUCHESS BY DACIA MARAINI

This immersive novel set in 18th-century Sicily is written by one of Italy's most engaging contemporary authors, the daughter of a Sicilian princess. The delicately narrated story is told through the eyes of the deaf and mute Marianna, and describes her growth from childhood trauma to eventual triumph as a mature woman. The world painted here is bleak and corrupt but also splendid and full of fascinating detail.

SIRACUSA BY DELIA EPHRON

A rollicking tale of suspense and family secrets, this novel follows a group of Americans on holiday in Sicily. Told from their different perspectives, events soon get out of hand, dragging the reader into a tangle of betrayal and dark morality. The dialogue is sharp, the plot well-paced, and there are plenty of surprises along the way. With its Siracusa setting, this makes an utterly engrossing holiday read.

SICILY, A SHORT HISTORY BY JOHN JULIUS NORWICH

Told in an anecdotal style, this volume is short on detail but packs a lot in, from the first Greek settlements to the growth of the Mafia. It's a turbulent story, most engaging when chronicling the Norman period, when Sicily was a beacon of multicultural harmony and artistic achievement. The final impression the reader is left with is the suffering that the island's population have had to endure at the whims of its corrupt and violent overlords.

MIDNIGHT IN SICILY BY PETER ROBB

In this deeply researched and highly readable study, Robb paints a vivid picture of the murky nexus of criminality and politics in Sicily. Its starting point is the kiss exchanged between Mafia boss Salvatore Riina and Giulio Andreotti, seven-time prime minister of Italy, but the book takes in many other themes, not least Sicily's art and food scenes, citing such cultural icons as Lampedusa, Sciascia, and Guttuso.

Chapter 2

TRAVEL SMART

Updated by
Robert Andrews

★ **REGIONAL CAPITAL:**
Palermo

👥 **POPULATION:**
4,840,876

💬 **LANGUAGE:**
Italian

$ **CURRENCY:**
Euro

📠 **COUNTRY CODE:**
39

⚠ **EMERGENCIES:**
112

🚗 **DRIVING:**
On the right

⚡ **ELECTRICITY:**
220v/50 cycles; electrical
plugs have two round prongs

🕐 **TIME:**
6 hours ahead of New York

🌐 **WEB RESOURCES:**
www.italia.it;
www.visitsicily.info;
www.beniculturali.it

Know Before You Go

An increasingly popular destination in Europe, Sicily has lots of notable attractions and can be a little overwhelming for a first-time visitor. Here are some key tips to help you navigate your trip, whether it's your first time visiting or your 21st.

SAVING MONEY

It's a general rule that flights booked well ahead are the cheapest, and the same principle applies to booking hotels and rental cars, too; you'll find the lowest rates for all of these outside the summer months in Sicily.

Sicilian cities all have good public transport options that cost a fraction of taxis. The airports, too, have good public transport connections to the nearest cities. If you do prefer to travel into town by taxi, look out for shared taxis at Palermo and Catania airports, where drivers wait for at least five passengers before setting off to the city center, making specific stops as requested. The usual charge is around €8—again, much less than regular taxis.

For traveling around the island, trains are usually the cheapest option, and fares are lowest for tickets booked in advance; check the Trenitalia website for times and ticket prices. For travel to and between Sicily's islands, choose ferries rather than the faster hydrofoils if you're not pressed for time. Ferry travel is usually about half the cost but takes twice as long.

As for eating and drinking, try to avoid numerous bar-stops—snacks and drinks often add up to a major expense. It's in bars, though, that you might save on the cost of evening meals if you find places offering *apericena*, a mainland trend that is catching on in some of Sicily's towns and cities. A conflation of *aperitivo* and *cena* (supper), it offers a generous selection of snacks to accompany a glass of wine or beer in the evening. Only a few places offer this, but if you see it advertised you might as well take advantage of it if you don't need a full dinner.

When it comes to sightseeing, look out for passes allowing entry to two or more attractions at a lower cost than paying for them individually. These multiple-entry tickets are available in Palermo and Erice, among other places, and can be picked up at the sights themselves.

CULTURAL DIFFERENCES

The main cultural divides in Italy are between fast, fashionable urban life and the simpler, slower, and less sophisticated ways of the countryside as well as between the cooler, tidier, and more restrained North, and the more spontaneous, extroverted, and sometimes chaotic South. As far as the superficial texture of life goes, most Italians would agree with these broad distinctions on a theoretical level.

Other common generalizations are less reliable, however. For instance, it used to be said that Sicilians were louder, brasher, ruder, and more emotional than their more reserved compatriots in the north, and, while there may have been a grain of truth in this, it's also true that these stereotypes are less meaningful nowadays. Visitors to Sicily will find social interactions much smoother than they might once have been and standards of service noticeably improved. Veterans of traveling in northern Italy may still encounter a more relaxed attitude to driving regulations and waiting in line in the South, for example, but otherwise most cultural differences affecting tourists have been largely ironed out. Sicilian society today is as modern, dynamic, subtle, and savvy as anywhere else in the country—but perhaps with a little more heart.

TRAVELING WITH SPECIAL NEEDS

Sicily is one of the worst regions of Italy for travelers with special needs to transverse buildings, public transport, sidewalks, and archaeological sites. Little allowance is made for anyone with sight or mobility issues, though some improvements are gradually being implemented, mainly in tourist facilities and public transport.

Problems are particularly acute in towns with vehicles parked on pavements and villages with cobbled lanes, where even crossing a street can be hazardous. Partly compensating for these deficiencies is the kindness of employees and passersby to lend whatever support they can, but overall the best solution may be to stay in modern, better-equipped hotels and to make use of organized tours to avoid the worst pitfalls.

PUBLIC TRANSPORT

Cars are great for travel between towns and especially for getting to out-of-the-way places in between, but they have their downsides, too—mostly negotiating complicated traffic systems, coping with other, often impatient and intimidating road-users, the difficulties of parking, and ZTL areas of towns where traffic is restricted and unwitting infringement of the regulations will result in fines. When all these factors are taken into account, public transport is often the better alternative.

A good network of private bus companies connects most places in Sicily, information on which is usually available on websites and from information phone lines (personnel usually has some knowledge of English). Booking in advance is not usually possible, except for popular inter-city routes (between Palermo and Catania, for example). Services to smaller places may have sporadic schedules, however.

Train services are good and reliable on the coastal lines between Messina, Cefalù, and Palermo, and Messina, Catania, and Siracusa, and on the Palermo–Agrigento and Siracusa–Noto inland routes. Services are not so good on the less-used lines west of Palermo (to Trapani, Marsala, and Mazara del Vallo), and between Palermo and Enna. Always remember to punch, or "validate," your ticket from one of the machines in the station or on the platforms before travel.

City buses and tram systems are usually excellent ways to travel within the larger towns, with cheap fares and frequent services. The only negative is knowing which services to take and which stops to use, though both of these issues can be solved on the companies' websites and by asking drivers, many of whom speak basic English. Tickets for multiple journeys over a full day or days are an especially good value. Again, always remember to punch or "validate," your ticket at

of the machines inside the bus or tram as soon as you board.

Last, taxis can be a huge help in getting somewhere fast, and do not charge a lot within towns and cities. They can be booked on 24-hour phone lines.

HIKING IN SICILY

Hiking in Sicily has only recently become a popular activity, and the island is not as well-equipped with walking routes as some other regions of the Italian peninsula. The Madonie and Nebrodi mountain ranges on the north side of the island and Mount Etna on the east side have a good range of hiking trails, while shorter, more family-friendly walks exist on Capo Milazzo; the Egadi and Aeolian islands; nature reserves such as Vendicari and Riserva dello Zingaro; the Alcantara gorge; and Pantalica. Long-distance trails are rarer; one exception is the Magna Via Francigena, an old pilgrimage way that crosses the island between Palermo and Agrigento, passing through Corleone, and takes about eight days to complete.

Getting Here and Around

Air

There are no direct flights between North America and Sicily. Most nonstop flights between North America and Italy serve Rome's Aeroporto Internazionale Leonardo da Vinci (FCO), better known as Fiumicino, and Milan's Aeroporto Malpensa (MXP); airports in Venice, Pisa, and Naples also accommodate nonstop flights from the United States and Canada. Flying time to Milan or Rome is approximately 8–8½ hours from New York, 10–11 hours from Chicago, and 11½ hours from Los Angeles. Since air tickets are frequently sold at discounted prices, the cost of flights within Italy (even one-way) may compare favorably with train travel, and there are frequent internal flights from Milan, Rome, and other regional airports to Sicily's two major airports, Palermo's Falcone Borsellino Airport (PMO) and Catania's Fontanarossa Airport (CTA), and to Trapani-Birgi's Vincenzo Florio Airport (TPS).

There are also direct flights from all of London's airports to Palermo, Catania, and Trapani. Flight times are approximately three hours to each of these.

Internal flights operate between the airports of Palermo, Catania, and Trapani, and the islands of Lampedusa and Pantelleria. There are also flights (mostly seasonal) to these islands from mainland Italian cities.

AIRPORTS

Sicily's two main airports are well connected to their respective cities. You can take a Trenitalia train or a bus from Palermo's airport to the city center (both take about 45 minutes), and buses from Catania's airport to Catania's center (about 20 minutes). Regular and shared taxi services also operate, and there are

bus services linking the airports to other Sicilian destinations, too.

Both airports have shops, bars, and restaurant facilities, as well as information desks with multi-lingual staff. A helpful website for information (location, phone numbers, local transportation, etc.) about all of the airports in Italy is ⊕ *www.italia-nairportguide.com*.

Bus

Air-conditioned buses connect major and minor cities in Sicily and are often faster and more convenient than local trains—still single track on many stretches—but also slightly more expensive. Various companies serve different routes. SAIS runs frequently between Palermo and Catania, Messina, and other cities, in each case arriving at and departing from near the train stations.

Car

Driving is the ideal way to explore Sicily. Modern highways circle and bisect the island, making all main cities easily reachable. Along the north coast, the A20 autostrada (also known as E90) connects Messina, Cefalù, and Palermo while along the eastern coast, Messina, Taormina, Catania, and Siracusa are linked by the A18/E45. Running through the interior, from Catania to west of Cefalù, is the A19; threading west from Palermo, the A29/E933 runs to Trapani, with a leg stretching down to Mazara del Vallo. In general, the south side of the island is less well served, though the extension of the A18 to Gela is under construction, while stretches of the SS115 west of Agrigento are relatively fast and traffic-free. The A18 and A20 autostradas are subject to tolls.

You'll likely hear stories about the dangers of driving in Sicily. In the big cities—especially Palermo, Catania, and Messina—streets can be a honking mess, with lane markings and stop signs taken as mere suggestions; you can avoid the chaos by driving through at off-peak times or on weekends. However, once outside the urban areas and resort towns, most of the highways and regional state roads are a driving enthusiast's dream—they're winding, sparsely populated, and reasonably well maintained, with striking new views around many bends. Obviously, don't leave valuables in your car, and make sure baggage is stowed out of sight, if possible.

CAR RENTALS

Most of the major international rental companies are represented in Sicily, though these are mostly concentrated in the airports and bigger towns. In addition to these are Italian companies and local outfits, and the latter are usually the only ones present in small towns and resorts.

Rental rates can be surprisingly inexpensive in the low season, and all rates are generally lowest when cars are picked up from airports as opposed to town centers. Always try to book online and as far in advance as possible for the best prices. A supplementary charge is incurred when dropping off a rental vehicle at a different place from where it was collected. Child seats and GPS devices are usually available, but cost extra.

RULES OF THE ROAD

Driving in Sicily is most pleasurable when you're outside towns and cities. The traffic in Palermo, Messina, and Catania can be atrocious, especially during rush hours (roughly between 8 and 9, and 5 and 7), and complicated one-way systems, pedestrianized areas, and road work will add to the stress. Be aware of ZTLs (*zone di traffico limitato*, or limited traffic zones), which are very common in town centers and in resorts during the summer. There should be notices advising when these are in operation, and any infringement is likely to be caught on camera and result in a fine (which will be passed on to you by your rental company, plus a hefty administrative supplement). Historic centers are often closed to all private cars unless in possession of special permits.

As for parking, this can also be a major headache-inducing factor. Leaving your vehicle in a car park is the best solution, but if one is not available, you should bear in mind that street-parking between blue lines is charged (pay at a meter), yellow lines are reserved for specific groups, and white lines are free, but usually hard to find.

Drivers should be aware of speed limits, and also of specifically Italian driving habits; for example, flashing headlights should be a warning that the driver wants priority, and all other cars and pedestrians should steer clear (rather than giving you priority, as it is intended in some countries).

Getting Here and Around

⭘ Ferries and Hydrofoils

There's an excellent network of ferries and hydrofoils that link Sicily with the Italian mainland and even with the North African coast. The network also connects Sicily with its own outlying islands.

Anyone driving down the mainland to Sicily will make use of the car ferries operated by Blu Ferries and Caronte & Tourist, which, together with passenger-only Blu Jet hydrofoils, constantly ply between Villa San Giovanni in Calabria, and Messina on Sicily's northeastern corner. The crossing only takes around 20 minutes on hydrofoils or 40 minutes on the car ferries. Train travelers will stay on board as their train is separated in order to fit onto larger ferries for this crossing.

You can also reach Sicily by sea on a variety of routes. Grandi Navi Veloci ferries connect Palermo with Genoa (20 hours, 30 minutes), Naples (11 hours), and Civitavecchia near Rome (13 hours) while Grimaldi Lines ferries link the Sicilian capital with Cagliari in Sardinia (12 hours), Tunis (10–13 hours), and Salerno (9–10 hours). Tirrenia ferries also operate ferries between Palermo and Naples, and Caronte & Tourist ferries run between Salerno and Messina.

Once in Italy, you can use Siremar ferries or the faster but more expensive Liberty Lines hydrofoils to reach the Egadi Islands and Pantelleria from Trapani, Ustica from Palermo, and Lampedusa from Porto Empedocle, near Agrigento.

Frequent Siremar ferries and Liberty Lines hydrofoils connect Milazzo, on Sicily's north coast, with the Aeolian Islands, and they also run between the Aeolians

themselves. Liberty Lines operates a less frequent hydrofoil service between Messina with the Aeolians, and the islands can also be reached from Naples on Siremar ferries and SNAV hydrofoils.

🚕 Taxis and Ride-sharing

Taxis are available at all airports, outside train and bus stations, and in city centers. Always insist on using the meter, or agree on a price beforehand. Drivers are well used to carrying foreigners and usually speak English. Ride-sharing apps like Uber and Lyft do not currently operate in Sicily, but may eventually do so in the future.

🚆 Train

There are direct express trains from Rome to Palermo, Catania, and Siracusa. The Rome–Palermo and Rome–Siracusa trips take at least 11 hours. After Naples, the run is mostly along the coast, so try to book a window seat on the right if you're not on an overnight train. At Villa San Giovanni, in Calabria, the train is separated and loaded onto a ferryboat to cross the strait to Messina—a favorite for kids.

There are no high-speed lines within Sicily, but main lines connect Messina, Taormina, Siracusa, Catania, and Palermo. The Messina–Palermo run, along the northern coast, and Messina–Taormina, along the eastern coast, are especially scenic. Secondary lines are generally very slow and may be unreliable. For schedules, check the website of the Italian state railway, Trenitalia.

Essentials

Dining

As befits a major city, Palermo has a huge selection of interesting and varied restaurants, while Catania is best known for its high-quality seafood. In the tourist-heavy coastal towns, dining can be hit or miss, while inland there has been a mini-explosion of new-wave gourmet restaurants in the Baroque towns of Ragusa, Modica, and especially Noto, as well as some intriguing options popping up on Mount Etna.

In the west of the island and on the Egadi Islands, Pantelleria, and Lampedusa, expect to find a Sicilian variant of North African couscous on the menus, often made with seafood and well worth sampling. In the countryside, *agriturismi* (farm B&Bs), country hotels, and wineries are your best bets for a good meal.

Special dietary needs are often catered for, but vegetarians and vegans will find very little choice beyond soups, salads, pastas, and grilled vegetables.

Dining etiquette in Sicily is no different from in other Italian regions. Unless it's for work, meals tend to be relaxed, often drawn-out affairs, perhaps starting with antipasti, then either a pasta or rice or soup to follow, going on to a main course and sometimes a dessert. Don't feel obliged to go the whole hog, though—many skip the starters or main altogether. Seafood is usually priced by weight, as so much per *etto* (1 *etto* is 100 grams). At seafood restaurants, whatever is available will often be displayed in a chiller cabinet, and it's perfectly acceptable to get up and examine the display to indicate what you wish to order.

Restaurants open for business at around 12:30 pm and then 7:30 pm; last orders are taken at around 2 in the afternoon and 10 in the evening, though there is very rarely any pressure on diners to pay the check and leave after those times. In summer these hours will often be extended.

Cover charges of €1.50–€2.50 per person is usually added to the final bill, and will include a basket of bread. Credit cards are almost always accepted, though not always American Express. Smoking is banned indoors, but may be allowed on outdoor terraces—check first.

✚ Health and Safety

Most pharmacies in Sicily are able to advise on minor ailments, and in cities, there will always be out-of-hours and nighttime services available (look for addresses and times on pharmacy doors). Otherwise, head for the local Guardia Medica (emergency medical clinic), or call the Pronto Soccorso (first aid) services by dialing 118.

Gone are the days when Sicily was synonymous with petty delinquency, but it still pays to observe commonsense practices. The same simple rules apply in Sicily that you will have followed for traveling in most other countries: don't flash your cash as waving wads of banknotes or having expensive jewelry visible will get you noticed and may make you a target; carry handbags and shoulder bags slung across your body rather than dangling on one side and make sure these are firmly closed; use hotel safes for storing valuables when you are out and about; have alternative and back-up methods for day-to-day payments; have copies of your passport and driving license available; avoid badly lit neighborhoods at night; and be wary of "interesting" offers and possible scams. You should be particularly alert when using public transport, and drivers should never leave valuable items

Essentials

visible inside a car or leave a car unattended for even a few seconds when it is unlocked or with the windows open. All that said, very few visitors to Sicily ever fall victim to crime.

COVID-19

COVID-19 has disrupted travel since March 2020, and travelers should expect sporadic ongoing issues. Always travel with a mask in case it's required, and keep up to date on the most recent testing and vaccination guidelines for Italy. Check out the websites of the CDC and the U.S. Department of State, both of which have destination-specific, COVID-19 guidance. Also, in case travel is curtailed abruptly again, consider buying trip insurance. Just be sure to read the fine print: not all travel-insurance policies cover pandemic-related cancellations.

◉ Hours of Operation

In Palermo, most commercial sites and offices in Sicily open at 8 or 9 in the morning and work right through until around 6. Summer sees a slight extension of these hours, perhaps with a couple of hours off in the afternoon, and in winter most outdoor attractions close earlier. Note that many state-run museums and galleries are closed on Monday.

On islands and holiday resorts, many hotels and restaurants remain closed throughout the winter season (roughly between mid-October and Easter). Apart from these places, most restaurants in Sicily have a period during the year when they are closed for two- to four weeks,

and often in November or February. For the rest of the year, restaurants are usually closed for one day of the week (frequently on Monday) except in peak season, when they are allowed to remain open daily. Very few restaurants serve meals all day; most kitchens are open 12:30–2:30 and 7:30–10:30, though closing time for customers may be much later, and in winter kitchens tend to close earlier in the evening.

As elsewhere in Italy, most churches open roughly 7:30–noon and 4–7. Sightseeing visits during church services are bad etiquette and you may be asked to enter no farther than the door or return later.

🛏 Lodging

High-quality and boutique hotels tend to be confined to the major cities and resorts of Palermo, Catania, Taormina, and Siracusa, The southeast towns of Modica, Ragusa, and Noto also offer some very classy and charming accommodations but are mostly small in scale. B&Bs exist everywhere, with the greatest choice in Palermo, Catania, and Taormina, including both period and more modern designer places. Beach resorts tend to have a range of options, while rural lodgings may include the odd swanky estate but are mostly confined to *agriturismi* (rural bed-and-breakfasts), ranging from quite basic to extensive spreads, and usually offering all-inclusive, full-board plans that can make for some of Sicily's most memorable meals.

Tipping

In restaurants in Sicily, a service charge of 10%–15% may appear on your check, but it's not a given that your server will receive this; consider leaving an additional tip of 5%–10% (in cash) for good service. At a hotel bar, tip €1 and up for a round or two of drinks. Taxi drivers also appreciate a euro or two, particularly if they help with luggage.

In hotels, give the *portiere* (concierge) about 10% of the bill for services or €3–€5 for help with dinner reservations and such. In moderately priced hotels, leave housekeeping about €1 per day, and tip a minimum of €1 for valet or room service. In expensive hotels, double these amounts.

Sightseeing guides should receive €1.50 per person for a half-day group tour, more if the tour is longer and/or they're especially knowledgeable.

Visitor Information

The main online resource for tourist information in Sicily is ⊕ *www.visitsicily.info.* Sicily's major airports and most towns and cities have a tourist information office, but these may close out of season in smaller places. In Palermo, there are several information points, only one of which stays open all day every day, near the Martorana church in Piazza Bellini (⊠ *Via Maqueda 189,* ☎ *091/740–82020).* Here you can pick up timetables, transport details, and lots of other information on sights and events from the multilingual staff.

When to Go

Sicily's high season (mid-June through mid-September) is hot, expensive, and busy. During the peak season from late July to late August, beaches are crowded, and hotels and restaurants are often booked up, so advance reservations are necessary—often several weeks or even months for hotels and a day or two for restaurants.

April–May and mid-September–October are the ideal months for more temperate weather, more elbow room on the beaches, and more capacity and availability at hotels and restaurants. Just keep in mind the Easter period (lasting a few days around Good Friday) can be very busy, and some resort destinations may close in October.

The winter months of November through March see many places outside the cities closed, if only for a few weeks, while tourist facilities at most of Sicily's beach resorts and on all the offshore islands shut down for the entire period. Flights, accommodation rates, and car rentals are at their lowest at this time of year, but bear in mind that November and December see a lot of rain while January and February are the coldest months.

Helpful Italian Phrases

BASICS

Yes/no	Sí/No	see/no
Please	Per favore	pear fa-**vo**-ray
Thank you	Grazie	**grah**-tsee-ay
You're welcome	Prego	**pray**-go
I'm sorry (apology)	Mi dispiace	mee dis-pee-**atch**-ay
Excuse me, sorry	Scusi	**skoo**-zee
Good morning/ afternoon	Buongiorno	bwohn-**jor**-no
Good evening	Buona sera	**bwoh**-na **say**-ra
Good-bye	Arrivederci	a-ree-vah-**dare**-chee
Mr. (Sir)	Signore	see-**nyo**-ray
Mrs. (Ma'am)	Signora	see-**nyo**-ra
Miss	Signorina	see-nyo-**ree**-na
Pleased to meet you	Piacere	pee-ah-**chair**-ray
How are you?	Come sta?	ko-may-**stah**
Hello (phone)	Pronto?	**proan**-to

NUMBERS

one-half	mezzo	**mets**-zoh
one	uno	**oo**-no
two	due	**doo**-ay
three	tre	Tray
four	quattro	**kwah**-tro
five	cinque	**cheen**-kway
six	sei	Say
seven	sette	**set**-ay
eight	otto	**oh**-to
nine	nove	**no**-vay
ten	dieci	dee-**eh**-chee
eleven	undici	**oon**-dee-chee
twelve	dodici	**doh**-dee-chee
thirteen	tredici	**trey**-dee-chee
fourteen	quattordici	kwah-**tor**-dee-chee
fifteen	quindici	**kwin**-dee-chee
sixteen	sedici	**say**-dee-chee
seventeen	dicissette	dee-chah-**set**-ay
eighteen	diciotto	dee-chee-**oh**-to
nineteen	diciannove	dee-chee-ahn-**no**-vay
twenty	venti	**vain**-tee
twenty-one	ventuno	**vent**-oo-no
thirty	trenta	**train**-ta
forty	quaranta	kwa-**rahn**-ta
fifty	cinquanta	cheen-**kwahn**-ta
sixty	sessanta	seh-**sahn**-ta
seventy	settanta	seh-**tahn**-ta
eighty	ottanta	o-**tahn**-ta
ninety	novanta	no-**vahn**-ta
one hundred	cento	**chen**-to
one thousand	mille	**mee**-lay
one million	un milione	oon **mill**-oo-nay

COLORS

black	Nero	**nair**-ro
blue	Blu	bloo
brown	Marrone	ma-**rohn**-nay
green	Verde	**ver**-day
orange	Arancione	ah-rahn-**cho**-nay
red	Rosso	**rose**-so
white	Bianco	bee-**ahn**-koh
yellow	Giallo	**jaw**-low

DAYS OF THE WEEK

Sunday	Domenica	do-**meh**-nee-ka
Monday	Lunedi	loo-ne-**dee**
Tuesday	Martedi	mar-te-**dee**
Wednesday	Mercoledi	**mer**-ko-le-**dee**
Thursday	Giovedi	jo-ve-**dee**
Friday	Venerdì	ve-ner-**dee**
Saturday	Sabato	**sa**-ba-toh

MONTHS

January	Gennaio	jen-**ay**-o
February	Febbraio	feb-**rah**-yo
March	Marzo	**mart**-so
April	Aprile	a-**pril**-ay
May	Maggio	**mahd**-joe
June	Giugno	**joon**-yo
July	Luglio	**lool**-yo
August	Agosto	a-**gus**-to
September	Settembre	se-**tem**-bre
October	Ottobre	o-**toh**-bre
November	Novembre	no-**vem**-bre
December	Dicembre	di-**chem**-bre

USEFUL WORDS AND PHRASES

Do you speak English?	Parla Inglese?	**par**-la een-**glay**-zay
I don't speak Italian	Non parlo italiano	non **par**-lo ee-tal-**yah**-no
I don't understand	Non capisco	non ka-**peess**-ko
I don't know	Non lo so	non lo **so**
I understand	Capisco	ka-**peess**-ko
I'm American	Sono Americano(a)	**so**-no a-may-ree-**kah**-no(a)
I'm British	Sono inglese	so-no een-**glay**-zay
What's your name?	Come si chiama?	**ko**-may see kee-**ah**-ma
My name is ...	Mi chiamo...	mee kee-**ah**-mo
What time is it?	Che ore sono?	kay o-ray **so**-no
How?	Come?	**ko**-may
When?	Quando?	**kwan**-doe
Yesterday/today/ tomorrow	Ieri/oggi/domani	**yer**-ee/ o-jee/ do-**mah**-nee

This morning	Stamattina/Oggi	sta-ma-**tee**-na/ **o**-jee
Afternoon	Pomeriggio	po-mer-**ee**-jo
Tonight	Stasera	sta-**ser**-a
What?	Che cosa?	kay **ko**-za
What is it?	Che cos'è?	kay ko-**zey**
Why?	Perchè?	pear-**kay**
Who?	Chi?	**Kee**
Where is ...	Dov'è...	doe-**veh**
the train station?	la stazione?	la sta-tsee-**oh**-nay
the subway?	la metropolitana?	la may-tro-po-lee-**tah**-na
the bus stop?	la fermata dell'autobus?	la fer-**mah**-ta del-ow-tor-**booss**
the airport	l'aeroporto	la-er-roh-**por**-toh
the post office?	l'ufficio postale	loo-**fee**-cho po-**stah**-lay
the bank?	la banca?	la **bahn**-ka
the hotel?	l'hotel...?	lo-**tel**
the museum?	Il museo	eel moo-**zay**-o
the hospital?	l'ospedale?	lo-spay-**dah**-lay
the elevator?	l'ascensore	la-shen-**so**-ray
the restrooms?	...il bagno	eel **bahn**-yo
Here/there	Qui/là	kwee/la
Left/right	A sinistra/a destra	a see-**neess**-tra/a **des**-tra
Is it near/far?	È vicino/lontano?	ay vee-**chee**-no/ lon-**tah**-no
I'd like ...	Vorrei...	vo-**ray**
a room	una camera	**oo**-na **kah**-may-ra
the key	la chiave	la kee-**ah**-vay
a newspaper	un giornale	oon jore-**nah**-vay
a stamp	un francobollo	oon frahn-ko-**bo**-lo
I'd like to buy ...	Vorrei comprare...	vo-**ray** kom-**prah**-ray
a city map	una mappa della città	**oo**-na **mah**-pa **day**-la chee-**tah**
a road map	una carta stradale	**oo**-na **car**-tah stra-**dahl**-lay
a magazine	una revista	**oo**-na ray-**vees**-tah
envelopes	buste	**boos**-tay
writing paper	carta de lettera	**car**-tah dah **leyt**-ter-rah
a postcard	una cartolina	**oo**-na car-tog-**leen**-ah
a ticket	un biglietto	oon bee-**yet**-toh
How much is it?	Quanto costa?	**kwahn**-toe **coast**-a
It's expensive/cheap	È caro/economico	ay **car**-o/ ay-ko-**no**-mee-ko
A little/a lot	Poco/tanto	**po**-ko/**tahn**-to
More/less	Più/meno	pee-**oo**/**may**-no

Enough/too (much)	Abbastanza/ troppo	a-bas-**tahn**-sa/tro-po
I am sick	Sto male	sto **mah**-lay
Call a doctor	Chiama un dottore	kee-**ah**-mah-oondoe-**toe**-ray
Help!	Aiuto!	a-**yoo**-to
Stop!	Alt!	ahlt

DINING OUT

A bottle of ...	Una bottiglia di...	**oo**-na bo-**tee**-lee-ah dee
A cup of ...	Una tazza di...	**oo**-na **tah**-tsa dee
A glass of ...	Un bicchiere di...	oon bee-key-**air**-ay dee
Beer	La birra	la **beer**-rah
Bill/check	Il conto	eel **cone**-toe
Bread	Il pane	eel **pah**-nay
Breakfast	La prima colazione	la **pree**-ma ko-la-**tsee**-oh-nay
Butter	Il Burro	eel **boor**-roh
Cocktail/aperitif	L'aperitivo	la-pay-ree-**tee**-vo
Dinner	La cena	la **chen**-a
Fixed-price menu	Menù a prezzo fisso	may-**noo** a **pret**-so **fee**-so
Fork	La forchetta	la for-**ket**-a
I am vegetarian	Sono vegetariano(a)	**so**-no vay-jay-ta-ree-**ah**-no/a
I cannot eat ...	Non posso mangiare	non **pose**-so mahn-gee-**are**-ay
I'd like to order	Vorrei ordinare	vo-**ray** or-dee-**nah**-ray
Is service included?	Il servizio è incluso?	eel ser-**vee**-tzee-o ay een-**kloo**-zo
I'm hungry/thirsty	Ho fame/sede	oh **fah**-meh/**sehd**-ed
It's good/bad	È buono/cattivo	ay **bwo**-bo/ka-**tee**-vo
It's hot/cold	È caldo/freddo	ay **kahl**-doe/**fred**-o
Knife	Il coltello	eel kol-**tel**-o
Lunch	Il pranzo	eel **prahnt**-so
Menu	Il menu	eel may-**noo**
Napkin	Il tovagliolo	eel toe-va-lee-**oh**-lo
Pepper	Il pepe	eel **pep**-peh
Plate	Il piatto	eel pee-**aht**-toe
Please give me ...	Mi dia...	mee **dee**-a
Salt	Il sale	eel **sah**-lay
Spoon	Il cucchiaio	eel koo-kee-ah-yo
Tea	tè	tay
Water	acqua	**awk**-wah
Wine	vino	**vee**-noh

Great Itineraries

The Best of Sicily

While it can be said that one might never have enough time in Sicily, a week here should be enough to spend some time in its major cities and towns, see the essential sights, and truly experience the Sicilian way of life. Think of this itinerary as a rough draft for you to amend according to your interests and time constraints. Driving is the only viable way to take in every place mentioned here, but you could use public transport if you stick to the major stops, and it makes sense to abandon the car altogether within bigger towns and cities.

DAY 1: PALERMO

After arriving in Palermo's airport or seaport, take the train or a taxi to your accommodations. After checking in and freshening up, you'll be ready to plunge into the Vucciria or Ballaro markets for an invigorating immersion in the city's beating heart. If it's the morning, have a snack lunch of market specialties before returning to your hotel for a rest; if it's the afternoon, a postperambulation rest may still be in order.

Afterward, join the evening throng outside the Teatro Massimo and have a drink at a bar before dinner.

Logistics: If you have a car, stow it for the duration of your stay in Palermo (or don't pick up your rental until you leave for your next stop); driving through the city is simply not worth the hassle.

DAY 2: PALERMO AND MONREALE

Dedicate the morning to one of Palermo's greatest sights, the **Palazzo Reale**, the highlight of which is the richly mosaic-ed **Cappella Palatina**. If there's time afterward, take in the nearby church of **San Giovanni degli Eremiti**, whose red domes and peaceful cloister are a reminder of the city's Arab past. For lunch, treat yourself to a typically Sicilian *arancino* or two.

Spend the afternoon at **Monreale**, a short way out of town, where the richly ornamented **Duomo** offers another angle on the glorious synthesis of different cultures that thrived under Norman rule. Don't forget the adjacent **cloister**, with its 216 double columns and idiosyncratically carved capitals.

To wind down the day, head back into Palermo for a stroll along **Corso Vittorio Emanuele** and around the illuminated statuary of **Piazza Pretoria** before a dinner of *pasta con le sarde*, Palermo's signature dish.

Logistics: The Palazzo Reale is easily accessible on foot, but you'll need to drive or take a bus or taxi to Monreale and back.

DAY 3: CEFALÙ AND TAORMINA

Leave Palermo behind and head east along the coast to **Cefalù** for a visit to another magnificent Arab-Norman cathedral, allowing an interesting comparison to the one in Monreale. Have a wander through the seaside town's intricate, boutique-filled lanes, ending up on the seafront for a swim at the lovely beach— if you have a bathing suit handy—or a drink, followed by lunch overlooking the bay.

In the afternoon, continue your progress east along the Tyrrhenian Coast, looking out to sea for glimpses of the **Aeolian Islands.** At **Messina**, on Sicily's northeastern point, have a pause to admire the sublime views across the Strait of Messina to the mountains of Calabria before carrying on south down the Ionian coast to **Taormina**.

Once you arrive at this iconic hilltop town, check into your hotel and slip into something stylish to join the fashionable parade along Corso Umberto, stopping for an evening drink before enjoying a fabulous meal, preferably with views over the coast.

Logistics: The nonstop drive from Cefalù to Taormina should take around 2 hours 30 minutes along the Tyrrhenian and Ionian coasts, but if you are willing to endure a longer journey, you might consider a very different, inland route, heading south from Cefalù through the Madonie Mountains to the SS120. The eastward section of this road takes in some stupendous mountain scenery as it winds through (or past) the remote hilltop villages of Gangi, Nicosia, Troina, and Cesarò. The dramatic silhouette of Mount Etna is a constant and growing presence, and you'll finally arrive at the volcano's foothills around Randazzo before reaching Taormina. The whole trip might take a little under five hours, though, so it should not be undertaken lightly.

DAY 4: TAORMINA
After breakfast, explore Taormina's specific attractions, most splendid of which is the superbly sited **Teatro Greco**. Have a picnic lunch in the shady and usually calm **Villa Comunale**.

In the afternoon jump on the **Funivia** to explore **Taormina Mare**, the site of the resort's bijou beach and a nature reserve on the aptly named **Isolabella** ("beautiful island"). If you still have the energy, head back up to Taormina and venture 5 km (3 miles) inland to lofty **Castelmola** to take in the stunning panorama, perhaps accompanied by a glass of cool almond wine.

After an evening meal, you might finish off your day with a concert or dramatic performance at Taormina's Teatro Greco.

Logistics: Before your arrival in Taormina, check with your hotel what, if any, parking arrangements they have. If none, you can take advantage of one of the town's capacious car parks as street-parking is virtually impossible.

DAY 5: SIRACUSA
Drive down the coast past Mount Etna and the sprawling city of Catania to **Siracusa,** one of Greece's earliest colonies in southern Italy. Here, you can start your sightseeing tour on the island of **Ortigia**, a tightly packed labyrinth of streets with the broad and graceful **Piazza del Duomo** at its heart. The **Duomo** itself deserves a

Great Itineraries

thorough examination, allowing you to unpick the various strands of Siracusa's history encapsulated in one building. Make sure your wanderings bring you to the delightful **Fonte Aretusa**, a freshwater spring close to the harbor that's rich with legend. Here, or on the harborside itself, would be a great lunch spot.

Devote the afternoon to the **archaeological park** on the mainland, whose centerpiece is the impressive **Greek theater**, though other sights here are equally enthralling, not least the intriguing **Orecchio di Dionisio**, or "Ear of Dionysius," famous for its ear-shape entrance and unusual acoustics. If there's time afterward, it's well worth visiting the nearby **Museo Archeologico**, one of Sicily's greatest archaeological collections that will help to put everything you've seen into context.

If your visit to Siracusa coincides with the annual program of classical tragedies performed in the Greek theater, you might remain in this part of town in order to attend; otherwise head back to Ortigia for supper, followed by a moonlit stroll along the harborfront.

Logistics: The Taormina–Siracusa drive takes around 1 hour, 30 minutes on autostrada A18 (with tolls). Ortigia is mainly car-free; most drivers use the large Talete car park on the island's east side. A city map would be useful here. It's easy to take a bus or taxi from Ortigia to the archaeological park.

DAY 6: NOTO, MODICA, AND RAGUSA

From Siracusa, drive 38 km (23 miles) southwest to the town of **Noto**. The highlights here are the **cattedrale** and the **Palazzo Nicolaci di Villadora**, two masterpieces of Baroque architecture, but the true joy is really in wandering the town's harmonious streets. Have a snack

lunch here before setting off on SS115 and SP17 to **Modica**, another gorgeous Baroque town. Stop here long enough to visit the lovely 18th-century church of **San Giorgio** and to pick up some of the town's famed chocolate.

From Modica, it's a brief drive to Ragusa, the third of the region's Baroque gems, where another church of **San Giorgio** is the main draw. Spend the night in Ragusa, or else drive on to your next stop, **Agrigento** to find accommodations there.

Logistics: From Siracusa, you can reach Noto in around 40 minutes by car. The drive between Noto and Modica also takes around 40 minutes, and from Modica to Ragusa it's 25 minutes on SS115. Stay on SS115 from Ragusa to reach Agrigento, a drive of around 2 hours, 20 minutes.

DAY 7: AGRIGENTO AND PALERMO

It will take you a whole morning to tour Agrigento's celebrated **Valle dei Templi**, one of the wonders of the classical world. This captivating ensemble of Greek monuments is located on a rise overlooking the sea, just outside the town.

Once you've had your fill, head north across the island's interior back to Palermo, for your onward travel back home. Alternatively, continue westward on SS115 to **Sciacca** for lunch before taking SS188 and SS624 north to Palermo.

Logistics: The drive from Agrigento to Palermo on the straight, fast SS189 and SS124 roads takes just under 2 hours, 15 minutes. If you drive to Sciacca on SS115 (around 1 hour), then head north on SS624, the total Agrigento–Palermo drive-time is about the same, to which you should add any time spent in Sciacca itself.

On the Calendar

February

Carnevale di Acireale. Carnival is celebrated with great vigor throughout Sicily, but Acireale's carnival celebrations are known as being the island's best, with fantastical floats, entertaining parades, and thousands of revelers packing the streets of the coastal town. The exact dates depend on Easter, but events usually take place in February, over the course of three weekends before the start of Lent (Ash Wednesday). ⊕ *www.carnevaleacireale.eu.*

Festa di Sant'Agata. Between February 3 and 5, Catania's primary festival dedicated to its patron Sant'Agata takes over the city. The relics of the martyr are paraded through the streets accompanied by thousands of devout followers, and gigantic, elaborately decorated candlesticks are carried for hours at a time by representatives of the city's trades amid similarly enthusiastic crowds. ⊕ *www.festadisantagata.it.*

Sagra del Mandorlo in Fiore. In late February and early March, when most of the almond trees are in blossom, Agrigento hosts the Sagra del Mandorlo in Fiore, with international folk dances, a costumed parade, and the sale of marzipan and other sweet treats made from almonds. ⊕ *www.mandorloinfiore.online.*

April

Processione dei Misteri. Easter, a moveable feast but usually taking place in April, sees life-size wooden statues representing figures from the Passion of Christ carried shoulder-high through the streets of Trapani on Good Friday. Each of the 20 groups of figures is associated with one of the town's traditional trades, such as fishermen and saltworkers, and are paraded by members of the relevant guilds draped in purple robes and cowls. The procession takes around 10 hours, between 2 pm and midnight. Equally dramatic events take place in other Sicilian towns around Easter—those in Taormina are especially impressive.

May

Greek Drama at Siracusa. Classical Greek dramas are performed at Siracusa's grand Teatro Greco from mid-May to early July. ⊕ *www.indafondazione.org.*

Festa della Madonna a Cavallo. In Scicli, the last Saturday in May brings the festival of the town's savior, Madonna delle Milizie (Virgin Mary of Militias), celebrating the supposed moment in the 11th century when the Virgin Mary descended on horseback to rescue the Norman-ruled town from a Saracen invasion. The weekend festival includes parading a statue of the Madonna on horseback through the main piazza to intervene in a mock battle before reveling in salvation by indulging in a sweet pastry towering with whipped cream, known as a *testa di turco*. ⊕ *www.comune.scicli.rg.it.*

June

Taormina Arte. In the wake of the town's film festival, Taormina Arte (aka TaoArte) features a full program of theater, music, and dance events from June to early October, with the Teatro Antico one of the main venues. ⊕ *www.taoarte.it.*

Taormina Film Festival. Sicily's famous festival takes place in the panoramic Teatro Antico over a week in late June and early July. ⊕ *www.taorminafilmfest.it.*

On the Calendar

July

Festa di Santa Rosalia. Taking place July 10–15, Palermo's most important festival celebrates its patron saint's rescue of the city from plague in 1624. Events include a long parade from the Palazzo dei Normanni along Corso Vittorio Emanuele to the seafront, headed by a candlelit statue of the saint borne aloft. There are also puppet reenactments of the saint's miracles, in addition to concerts, exhibitions, and gastronomic events. The celebrations culminate in a spectacular display of fireworks over the harbor. The liturgical part of the festival takes place on the anniversary of the saint's death, September 4, when a pilgrimage on foot is made to her sanctuary on Monte Pellegrino.

August

Ferragosto. The feast of the Assumption, held on August 15 (though festivities often extend a week or more on either side), is celebrated all over Sicily, but rarely reaches such spectacular heights as in Messina, where late night fireworks dramatically light up the Strait separating Sicily from the mainland. During the day, the *Vara*, a heavy carriage 14 meters tall and elaborately adorned with cherubs and angels, is hauled through town by teams of sweating penitents.

Festa dei Giganti. Between August 10 and 14, giant statues of Messina's legendary founders, Mata and Grifone, both mounted on huge steeds, are wheeled through the city accompanied by cheering crowds.

Palio dei Normanni. Held in the historic center of Piazza Armerina on August 12–14, the Norman Palio features medieval jousting, music, and a procession of locals in the garb of knights and nobles along the town's narrow streets. The colorful procession ends at the Duomo, where homage is paid to Count Roger and the keys to the city delivered to him. ⊕ *www.comune.piazzaarmerina.en.it.*

September

Couscous Fest. The principal festival at the beach resort of San Vito Lo Capo, in Sicily's far west, is dedicated to couscous, prepared and available to sample in innumerable ways. It's not just about food, as the town pulls out all the stops with music, dancing, and fireworks until late, taking place over 10 days in mid- to late September. ⊕ *www.couscousfest.it.*

December

Festa di Santa Lucia. The feast of Siracusa's patron, Santa Lucia, is held from December 13 to 20 at the Church of Santa Lucia alla Badia. A splendid silver statue of the saint is carried from the church to the Duomo: a torchlight procession and band music accompany the bearers, while local families watch from their balconies. ⊕ *www.basilicasantalucia.com.*

Did You Know?

Selinunte is Europe's largest archaeological park, with over 2,500 years of history spread over 600 acres on Sicily's southwestern coast.

Contacts

Air

AIRPORTS Aeroporto Vincenzo Florio Trapani Birgi. ✉ *Contrada Birgi Nivaloro, Trapani* ☎ *0923/610111* ⊕ *www.airgest.it.* **Catania-Fontanarossa Airport.** ✉ *Via Fontanarossa, Catania* ☎ *095/7239111* ⊕ *www.aeroporto. catania.it/en.* **Lampedusa Airport.** ✉ *Contrada Cala Francese, Lampedusa* ☎ *0922/970731.* **Palermo Airport.** ☎ *800/541880* ⊕ *www.aeroportodipalermo.it.* **Pantelleria Airport.** ✉ *Contrada Margana* ☎ *0923/911172* ⊕ *www. aeroportodipantelleria.it.*

Bus

CONTACTS AST. ☎ *091/6800011* ⊕ *www. aziendasicilianatrasporti. it.* **Autoservizi Russo.** ☎ *0924/31364* ⊕ *www. russoautoservizi. it.* **Autoservizi Salemi.** ☎ *0923/981120* ⊕ *www. autoservizisalemi.it.* **Prestia & Comandè.** ☎ *091/580457* ⊕ *www.prestiaecomande. it.* **SAIS.** ☎ *800/211020* toll-free ⊕ *www.saisautolinee.it.* **Segesta Autolinee.** ☎ *06/164160* ⊕ *www. segesta.it.* **Tarantola e Cuffaro.** ☎ *0924/31020* ⊕ *www.tarantolacuffaro.it.*

Car

LOCAL RENTAL CAR COMPANIES AG Transfers. ✉ *Aeroporto Fontanarossa, Catania* ☎ *095/349330* ⊕ *www.agtransfers.it.* **Maggiore.** ✉ *Via Vittorio Emanuele II 75, Messina* ☎ *090/675476* ⊕ *www. maggiore.it.* **Riolo Rent.** ✉ *Viale Regione Siciliana 1514, Palermo* ☎ *800/180477.* **Sicily Rent Car.** ✉ *Aeroporto Falcone e Borsellino, Palermo* ☎ *091/203374* ⊕ *www. sicilyrentcar.it.* **Lacauto.** ✉ *Aeroporto Fontanarossa, Catania* ☎ *095/346893* ⊕ *www.locautorent.com.* **Noleggiare.** ✉ *Aeroporto Fontanarossa, Catania* ☎ *392/8173940* ⊕ *www. noleggiare.it.* **Speed Rent.** ✉ *Via Pergusa 58, Enna* ☎ *0935/1980167* ⊕ *www. speedrentsicily.it.* **HSA Rent A Car.** ✉ *Via La Farina 13, Messina* ☎ *090/9020692* ⊕ *www.hsarentacar.it.* **WayCar.** ✉ *Via Piersanti Mattarella 33, San Vito Lo Capo* ☎ *389/7908495* ⊕ *www.waycar.it.* **Sicily By Car.** ✉ *Corso Umberto 90, Siracusa* ☎ *0931/483044* ⊕ *www.sicilybycar. it.* **Syracuse Rent Car.** ✉ *Lungomare di Levante Elio Vittorini 8, Siracusa* ☎ *329/3846935* ⊕ *www. syracuse-rentcar.com.* **Etna Rent.** ✉ *Via Apollo Arcageta 12, Taormina*

☎ *0942/51972* ⊕ *www. taorminarent.it.* **Rent Car Seminara.** ✉ *Contrada Mastrissa, Taormina* ☎ *0942/625628* ⊕ *www. rentcarseminara.com.* **Ruggirello.** ✉ *Corso Italia 70, Trapani* ☎ *0923/360612* ⊕ *www.autonoleggioruggirello.it.*

Ferries and Hydrofoils

CONTACTS Blu Ferries. ☎ *090/6786626* ⊕ *www. bluferries.it.* **Caronte & Tourist.** ☎ *090/5737* ⊕ *www. carontetourist.it.* **Liberty Lines.** ☎ *0923/022022* ⊕ *www.libertylines.it.* **Blu Jet.** ☎ *340/9848540* ⊕ *www.blujetlines.it.* **Siremar.** ☎ *090/364601* ⊕ *www.siremar.it.* **GNV.** ☎ *010/2094591* ⊕ *www.gnv.it.* **SNAV.** ☎ *081/4285555* ⊕ *www. snav.it.* **Grimaldi Lines.** ☎ *081/496444* ⊕ *www. grimaldi-lines.com.* **Pellaro.** ☎ *081/496444* ⊕ *www. pellaro.net.* **Tirrenia.** ☎ *0781/1889026* ⊕ *www. tirrenia-traghetti.it.*

Trains

Trenitalia. ☎ *892021 within Italy* ⊕ *www.trenitalia. com.*

Chapter 3

PALERMO AND WESTERN SICILY

3

Updated by
Robert Andrews

⊙ Sights	🎔 Restaurants	🛏 Hotels	🛍 Shopping	🍸 Nightlife
★★★★★	★★★★☆	★★★★☆	★★★☆☆	★★★★☆

WELCOME TO PALERMO AND WESTERN SICILY

TOP REASONS TO GO

★ **Palermo's multicultural heritage:** Virtually every great European empire ruled Sicily's strategically positioned capital at some point, and it shows most of all in the city's diverse architecture, from Byzantine and Arab-Norman to Baroque.

★ **Riserva dello Zingaro:** Escape the hubbub amid the pristine environment of this nature reserve, a tranquil blend of undeveloped coast and wild mountain scenery.

★ **San Vito Lo Capo:** By common consent, the fine sandy bay at this out-and-out holiday town constitutes one of Sicily's finest beaches. It's an essential component of San Vito's appeal, which also includes September's exuberant couscous festival.

★ **The ruins of Segesta:** Greek temples don't come much more perfectly preserved than this one, poised above the countryside in majestic isolation.

1 Palermo. The unmissable capital of the island and the most theatrical of Sicilian cities.

2 Monreale. Home to arguably the grandest of Sicily's Arab-Norman cathedrals.

3 Bagheria. Once the abode of princes, a small town that now has a remarkable museum dedicated to its native son, the artist Renato Guttuso.

4 Mondello. Palermo's seaside satellite, ideal for an afternoon on the beach or an evening among the milling crowds.

5 Ustica. A remote isle north of Palermo with gorgeous sea views.

6 Corleone. An inland center famed for its Mafia connections, now home to a museum illustrating Cosa Nostra's atrocities and the fightback against organized crime.

7 Gibellina. An earthquake-struck village with one astounding work of landscape art.

8 Segesta. A beautifully preserved temple owing much of its powerful impact to its isolated hillside location.

9 Castellammare del Golfo. A peaceful fishing port and resort.

Isola Levanzo
Isola Marettimo
ISOLA EGADI
Marettimo
Isola Favignana
Favignana
Isola Grande
Mozia Island
Marsala

0   10 mi
0   10 km

10 Scopello. A postcard-pretty village, with tall rocky stacks sprouting out of the sea nearby.

11 Riserva Naturale dello Zingaro. Far from the urban bustle, a stretch of uncontaminated coast that is a balm for body and soul.

12 San Vito Lo Capo. A full-on beach resort with everything you need for an intense summer spree.

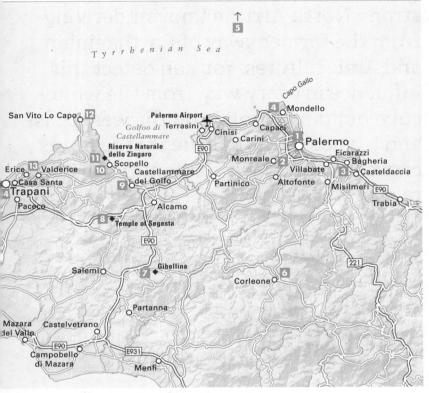

13 Erice. A warren of beautifully preserved medieval streets in a hilltop village, thick with atmosphere.

14 Trapani. Built on a curving promontory with the sea on either side, with a lively old town that makes an appealing base for exploring farther afield.

15 Favigana. The largest of the Egadi Islands, with the archipelago's finest beaches.

16 Levanzo. An Egadi island with a brilliant array of prehistoric cave art.

17 Marettimo. The most remote of the Egadi Islands and a well-guarded secret among lovers of solitude and wilderness.

18 Marsala. A coastal town best known for its fortified wine and recovered Punic warship on display.

19 Mozia Island. Once a Carthaginian base, now a fascinating archaeological site.

Palermo and western Sicily have a character very distinct from Sicily's other regions, a difference attributable to its strong North African imprint deriving from the former sway of Carthaginian and Arab cultures. You can detect this influence in every way, from the white-cube buildings prolific on the west coast and islands to the cuisine that features couscous and sweet elements such as raisins.

The stamp of other cultures is very much in evidence, too, not least in Palermo where the synthesis of Greek, Jewish, Arab, and Norman is evident in the great monuments and churches of Palermo and Monreale, embellished by some of the most beautiful mosaics and calligraphic designs to be found anywhere in Europe. The red domes of Palermo's churches of San Cataldo and San Giovanni degli Eremiti would not look out of place in Tunis, nor would the glittering mosaics appear unusual in Constantinople or Ravenna. Palermo also has some of Italy's grandest examples of Baroque architecture, but you can find much humbler and more engaging Baroque artistry hidden away in the private oratories adorned with the sculptures of the master of stucco, Giacomo Serpotta, and in the playful statuary of Bagheria's Villa Palagonia.

Outside Palermo, Sicily's Greek heritage is showcased in the temple at Segesta—one of the finest Greek temples anywhere—while Greek, Carthaginian, and Roman traces can be found on Mozia island. As for the Norman presence, this is evident throughout the west, from the ruined castles and bastions of such towns and villages as Castellammare del Golfo and Caltabellotta to the stark, medieval flavor of hilltop Erice.

There's a rougher and rawer style to the western landscape, too, which you can experience in the wilderness of the Riserva dello Zingaro nature reserve on the Golfo di Castellammare. Ustica island and the Egadi Islands have something of this untrammeled flavor, too, with human settlement confined to small huddles of dwellings and the rest given over to barren rock and scrubland. The pristine waters here are popular with snorkelers and divers.

Urban culture is very much in evidence in the west-coast towns of Trapani and Marsala, in both of which you'll find elegant architecture and bustling evening promenades. Holiday crowds predominate in the region's premier beach resort,

San Vito Lo Capo, on the northwestern tip of the island, though in winter you'll find little movement of any kind here.

In the less populated interior, towns and villages are few and far between. It's worth the trek into the rolling countryside south of Palermo to wander the streets of Corleone, a provincial center that once had dark associations with organized crime and now holds a compelling exhibition that graphically tells the story of Sicily's Cosa Nostra.

Planning

When to Go

Palermo is an all-year-round city whose attractions normally have the same time-tables no matter the season. Accommodations are available throughout the year, though some restaurants take advantage of the quiet months of January and February to allow their staff well-earned rests and undertake any renovations and maintenance required. The above is also true for the other major towns in the region, like Trapani and Marsala. However, when it comes to the islands (the Egadi archipelago and Ustica), you'll find almost everywhere closed between October and Easter, with a severely limited choice of places to eat and sleep. The same applies to the out-and-out summer resort of San Vito Lo Capo as well as the tourist magnet of Erice, which is often shrouded in mist during the winter months.

A visit in spring would enable you to appreciate the coasts and countryside at their best, not least the Zingaro nature reserve. Make sure you reserve accommodations well ahead if you are thinking of visiting the islands and coastal resorts during the peak summer months, and avoid this period altogether if you want a little more elbow room on the beaches.

Planning Your Time

As the island's capital, Palermo has western Sicily's richest mix of attractions, restaurants, and nightlife, and also makes a great base for visiting outlying destinations such as Monreale, Mondello, Bagheria, and Ustica. You could comfortably spend up to a week here without exhausting the local sights, though two or three days would be enough to take in the essentials.

If you plan to tour the whole region, you might allow about a week if you're content to make more or less cursory visits to the destinations covered here, or two weeks if you wish to travel at a more relaxed pace.

Most people start in the capital and venture forth from there. The coastal towns of Trapani and Marsala make useful overnight stops, and you could comfortably take in their main attractions in a morning or afternoon each. These are also viable bases for explorations farther afield, like Mozia and the Egadi Islands. On the other hand, the Egadi Islands make ideal places to unwind with a bit of relaxing beach time, as does Ustica, so you may decide to stay longer in these places. Castellammare del Golfo, Scopello, and San Vito Lo Capo would merit one or two days each, more if you wish to explore the Zingaro nature reserve.

One way to take in Western Sicily would be to head south from Palermo, perhaps making a brief stop at Corleone, then continue on to the south coast and work around the coast clockwise, making inland excursions to Erice and Segesta. The alternative, of course, would be to head west and follow the coast counterclockwise.

Getting Here and Around

AIR

Western Sicily holds two of the island's regional airports, outside the cities of Palermo and Trapani, both of which handle international flights as well as regular flights to and from other Italian cities such as Milan, Rome, and Naples, and to Sicily's far-flung isles of Pantelleria and Lampedusa.

There are good transport services from the airports to Palermo and Trapani city centers, and less frequent bus services to some other towns.

CONTACTS Falcone Borsellino Airport.
✉ *Palermo* ☎ *091/7020111, 800/541880 toll-free* ⊕ *www.aeroportodipalermo. it.* **Trapani–Birgi Airport.** ✉ *Trapani* ☎ *0923/610111* ⊕ *www.airgest.it.*

BOAT

Siremar (ferries) and Liberty Lines (hydrofoils) link Palermo with Ustica, and Trapani and Marsala with the Egadi islands of Favignana, Levanzo, and Marrettimo. Ferries are generally half the price, but take twice as long as hydrofoils.

CONTACTS Liberty Lines. ☎ *0923/022022* ⊕ *www.libertylines.it.* **Siremar.** ☎ *090/364601* ⊕ *www.siremar.it.*

BUS

Air-conditioned buses connect Palermo and all the major towns of the region and are often faster and more convenient than local trains, but also slightly more expensive. Various companies serve the different routes. SAIS Autolinee operates a frequent service between Palermo and Catania, Messina, and mainland cities, in each case arriving at and departing from near the train stations. Salemi connects Palermo with Marsala and Trapani. Prestia & Comandè serves the Palermo–Palermo Airport route. Segesta travels between Palermo and Trapani while AST links Palermo with Monreale and Corleone,

and Trapani with Erice, Castellammare del Golfo, and San Vito Lo Capo.

CONTACTS Autoservizi Salemi.
☎ *0923/981120* ⊕ *www.autoservizis-alemi.it.* **AST.** ☎ *0916/208111* ⊕ *www. aziendasicilianatrasporti.it.* **Prestia & Comandè.** ☎ *091/580457* ⊕ *www. prestiaecomande.it.* **SAIS Autolinee.**
☎ *091/2776999* ⊕ *www.saisautolinee.it.*

CAR

While you don't need a car in Palermo, driving is a good way to explore the rest of western Sicily. Along with the autostrada network, which links Palermo to Messina, Catania, Trapani, and Marsala, there is a good set of major roads connecting the coastal towns. Avoid, if you can, minor country roads, colored white on maps and called *strade bianche* ("white roads"), as these can be atrocious—pitted with potholes, heaps of rubble, and landslips—especially at night or after a rainstorm.

TRAIN

A good and frequent train service runs along Sicily's northern coast between Palermo and Messina, taking in Bagheria and Cefalù. Single-track local trains connect Palermo with Castellammare del Golfo, Trapani, and Agrigento, but these are slow and infrequent.

CONTACTS Trenitalia. ☎ *892021 within Italy* ⊕ *www.trenitalia.com.*

Hotels

Palermo has a huge selection of lodgings to suit every taste and pocket, ranging from apartment B&Bs to glitzy and luxurious hotels, often oozing historic character. Few of these are equipped with restaurants, but this should not be an issue with the abundance of eateries in every neighborhood.

Outside the capital, you'll find discreet hideaways in places like Erice and Scopello, as well as secluded villas with acres of grounds. Strangely, few places in coastal towns and resorts face the sea, but many of these have access to private beaches. The islands—Ustica and the Egadis—have a much smaller range of accommodations, usually only open between Easter and October, and what there is fills up months ahead for summer stays. You'll need your own transport to overnight in rural areas, but these generally have their own restaurants and more spacious facilities.

Restaurants

Restaurants in western Sicily demonstrate a passion for seafood as strong as anywhere else on the island. Other than this, though, you can expect to find dishes unavailable on menus elsewhere, for example, Palermo's signature dishes of *macco di fave,* a soup with broad beans and wild fennel, or the Arab-influenced *pasta con le sarde,* with sardines, fennel, raisins, and pine nuts.

For snacks, Palermo's street food like *pane con le milza* (*pani ca meusa* in dialect), a panino stuffed with spleen of veal, and *sfincione,* a sort of pizza seasoned with tomato sauce, onion, caciovallo cheese, and anchovies, is available from stalls in markets, and well worth sampling.

North African–inspired couscous is widely available in the region, especially in the two westernmost towns of Trapani and Marsala and on the Egadi Islands, where it is often prepared with seafood. Trapani's *pesto alla trapanese,* with fresh basil, almonds, garlic, olive oil, cheese, and fresh tomatoes, also makes a delicious pasta topping.

Increasingly you'll find a few gluten-free choices on the region's menus, though vegetarians may have a tough time varying their diet, as little is available for them beyond soups, grilled vegetables, and salads.

RESTAURANT AND HOTEL PRICES

Restaurant prices in the reviews are the average cost of a main course at dinner, or if dinner is not served, at lunch. Hotel prices in the reviews are the lowest cost of a standard double room in high season. Restaurant and hotel reviews have been shortened. For full information, visit Fodors.com.

What it Costs In Euros			
$	$$	$$$	$$$$
RESTAURANTS			
under €15	€15–€22	€23–€30	over €30
HOTELS			
under €125	€125–€225	€226–€350	over €350

Palermo

Once the intellectual capital of southern Europe, Palermo has always been at the crossroads of civilization. Favorably located on a crescent bay at the foot of Monte Pellegrino, it has attracted almost every culture touching the Mediterranean world. To Palermo's credit, it's absorbed these diverse cultures into a unique personality that's at once Arab and Christian, Byzantine and Roman, Norman and Italian. The city's heritage encompasses all of Sicily's varied ages, but its distinctive aspect is its Arab-Norman identity, an improbable marriage that, mixed in with Byzantine and Jewish elements, resulted in resplendent works of art. These are most notable in its churches, from small jewels such as San Giovanni degli Eremiti to larger-scale works such as the cathedral. No less noteworthy than the architecture is Palermo's chaotic vitality, on display at some of Italy's most vibrant outdoor markets, public squares, street bazaars, and food vendors, and, above all, in its grand, discordant symphony of motorists, motorcyclists, and pedestrians that triumphantly climaxes in the new town center each evening with Italy's most spectacular passeggiata.

Sicily's capital is a multilayered, vigorous metropolis with a strong historical profile; approach it with an open mind. You're likely to encounter some frustrating instances of inefficiency and, depending on the season, stifling heat. If you have a car, park it in a garage as soon as you can, and don't take it out until you're ready to depart.

Palermo is easily explored on foot, but you may choose to spend a morning taking a bus tour to help you get oriented. The Quattro Canti, or Four Corners, is the hub that separates the four sections of the old city: La Kalsa (the old Arab section) to the southeast, Albergheria to the southwest, Capo to the northwest, and Vucciria to the northeast. Each of these is a tumult of activity during the day, though at night the narrow alleys empty out and are best avoided in favor of the more animated avenues of the new city north of Teatro Massimo. Sights to see by day are scattered along three major streets: Corso Vittorio Emanuele, Via Maqueda, and Via Roma. The tourist information office in Piazza Bellini will give you a map and a valuable handout that lists opening and closing times, which sometimes change with the seasons.

GETTING HERE AND AROUND

Palermo is home to one of Sicily's two major international airports, Aeroporto di Falcone Borsellino at Punta Raisi, 30 km (18 miles) west of town, and as such is a main gateway for those arriving in Sicily by plane. Along with international flights, there are regular connections from and to other Italian cities such as Milan, Rome, and Naples, as well as to Sicily's far-flung isles of Pantelleria and Lampedusa.

Trains run from the station below Palermo's airport to the city center every half hour or so, with tickets dispensed from machines. Don't forget to validate your ticket before travel by punching it at one of the station's machines. Prestia e Comandè buses run every 30 minutes to Piazza Ruggero Settimo in the city center. A taxi from Palermo's airport to the center should cost €40–€50, while shared taxis cost €8 per person, with drop-offs at a range of points within the city (though you may have to wait for the minimum of five passengers before setting off). Journey time by taxi or bus between Palermo airport and city center is 30 minutes to one hour, depending on traffic; by train, it's around one hour, with stops within walking distance of Palazzo Reale and Via della Libertà before reaching the main station.

You'll find you can walk to most spots within central Palermo, though it's worth taking advantage of city bus services, run by AMAT, for longer stretches—for example, between the main train station and Piazza Castelnuovo (Bus 101); between the main train station and Piazza dell'Indipendenza, for the Palazzo Reale (Bus 109); and out to Monreale (Bus 389 from Piazza dell'Indipendenza) and Mondello (Bus 806 from the Politeama or Viale della Libertà).

Bus tickets can be purchased from kiosks and shops showing the AMAT sticker and cost €1.40 for any journeys made within 90 minutes (timed from when you punch your ticket in the machine onboard the bus); €3.50 for tickets lasting an entire day; €6 for tickets lasting two days; €8 for three days; and €16.50 for a week.

VISITOR INFORMATION

CONTACTS Palermo Tourism Office. ⊠ *Piazza Bellini, Quattro Canti* ☎ *091/7408020 Piazza Bellini, 091/591698 airport* ⊕ *www.cittametropolitana.pa.it/turismo.*

Did You Know?

At Palermo's Museo Archeologico Regionale Salinas (the oldest public museum in Sicily), you can view a wonderful collection of excavated pieces from different regions in Sicily and relax in the peaceful, plant-filled courtyard.

Palermo

Sights ▼

1	Catacombe dei Cappuccini	A7
2	Cattedrale	F7
3	Chiesa del Gesù	G7
4	La Martorana	G7
5	Museo Archeologico Regionale Salinas	G5
6	Museo Internazionale delle Marionette Antonio Pasqualino	I5
7	Oratorio del Rosario di San Domenico	H5
8	Oratorio di Santa Cita	H5
9	Palazzo Abatellis	J6
10	Palazzo Butera	J5
11	Palazzo Reale	E7
12	Piazza Pretoria	G6
13	Quattro Canti	G6
14	San Cataldo	G6
15	San Giovanni degli Eremiti	E8
16	Santa Caterina	G6
17	Teatro Massimo	F5

Restaurants ▼

1	Casa del Brodo	H6
2	Comparucci	E3
3	MadoniEAT	J5
4	MEC Restaurant	F7
5	Osteria dei Vespri	H7
6	Ristorante Cin Cin	E2

Quick Bites ▼

1	Antica Focacceria San Francesco	H6
2	Café Latino	G6
3	Cappadonia	F6
4	Pani Cà Meusa	I5

Hotels ▼

1	Eurostars Centrale Palace	G6
2	Grand Hotel Piazza Borsa	H6
3	Hotel Principe di Villafranca	D3
4	La Dimora del Genio	H7
5	Le Terrazze	F7
6	Massimo Plaza Hotel	F5
7	Palazzo Pantaleo	F4
8	Villa Igiea	G1

Sights

Catacombe dei Cappuccini

CEMETERY | The spookiest sight in all of Sicily, this 16th-century catacomb houses over 8,000 corpses of men, women, and young children—some in tombs but many mummified and preserved—hanging in rows on the walls, divided by social caste, age, or gender. Most wear signs indicating their names and the years they lived, and many are Capuchin friars, who were founders and proprietors of this bizarre establishment from 1599 to 1911. The site is still managed by the nearby Capuchin church, but was closed to new corpses when an adjacent cemetery was opened, making the catacombs redundant. Though memorable, this is not a spot for the faint of heart; children might be frightened or disturbed. ⊠ *Piazza Cappuccini 1, off Via Cappuccini, Near Palazzo Reale* ☎ *091/6527389* ⊕ *www.catacombepalermo.it* ⛶ *€3.*

Cattedrale

CHURCH | This church is a lesson in Palermitano eclecticism—originally Norman (1182), then Catalan Gothic (14th to 15th century), then fitted out with a Baroque and neoclassical interior (18th century). Its turrets, towers, dome, and arches come together in the kind of meeting of diverse elements that King Roger II (1095–1154), whose tomb is inside along with that of Frederick II, fostered during his reign. The exterior is more intriguing than the interior, but the back of the apse is gracefully decorated with interlacing Arab arches inlaid with limestone and black volcanic tufa. It's possible to visit the cathedral's roof for some fabulous city views. ⊠ *Corso Vittorio Emanuele, Palermo* ☎ *091/334373* ⊕ *www.cattedrale.palermo.it* ⛶ *Free; €12 treasury, crypt, royal tombs, and roof visit; €7 treasury, crypt, and tombs; €2 royal tombs only.*

Chiesa del Gesù

CHURCH | It is more than worth the short detour from the lively Ballarò Market to step into the serene Baroque perfection of Chiesa del Gesù (Church of St. Mary of Gesù). The ornate church was built by the Jesuits not long after their arrival in Palermo in the late 16th century, and was constructed at the site of their religious seat in the city, so the chuch is also sometimes known as Casa Professa (mother house). The interior is almost completely covered with intricate marble bas-reliefs and elaborate black, tangerine, and cream stone work. The splendid church was severely damaged in World War II, but careful restoration has returned it to its shiny, swirling glory. ⊠ *Piazza Casa Professa 21, Palermo* ☎ *338/4512011* ⛶ *Free.*

★ La Martorana

(*Santa Maria dell'Ammiraglio*)
CHURCH | One piazza over from the dancing nymphs of Fontana Pretoria, this church, with its elegant Norman campanile, was erected in 1143 but had its interior altered considerably during the Baroque period. High along the western wall, however, is some of the oldest and best-preserved mosaic artwork of the Norman period. Near the entrance is an interesting mosaic of King Roger II being crowned by Christ. In it Roger is dressed in a bejeweled Byzantine stole, reflecting the Norman court's penchant for all things Byzantine. Archangels along the ceiling wear the same stole wrapped around their shoulders and arms. The much plainer San Cataldo is next door. ⊠ *Piazza Bellini 3, Quattro Canti* ☎ *345/8288231* ⛶ *€2* ☉ *Closed Sun. and Mon.*

Museo Archeologico Regionale Salinas (*Salinas Regional Museum of Archaeology*)

HISTORY MUSEUM | This archaeology museum is the oldest public museum in Sicily, with a small but excellent collection, including a marvelously reconstructed

The church La Martorana contains some of the oldest and best preserved mosaic artwork of the Norman period in Italy.

Doric frieze from the Greek temple at Selinunte, which reveals the high level of artistic culture attained by the Greeks in Sicily some 2,500 years ago. There are also lion's head water spouts from 480 BC, as well as other excavated pieces from around Sicily, including Taormina and Agrigento, which make up part of an informative exhibition on the broader history of the island. After admiring the artifacts, wander through the two plant-filled courtyards, and be sure to check the website for special culture nights, when the museum is open late to host musical performances. ⊠ *Piazza Olivella 24, Via Roma, Olivella* ☎ *091/6116807* 🖶 *€6* ⊘ *Closed Mon.*

Museo Internazionale delle Marionette Antonio Pasqualino

OTHER MUSEUM | FAMILY | This collection of more than 4,000 masterpieces showcasing the traditional Opera dei Pupi (puppet show), both Sicilian and otherwise, will delight visitors of all ages with their glittering armor and fierce expressions. The free audio guide to the colorful displays is only available in Italian, but the well-designed exhibits include video clips of the puppets in action, which requires no translation. There are also regular live performances in the museum's theater (stop by or call in advance to check times), which center on the chivalric legends of troubadours of bygone times. The museum can be hard to find: look for the small alley just off Piazzetta Antonio Pasqualino 5. ⊠ *Piazzetta Antonio Pasqualino 5, near Via Butera, Kalsa* ☎ *091/328060* ⊕ *www. museodellemarionette.it/en* 🖶 *€5* ⊘ *Closed Sat.*

Oratorio del Rosario di San Domenico

CHURCH | Despite its grand facade and airy interior, the church of San Domenico itself holds little interest for anyone who isn't excited by the tombs of Sicilian notables, but the eponymous oratory, located behind the church, constitutes one of Palermo's great unsung treasures. The private chapel is generously adorned with sumptuous, creamy white stuccos, exquisitely crafted by Giacomo Serpotta (1656–1732) and depicting figures representing Patience, Obedience, Humility, Liberty, Justice, and more. Unusually, these allegorical figures take the form of elegant society ladies—something which would never have been possible in a public place of worship like a church. A QR code shown at the ticket office will allow you to download an app that provides background information on what you're looking at, such as the numerous symbols incorporated into each of the sculptures, including the gold-colored lizard on Fortitude's column, a puny reference to the artist himself, whose name resembles the Sicilian dialect word for "lizard." Around the allegorical figures cavort a host of playful *putti* (cherubs), some of them playing musical instruments, while the 1628 painting above the altarpiece, *Madonna and Saints*, is the work of Anthony van Dyck. ⊠ *Via dei Bambinai 2, Vucciria* ☎ *091/332779* 🎫 *€4; €6 with admission to Oratorio di Santa Cita.*

Oratorio di Santa Cita

CHURCH | Hidden behind high walls and accessed through a courtyard, the oratory—or private chapel—of Saint Cita boasts one of the finest collections of the graceful white stuccos for which their creator, Giacomo Serpotta (1656–1732), is famous. The centerpiece is an amazingly elaborate rendering of the Battle of Lepanto, at which the Ottoman Turkish fleet was defeated by combined Christian forces in 1571. The walls are inset with a series of Biblical scenes from the life of Jesus. To leaven the solemnity of such scenes, however, Serpotta has introduced some of his most fetching portrayals of the ordinary people of Palermo, from street urchins to wizened old men and sophisticated ladies, while an army of mischievous *putti* (cherubs) interweaves among them. ⊠ *Via Valverde 3, Vucciria* ☎ *091/7853181* 🎫 *€4; €6 with admission to Oratorio del Rosario di San Domenico.*

Palazzo Abatellis

ART MUSEUM | Housed in this late-15th-century Catalan Gothic palace with Renaissance elements is the Galleria Regionale. Among its treasures are the *Annunciation* (1474), a painting by Sicily's prominent Renaissance master Antonello da Messina (1430–79), and an arresting fresco by an unknown 15th-century painter, titled *The Triumph of Death*, a macabre depiction of the plague years. ⊠ *Via Alloro 4, Kalsa* ☎ *091/6230011* 🎫 *€8* ⊘ *Closed Mon.*

★ Palazzo Butera

ART MUSEUM | Dating from the 18th century but closed for most of the last four decades, the Palazzo Butera has reopened following a complete face-lift and conversion into one of Sicily's (and Italy's) most imaginative museum collections. Its labyrinthine rooms now display a heady mixture of old and new art. The collection's strength lies in its bold juxtapositions, with works by an international roster of experimental modern artists of the likes of Gilbert and George, and David Tremlett, exhibited alongside classical landscapes and graceful Sicilian furniture from the 19th century. Painted ceilings remain from the palace's Baroque beginnings, some of them artfully peeled back to reveal the wooden construction behind them. Diverse temporary exhibitions displayed on the ground floor add to the mix. There's a lot to take in, but if you need a break from all the hectic creativity, head for the terrace, accessed from the second floor, which provides benches and a walk around one of the two courtyards as well as views over the harbor. You can get even better views from the viewing platform reached from the roof, while further up, steps lead to a lofty view of the harbor, Monte Pellegrino, and, inland, the whole of the Conca d'Oro bowl in which the city sits. ⊠ *Via Butera 18, Kalsa* ☎ *091/7521754* ⊕ *www.palazzobutera.it* 🎫 *€7.50* ⊘ *Closed Mon.*

★ **Palazzo Reale** (*Royal Palace*)
CASTLE/PALACE | This historic palace, also called Palazzo dei Normanni (Norman Palace), was the seat of Sicily's semiautonomous rulers for centuries; the building is a fascinating mesh of 10th-century Norman and 17th-century Spanish structures. Because it now houses the Sicilian Parliament, parts of the palace are closed to the public from Tuesday to Thursday when the regional assembly is in session. The must-see Cappella Palatina (Palatine Chapel) remains open. Built by Roger II in 1132, it's a dazzling example of the harmony of artistic elements produced under the Normans and the interweaving of cultures in the court. Here the skill of French and Sicilian masons was brought to bear on the decorative purity of Arab ornamentation and the splendor of 11th-century Greek Byzantine mosaics. The interior is covered with glittering mosaics and capped by a splendid 10th-century Arab honeycomb stalactite wooden ceiling. Biblical stories blend happily with scenes of Arab life—look for one showing a picnic in a harem—and Norman court pageantry.

Upstairs are the royal apartments, including the Sala di Re Ruggero (King Roger's Hall), decorated with ornate medieval mosaics of hunting scenes—an earlier (1120) secular counterpoint to the religious themes seen elsewhere. During the time of its construction, French, Latin, and Arabic were spoken here, and Arab astronomers and poets exchanged ideas with Latin and Greek scholars in one of the most interesting marriages of culture in the Western world. From Friday to Monday, the Sala is included with entry to the palace or chapel; it sometimes hosts special art exhibits. ⊠ *Piazza del Parlamento, Near Palazzo Reale* ☎ *091/7055611* ⊕ *www.federicosecondo. org* ⊠ *€19 Fri.–Mon.; €16 Tues.–Thurs.* ⊙ *Royal Apartments closed Tues.–Thurs.*

Piazza Pretoria
FOUNTAIN | The square's centerpiece, a lavishly decorated fountain with 500 separate pieces of sculpture and an abundance of nude figures, so shocked some Palermitans when it was unveiled in 1575 that it got the nickname "Fountain of Shame." It's even more of a sight when illuminated at night. ⊠ *Piazza Pretoria, Quattro Canti.*

Quattro Canti
STREET | The Four Corners is the decorated intersection of two main thoroughfares: Corso Vittorio Emanuele and Via Maqueda. Four rather exhaust-blackened Baroque palaces from Spanish rule meet at concave corners, each with its own fountain and representations of a Spanish ruler, patron saint, and one of the four seasons. Today it's often a venue for buskers and other street performers. ⊠ *Palermo.*

San Cataldo
CHURCH | Three striking Saracenic scarlet domes mark this church, built in 1154 during the Norman occupation of Palermo. The church now belongs to the Knights of the Holy Sepulchre and has a spare but intense stone interior. ⊠ *Piazza Bellini 3, Kalsa* ☎ *091/6077111* ⊠ *€2.50.*

San Giovanni degli Eremiti
CHURCH | Distinguished by its five reddish-orange domes and stripped-clean stone interior, this 12th-century church was built by the Normans on the site of an earlier mosque—one of 200 that once stood in Palermo. The emirs ruled Palermo for nearly two centuries and brought to it their passion for lush gardens and fountains. One is reminded of this while sitting in San Giovanni's delightful cloister of twin half columns, surrounded by palm trees, jasmine, oleander, and citrus trees. ⊠ *Via dei Benedettini 14–20, Near Palazzo Reale* ☎ *091/6515019* ⊠ *€6.*

Palermo's Multicultural Pedigree

Palermo was first colonized by Phoenician traders in the 6th century BC, but it was their descendants, the Carthaginians, who built the important fortress here that caught the covetous eye of the Romans. After the First Punic War, the Romans took control of the city in the 3rd century BC. Following several invasions by the Vandals, Sicily was settled by Arabs, who made the country an emirate and established Palermo as a showpiece capital that rivaled both Córdoba and Cairo in the splendor of its architecture. Nestled in the fertile Conca d'Oro (Golden Conch) plain, full of orange, lemon, and carob groves and enclosed by limestone hills, Palermo became a magical world of palaces, mosques, minarets, and palm trees.

It was so attractive and sophisticated a city that the Norman ruler Roger de Hauteville (1031–1101) decided to conquer it and make it his capital (1072). The Norman occupation of Sicily resulted in Palermo's golden age (1072–1194), a remarkable period of enlightenment and learning in which the arts flourished. The city of Palermo, which in the 11th century counted more than 300,000 inhabitants, became the European center for the Norman court and one of the most important ports for trade between the East and West.

Eventually the Normans were replaced by the Swabian ruler Frederick II (1194–1250), the Holy Roman Emperor, and incorporated into the Kingdom of the Two Sicilies. You'll also see plenty of evidence in Palermo of the Baroque art and architecture of the long Spanish rule. The Aragonese viceroys also brought the Spanish Inquisition to Palermo, which some historians believe helped foster the protective secret societies that evolved into today's Mafia.

Santa Caterina

CHURCH | The walls of this splendid Baroque church (1596) in Piazza Bellini are covered with extremely impressive decorative 17th-century inlays of precious marble. There is also a bakery selling delicacies made using the nuns' recipes. ✉ *Piazza Bellini, Quattro Canti* ☎ *091/2713837* ⊕ *www.monasterosantacaterina.com* 🎟 *€3; €10 combined ticket, includes church, monastery, and rooftop.*

Teatro Massimo

PERFORMANCE VENUE | Construction of this formidable neoclassical theater, the largest in Italy, was started in 1875 by Giovanni Battista Basile and completed by his son Ernesto in 1897. A reconstruction project started in 1974 ran into severe delays, and the facility remained closed until just before its centenary, in 1997.

Its interior is as glorious as ever, but the exterior remains more famous thanks to *The Godfather Part III*, which ended with a famous shooting scene on the theater's steps. Visits, by 30-minute guided tour only, are available in five languages, including English. ✉ *Piazza Verdi 9, at top of Via Maqueda, Olivella* ☎ *091/6053267 tours, 091/8486000, 091/6053580 ticket office* ⊕ *www.teatromassimo.it* 🎟 *€10.*

🍴 Restaurants

Casa del Brodo

$$ | **SICILIAN** | On the edge of the Vucciria, this is one of Palermo's oldest restaurants, dating back to 1890, and still dear to the hearts of locals for its wintertime namesake dish, tortellini *in brodo* (in beef broth), the specialty of the house. There's an extensive antipasto

Palermo's Four Corners (Quattro Canti) is a popular spot for walkers and street performers.

buffet, and you can't go wrong with the *fritella di fave, piselli,*and *carciofi e ricotta* (fried fava beans, peas, artichokes, and ricotta). **Known for:** good choice of meat dishes; tortellini in brodo; large selection of antipasti. [$] *Average main: €15* ✉ *Corso Vittorio Emanuele 175, Vucciria* ☎ *091/321655* 🌐 *www.casadelbrodo.it* 🕓 *Closed Jan., Tues. in Oct.–May, and Sun. in June–Sept.*

★ Comparucci

$ | PIZZA | One of Palermo's best modern pizzerias serves delicious Neapolitan pies from a big oven in the open kitchen—the genius is in the crust, which is seared in a matter of seconds. The owners make their money on a quick turnover (so don't expect a long, leisurely meal), but the pizza is delicious and the place often serves until midnight—later than almost any other restaurant in the neighborhood. **Known for:** late-night dining; outdoor seating in summer; pizza, pizza, and more pizza. [$] *Average main: €8* ✉ *Via Messina 36e, Libertà* ☎ *091/6090467* 🌐 *www.comparucci.it* 🕓 *No lunch.*

★ MadoniEAT

$ | SICILIAN | Only the finest agricultural produce of the nearby Madonie mountains goes into the simple but fabulous dishes served in this informal eatery attached to the Palazzo Butera art gallery. The frequently changing menu—dependent on the season and what's available from their suppliers—might include chicken breasts in orange sauce and almonds; vegetarian meatballs with ricotta cheese; or sausages braised in red wine with kale. **Known for:** seasonal, fresh, and locally produced ingredients; gourmet sandwiches; convenient for lunch after a visit to Palazzo Butera. [$] *Average main: €11* ✉ *Palazzo Butera, Via Butera 20, Kalsa* ☎ *091/7521749* 🌐 *www.madonieat.com* 🕓 *Closed Mon. and 2 wks in Jan. No dinner.*

★ MEC Restaurant

$$$$ | SICILIAN | Here's a novelty for Palermo in the form of a superb modern restaurant located within a museum dedicated to Steve Jobs and Apple products, a surprisingly successful combination;

you not only have the ability to revisit ancient IT devices and learn about the history of the tech company, but the food is pretty excellent. Each of the dishes is a revelation, from the sea-urchin ice cream to the ravioli with stewed veal cheek and the lamb sirloin, while vegetarian options are as good as any that Palermo has to offer. **Known for:** restaurant and museum in one gorgeous historic building; attentive service; innovative modern dishes. $ *Average main: €40* ✉ *Via Vittorio Emanuele 452, Quattro Canti* ☎ *091/9891901* ⊕ *www.mecrestaurant.it* ⊗ *Closed Sun. No lunch.*

Osteria dei Vespri

$$$ | SICILIAN | This popular eatery occupies a cozy-but-elegant space on an unheralded piazza in the historic city center and splits its offerings between the winter menu (November–March) with traditional osteria fare, and a special larger tasting menu built around seasonal ingredients for the summer. Local seafood is a big draw here, and the house-made pastas won't disappoint, especially when paired with a selection from the extensive wine list. **Known for:** impressive wine cellar; local seafood; tasting menus with local ingredients. $ *Average main: €25* ✉ *Piazza Croce dei Vespri 6, Kalsa* ☎ *091/6171631* ⊕ *www.osteriadeivespri. it* ⊗ *No dinner Sun. No lunch Mon. in Nov.–Apr.*

Ristorante Cin Cin

$$ | SICILIAN | The Sicilian-born owner of this charming restaurant near Palermo's main shopping street is known for creating lighter and more modern versions of traditional Sicilian dishes, including exemplary pasta with ultrafresh seasonal ingredients and creative takes on seafood-based main dishes. Don't miss the signature dessert, a heavenly semifreddo with flavors like pistachio and cinnamon, chocolate and hazelnut, and Marsala wine and raisin—and perhaps learn some of the secrets with a chef's private cooking class. **Known for:** top-notch cooking

classes; delicious semifreddo; modernized Sicilian flavors. $ *Average main: €16* ✉ *Via Manin 22, Libertà* ☎ *091/6124095* ⊕ *www.ristorantecincin.com* ⊗ *Closed Sun. and Feb. No lunch.*

☕ Coffee and Quick Bites

Antica Focacceria San Francesco

$ | SICILIAN | Turn-of-the-20th-century wooden cabinets, marble-top tables, and cast-iron ovens characterize this neighborhood bakery, celebrated for its Sicilian snacks and inexpensive meals. The big pot on the counter holds the delicious regional specialty *pani cà meusa* (boiled calf's spleen with caciocavallo cheese and salt), but the squeamish can opt for chickpea fritters or an enormous arancina (stuffed, fried rice ball). **Known for:** meat and pasta specialties; historic atmosphere; Sicilian street food. $ *Average main: €12* ✉ *Via A. Paternostro 58, Kalsa* ☎ *091/320264* ⊕ *www.anticafocacceria.it* ⊗ *Closed Jan. and Feb.*

Café Latino

$ | CAFÉ | Just steps away from Quattro Canti, this smart snack stop has everything you could want to accompany a break from sightseeing: panini, house-made pastries and biscuits, ice cream, and good coffee. There are tables in the cozy interior and out on the pavement, and pastas, pizzas, and salads are also served if you want something more substantial. **Known for:** range of snacks and meals; relaxed setting; handy, central spot for a break. $ *Average main: €5* ✉ *Corso Vittorio Emanuele 276, Quattro Canti* ☎ *091/580910.*

Cappadonia

$ | ICE CREAM | FAMILY | After experiencing the cozy but basic trattorias located down Palermo's twisting alleyways, take a sweet break at this modern gelateria along the main drag, which serves exceptional gourmet ice cream. The flavors change with the seasons, but don't miss the tangerine sorbetto that bursts

Desserts in Sicily

Sicily is famous for its desserts, none more so than the wonderful cannoli (singular *cannolo*), whose delicate pastry shells and just-sweet-enough ricotta filling, and local pistachio crumbles barely resemble their foreign impostors. They come in all sizes, from pinkie-size bites to holiday cannoli the size of a coffee table, but all should be freshly made to order (*espressi*).

Even your everyday bar will display a window piled high with dozens of varieties of ricotta-based desserts, including delicious fried balls of dough, like the cream-filled iris of Catania. The traditional cake of Sicily is the *cassata siciliana*, a rich, chilled sponge cake with sheep's-milk ricotta and candied fruit. Often bright green

thanks to a colored almond-based frosting, it's the most popular dessert at many Sicilian restaurants, and you shouldn't miss it. From behind bakery windows and glass cases beam tiny marzipan sweets fashioned into brightly colored apples, cherries, and even hamburgers and prosciutto.

If it's summer, do as the locals do and dip your morning brioche—the best in Italy—into a cup of brilliantly refreshing coffee- or almond-flavored granita (Italian shaved ice). Indeed, top-quality frozen treats remain prevalent throughout the island; the world's first granita is said to have been made by the Romans from the snow on the slopes of Mt. Etna mixed with fruit from the countryside.

with sweet citrus tang or the classic zabaglione custard. **Known for:** central location; delicious ice cream; seasonal flavors. $ *Average main: €3* ⊠ *Via Vittorio Emanuele 401, Palermo* ☎ *392/5689784, 392/5759351* ⊕ *cappadonia.it* ⊙ *Closed Nov.–Feb.*

Pani Cà Meusa
$ | **SANDWICHES** | A civic institution facing Palermo's old fishing port, this standing-room-only joint has been serving its titular calf's spleen sandwich for more than 70 years. The original owner's grandsons still produce this local specialty sprinkled with a bit of salt and some lemon and served with or without cheese to a buzzing crowd of Palermo's well-weathered elders. **Known for:** no seating; a bit of Sicilian history; calf's spleen sandwich that might be the best in town. $ *Average main: €2* ⊠ *Via Cala 62, Porta Carbone, Kalsa* ☎ *091/323433* ⊙ *Closed Sun.*

🛏 Hotels

★ Eurostars Centrale Palace
$ | **HOTEL** | A stone's throw from Palermo's main historic sites, this is the only hotel in the heart of the old town that was once a stately private palace; built in 1717, it weaves old-world charm with modern comfort. **Pros:** great rooftop restaurant; comfortable rooms; location in the center of it all. **Cons:** some rooms have no views; very limited parking; showing its age a bit. $ *Rooms from: €116* ⊠ *Corso Vittorio Emanuele 327, Quattro Canti* ☎ *091/336666* ⊕ *www. eurostarscentralepalace.com* ➵ *104 rooms* ⊙ *Free Breakfast.*

Grand Hotel Piazza Borsa
$$ | **HOTEL** | Cleverly converted from three historic buildings—a bank, a palazzo, and a monastery—this hotel is ideally located in a quiet corner of the old town, just off the central axis of Corso Vittorio Emanuele. **Pros:** quiet but central location;

wellness center with fitness equipment, rare for Sicily hotels; interesting architecture. **Cons:** building feels a bit sterile; some noise issues in rooms; somewhat indifferent staff. $ *Rooms from: €145* ✉ *Via dei Cartari 18, Kalsa* ☎ *091/320075* ⊕ *piazzaborsa.it* ⇆ *127 rooms* ⦿ *Free Breakfast.*

Hotel Principe di Villafranca

$$ | HOTEL | Contemporary art mixed with antique furnishings, creamy marble floors, and vaulted ceilings evoke a luxurious private home in a residential area near Palermo's glitzy shopping district. **Pros:** appealing design; quiet, center-adjacent location; well-maintained building. **Cons:** immediate surroundings lack character; car park has just four spaces; some rooms and bathrooms on the small side. $ *Rooms from: €148* ✉ *Via G. Turrisi Colonna 4, Libertà* ☎ *091/6118523* ⊕ *www.principedivillafranca.it* ⇆ *32 rooms* ⦿ *Free Breakfast.*

La Dimora del Genio

$ | B&B/INN | Stepping into this charming apartment off Piazza della Rivoluzione is like entering a different time zone: a taste of Old Palermo where the elegant furnishings evoke a romantic world you might think only exists today in novels. **Pros:** spacious rooms; lively neighborhood; antique character. **Cons:** only two rooms that book up quickly; decor can be a bit somber; lots of steps and no elevator. $ *Rooms from: €120* ✉ *Via Garibaldi 58, Kalsa* ☎ *347/6587664* ⊕ *www. ladimoradelgenio.it* ⇆ *2 rooms* ⦿ *Free Breakfast.*

★ Le Terrazze

$ | B&B/INN | Although just steps from the bustling Cattedrale area, complete calm envelops this small, beautifully restored B&B, named for its five lush roof terraces, all with sublime views. **Pros:** convenient location; period-style rooms; in summer, breakfast is served on the glorious rooftop. **Cons:** Wi-Fi sometimes patchy; books up quickly; parking can be difficult. $ *Rooms from:*

€110 ✉ *Via Pietro Novelli 14, Albergheria* ☎ *091/6520866, 320/4328567* ⊕ *www. leterrazzebb.it* ▭ *No credit cards* ⇆ *2 rooms* ⦿ *Free Breakfast.*

Massimo Plaza Hotel

$$ | HOTEL | Small and select, this hotel enjoys one of Palermo's best locations—opposite the Teatro Massimo, on the border of the old and new towns—and has guest rooms that are spacious, comfortably furnished, and well insulated from the noise on pedestrianized Via Maqueda. **Pros:** central location; tasty breakfast made to order; low-season bargains. **Cons:** cheaper rooms have no views; in pedestrian zone, so vehicles have to keep their distance; 21 steps (no elevator) up to the rooms. $ *Rooms from: €191* ✉ *Via Maqueda 437, Olivella* ☎ *091/325657* ⊕ *www.massimoplazahotel.com* ⇆ *11 rooms* ⦿ *Free Breakfast.*

★ Palazzo Pantaleo

$ | B&B/INN | Accessed from a quiet courtyard situated between Palermo's two great theaters, with large, airy rooms and a charming host, this top-floor apartment is part of a beautifully renovated palazzo dating from the mid-19th century. **Pros:** pleasant and welcoming host; free private parking; very close to airport bus stop. **Cons:** a little hard to find; occasional noise intrusion from other guests; often booked up. $ *Rooms from: €110* ✉ *Via Ruggero Settimo 74, Libertà* ☎ *335/7006091* ⊕ *www.palazzopantaleo. it* ⇆ *7 rooms* ⦿ *Free Breakfast.*

★ Villa Igiea

$$$$ | HOTEL | Although recently renovated, this grande dame set in a private tropical garden at the edge of the bay—a local landmark for a century—still maintains a somewhat faded aura of luxury and comfort and retains its essential character. **Pros:** secluded setting; free shuttle to city center in the summer; historic building with lots of atmosphere. **Cons:** a bit far from Palermo attractions; no amenities in the nearby area; price range out of reach for most. $ *Rooms* *from: €680* ✉ *Salita Belmonte 43, Palermo* ☎ *091/2570050* ⊕ *villa-igiea.com* ⊘ *Closed early Nov.–mid-Mar.* ➿ *100 rooms* ⦿❘ *Free Breakfast.*

Nightlife

Each night between 6 and 9, Palermitans of all ages gather to shop, socialize, flirt, and plan the evening's affairs in an epic passeggiata along Via Maqueda and its northern extension Via Ruggiero Settimo, filling Piazza Ruggiero Settimo in front of Teatro Politeama. Some trendy bars also line Via Principe di Belmonte, intersecting with Via Roma and Via Ruggiero Settimo.

BARS AND CAFES
★ Bocum Fuoco
COCKTAIL LOUNGES | This multilevel cocktail bar between the Vucciria market and the marina is serious about mixology and has created a dedicated oasis in the city's trendiest area. Linger over complex cocktails while lounging on vintage chairs under sparkling chandeliers, all while rubbing elbows with Palermo's cool crowd as records spin on the retro turntable in the corner. A short menu of pasta, meat, and seafood dishes is also available. ✉ *Via dei Cassari 6, Vucciria* ☎ *091/332009* ⊕ *www.bocum.it.*

Santa Monica
PUBS | Immensely popular with the twenty- and thirtysomething crowd, who belly up to the bar for pizza, crepes, and excellent German-style draft beer, this pub is also a good place to watch televised soccer. ✉ *Via E. Parisi 7, Libertà* ☎ *091/324735* ⊕ *www.santamonicaris-torante.it.*

Performing Arts

Figli d'Arte Cuticchio Association
PUPPET SHOWS | FAMILY | Palermo's tradition of puppet theater holds an appeal for children and adults alike, and street artists often perform outside the Teatro Massimo in summer. One of the most celebrated examples of the folk tradition is performed by the Figli d'Arte Cuticchio association, which hosts classic puppet shows from September to June. ✉ *Via Bara all'Olivella 95, Olivella* ☎ *091/323400* ⊕ *www.figlidartecuticchio. com* ➿ *€10.*

★ Teatro Massimo
CONCERTS | As the biggest theater in Italy, Teatro Massimo is truly larger than life. Concerts and operas are presented throughout the year, though in summer concerts are usually held outdoors. An opera at the Massimo is an unforgettable Sicilian experience. ✉ *Piazza Verdi, at top of Via Maqueda, Palermo* ☎ *091/6053580 tickets, 091/8486000 general information, 091/6053267 tours* ⊕ *www. teatromassimo.it* ➿ *Performances from €22, tours €8.*

Teatro Politeama Garibaldi
CONCERTS | The shamelessly grandiose, neoclassical Teatro Politeama Garibaldi, home of the Orchestra Sinfonica Siciliana, stages a season of opera and orchestral works from October through June. ✉ *Piazza Ruggiero Settimo, Libertà* ☎ *091/6072532* ⊕ *www.orchestrasinfon-icasiciliana.it.*

Shopping

North of Piazza Castelnuovo, Via della Libertà and the surrounding streets represent the luxury end of the shopping scale. A second nerve center for shoppers is the pair of parallel streets connecting modern Palermo with the train station, Via Roma and Via Maqueda, where boutiques and shoe shops become increasingly upscale as you move from the Quattro Canti past Teatro Massimo to Via Ruggero Settimo.

Ballarò Market
MARKET | Wind your way through the Albergheria district and this historic market, where the Saracens did their shopping in the 11th century—joined by the Normans in the 12th. The market's

name is said to come from nearby Monreale, named Bahlara when Arab traders resided there, and it remains faithful to their original commerce of fruit, vegetables, and grain. These days the stalls are dotted with bars and outdoor restaurants where you can sample the produce, but the market has lost none of its authenticity—just keep a close eye on your belongings in the crowd. And go early: the action dies out by 4 pm most days. ⊠ *Ballarò Market, Albergheria* ✛ *Between La Martorana and Quattro Canti.*

Enoteca Picone

WINE/SPIRITS | The best wineshop in town has been family run for four generations and stocks a fantastic selection of Sicilian and national wines. Although service can be curt, you can taste a selection of wines by the glass in the front of the store. There are tables in the back, where meats and cheeses are also served. ⊠ *Via Marconi 36, Libertà* ☎ *091/331300* ⊕ *www.enotecapicone.it.*

I Peccatucci di Mamma Andrea

FOOD | The charming "Mamma Andrea's Small Sins" sells a plethora of mouthwatering original creations, including jams, preserves, chocolates, and Sicilian treats like the superb marzipan *frutta martorana* (fruits and vegetables). ⊠ *Via Principe di Scordia 67, on Piazza Florio, Libertà* ☎ *091/6111654* ⊕ *www.mammaandrea. com.*

Mercato del Capo

MARKET | Umbrella-covered stands crowd the narrow streets along Via Porta Carini and Via Beati Paoli, which are soon clogged with locals stopping to check out the daily fresh catch or haggle over household items at this traditional market. Less touristed than Palermo's other famous food markets, the atmosphere is lively without feeling showy, and there are excellent street food options tucked along the main artery—particularly the unmissable arancini at Da Arianna, a low-key eatery in the heart of the market. ⊠ *Via Porta Carini, Capo.*

Pasticceria Alba

FOOD | One of the most famous sweets shops in Italy, this is the place to find pastry favorites like cannoli and cassata siciliana, as well as excellent gelato in summer. There is also an on-site restaurant pizzeria. ⊠ *Piazza Don Bosco 7/C, off Via della Libertà near La Favorita Park, Libertà* ☎ *091/309016* ⊕ *www.baralbadonbosco.it.*

Tanto di Coppola

HATS & GLOVES | The *coppola*, or flat cap, is as Sicilian as cassata ice cream, though this traditional workingman's headwear has become something of a rarity in recent decades. Here, though, it makes a triumphant revival, lovingly transformed into something more akin to a fashion accessory while retaining its original style and function. You'll find every variation of it in this shop, from the sober and utilitarian to the colorful and outrageous, but always "handmade in Sicily" and even made to order. ⊠ *Via Bara all'Olivella 72, Olivella* ☎ *091/324428* ⊕ *www.tantodicoppola.it.*

Vincenzo Argento e Figli

CRAFTS | The Argento family has been in the puppet business since the late 19th century, and the tradition is alive and well in the hands of Vincenzo, whom you can see at work in his tiny workshop, or *laboratorio artistico*, near the Cathedral. Here you will find puppets in all stages of production, with plenty of examples for sale in all their finery. ⊠ *Via Vittorio Emanuele 445, Quattro Canti* ☎ *091/6113680.*

Vucciria Market

MARKET | It's easy to see how this market got its name—*vucciria* translates to "voices" or "hubbub." Though now just as frequented by tourists as it is by locals, Palermo's most established outdoor market, in the heart of the old town, is a maze of side streets around Piazza San Domenico, where hawkers deliver incessant chants from behind stands brimming with mounds of olives, blood oranges, fennel, and long-stem artichokes. Morning is the best time to see the market in full swing, but it takes on more of a street food atmosphere at night, when no-name bars open to sell cheap cocktails to the crowds gathering around the smoking grills that are wheeled outside after dark. ⊠ *Vucciria Market, Vucciria.*

Monreale

10 km (6 miles) southwest of Palermo.

Only a short drive or bus ride from Palermo, the sleepy town of Monreale is well worth the effort of a visit just to see the spectacular gold mosaics inside its Duomo. Try to arrive early in the morning or later in the afternoon to avoid the tour bus hordes.

GETTING HERE AND AROUND
You can reach Monreale on frequent AMAT buses that depart from Palermo's Piazza Indipendenza or on AST buses from Piazza Giulio Cesare, outside the central station. From Palermo, drivers can follow Corso Calatafimi west, though the going can be slow. Park in the car park a little way outside Monreale's center.

Sights

Cloister
RELIGIOUS BUILDING | The lovely cloister of the abbey adjacent to the Duomo was built at the same time as the church but enlarged in the 14th century. The beautiful enclosure is surrounded by 216 intricately carved double columns, every other one decorated in a unique glass mosaic pattern. Afterward, don't forget to walk behind the cloister to the belvedere, with stunning panoramic views over the Conca d'Oro (Golden Conch) valley toward Palermo. ⊠ *Piazza del Duomo, Monreale* ☎ *091/7489995* 🎫 *€6; €10 with Duomo.*

★ Duomo
CHURCH | Monreale's splendid cathedral is lavishly executed with mosaics depicting events from the Old and New Testaments. It's a glorious fusion of Eastern and Western influences, widely regarded as the finest example of Norman architecture in Sicily. After the Norman conquest of Sicily, the new princes showcased their ambitions through monumental building projects. William II (1154–89) built the church complex with a cloister and palace between 1174 and 1185, employing Byzantine craftsmen.

The major attraction is the 68,220 square feet of glittering gold mosaics decorating the cathedral interior. Christ Pantocrator dominates the apse area; the nave contains narratives of the Creation; and scenes from the life of Christ adorn the walls of the aisles and the transept. The painted wooden ceiling dates from 1816–37 while the roof commands a great view (a reward for climbing 172 stairs). The wood and metal organ, the only one in Europe with six keyboards and 10,000 pipes, was restored after lightning damage in 2015, and played by Mick Jagger on a private visit in 2021.

Bonnano Pisano's bronze doors, completed in 1186, depict 42 biblical scenes and are considered among the most important medieval artifacts still in existence. Barisano da Trani's 42 panels on the north door, dating from 1179, present saints and evangelists. ⊠ *Piazza del Duomo, Monreale* ⊕ *www.monrealeduomo.it* 🎫 *€4; €10 with Cloister.*

🍴 Restaurants

La Botte 1962
$$ | SICILIAN | It's worth the short drive or inexpensive taxi ride from Monreale to reach this restaurant, which is famous for well-prepared local specialties (just keep in mind it has limited open hours, so call before you come). Seafood dishes include *bavette don Carmelo*, a narrow

version of tagliatelle with a sauce of swordfish, squid, shrimp, and pine nuts while other favorites include *involtini alla siciliana* (meat roulades stuffed with salami and cheese). **Known for:** hazelnut semifreddo with hot chocolate dessert; good value set menus; sophisticated cooking and local wines. [$] *Average main: €16* ✉ *Contrada Lenzitti 20, SS186 KM 10, Monreale* ☎ *091/414051, 338/4383962* 🌐 *www.mauriziocascino.it* 🕒 *Closed Mon.–Thurs. (except by advance booking of at least 4 days) and Aug.–early Sept. No lunch Fri. and Sat. No dinner Sun.*

Le Barrique
$ | SICILIAN | Steps away from the Duomo's exquisitely patterned apse, this backstreet wine bar, restaurant, and deli entices you in with offers of wine, beer, and food. You won't be disappointed thanks to the top-quality fare, whether you order a bulging panino, a *tagliere* (tray) of cold meats, cheeses, and preserves, or a more substantial dish of veal or pork *involtini* (roulades) or house-made sausages. **Known for:** quality meats and cheeses; late night hours; good range of antipasti. [$] *Average main: €13* ✉ *Via Arcivescovado 4, Monreale* ☎ *393/5580298* 🕒 *Closed Mon. and 2 wks in Jan. and Feb.*

🛏 Hotels

Opera Boutique Rooms
$ | B&B/INN | This smart and central B&B offers a calm alternative to staying in Palermo whether or not you're primarily here to visit Monreale. **Pros:** varied and abundant breakfasts; location close to the Duomo; wonderful sauna. **Cons:** steep steps to climb and no elevator; no parking; occasional noise from adjacent rooms. [$] *Rooms from: €80* ✉ *Via Giuseppe Verdi 4, Monreale* ☎ *366/1270447* 🌐 *www.operaboutiquerooms.com* 🔑 *6 rooms* 🍴 *Free Breakfast.*

Bagheria

15 km (9 miles) east of Palermo.

Bagheria was a favorite summer haunt of Palermo's nobility in the 17th and 18th centuries, studded with a fabulous collection of Baroque mansions. Most of these were subsequently allowed to fall into ruin and Bagheria itself became notorious for its illegal building developments and Mafia activities. Today, an air of neglect hangs over the place, but some traces of its former glory have survived and two of its palaces, Villa Cattolica and Villa Palagonia, are now open to the public, holding, respectively, an important collection of 20th-century Sicilian art and a bizarre assemblage of grotesque statuary. For these alone, Bagheria makes an intriguing excursion, well worth a morning or afternoon off-the-beaten-track.

The town is also where Giuseppe Tornatore's nostalgic movie, *Cinema Paradiso*, was set and filmed, and was the locale of Dacia Maraini's delightful childhood memoir, *Bagheria*.

GETTING HERE AND AROUND

Bagheria is an exit on the A19 autostrada and can also be reached by car along SS113. There are regular AST buses from Palermo and it's a stop on the main Palermo–Cefalù train route as well. From Bagheria's train station, you can walk to Villa Cattolica in 10 minutes, and, in the opposite direction, to Villa Palagonia in the center of town in 30 minutes.

👁 Sights

Museo Guttuso
ART MUSEUM | One of Bagheria's most impressive palaces, Villa Cattolica has been meticulously renovated and converted into a gallery devoted to the artist Renato Guttuso (1911–87), who was born in the town. Guttuso's fierce, expressionist style and vivid sense of color made him one of Sicily's most renowned

modern artists, and the gallery traces his career from his earliest sketches in the 1920s and 1930s to his later bold canvases, including his last work, a huge collective portrait of his mistresses and muses. Guttuso started his career painting *carretti* (farmer's carts) in the traditional style and the first rooms feature a collection of painted carts. The gallery also hosts work by Guttuso's peers and contemporaries, and a separate building holds an exhibition of Italian film posters, including one for the film *Kaos*, designed by Guttuso. The artist's tomb lies in the villa's garden. ✉ *Via Ramacca 9* ☎ *366/8035918* 🌐 *www.museoguttuso.com* 🎫 *€6* 🕓 *Closed Mon.*

★ Villa Palagonia

HISTORIC HOME | Probably the most intriguing of all Bagheria's villas is the Villa Palagonia, which can either be viewed as a delightful flight of whimsy or the product of a disturbed mind. The villa was erected in 1705 by Francesco, Prince of Palagonia, and his architect, Tommaso Napoli, but what makes it stand out today is the work of Francesco's grandson, Ferdinando, a hunchback who commissioned a weird assembly of sculptures depicting monsters and bizarre figures said to be caricatures of his wife's lovers. Visitors will see a parade of them on either side of the front and back entrances as well as atop the walls of the surrounding garden, a grotesque gallery of monsters, gnomes, and gargoyles. Only 64 of the original statues remain—they are once said to number 200—and these are in a poor state of repair.

You'll find the same air of dereliction when you climb the once-grand double staircase to enter the palace itself, where only five rooms are currently open to the public. Most striking of these is the Salone degli Specchi, a large hall whose domed ceiling is covered in mirrors, now cracked and fogged. Along the marbled walls here and in other rooms are arrayed flamboyant busts, faded frescoes, and trompe l'oeil effects that recall the grandeur that the villa must once have embodied, though you'll come away with a sense of wistful regret that more care has not been taken to restore and maintain this peculiar place. ✉ *Piazza Garibaldi 3, Palermo* ☎ *091/932088* 🌐 *www.villapalagonia.it* 🎫 *€6.*

🍴 Restaurants

★ Osteria Can Caus

$ | **SICILIAN** | This welcoming *osteria* near the train station makes a perfect lunch stop. With friendly staff and an appealing modern interior—red-tiled floor, chic basket lampshades, and rows of hanging wine bottles—it serves up inexpensive but expertly prepared dishes of local specialties such as risotto with prawns and artichoke cream, and *baccalà su macco de fave* (salted cod on a bean and fennel stew). **Known for:** local dishes and wine; good desserts; chic interior. [$] *Average main: €11* ✉ *Corso Butera 9, Palermo* ☎ *333/6790636* 🕓 *Closed Mon. No dinner Sun.*

Mondello

10 km (6 miles) north of Palermo.

Beyond the hulking elevation of Monte Pellegrino, the seaside resort of Mondello offers a refreshing break from the heat and crowds of Palermo in the summer months. With its long sandy beach and parade of bars and ice-cream parlors, at its best it's a fun getaway for an evening of carefree entertainment, while at its worst it teeters on the tacky, its blitz of stalls, hot dog and burger bars, and noisy revving scooters sometimes oppressive. Avoid the weekend if you want a quieter time. In winter, it's positively serene, though you'll find some of the hotels and restaurants are closed.

The seaside town of Mondello makes a nice break from the chaos and crowds of Palermo.

By day, the main magnet is, naturally, the beach, which is divided between *spiagge libere* (free to use, but without any facilities) and sectioned-off private lidos where you pay a daily rate for access. Away from the beach, there's nothing specific to see in Mondello, but the pleasure is all in perambulating or cruising up and down the promenade, admiring—or wincing at—the monumental pavilions that line the seafront, some in art deco or art nouveau style, and some undeniably kitsch. Whatever your take on the architecture, you can't fail to be impressed by the soaring proximity of Monte Pellegrino.

GETTING HERE AND AROUND

From Via Filippo Turati in Palermo, next to the Politeama Theater, Bus 806 leaves for Mondello every 20 minutes. The ride takes around 35 minutes.

Beaches

Mondello Beach

BEACH | FAMILY | The town's beach is a 2-km (1-mile) stretch of sand, unusually clean for its proximity to the city. You can choose between public areas or private lidos where you can rent sun-loungers and a parasol and gain access to washing facilities with hot showers and changing rooms (expect to pay €15–€20 for an entire day, though afternoon rates may be reduced). The private beaches are also noticeably tidier and are patrolled by lifeguards. All the beaches get very busy on weekends but you should always be able to find space. **Amenities:** food and drink; lifeguards; washing facilities. **Best for:** water sports; swimming; walking. ⊠ *Via Regina Elena, Mondello.*

Restaurants

Charleston

$$$$ | SICILIAN | For fine dining in Mondello, you can't go wrong with Charleston, a local institution where the dishes are of the highest quality and the white-gloved waiters offer impeccable service. Partly hidden behind a low white wall directly opposite the beach, the restaurant is an odd combination of the traditional and the contemporary, as the setting is stately and refined while the menu has the minimalist yet adventurous quality of cutting-edge cuisine. **Known for:** prestige institution; sophisticated setting; high-concept dishes like swordfish wrapped with cheese, sultanas, and pine nuts. [$] *Average main: €70* ⊠ *Viale Regina Elena 37/39, Mondello* ☎ *091/450171* ⊕ *www.ristorantecharleston.com* ⊗ *Closed Sun. and Nov.–Mar.*

L'Angolo di Mondello

$$ | SEAFOOD | Seafood is the cuisine of choice in Mondello, though the quality on offer at many of the seafront restaurants can be patchy, to say the least, but you'll find no complaints at this family-run trattoria. With a smart, modern interior and an outdoor terrace, it has an upbeat ambience and a helpful English-speaking staff. **Known for:** fresh high-quality seafood; long list of antipasti; good-time atmosphere. [$] *Average main: €18* ⊠ *Via Mondello 15, Mondello* ☎ *091/6377921* ⊗ *Closed Wed. and Nov.*

🛏 Hotels

B&B Mondello Resort

$$ | B&B/INN | FAMILY | You'll feel indulged at this sequestered B&B located in a quiet lane a 15-minute walk from Mondello's seafront. **Pros:** lovely garden; helpful hosts; large pool. **Cons:** four-night minimum stay in summer; distant from the center of the action in Mondello; high prices. [$] *Rooms from: €142* ⊠ *Villa Dena, Viale Egle 7, Mondello* ☎ *339/5886611* ⊕ *www.bbmondelloresort.it* 🍽 *5 rooms* ❍ *Free Breakfast.*

Ustica

60 km (37 miles) north of Palermo.

Only 5 km (3 miles) in diameter, the isle of Ustica (pronounced with the emphasis on the first syllable) was used to hold prisoners until the 1950s, and still appears completely cut off from the currents of Palermo, to which it is umbilically attached by a regular ferry and hydrofoil service.

It is this very remoteness in the middle of the Tyrrhenian Sea that makes the island a favorite getaway for Palermitani, who come here in droves on weekends and daily during the summer months. To cater for this influx, there are numerous bars and restaurants in the only town on the island, also called Ustica. Since most visitors are day-trippers, there's a smaller choice of accommodations. Come in winter, however (roughly between November and March), and you'll find almost everything shut down, with only a handful of restaurants and bars open and at most a couple of accommodation options. If you have any choice, May, June, or September would be the ideal months to visit, avoiding the worst of the crowds while still finding a good selection of facilities open for business.

Once you're here, the main recreations boil down to exploring the main town with its souvenir and craft shops, lounging by the port, embarking on boat tours around the island, and tackling the footpaths that wind around Ustica's perimeter. You could complete a circuit of the island in two- to three-hours, and there are a few detours that allow you to take short-cuts or branch off along inland routes. Just be sure to bring headwear, as the island is mainly tree-less and unshaded.

Despite it being an island, Ustica has little to offer in the way of beaches—the few that exist are narrow and rocky, while the seabed is sharp with volcanic stones (so gear up with water shoes if you're planning to swim). Snorkeling and scuba diving are popular pursuits as the island's waters are kept crystal-clear thanks to Ustica's protected status—the island became Italy's first marine protected area in 1986.

GETTING HERE AND AROUND

Siremar ferries (3 hours) and Liberty Lines hydrofoils (90 minutes) travel daily between Palermo and Ustica.

Restaurants

★ Il Terrazzino

$$ | SICILIAN | Centrally located on the main piazza in Ustica town, this trattoria's outdoor terrace is a marvelous spot for feeling like you're in the thick of local life while enjoying first-class food. Seafood is the main feature, of course, on a menu that combines traditional dishes, such as prawn ravioli, with more adventurous juxtapositions, like the antipasto of grilled octopus with lentil purée. **Known for:** great location; convivial ambience; fresh seafood. $ *Average main: €18* ✉ *Piazza Umberto I, Ustica* ☎ *388/8990301* 🕐 *Closed Oct.–Mar.*

Rosso di Sera

$$ | SICILIAN | With its covered terrace overlooking the port, Rosso di Sera combines great food with a laid-back atmosphere conducive to feelings of well-being and positivity. Well-presented dishes such as *busiate* pasta with rockfish—or with any other fish that has been freshly caught—and *polpette di melanzane* (eggplant balls) are fresh and succulent, and you'll be tempted desserts like *cannoli* and ricotta mousse. **Known for:** splendid harbor view; booking ahead necessary for a terrace table; fresh seafood. $ *Average main: €18* ✉ *Via Vittorio Emanuele 11, Ustica* ☎ *331/7767115* 🕐 *Closed Oct.–Mar.*

🛏 Hotels

Residence Stella Marina

$ | APARTMENT | In a prime position overlooking the port, this residence is the best option for spending a few days on Ustica. **Pros:** perfect location; access to private lido; unbeatable harbor views. **Cons:** some rooms are small and viewless; two-night minimum; unimaginative breakfasts. $ *Rooms from: €109* ✉ *Via Cristoforo Colombo 35, Ustica* ☎ *338/5358588* ⊕ *www.stellamarinaustica.it* 🕐 *Closed Nov.–Feb.* 🛏 *11 rooms* 🍽 *Free Breakfast.*

🏃 Activities

★ Orca Diving Ustica

DIVING & SNORKELING | Enjoying the benefits of its marine protected area, Ustica enjoys some of the best diving in the Mediterranean, as its clean and clear waters are perfect for viewing a range of underwater life and a stunning marine landscape. Orca Diving Ustica, based near the port, takes care of everything, from tuition to equipment hire, delicious snacks between the dives, and even transport and accommodation. The friendly and professional staff have access to a range of excellent diving sites. ✉ *Via Cristoforo Colombo 39, Ustica* ☎ *334/2161588* ⊕ *www.orcadivingustica.com* 🤿 *From €45.*

Corleone

60 km (37 miles) south of Palermo.

A journey to the inland town of Corleone is like crossing into another era, traversing an empty landscape largely unchanged for decades. The town itself is small and provincial (population around 11,000), an agricultural center with nothing in common with Palermo's zippy, cosmopolitan flavor.

Long before Mario Puzo borrowed the name for his fictional Godfather, Don Corleone, the town was notorious for its Mafia associations. The Corleonese clan was one of the most powerful Mafia groups in Sicily, whose bosses included Luciano Leggio, responsible for the murder of the trade union leader Placido Rizzoto in 1948, and Leggio's successors, Salvatore Riina and Leoluca Bagarella (both implicated in the murders of the judges Giovanni Falcone and Paolo Borsellino in 1992).

Visitors to Corleone today will find little evidence of present-day criminality, though the town's main attraction, a museum of the Mafia, poignantly preserves the memories of both the outlaws who put the town on the map and their victims.

GETTING HERE AND AROUND

A drive from Palermo takes about 1 hour and 15 minutes to reach Corleone, using the A19 autostrada eastward, then south onto SS121 and SS118. Four or five AST buses a day take around 90 minutes to reach Corleone from Palermo.

◉ Sights

★ **C.I.D.M.A.** (*The Centro Internazionale di Documentazione sulla Mafia e del Movimento Antimafia*)

HISTORY MUSEUM | Housed, perhaps appropriately, in an ex-orphanage in the center of Corleone, the Centro Internazionale di Documentazione sulla Mafia e del Movimento Antimafia, or C.I.D.M.A., chronicles the dark history of the criminal organization that has been identified with Sicily for much of the 20th century. Most of the story is told through a moving exhibition of black-and-white photographs, almost all taken by Letizia Battaglia, who bravely made it her life's work to record the Mafia's activities in Sicily, in particular the arrests of Mafia operatives and the deaths of their victims. One room holds the vast collection of files

used in the Maxi-Trial of Mafia suspects that took place between 1986 and 1992, which directly led to the murders of the judges Giovanni Falcone and Paolo Borsellino, who are also remembered here. There is space given to the *pentito* (informant) Tomasso Buscetta, whose testimony resulted in a slew of arrests, but whose entire family was wiped out by vengeful hitmen . It's a sad and sobering experience to hear about such atrocities, and a visit to the center is best undertaken with a guide, without whose explanations you would miss much essential information. Call ahead to book a guided tour (available in English). ✉ *Via G. Valenti 7, Corleone* ☎ *340/4025601, 091/84524295* ⊕ *www.cidmacorleone.it* 🖃 *€8* ⊗ *Closed Sun.*

🍴 Restaurants

Al Capriccio

$ | SICILIAN | As befits a simple trattoria in a traditional provincial town, this is an unashamedly old-fashioned place, unswayed by any desire to innovate, instead relying on time-tested local recipes that have satisfied generations of customers. Take the signature dish: Spaghetti Corleone, a hearty concoction of tomato, garlic, ham, and egg piled on a generous helping of pasta. **Known for:** simple country cooking; moderate prices; traditional ambience. 💲 *Average main: €12* ✉ *Via Sant'Agostino 41, Corleone* ☎ *091/8467938* ⊗ *Closed Tues.*

🛏 Hotels

Azienda Agricola Ridocco del Conte Lo Bue di Lemos

$ | B&B/INN | This family-run agriturismo is set on a working farm surrounded by gently rolling hills, 4 km (2½ miles) southwest of Corleone. **Pros:** quiet and peaceful rural surroundings; delicious evening meal available; comfortable accommodations. **Cons:** approach road is a little rocky; your own transport is necessary;

Tyrrhenian Sea

no facilities nearby. 💲 *Rooms from: €80* ✉ *Contrada Ridocco, Campofiorito, Corleone* ☎ *339/6240195, 091/8461575* 🌐 *www.ridocco.com* 🛏 *4 rooms* 🍽 *Free Breakfast.*

Gibellina

45 km (28 miles) west of Corleone.

In January 1968, a devastating earthquake struck the Belice valley in western Sicily, killing between 230 and 500 of the local inhabitants and making around 100,000 homeless. The epicenter was near the village of Gibellina, which was completely destroyed. Survivors from the village were relocated to a new settlement, Gibellina Nuova, 18 km (11 miles) northwest, whose wide, empty streets are today adorned with abstract sculptures, huge white spheres, giant plows, and other items frozen in the image of what appeared futuristic in the 1970s. However, on the original site of the village, now known as Gibellina Vecchia, the local administration decided to commemorate the destruction by leaving many of the earthquake's ruins in their shattered state—still visible today and known as the Ruderi di Gibellina—and by commissioning a gigantic piece of land art by the Italian artist Alberto Burri (1915–95). Said to be one of the largest works of art ever realized, the project, known as *Il Cretto di Burri*, involved pouring tons of concrete over an entire hillside, with channels carved through the mantle to recall the village's former layout. The work was begun in 1985, interrupted five years later due to lack of funds, and not finally completed until 2015, 20 years after the artist's death.

The gray-white expanse of concrete makes a disconcerting sight that draws a trickle of curious visitors to this out-of-the-way spot, particularly fans of large-scale art statements. You may be inspired or appalled by it, either way it's worth a detour if only for the photo opportunities—and children will adore playing hide-and-seek within the modern concrete maze. It's always open and free to enter, but there are no facilities of any kind at the site barring the occasional snack stall.

Segesta

70 km (43 miles) northeast of Corleone, 85 km (53 miles) southwest of Palermo.

Segesta is the site of one of Sicily's most impressive temples, constructed on the side of a barren windswept hill overlooking a valley of giant fennel. Virtually intact today, the temple is considered by some to be finer in its proportions and setting than any other Doric temple left standing.

GETTING HERE AND AROUND

At least four Tarantola e Cuffaro buses travel from Trapani to Segesta every day but Sunday. About as many trains from Palermo and Trapani stop at the Segesta–Tempio station, a 20-minute uphill walk from Segesta. The site is easily reached via the A29 autostrada.

BUS CONTACT Tarantola e Cuffaro.
☎ 0924/31020 ⊕ www.tarantolacuffaro.it.

Sights

★ Tempio Dorico (*Doric Temple*)
RUINS | Segesta's imposing temple was actually started in the 5th century BC by the Elymians, who may have been refugees from Troy—or at least non-Greeks, since it seems they often sided with Carthage. In any case, the style of the temple is in many ways Greek, but

it was never finished; the walls and roof never materialized, and the columns were never fluted.

Wear comfortable shoes, as you need to park your car in the lot at the bottom of the hill and walk about five minutes up to the temple. If you're up for a longer hike, a little more than 1 km (½ mile) away near the top of the hill are the remains of a fine theater with impressive views, especially at sunset, of the plains and the Bay of Castellammare (there's also a shuttle bus to the theater for €2 that leaves every 15–30 minutes). Concerts and plays are staged here in summer.
⊠ *Calatafimi-Segesta* ☎ *0924/952356* ⊕ *www.parcodisegesta.com* ⍾ *€6.*

Castellammare del Golfo

20 km (12 miles) north of Segesta, 60 km (37 miles) west of Palermo.

Of the series of seaside towns and resorts strung along the coast west of Palermo, Castellammare del Golfo is the biggest and the most attractive. Its long harborfront looks out onto a phalanx of gleaming yachts and fishing boats and is backed by smart bars and restaurants. At one end stands the heavily restored Norman castle from which the town takes its name, now hosting occasional exhibitions. High above, the broad Largo Petrolo offers compelling sea views and is a venue for lively *passeggiatas* and, in summer, crafts markets.

Although lacking many specific sights, Castellammare has an easy-going vibe and a good selection of hotels and restaurants that make it an attractive destination for a few nights. It's also a useful base for exploring the nearby tourist magnet of Scopello, the nature reserve of Lo Zingaro, and the alluring beaches in the vicinity.

Castellammare del Golfo's charming harborfront makes it one of the prettiest towns in this part of Sicily.

GETTING HERE AND AROUND

Castellammare is easily reached by car from the A28 autostrada. Russo buses connect the town with Palermo and Scopello, and (in summer) with Lo Zingaro nature reserve.

BUS CONTACT Autoservizi Russo. ☎ *0924/31364* 🌐 *www.russoautoservizi.it.*

🍴 Restaurants

★ Grani da Re

$ | PIZZA | Top-quality local ingredients are used in this modern, brightly lit pizzeria, where a vast range of pizzas are served, including seasonal, gourmet, and gluten-free varieties. The eclectic menu also takes in delicious antipasti, meat and seafood burgers, pastas, and seafood dishes. **Known for:** fantastic range of pizzas; modern setting; good beer menu. [$] *Average main: €12* ✉ *Via Giacomo Medici 30, Castellammare del Golfo* ☎ *0924/511016* 🕒 *Closed Tues. No lunch Mon.–Sat.*

La Tonnara

$$ | SEAFOOD | If it's seafood you're looking for, you'll feel at home at this harborside fish restaurant, where the day's catch is displayed in a chiller at the front. Couscous features among the starters, as does the outstanding *busiate con gambero, pistacchio e bottarga* (pasta with prawns, chopped pistachios, and tuna roe); mains change daily, but tuna cooked in citrus and the grilled swordfish are usually on the menu. **Known for:** fresh fish dishes; good wine list; pleasant outdoor terrace. [$] *Average main: €16* ✉ *Via Don Leonardo Zangara 29, Castellammare del Golfo* ☎ *0924/32443.*

🛏 Hotels

Hotel Al Madarig

$ | HOTEL | Spread along one side of the wide expanse of Largo Petrolo, this smart, two-story hotel has warm colors and a welcoming, intimate atmosphere. **Pros:** obliging, multilingual staff; free beach shuttle service; convenient location. **Cons:** some rooms are small; slightly dated in parts; very limited parking. $ Rooms from: €96 ✉ Largo Petrolo 7, Castellammare del Golfo ☎ 334/2479378, 0924/33533 ⊕ www.almadarig.com ☞ 33 rooms ⦿ Free Breakfast.

Hotel Cala Marina

$ | **HOTEL** | On the edge of town, overlooking a small beach at the western end of the harbor, this small and chic hotel stands a little apart from the quayside activity, and is all the better for it. **Pros:** beach transfers available; great seafront position close the action but still quiet; pleasant terrace for breakfast and drinks. **Cons:** only three harborfront rooms; poor soundproofing in some rooms; most rooms are small. $ Rooms from: €110 ✉ Don Leonardo Zangara 1, Castellammare del Golfo ☎ 0924/531841 ⊕ www. hotelcalamarina.it ☉ Closed mid-Oct.– mid-Mar. ☞ 15 rooms ⦿ Free Breakfast.

Scopello

10 km (6 miles) northwest of Castellammare del Golfo, 80 km (50 miles) west of Palermo

Located on the craggy coast of the Golfo di Castellammare and originally inhabited by workers of the nearby *tonnara,* or tuna fishery, the village of Scopello has been tidied up and endowed with a sprinkling of fashionable restaurants and hotels, attracting day-trippers aplenty. Many are here primarily to have a coffee and a wander through its quaint lanes before or after taking a selfie against the background of the highly photogenic fishery, with its spires of rock topped by ruined structures. Others are drawn to the golden-sand beaches in the vicinity or the Zingaro nature reserve, whose southern entrance lies just beyond the *tonnara.* Scopello is at its best, though, after the crowds have departed, and you might consider an overnight stay or at

the very least a meal in one of its lively restaurants. Avoid weekends and the peak summer period to enjoy a more laid-back visit.

Most of the activity is concentrated in and around the main Piazza Fontana, on one side of which sits the gateway to the enclosed courtyard of the village's 18th-century manor house, now the location of crafts and souvenir shops, bars, and restaurants.

The nearby *tonnara* is theoretically open for visits, though it's usually in the off-season or when it's used for events. The structure even has a small shingle beach which you will be tempted to use. There's little to see inside, but it's an irresistible vantage point for views of the towering rock stacks lying around it.

GETTING HERE AND AROUND
Scopello is best reached by car along an easy (and scenic) coastal road from Castellammare del Golfo. Three Tarantola e Cuffaro buses daily connect the village with Castellammare.

BUS CONTACT Tarantola e Cuffaro. ☎ 0924/31020 ⊕ www.tarantolacuffaro.it.

 Restaurants

Torre Bennistra

$$ | **SEAFOOD** | Part of a hotel, this restaurant relies on its 180-degree views of the sea to pull in diners, but foodies won't be disappointed either. The emphasis is on fresh fish and local ingredients, and the seafood choices are always beautifully prepared and presented, like the *spaghetti cozze e vongole* (with mussels and clams) and tuna dishes. **Known for:** romantic atmosphere, especially on the scenic terrace; stunning views; conscientious service. $ *Average main: €18* ✉ *Via Natale di Roma 19, Scopello* ☎ *0924/541128* ⊕ *www.hoteltorrebennistra.it* ☉ *Closed Oct.–Apr.*

Hotels

Hotel La Tavernetta

$$$ | **HOTEL** | This boutique hotel might be in the center of Scopello, but once within its secluded grounds, you might believe you're in the open countryside. **Pros:** central but secluded; beautiful grounds including a gorgeous garden with pool and views; courteous multilingual staff. **Cons:** no single-night stays; difficult to approach by car; inflated rates. [$] *Rooms from: €230* ✉ *Via Armando Diaz 3, Scopello* ☎ *333/5736045, 0924/541129* 🌐 *www.albergolatavernetta.it* 🕒 *Closed mid-Oct.–mid-Apr.* 🛏 *22 rooms* 🍴 *Free Breakfast.*

Riserva Naturale dello Zingaro

28 km (20 miles) northeast of Scopello.

One of Sicily's best natural areas, Riserva Naturale dello Zingaro is the perfect place to commune with nature amid some true peace and quiet.

GETTING HERE AND AROUND

Scopello, Castellammare del Golfo, and San Vito Lo Capo are the best bases for exploring the reserve. Drivers can park outside the reserve's entrances on the Castellammare del Golfo and San Vito Lo Capo sides. Russo buses operate in summer (July–mid-September) from Castellammare to the southern entrance of the reserve.

BUS CONTACT Autoservizi Russo. ☎ *0924/31364* 🌐 *www.russoautoservizi.it.*

Sights

★ Riserva Naturale dello Zingaro

NATURE PRESERVE | Extending for 7 km (4½ miles) along the western edge of the Golfo di Castellammare, the Riserva dello Zingaro nature reserve is one of the few stretches of coastline in western Sicily that is not built up. It's only accessible on foot, using a good choice of paths, and offers exhilarating views and some fabulous small beaches. The best time to visit is late spring when both wildflowers and birds are plentiful.

The reserve's two entrances are roughly 1 km (0.6 miles) north of Scopello and, at its northern end, 12 km (7½ miles) east of San Vito Lo Capo. Entry costs €5 per person. The reserve is open daily (until 6) all year, and in winter (Oct.–May) it is possible to stay overnight in very rudimentary shelters for up to two nights. The shelters, which lack electricity, gas, heating, beds, toilets, and drinking water, can be booked for €10 per person per night via the reserve's website.

Route maps can be picked up from either of the entrances. There are three main routes, color-coded green (for the coastal trail), yellow (for the central trail), and orange (for the high trail). A few trails connect the routes, but these are not always where you might want them. The coastal trail is the easiest, while the high trail is the hardest.

The terrain is mostly rock and scrub, with little shade. Along with the variety of vegetation, there is plenty of unusual wildlife to look out for, including buzzards, kestrels, hoopoes, owls, and the rare Bonelli's eagle. Bees, grasshoppers, and lizards are ubiquitous, and snakes (mostly harmless) are also common. You can pick up illustrated guides to the reserve's flora and fauna at the two entrances.

The Riserva Naturale dello Zingaro, with its many walking paths, is one of the few untouched stretches of coastline in western Sicily.

The only food and refreshments you'll find are also at the two entrances, where you can fill up your water flasks. Be sure to carry plenty of water, and you should also come equipped with sun protection and sturdy footwear (sandals are definitely not recommended). ⊠ *Riserva Naturale dello Zingaro, Riserva Naturale dello Zingaro* ☎ *0924/35108* ⊕ *www. riservazingaro.it* ✉ *€5.*

San Vito Lo Capo

43 km (26 miles) north of Scopello.

Ask any Sicilian about the island's best beach, and the chances are they will nominate the long curve of fine, white sand at San Vito Lo Capo as a primary candidate. The beach is the main reason for the growth of the settlement, a sprawl of low, white, mainly modern buildings just west of the cape, Capo San Vito, that gives the town its name. Other less accessible and far less crowded beaches can be discovered a short distance out of town.

Apart from sea and sand, San Vito Lo Capo's appeal resides in the stark landscape surrounding it, a rugged, brown terrain, the vast majority undeveloped and imbued with a barren, other-worldly character. It is the contrast between this almost primeval setting and the predominantly modern look of San Vito Lo Capo that gives the place its unique appeal.

San Vito is not all modern in style, however there are traces of an older, Arab-influenced culture, like in the 15th-century Santuario di San Vito in the town center, with its square, fortress-like appearance, and the Arab-Norman Santa Crescenzia chapel, on the main SP16 road, which you can't fail to spot on your way into town.

Moorish influence is also evident in San Vito's signature dish: North African couscous prepared with fish instead of meat. You'll find it on the menus of most of the resort's restaurants, and it's a must-try. In mid- to late-September, the town hosts the 10-day Cous Cous Fest (⊕ *www. couscousfest.it*), a serious international competition and festival with live music and plenty of free tastings.

As the summer progresses, so does the size and intensity of the evening *passeggiata* along pedestrianized Via Savoia. In addition to the couscous festival, there are regular organized events throughout the season, with a full program of concerts and other performances—mostly free, outdoors, and lasting late into the evening—to keep its multigenerational visitors entertained. Many of these take place outside the Santuario di San Vito.

San Vito Lo Capo is also one of the bases for exploring the Riserva dello Zingaro nature reserve, stretching between here and Scopello. Follow signs east of town to find the entrance, 12 km (7½ miles) away.

Note that car traffic in the center of town is restricted in summer, and you are likely to incur a fine if you do not have permission to enter the ZTL restricted area. Check with your accommodations before arrival about which roads you can use.

GETTING HERE AND AROUND

San Vito Lo Capo is only approachable from the west coast, using SP16. The town is connected to Trapani by AST buses and to Palermo and Castellammare del Golfo by less frequent Russo buses.

BUS CONTACTS AST. ☎ *0923/21021* 🌐 *www.astsicilia.it.* **Autoservizi Russo.** ☎ *0924/31364* 🌐 *www.russoautoservizi.it.*

Beaches

★ San Vito Lo Capo Beach

BEACH | FAMILY | There are numerous small, niche swimming spots in the Capo San Vito area, but the grandest and by far the most popular beach of all—and the centerpiece of the whole town—is San Vito Lo Capo's beach, a blissful arc of silky, white sand at the foot of Monte Monaco. Most of its length of nearly 3 km (1.8 miles) is public and free to use, but sections have been roped off as private lidos, where you'll pay €15–€20 for a full day's use of sunbeds and a parasol, plus access to bars and bathroom facilities. Needless to say, both public and private beaches get intensely crowded in July and August, which is the perfect time to seek out all those other lesser-known beaches in the vicinity. **Amenities:** food and drink; lifeguards; toilets. **Best for**: families; swimming; watersports; walking. ✉ *San Vito Lo Capo.*

Restaurants

Pomelia

$ | PIZZA | This is that rare creature, a great pizzeria that also produces main meals of quality and undoubted flair. The pizzas are available in "gourmet" or "classic" varieties, both making good use of fresh local ingredients with a light, crispy base. **Known for:** excellent pizzas using fresh ingredients; small space that books up quickly (so reserve ahead); fresh seafood. [$] *Average main: €12* ✉ *Via Dogana 24, San Vito Lo Capo* ☎ *371/3061993* 🕒 *No lunch weekdays.*

Ristorante Rais

$$ | SICILIAN | Founded by a locally born sister-and-brother team, this restaurant just steps away from the beach has one eye on tradition and one on innovative and creative cuisine. Intriguing taste combinations are well-judged, though you can be equally satisfied with a simple but delicious plate of spaghetti with tuna or grilled fish, as even the plainest dishes are surprisingly tasty. **Known for:** innovative cuisine; excellent wine list; three versions of couscous. [$] *Average main: €16* ✉ *Via Principe Tommaso 8, San Vito Lo Capo* ☎ *340/0902838* 🌐 *www.sanvitolocaporais.it.*

Coffee and Quick Bites

L'Angolo DiVino
$ | **SICILIAN** | This salumeria and enoteca with outdoor tables is a great choice for a midday snack of cold cuts, perhaps accompanied by a glass of cool white wine chosen from the formidable wine list. Your *tagliere* (tray) might include various hunks of local cheeses, a selection of salamis and hams, and a bowl of olives. **Known for:** casual outdoor snacks and drinks; seasoned bread topped with tomato, onion, anchovies, and capers; craft beers. [$] *Average main: €7* ✉ *Via Generale Arimondi 86, San Vito Lo Capo* ☎ *345/8383508* 🕒 *Closed Oct.–Apr.*

Hotels

Riva del Sole
$$ | **HOTEL** | Just steps away from the beach, this small, family-run lodging has a warm, friendly character, with public areas and guest rooms enlivened by colorful, Middle Eastern-style ceramic tiles. **Pros:** good choices at breakfast; private beach; spacious rooms with air-conditioning. **Cons:** no elevator; limited availability for rooms and private beach facilities; rooms near reception may suffer noise. [$] *Rooms from: €130* ✉ *Via Generale Arimondi 11, San Vito Lo Capo* ☎ *0923/972629* 🌐 *www.hotelrivadelsole.it* 🛏 *13 rooms* 🍴 *Free Breakfast.*

Trigrana Vacanze Hotel
$ | **HOTEL** | **FAMILY** | Lying 5 km (3 miles) outside the hustle and bustle of San Vito in the Castelluzzo neighborhood, this hotel has gardens planted with olive trees and is surrounded by wonderful scenery. **Pros:** good for families; low rates; stunning scenery. **Cons:** entrance is on a busy road; away from town's amenities; no pool. [$] *Rooms from: €87* ✉ *Viale Cristoforo Colombo 543/A, Castelluzzo, San Vito Lo Capo* ☎ *0923/973619* 🌐 *www.hoteltrigrana.it* 🛏 *8 rooms* 🍴 *Free Breakfast.*

Erice

38 km (24 miles) south of San Vito Lo Capo, 15 km (9 miles) northeast of Trapani.

Perched 2,450 feet above sea level, Erice is an enchanting medieval mountaintop aerie of palaces, fountains, and cobblestone streets. Shaped like an equilateral triangle, the town was the ancient landmark Eryx, dedicated to Aphrodite (Venus). When the Normans arrived, they built a castle on Monte San Giuliano, where today there's a lovely public park with benches and belvederes offering striking views of Trapani, the Egadi Islands offshore, and, on a very clear day, Cape Bon and the Tunisian coast. Because of Erice's elevation, clouds conceal much of the view for most of winter. Sturdy shoes (for the cobblestones) and something warm to wear are recommended.

GETTING HERE AND AROUND

Make your approach via Trapani, which is on the A29 autostrada and well connected by bus and train with Marsala and Palermo. In late March to early January, a *funivia* runs from the outskirts of Trapani to Erice (Monday 2–9, Tuesday to Friday 8:30–8, weekends 9:30–8:30; extended hours from late June to mid-September; see 🌐 *www.funiviaerice.it* for details). Going by car or bus from Trapani takes around 40 minutes. By car, take the route via Valderice, not the "direct route," to avoid an extremely winding and steep country road. Buses depart from the terminal on Trapani's Piazza Malta.

Sights

Castello di Venere
CASTLE/PALACE | Built over an ancient temple dedicated to Venus (hence the name), the ruined Castello di Venere dates from Norman times and is erected in a position to afford the best possible views of the sea and coast. For this reason alone

it's worth the 20-minute walk to the southeastern corner of Erice's triangular layout. There's plenty of background to absorb from the information boards (also in English), but not much to see inside, so it's all about the spectacular vistas where you can take in Trapani, the salt pans, and the Egadi Islands. ✉ *Largo Castello, Erice* ☎ *320/8672957* 🌐 *www.fondazioneericearte.org* 🎫 *€4* 🕒 *Closed weekdays Nov.–Mar.*

Real Duomo and Torre di Re Fernando

RELIGIOUS BUILDING | Just inside Porta Trapani, the western entrance that most people use to access Erice, the first sight that confronts visitors to the town is the dramatic ensemble of the Real Duomo, Erice's main church, and its detached belltower, the Torre di Re Fernando. Both are battlemented and retain a formidable Gothic appearance. The church, dating from around 1314, contains traces of a fresco of an angel dating from its original construction, visible in the sanctuary on the left-hand side of the nave. The belltower was orignally built by the Aragonese as a lookout tower in the late 13th century, and its 108 steps can be climbed for splendid bird's-eye views. ✉ *Via Chiaramonte, Erice* ☎ *0923/869123* 🌐 *www.ericelamontagnadelsignore.it* 🎫 *€3 church, €3 belltower* 🕒 *Closed early Jan. and Feb.*

🍴 Restaurants

Monte San Giuliano

$$ | **SICILIAN** | At this traditional restaurant located on a side street near the main piazza, you can sit on a tree-lined patio overlooking the sea or in the white-walled dining room and munch on free panelle (chickpea fritters) while waiting for your main dish, which will be served tableside, spooned from the cooking pots to your plate by the friendly staff. The pastas are exemplary (there are even gluten-free options), but the specialty is the seafood couscous, served with a bowl of fish broth on the side. **Known for:** extensive and interesting wine list; charming setting; great pasta and couscous. [$] *Average main: €16* ✉ *Vicolo San Rocco 7, Erice* ☎ *334/1396763, 0923/869595* 🌐 *www.montesangiuliano.it* 🕒 *Closed Mon., 6 wks in Jan. and Feb., and 4 wks in Nov. and Dec.*

Osteria di Venere

$$ | **SICILIAN** | Housed in the former church of Sant'Alberto, with some of its old stone walls left exposed, this restaurant (a cut above what you might expect from an "osteria") flaunts its authentically traditional character. The menu shows the same respect for local cuisine, but dishes are enlivened by a fresh, modern approach, including old favorites like caponata, antipasto rustico, creamy risottos, and seafood pastas—all highly rated by locals as well as tourists. **Known for:** traditional, local dishes revisited; open all year; fantastic desserts. [$] *Average main: €15* ✉ *Via Roma 6, Erice* ☎ *0923/869362* 🌐 *www.osteriadivenere.it.*

☕ Coffee and Quick Bites

★ La Tonda Fritta

$ | **SICILIAN** | Arancine—fried rice balls—are ubiquitous all over Sicily, but rarely do you find them prepared while you wait or offered in such a range as in this little snack shop near Porta Trapani. The menu lists more than 35 varieties, which include swordfish, smoked salmon, and curry fillings, as well as vegetarian and vegan options. **Known for:** more than 35 types of arancine; fast service; great snacks on the go. [$] *Average main: €3* ✉ *Via Vittorio Emanuele 100, Erice* ☎ *328/1378708* 🌐 *www.la-tonda-fritta.jimdosite.com* 🕒 *Closed Nov.–Feb.*

Pasticceria Grammatico

$ | **BAKERY** | Fans of Sicilian sweets make a beeline for this place, run by Maria Grammatico, who gained international fame with *Bitter Almonds,* her life story of growing up in a convent orphanage cowritten with Mary Taylor Simeti. Her almond-paste creations are works of art, molded into striking shapes, including dolls and animals. **Known for:** uniquely shaped desserts; nice views; delicious sweets. [$] *Average main: €5* ✉ *Via Vittorio Emanuele 14, Erice* ☎ *0923/869390* 🌐 *www.mariagrammatico.it.*

Hotels

Hotel Elimo
$ | **HOTEL** | Like the town of Erice itself, the Hotel Elimo is old-fashioned and yet full of charm; eccentric knickknacks and artwork fill the lobby, and the homey guest rooms are all different, many boasting terraces with views of either the cobblestone streets or the valleys below (when they're not shrouded by clouds). **Pros:** convenient location; great on-site restaurant; lots of character. **Cons:** noise in some rooms; small bathrooms; rooms can feel a bit musty. [$] *Rooms from: €85* ✉ *Via Vittorio Emanuele 75, Erice* ☎ *0923/869377* 🌐 *www.hotelelimo.it* 🕒 *Closed Jan. and Feb.* 🛏 *21 rooms* 🍴 *Free Breakfast.*

Moderno
$ | **HOTEL** | This delightful hotel has a creaky old feel to it, but that's part of the charm—the lobby area, scattered with books, magazines, and tchotchkes, calls to mind an elderly relative's living room; but the rooms themselves are simple, light, and comfortable. **Pros:** central location; well-regarded restaurant; great rooftop terrace. **Cons:** old-fashioned feel not for everyone; street-facing rooms can be noisy; very modest rooms. [$] *Rooms from: €90* ✉ *Via Vittorio Emanuele 67, Erice* ☎ *0923/869300* 🌐 *www.hotelmodernoerice.it* 🛏 *40 rooms* 🍴 *Free Breakfast.*

Shopping

Ceramica Ericina
CERAMICS | Among Italians, Erice is known for the quality and delicate floral designs of its majolica ceramics, well represented in this ceramics store off Piazza San Domenico, one of the best in town. ✉ *Via Gian Filippa Guarnotti 20, Erice* ☎ *0923/869126.*

Trapani

11 km (7 miles) southwest of Erice, 30 km (19 miles) northwest of Segesta, 75 km (47 miles) southwest of Palermo.

The provincial capital of Trapani (both province and city share the same name) was originally founded by the ancient Elymians, who claimed descent from the Trojans, as a port for Eryx (Erice). Its Greek name, Drepanon, meaning "sickle," refers to the long, curving limb of land trailing into the sea on which the city is built. Much of its later wealth was founded on the salt pans lying to the south that are still active today.

Although the outskirts of town are uninspiring, Trapani's old town has a busy, buzzy feel to it, especially in the evenings when families crowd the main, pedestrianized Corso Vittorio Emanuele and bars and restaurants spill onto the street. Via Garibaldi, linking the old and new districts, is also a busy shopping and promenading thoroughfare. North of the hydrofoil port, the old Jewish quarter is a warren of somewhat down-at-heel alleys centered on the 16th-century Palazzo della Giudecca on Via della Giudecca.

Linked to Palermo and Mazara del Vallo by autostrada A20, the town has its own airport and is also an important nexus for trips to Erice, Mozia, San Vito Lo Capo, and the Egadi Islands.

GETTING HERE AND AROUND

Trapani's airport is located in Birgi, 15 km (9 miles) to the south. The town is linked to Palermo by the A29 autostrada and by infrequent slow trains. Most using public transport travel on the much faster bus services, which all terminate at Piazza Malta, though fast buses from the airport, Palermo, Palermo airport, and Agrigento also make a stop at the ferry and hydrofoil port.

With much of the old town closed to traffic and available parking spots hard to find, drivers should take advantage of the large and inexpensive car park on Piazza Vittorio Emanuele, at the bottom of Via Garibaldi. The old town is easy to negotiate on foot, though visitors to the Museo Pepoli and Santuario Annunziata should either drive or make use of the frequent city bus services.

Tickets to the Egadi islands can be picked up from the ticket offices at the port or from the Egatour agency, which also offers island tours, tickets for Pantelleria, and bus tickets.

AIRPORT CONTACT Trapani–Birgi Airport.
⊠ *Trapani* ☎ *0923/610111* ⊕ *www.airgest. it.*

Sights

Museo Regionale Pepoli

ART MUSEUM | Trapani's foremost museum collection is located in a former Carmelite monastery that was attached to the important religious site of Santuario dell'Annunziata. The art sections take in some excellent examples of medieval and Renaissance art, including statuary by Antonello Gagini and a painting by Titian. Among the archaeological exhibits is a selection of low-key finds from Mozia and Selinunte. There's also a guillotine from 1800, and a good collection of memorabilia from Garibaldi's Sicilian campaign against the Bourbons in 1860.

The usual entrance to the museum is in the Villa Pepoli public garden; when this is closed enter from Via Madonna, behind the garden. ⊠ *Via Conte Agostino Pepoli 180, Trapani* ☎ *0923/553269* ⊠ *€6* ⏱ *Closed Mon.*

Santuario dell'Annunziata

RELIGIOUS BUILDING | This sanctuary dedicated to the Virgin Mary and local saints is one of Sicily's most revered religious sites, visited by devout pilgrims from all over the country. The complex was originally built for the Carmelite religious order in 1332, and its most treasured object is the life-size statue of the Madonna di Trapani, serenely smiling and holding the infant Jesus, thought to be the work of Nino Pisano or his studio. The importance of the sanctuary to the local fishing community is shown in the chapel dedicated to sailors, displaying scallop-shell motifs over every window as well as over the altar itself, and in one chapel dedicated to fishermen, dating from the 16th century. A separate room holds numerous ex-voto paintings of sailing vessels beset by stormy waters. ⊠ *Via Conte Agostino Pepoli 178, Trapani* ☎ *0923/539184* ⊕ *www.madonnaditrapani.it* ⊠ *Free.*

Restaurants

Ai Lumi

$ | SICILIAN | This popular restaurant on the pedestrianized Corso Vittorio Emanuele occupies some former stables, though the modern art on the walls and its candlelit tables evoke far more romantic associations. Dishes are predominantly local and sea-based, like a delicious fish couscous, *ghiotta di pesce misto* (mixed seafood in a rich sauce of tomatoes, olives, and capers), and swordfish involtini (roulades) served with orange. **Known for:** quirky interiors; fast service; delicious local dishes. $ *Average main: €14* ⊠ *Corso Vittorio Emanuele 75, Trapani* ☎ *0923/872418.*

Favignana is the largest of the three islands that make up the Egadi archipelago.

Cantina Siciliana

$ | **SICILIAN** | Not many tourists find their way to this traditional trattoria deep in the heart of Trapani's old Jewish quarter, but those that do will find themselves in a typical rustic ambience, surrounded by a small army of Sicilian puppets hanging from the ceiling, shelves full of wine bottles, copper pots and pans on the walls, and even an intact Sicilian cart. The menu focuses on traditional island dishes, of course, including grilled or fried squid and swordfish prepared with oregano from Pantelleria and capers from the Aeolian islands. **Known for:** strong local character; great wine list; seafood dishes. [$] *Average main: €14* ✉ *Via Giudecca 36, Trapani* ☎ *0923/28673* 🌐 *www.cantinasiciliana.it* 🕒 *Closed Wed. Oct.–Mar.*

Coffee and Quick Bites

★ **Meno Tredici**

$ | **ICE CREAM** | **FAMILY** | There's a regular trickle of locals to this gelateria conveniently located opposite the hydrofoil port. Most opt for the local favorite: ice cream in a brioche with a couple of wafer biscuits poking out. **Known for:** tangy ice creams; tasty desserts; thirst-quenching granitas. [$] *Average main: €3* ✉ *Via Staiti 61, Trapani* ☎ *0923/1781797* 🌐 *www.gelateriamenotredici.it.*

Hotels

Hotel San Michele

$ | **HOTEL** | It's a revelation to find this smart boutique hotel buried within Trapani's rather neglected former Jewish neighborhood, but once within its doors you'll find everything clean, calm, and orderly, with soothing colors and well-equipped guest rooms. **Pros:** convenient for the hydrofoil dock; valet parking; helpful staff. **Cons:** shabby neighborhood; poor soundproofing in some rooms; a little difficult to find. [$] *Rooms from: €96* ✉ *Via San Michele 16, Trapani* ☎ *0923/23470* 🌐 *www.sanmicheletp.it* 🕒 *Closed Jan. and Feb.* 🛏 *21 rooms* 🍴 *Free Breakfast.*

La Gancia

$$ | HOTEL | Although detached from the town's hubbub, this residence is actually in a central location on Trapani's northern waterfront, with wonderful coastal views. **Pros:** fantastic breakfast experience; seaside views; central but sequestered feel. **Cons:** some rooms are dark with small windows; not staffed at night; no nearby parking. $ *Rooms from: €145* ⊠ *Piazza Mercato del Pesce, Trapani* ☎ *0923/438060* ⊕ *www.lagancia. com* ☾ *Closed early Oct.–late Feb.* ⤵ *20 rooms* ⦿ *Free Breakfast.*

Room of Andrea

$$ | HOTEL | A 19th-century palazzo is now home to this hotel opposite a public garden in central Trapani, which provides pampering accommodation in swish surroundings. **Pros:** characterful surroundings and decor; small rooftop pool; good location. **Cons:** better rooms are overpriced in high season; no hotel parking; most rooms lack much of a view. $ *Rooms from: €139* ⊠ *Viale Regina Margherita 31, Trapani* ☎ *0923/365728* ⊕ *www.roomofandrea.it* ⤵ *45 rooms* ⦿ *Free Breakfast.*

🛍 Shopping

Colomba Shop

SOUVENIRS | Giovanna Colomba is the creative force behind this store near the hydrofoil port, where typical Sicilian motifs and artifacts are given a vibrant new style. There is no single theme to the choice of objects on sale, which include eye-catching handbags decorated with citrus fruits, flamboyant ceramics, colorful cushions, and T-shirts with floral designs, but all share a very Sicilian exuberance as well as respect for local tradition and quality of manufacture. ⊠ *Corso Italia 19, Trapani* ☎ *388/1926471* ⊕ *www.colombashop.it.*

Favignana

1 hour, 20 minutes from Trapani by ferry.

The three islands of the Egadi archipelago ("Egadi" is pronounced with the emphasis on the first syllable) lurk off Sicily's western coast like a trio of giant whales. Dotted with white-walled and blue-shuttered dwellings, the islands' rugged slopes appear barren and inhospitable from afar, but in summer crowds of vacationers make their way here, attracted to the relaxed atmosphere and the refuge they provide from Sicily's overheated towns and cities. Just keep in mind that none of the islands are famed for their beaches; the main draw is in exploring the coast on boat tours, rambling along the good supply of footpaths, and sampling the bar life and the North African–tinged cuisine of the restaurants in the evenings. Visitors will find significantly higher prices than on the mainland, however. Between October and Easter, of course, you won't find much movement at all, as most facilities are closed.

The archipelago is situated within Europe's largest protected marine reserve, and as such enjoys largely uncontaminated waters, much appreciated by water-sports enthusiasts.

The largest of the three isles, and the nearest to the coast, is Favignana, whose only town—also called Favignana—holds the majority of the archipelago's amenities, including bars, restaurants, and lodgings. Like the other islands, Favignana has little in the way of sights, though you can't fail to notice the imposing Art Nouveau Villa Florio in the center of town, once the home of Ignazio Florio, responsible for developing the local tuna fisheries at the end of the 19th century (his Stabilimento Florio fishery is visible across the bay and can be visited). Villa Florio, which includes a pleasant garden, today houses Favignana's town hall and is partly open for occasional exhibitions and other events.

The town has numerous bicycle and scooter rental outlets for launching out on Favignana's small network of roads. Most of the roads are on the eastern end of the island, allowing you to access some choice swimming spots, best among them Cala Rossa, reached along a rocky path, and the island's only sandy beach, Lido Burrone, where umbrellas and loungers can be rented in the season. Roads are sparser on the western half of Favignana; the main route burrows through the island's only elevation, Monte Santa Caterina, on its way to the tiny settlement of Pozzo Ponente on the western edge.

GETTING HERE AND AROUND

All three Egadi islands can be reached by ferry, operated by Siremar, or by the faster, more frequent (but more expensive) hydrofoil service operated by Liberty Lines. Both leave from the ferry and hydrofoil docks along Trapani's northern littoral.

FERRY CONTACTS Liberty Lines. ☎ *0923/022022* 🌐 *www.libertylines.it.* **Siremar.** ☎ *090/364601* 🌐 *www.siremar.it.*

Sights

Ex Stabilimento Florio delle Tonnare di Favignana e Formica

HISTORY MUSEUM | The entrepreneur Ignazio Florio played a leading part in the regeneration of Favignana's tuna fisheries in the 19th century, a tale told in his company's former fishery, a huge complex located on the outskirts of Favignana town, now converted into a museum. Hour-long guided tours take you through the fascinating history and gruesome methods of bluefin tuna fishing, including the ritualistic and bloody culmination of the fishing process, La Mattanza, or "The Killing." These traditional methods died out with the growth of modern industrial practices and overfishing. Tours must be booked a least a day in advance. There's also a separate section focusing on the Battle of Egadi (241 BC), which saw the defeat of the Carthaginians by a Roman fleet and their subsequent expulsion from Sicily. ✉ *Via Amendola 29, Favigana* ☎ *338/5365899* 🎫 *€6* 🕒 *Closed Oct.–Mar.*

Restaurants

A' Cialoma

$$ | SEAFOOD | This restaurant in Favignana's main square is a must for seafood-lovers. The short, daily changing menu is constructed around the catch of the day, from the grand portions of antipasti to the main courses, and all ingredients are strictly seasonal. **Known for:** large portions; charming ambience; fresh fish. [$] *Average main: €20* ✉ *Piazza Matrice 33, Favigana* ☎ *347/1784395* 🕒 *Closed Nov.–Apr.*

Hotels

★ **Cave Bianche Hotel**

$$$ | HOTEL | Tufa quarries are a feature of Favignana's landscape, and this designer hotel to the southeast of town has been built within one that has been abandoned. **Pros:** excellent restaurant; eco-friendly ethos; spectacular setting. **Cons:** austere modern design may not be to everyone's liking; guestrooms are a little basic; journey needed to get anywhere (though there is a free shuttle into town). [$] *Rooms from: €241* ✉ *Strada Comunale Fanfalo, Favigana* ☎ *0923/925451* 🌐 *www.cavebianchehotel.it* 🕒 *Closed Oct.–May* 🛏 *32 rooms* 🍴 *Free Breakfast.*

Hotel Aegusa

$$ | HOTEL | This attractive mid-range hotel in the center of Favignana town is in an old palazzo but has modern furnishings and fittings. **Pros:** central location; nice restaurant; spacious rooms. **Cons:** for longer stays only; front-facing rooms can get street noise; Wi-Fi service can

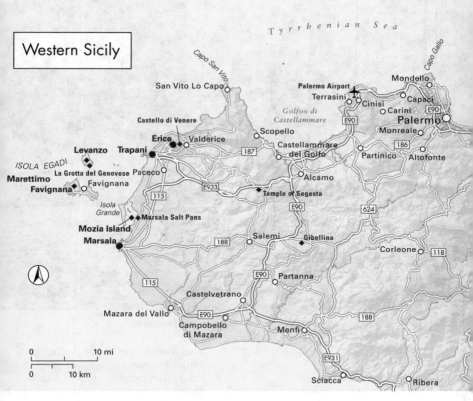

Western Sicily

Tyrrhenian Sea

be patchy. $ *Rooms from: €146* ✉ *Via Garibaldi 11, Favigana* ☎ *0923/921739* ⊕ *www.aegusahotel.it* ⊘ *Closed Nov.– late Apr.* ⤳ *15 rooms* ⦿ *Free Breakfast.*

Levanzo

40 minutes from Favignana by ferry; 1 hour, 30 minutes from Trapani by ferry.

Levanzo (with the accent on the first syllable) is the smallest of the Egadi islands and makes even Favignana, just 4 km (2½ miles) to the south, look positively metropolitan in comparison. As is the case for all the Egadi islands, everything is concentrated in the main, eponymous town, where the only accommodations and restaurants are. Levanzo's road

infrastructure is almost nonexistent— there's just one road that leads west of the port to the *faraglione*, a rocky spire sprouting out of the sea. A few footpaths will enable you to reach other parts of the island, including swimming spots such as Cala Tramontana and Cala Minnola, but don't expect to find any beaches.

Boat trips are available at the port to take you around the island, of which the most popular is the excursion to visit the famed Grotta del Genovese, where you can view paleolithic cave art.

GETTING HERE AND AROUND
Levanzo can be reached via regular ferry or hydrofoil service from Trapani or the other Egadi Islands.

Marettimo is the most remote of the Egadi Islands and the least developed.

Sights

La Grotta del Genovese

CAVE | Located on Levanzo's rugged northwestern coast, Italy's most important example of cave art, the Grotta del Genovese, displays a stunning set of paintings and incised drawings dating from the Upper Paleolithic and Neolithic eras. The guide explains in fascinating detail how the small red and black figures of animals, fish, and insect-like humans were created here between 10,000 and 15,000 years ago, and how they were discovered by a holidaymaker in 1949.

Transport to the grotto, which is privately owned, is included in the price of the ticket. Arriving by sea, a 20-minute ride, allows you to experience Levanzo's beautiful coast, but is not possible when the sea is at all rough as the boat must negotiate a narrow inlet in order to disembark passengers. The alternative is overland via Jeep, though this involves a downhill walk along a track for the last half mile. The whole excursion by boat or Jeep takes around 90 minutes. You can also make your own way here on foot along inland paths from Levanzo town, a walk of around one hour each way.

Visits to the site must be booked online, by email, or by phone at least 48 hours in advance, but ideally several days ahead during the busy summer months. Note that neither touching the engravings nor photographing them is allowed, and sturdy shoes are advised. ⊠ *Levanzo* ☎ *339/7418800, 331/1330259* ⊕ *www. grottadelgenovese.it* 🖃 *€15; €35 including transport.*

Hotels

Lisola Residence

$ | **APARTMENT** | Located not far from the port, Lisola Residence offers complete tranquillity in the form of charming, adults-only apartments that accommodate either two or four people, each retaining a degree of privacy from its neighbor. **Pros:** free jeep service to the port; perfect rustic setting; nice swimming pool. **Cons:** 10-minute walk to the port; minimal facilities; minimum-stay periods. [$] *Rooms from: €120* ✉ *Contrada Case, Levanzo* ☎ *351/6141337* 🌐 *www.lisola.eu* 🕒 *Closed Oct.–Apr.* 🛏 *7 apartments* 🍴 *No Meals.*

Marettimo

2 hours from Levanzo via ferry; 3 hours from Trapani via ferry.

The most remote of the Egadi Islands, Marettimo (pronounced with the emphasis on the "E") has the smallest population, the least development, and a complete absence of cars. It's a destination for lovers of seclusion and uncontaminated nature, and for those who can create their own entertainment. However, do not expect a wide choice of accommodations or dining options, especially not in the winter months when they dwindle to almost nothing.

Marettimo's indented coastline is pitted with sea caves and rocky coves sheltering a few minuscule beaches such as Cala Sarde and Cala Nera on the south coast, which can be reached on footpaths. Walkers can also use the island's tracks and pathways to reach the remains of the Castello di Punta Troia, a Saracen castle located on the north-eastern tip of the island. Underwater enthusiasts will appreciate the island's clear waters and 20-odd dive sites.

GETTING HERE AND AROUND

Marettimo can be reached via regular ferry or hydrofoil service from Trapani or the other Egadi Islands.

Hotels

La Tartaruga

$ | **B&B/INN** | There's nothing remote or rough-and-ready about this gorgeous B&B set in the higher part of Marettimo, where tasteful modern design combines with personable hosts to create the perfect island getaway. **Pros:** panoramic roof terrace; helpful hosts; brilliant breakfasts. **Cons:** lacks much privacy; no TVs in rooms; availability may be limited. [$] *Rooms from: €100* ✉ *Via Carlo Cavasino 4, Marettimo* ☎ *329/4116346* 🌐 *www.latartarugabedandbreakfast.it* 🕒 *Closed Nov.–Mar.* 🛏 *4 rooms* 🍴 *Free Breakfast.*

Activities

Blu Tek Diving

DIVING & SNORKELING | Discover Marettimo's best dive sites with this friendly crew, who will guide you around some unforgettable caves, reefs, flora, and fauna all while instructing you in some of the finer points of marine biology. A full day will take in two dives with a leisurely lunch or swim in between, and the boat is spacious and comfortable. ✉ *Marettimo* ☎ *329/6113675* 🌐 *www.blutekdiving.com* 🎟 *From €40.*

Marsala

30 km (19 miles) south of Trapani.

Marsala is readily associated with its world-famous, richly colored eponymous fortified wine, and your main reason for stopping may be to visit some of the many wineries in the area and sample the product. But this quiet seaside town, together with the nearby island of Mozia, was also once the main Carthaginian base in Sicily: it was from here that Carthage fought for supremacy over the island against Greece and Rome, leaving behind intriguing archaeological sites. In 1773, a British merchant named John Woodhouse happened upon the town and discovered that the wine here was as good as the port long imported by the British from Portugal. Two other wine merchants, Whitaker and Ingram, rushed in, and by 1800 Marsala was exporting wine all over the British Empire.

The city of Marsala is known as the producer of a famous fortified wine.

Later in the 18th century, Marsala played a significant role in the Risorgimento, the movement for Italian liberty. It was here that the swashbuckling national hero Giuseppe Garibaldi landed in 1860 with his thousand Redshirts to begin the campaign to oust the Bourbons from southern Italy.

GETTING HERE AND AROUND
Buses and trains from Palermo, Trapani, and Castelvetrano stop in Marsala. Drivers can take the coastal SS115.

VISITOR INFORMATION
CONTACT Marsala Tourism Office. ⊠ *Via XI Maggio 100,* ☎ *0923/714097* ⊕ *www. turismocomunemarsala.com.*

Sights

⭐ **Donnafugata Winery**
WINERY | A respected Sicilian wine producer, the 160-year-old Donnafugata Winery is open for tastings and tours of its *cantina* (wine cellar); reservations are required and can be made online or by phone. It's an interesting look at

the wine-making process in Sicily, and it ends with a sampling of several whites and reds, an optional food pairing, and a chance to buy a bottle. Don't miss the delicious, full-bodied red Mille e Una Notte, and the famous Ben Ryè Passito di Pantelleria, a sweet dessert wine made from dried grapes. ⊠ *Via Sebastiano Lipari 18, Marsala* ☎ *0923/724245* ⊕ *www.donnafugata.it* ⊠ *Tastings from €24* ⊘ *Closed Sun.*

⭐ **Marsala Salt Pans**
SCENIC DRIVE | Driving along the flat and winding coast road north of Marsala, you'll soon come across the extraordinary series of salt pans glistening in the shallows of Sicily's largest lagoon, the Stagnone di Marsala. The shallow depth of the lagoon, ranging from 2 to 6 feet, has made it perfect for the production of salt, and it has been put to this purpose since Phoenician times. The sheer flatness of the scene is varied only by the conical heaps of salt and a scattering of the disused windmills once used to supply power. The scene is still and

quiet most of the time, but you'll sometimes see pockets of activity, with full wheelbarrows of salt being hauled to the conveyor belts that create the mounds. The stacks of earthenware tiles you'll see everywhere are used to weigh down the salt to prevent it being from blown away by gusts of wind. It's an extremely photogenic tableau, with the light changing through the day and Mozia and the Egadi archipelago looming through the haze.

The narrow coastal road is one-way for much of its length, and the cycle track running alongside it enables the area to be comfortably toured on two wheels. ⊠ *Marsala.*

Museo Archeologico Baglio Anselmi

HISTORY MUSEUM | A sense of Marsala's past as a Carthaginian stronghold is captured by the well-preserved Punic warship displayed in this museum, along with some of the amphorae and other artifacts recovered from the wreck. The vessel, which was probably sunk during the great sea battle that ended the First Punic War in 241 BC, was dredged up from the mud near the Egadi Islands in the 1970s. There's also a good display of maritime and archaeological finds, as well as some Roman ruins with mosaics just beyond the museum's doors. ⊠ *Lungomare Boeo 30, Marsala* ☎ *0923/952535* ⌨ *€4* ⊘ *Closed Mon.*

Museo Garibaldino

HISTORY MUSEUM | A former Benedictine monastery off Piazza Repubblica is now the home of the Complesso Monumentale di San Pietro, a series of exhibition and conference rooms that include a collection of items relating to Giuseppe Garibaldi, the flamboyant hero of Italy's 19th-century war of independence. The resistance leader's name is ubiquitous in Marsala, for it was here that he disembarked his army of one thousand "red shirts" to battle against the Bourbons, a struggle that eventually led to a unified and independent Italy. Two rooms—including the monastery's

former refectory—display guns, swords, busts, paintings, photographs, and uniforms from the campaign, including examples of the famous red shirts worn by Garibaldi's fiercely loyal followers. A box in the center of the room holds the guerrilla general's own pistol.

Other parts of the museum complex hold archaeological fragments from Roman hypogea and necropolis in the area as well as traditional masks and costumes worn in Marsala's Easter Thursday procession. The wide central courtyard is the venue for concerts and open-air movies in the summer. ⊠ *Complesso Monumentale di San Pietro, Via Ludovico Anselmi Correale 12, Marsala* ☎ *0923/993181* ⊘ *Closed Sun. and Mon.*

San Tommaso di Canterbury

CHURCH | Dedicated to Thomas à Becket, the English saint famously martyred after provoking the fury of Henry II, Marsala's imposing Duomo is located in the heart of the old town, dominating a stately piazza that is also flanked by the 18th-century town hall. The church's grand Baroque facade is matched by its spacious and airy interior. The chapels on either side of the nave contain much work by Sicily's prolific Gagini family of sculptors. ⊠ *Piazza della Repubblica, Marsala* ☎ *0923/716295* ⊕ *www.chiesamadremarsala.eu* ⌨ *Free.*

 Restaurants

Trattoria Garibaldi

$ | **ITALIAN** | **FAMILY** | The word "trattoria" usually suggests somewhere casual and even slapdash and while this place has an informal feel, there is nothing at all lacking in the level of service or the quality of the food. Dating back to 1963, the place has a classic feel, as reflected on an extensive menu that focuses on fish (there's a display of what's on offer as you come in), but also includes very acceptable versions of old favorites such as lasagne, couscous, escalopes in Marsala

Did You Know?

One of the most stunning scenes in Sicily is the Marsala salt pans, located in the shallows of Sicily's largest lagoon, the Stagnone di Marsala and dotted with windmills that were once used to supply power to the area.

sauce, and, for dessert, *cassata siciliana*. **Known for:** authentic ambience; traditional dishes; family-friendly. 🟥 *Average main: €14* ✉ *Piazza Addolorata 37, Marsala* ☎ *0923/953006* 🕐 *No dinner Sun.*

☕ Coffee and Quick Bites

Busiate

$ | ITALIAN | If you want to expereince Italian street food, Marsala-style, try this small shop named for the ropelike pasta that is typical in Trapani province, and offered here in cartons for consuming either at one of the tables in the piazza outside or as you walk along. Order the type you prefer ("classic," wholefood, or gluten-free), choose your sauce, which could be seafood, meat, or vegetarian, and order whatever additions take your fancy, maybe fresh breadcrumbs with garlic, Sicilian pecorino, toasted pine nuts, or baked ricotta. **Known for:** tasty street food; customized choices; gluten-free options. 🟥 *Average main: €7* ✉ *Via Sebastiano Cammareri Scurti 3, Marsala* ☎ *334/5640801* 🕐 *Closed Sun. No dinner Mon.–Thurs.*

Gelateria del Cassaro

$ | ICE CREAM | FAMILY | There's usually a bit of a bustle in and around this ice-cream parlor near Piazza della Repubblica, popular with children and gelato fans of all ages. The ice creams are free of hydrogenated fats and come in an enticing range of flavors; popular choices include ricotta, pistachio, and, naturally, Marsala. **Known for:** use of nonhydrogenated fats; great granitas; child-friendly vibe. 🟥 *Average main: €4* ✉ *Via XI Maggio 51, Marsala* ☎ *380/3421078* ▤ *No credit cards.*

Hotels

★ Hotel Carmine

$$ | HOTEL | In a pedestrianized piazza in Marsala's old town and housed in a former convent, Hotel Carmine makes a stylish and atmospheric lodging. **Pros:** good spread for breakfast; central

but quiet location; historic ambience. **Cons:** limited parking; some rooms are dark; mosquitoes may be a problem in garden-facing rooms. 🟥 *Rooms from: €130* ✉ *Piazza Carmine 16, Marsala* ☎ *0923/711907* ⊕ *www.hotelcarmine.it* 🛏 *28 rooms* 🍽 *Free Breakfast.*

Villa Favorita

$$ | HOTEL | Some 2 km (1 mile) from downtown Marsala, this luxurious retreat with extensive semi-tropical gardens was built as a *baglio*, or wine estate, and it retains strong echoes of its 19th-century origins. **Pros:** sumptuous breakfasts; good-size pool; palatial setting. **Cons:** bit remote from town center and local attractions; wedding receptions and other events often take priority; intrusive music sometimes played in grounds. 🟥 *Rooms from: €135* ✉ *Via Favorita 27, Marsala* ☎ *0923/989100* 🕐 *Closed Oct.–Mar.* 🛏 *42 rooms and bungalows* 🍽 *Free Breakfast.*

Nightlife

Morsi e Sorsi

WINE BARS | This enoteca (wine bar) has a few tables indoors but most people choose to sit out in Piazza Vittoria opposite the grand Art Deco cinema Cine Impero. Apart from a range of wines (including, of course, Marsala) and cocktails, snacks are served—mainly pastas and meat dishes—and it stays open late. ✉ *Via Armando Diaz 66, Marsala* ☎ *351/9277763.*

Activities

Krivamar Elegant Tour

BOAT TOURS | Krivamar provides 90-minute boat tours of the Stagnone di Marsala lagoon (every 30 minutes, less frequently in winter) from the signposted Imbarcadero ferry embarcation point. The flat-keeled boats cruise among the small islands of the lagoon—including Mozia—with the guide pointing out such features as the sunken causeway that

On Mozia Island, the Museo Whitaker holds items excavated from the island itself, once an important Phoenician settlement.

once connected Carthaginian Mozia to the mainland. There's no need to book in advance, just show up ready to go.
✉ *Contrada Ettore Infersa 158, Marsala* ☎ *339/4904090* ⊕ *www.krivamar.com* 🎫 *€10.*

Stagnone Kitesurf

SURFING | The Stagnone of Marsala has become Sicily's premier kitesurfing location in recent years, ideal for its sheltered position. This outfit arranges courses for total beginners or those with more experience and also rents out equipment if you want to go out on your own. Windsurfing and stand-up paddling courses and equipment hire are also available.
✉ *Stagnone di Marsala, Contrada Birgi Clemente* ☎ *380/7193438* ⊕ *www.stagnonekitesurf.com* 🎫 *From €80.*

Mozia Island

23 km (14 miles) and 15-minute ferry south of Trapani.

Between Marsala and Trapani, the Stagnone Islands sit amid the shallow lagoon that forms part of a nature reserve, fringed by the eye-catching salt pans that dominate the local landscape. The best known of the islands is tiny Mozia, once an important Phoenician settlement, later fortified by the Carthaginians under whom it became one of the three main Punic strongholds in Sicily. Motya, as it was known, was completely destroyed by Dionysius of Syracuse in 397–396 BC, and its population transferred to the more defensible site of Lilybaeum (modern Marsala), after which most of the Carthaginian city vanished beneath fields and orchards. There was some Roman settlement here, but it was not until the 17th century that the island was identified as the site of ancient Motya, and not until it was acquired in the late 19th century by the Anglo-Sicilian polymath Joseph (or Giuseppe) Whitaker, scion of one of the most prominent Marsala wine dynasties, that excavations began.

The Fondazione Whitaker still owns the island and manages Mozia's excellent archaeological museum that displays some of the most significant finds dug up here (though many now reside in Palermo's archaeological museum).

GETTING HERE AND AROUND

Ferries operated by Arini e Pugliese and Mozia Line leave from two embarkation points signposted from the coast road opposite the islands in Marsala. Crossings are every 15 to 30 minutes—or in winter whenever there are enough people ready to board—and run all day until the island's closing time. Note that in winter, ferries only use the northernmost embarkation point.

FERRY CONTACTS Arini e Pugliese.
☎ *347/3430329* ⊕ *www.ariniepugliese. com.* **Mozia Line.** ☎ *338/7860474* ⊕ *www. mozialine.com.*

Sights

★ Museo Whitaker and Mozia Archaeological Site

RUINS | Joseph Whitaker's former home now holds the Museo Whitaker, displaying a good selection of the finds excavated from Mozia Island. As you enter you'll see useful aerial photographs and models showing the island now and as it might have looked under Carthaginian rule. Most of the exhibits consist of steles, pottery, painted vases, and a scattering of spearheads and jewelry, but the centerpiece is the so-called youth of Motya, an elegantly sinuous life-size statue of a poised young man, one hand resting on his hip, exuding a powerful air of self-assurance. The statue is also known as the "charioteer," though there is no evidence that this was his role.

Outside the museum, walk in any direction to take in the dispersed archaeological site. You can't go wrong tracing the perimeter of the island, which will bring you to the Tophet (shrine and burial ground) on the northern shore, and the Cappiddazzu sanctuary, close to where the youth of Mozia was unearthed. There is little above thigh-height until you come to such imposing structures as the north gate, the city's main entrance that stood at the end of a causeway (now submerged) that formerly linked it to the Sicilian mainland; the eastern tower; and the remains of the sturdy Carthaginian city walls. There are panels and charts throughout, providing explanations and background on what you're seeing.

Allow at least three hours for a thorough exploration of the museum and island, or longer if you want to bring a picnic lunch or pick up a snack at the café. Sunhats are strongly recommended. ⊠ *Mozia Island* ☎ *349/6256508* ⊕ *www.isoladimozia.it* ⊠ *€6.*

THE TYRRHENIAN COAST

Updated by
Rochelle Del Borrello

👁 **Sights**
★★★☆☆

🍴 **Restaurants**
★★★☆☆

🛏 **Hotels**
★★★☆☆

🛍 **Shopping**
★☆☆☆☆

🍸 **Nightlife**
★☆☆☆☆

WELCOME TO THE TYRRHENIAN COAST

TOP REASONS TO GO

★ **Beaches:** A true understated jewel of Sicily, this stunning panoramic coastline is dotted with rocky, sandy beaches and peaceful bays, perfect for swimming and lounging.

★ **No crowds:** This part of the island is largely ignored by the mass tourism industry and is far away from the hustle and bustle of the big cities. Here you can explore a more authentic part of Sicily, and interact with the locals to get a real sense of everyday life here.

★ **History:** Like the rest of Sicily, the Tyrrhenian Coast is basically an open-air museum. Nearly everywhere you look is filled with art-drenched churches, ornate palaces, medieval towers, and historic castles to visit.

★ **Food:** Food is the unofficial religion in Sicily, and the Tyrrhenian Coast will offer you perhaps the best seafood you will ever taste.

1 Termini Imerese. The stunning western gateway to the Tyrrhenian Coast.

2 Caccamo. A tiny mountain village with the largest castle in Sicily.

3 Cefalù. A fascinating medieval town nestled between the mountains and the coast.

4 Collesano. A small town that's an integral part of the historic car race, the Targa Florio, that weaves through the beautiful Madonie Mountains.

5 Castelbuono. A stunning ancient town considered one of the most beautiful hamlets in Italy.

6 Polizzi Generosa. A beautiful village once a residence to royalty, including Queen Elizabeth of Aragon and Emperor Charles V.

7 Petralia Sottana. A village with beautiful views and a surprising amount of medieval art and history.

8 Petralia Soprana. The highest point of the Madonie Mountains, offering a trip back into the middle ages with some of the best views in Sicily.

9 Gangi. A town filled with ancient stone houses reflecting a mesmerizing part of the island's history.

10 Castel di Tusa. A picturesque seaside town with hidden seaside hamlets, beaches, an open-air sculpture park, and castle ruins.

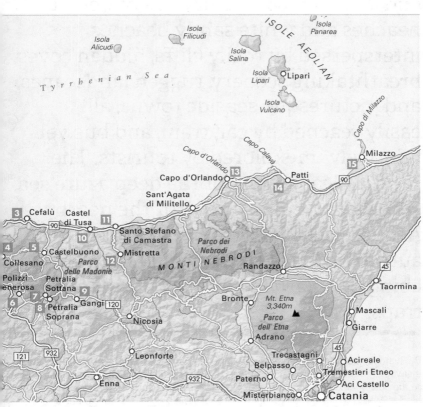

The suggestive coastline of the Tyrrhenian Sea on Sicily's northern end is dotted with a mixture of pebble beaches and white sandy beaches interspersed by rocky cliffs, hidden coves, breathtaking scenery, rugged landscapes, and picturesque seaside towns, all easily reached by car, train, and bus yet relatively unexplored by tourists. The crystal clear waters of the deep azure sea show off stunning views of the nearby Aeolian Islands. Here, you can enjoy an authentic Sicilian experience without being bombarded by crowds and tourist traps.

The historic nature of Sicily means there is always something interesting to see on the coast or in the nearby mountain villages, which will take you back in time and offer you ancient castles, palaces, and stunning panoramas. There is a delicious array of Sicilian food and cuisine to taste throughout the year as well. Many foods are associated with traditional religious celebrations, such as days related to local patron saints. Each town's seasonal food festival will reward you with the highest quality seasonal products and diverse tastes from every area. These religious and food celebrations are unforgettable experiences rich in Sicilian history, culture and history.

The Tyrrhenian Sea, or *Mar Tirreno* to Italians, is the section of the Mediterranean Sea located off the western coast of mainland Italy. It was named after the Tyrrhenians, or Etruscan people, an ancient tribe who inhabited the west coast of the Italian peninsula from Tuscany down towards southern Italy from 900 to 27 BC.

This area has been inhabited since prehistoric times and has a very long history. Thirteen different colonizers have invaded Sicily throughout known history, all hungry to take advantage of its strategic position in the Mediterranean. Everyone from the Phoenicians, Greeks, Romans, Byzantines, Arabs, Normans, French, Germans, Spanish, Italians and even the British have tried to make the island theirs, and each civilization left behind imprints of their culture on the island. From Greek temples and Roman villas to Norman cathedrals and Baroque churches, Sicily offers a head-spinning array of historical sights to see.

And the Tyrrhenian Coast has always been at the forefront of this history. Ever since the Greeks colonized Naxos near Taormina over in eastern Sicily, the cities on this stretch of coastline have been a hub of activity, trade, and commerce. The export of agricultural products from the center of the island allowed the region to develop a series of historically significant villages, hamlets, and fortresses. The result is an intriguing part of Sicily filled with precious historical artifacts, from churches filled with art to well-preserved defensive castles and palaces.

Besides all this fascinating history, the coastline also offers up rustic, off-the-beaten-track locations to explore, such as sleepy fishing villages and bustling seaside resort towns filled with a buzzing energy.

The compact geographic lay-out of the region means you can enjoy the richness of the coast, including the stunning beaches and the best seafood you will ever taste, along with the evocative beauty of its interior and its mountains dotted with intriguing villages to explore, often all on the same day. Enjoy a morning swim at the beach and take a short drive into the picturesque mountains, have a hearty lunch in a small family-run trattoria, and be back at the beach in time to see the sunset.

Planning

When to Go

Sicily isn't called the island of the sun for no reason. Even in the dead of winter, the coast will be bathed in splendid sunlight. If you want to make the most of your time at the beach, June or July is the best time to visit. August can get so hot and humid, it's uncomfortable, with most places lacking air-conditioning and crowds at their highest due to Italians going on summer holidays. September and October are still warm and a little less crowded than peak summer. Springtime in Sicily is also beautiful when the countryside blossoms and the immensely spectacular traditional Easter celebrations occur throughout the region.

Planning Your Time

The best way to start your Tyrrhenian Coast adventure is to fly directly to Palermo, the island's capital. It's actually possible to base yourself in Palermo and day-trip along the coast and inland to some of the beautiful villages and towns nearby, such as Cefalù. It's also easy to catch a train from Palermo toward Messina and stop at any of the dozens of seaside cities for a few days at the beach. But the ideal way to explore is by renting a car and driving all around the coast. For those short on time, you can make the drive from Palermo to Messina in less than three hours; taking a whole day to make the drive will allow you to make leisurely stops at some of the beaches and inland villages.

But you could also spend a whole week in just this region, exploring all the beauty and culture it has to offer. Base yourself in just one town the whole time (Cefalù, Castelbuono, or Capo d'Orlando are good options), making day trips to other stops on the coast and inland, or move around every two or three nights to a new base. Just make sure to get a good variety of sea and mountains.

Instead of heading back to Palermo again at the end of your trip, it is easy to continue toward Messina and explore other places like Taormina and Catania. You can even choose to fly out of Catania's Fontanarossa airport rather than having to double back the way you already came.

Getting Here and Around

AIR

Most major airlines fly to the Falcone Borsellino Airport in Palermo, where you can easily rent a car to explore the coast. Otherwise, you can take a bus (€6.30) or a taxi (€35–€45) from the airport to the city's central train station, where you can then catch trains on to the coast

You can also fly into Catania Fontanarossa airport, on the eastern side of the island, where car rentals are also widely available.

CONTACTS Catania Airport.
☎ 095/7239111 ⊕ www.aeroporto. catania.it. **Falcone Borsellino Airport.** ✉ Palermo ☎ 091/7020111, 800/541880 toll-free ⊕ www.aeroportodipalermo.it.

BUS

Local bus service is widely available from Palermo and Messina to most of the coast's towns and between the towns themselves.

CONTACTS Cuffaro Autolinee.
☎ 091/6161510 ⊕ www.cuffaro.info. **Magistro Autolinee.** ☎ 094/1562295 ⊕ www. magtour.it. **SAIS.** ☎ 800/211020 toll-free ⊕ www.saisautolinee.it.

CAR

This area is easy to explore by car, and having a vehicle is perhaps the best way to see all the region's towns and sights in the shortest amount of time. You can rent a car directly from the Palermo or Catania

airports, both of which feature most major car rental companies.

Traffic and driving in the bigger cities of Sicily is often chaotic, but things are much easier to navigate once outside of the cities. The highway system, or autostrada, is a toll-paying service; you will have to collect a ticket near the gate as you enter and stop and pay either at the automatic machines or in person at the gates when you exit. Payments are usually made in cash, so be sure to have some Euros with you.

TRAIN

Most towns on the Tyrrhenian Coast are served by Trenitalia, Italy's national trainline, which makes its way leisurely along the picturesque coastline from Palermo to Messina; ticket prices are very reasonable. Just remember that Italian trains are infamous for being slow and constantly delayed, so be sure to pack a lunch, have some patience, and don't hurry. While trains in Sicily often aren't the most time-effective way to get to where you're going, this particular route is an excellent way of savoring the landscape as the line is parallel to the seaside on one side and the mountains on the other.

CONTACTS Trenitalia. ☎ 892021 in Italy, 06/68475475 outside Italy ⊕ www. trenitalia.com.

Hotels

In the larger cities and more touristy destinations like Cefalù, you'll find many options for accommodations from five-star beach resorts and luxury apartments to simple inns, but in some of the smaller villages, lodging options might be much more limited. Agriturismos, or farm stays, are very popular and are often located in the countryside. An agriturismo is a great way to experience the landscape and taste the best of local cuisine.

The city of Termini Imerese is an important commercial port known for its natural springs.

Restaurants

While traveling along the coast, be ready to enjoy a vast array of fresh seafood, especially swordfish, tuna, and sardines, all made with simple and natural ingredients like olive oil and garlic. Practically every coastal town will have excellent seafood readily available while the region's mountain villages are famous for their traditional farming products such as cheeses, salami, fresh pork, tomatoes, eggplant, and other fruits and vegetables. In most towns, you'll find a diverse selection of casual trattorias and more expensive (and sometimes more upscale) restaurants as well as quick takeaway pizza places and bars offering coffee, pastries, and arancini.

RESTAURANT AND HOTEL PRICES

Restaurant prices in the reviews are the average cost of a main course at dinner, or if dinner is not served, at lunch. Hotel prices in the reviews are the lowest cost of a standard double room in high season. Restaurant and hotel reviews have been shortened. For full information, visit Fodors.com.

What it Costs in Euros			
$	$$	$$$	$$$$
RESTAURANTS			
under €15	€15–€22	€23–€30	over €30
HOTELS			
under €125	€125–€225	€226–€350	over €350

Tours

There are no major tour operators specializing in the Tyrrhenian Coast area, but most local tours or day trips can be booked through hotels or local travel agents, especially during the summer season.

Termini Imerese

38 km (24 miles) from Palermo, 260 km (161 miles) from Messina.

As the last town in the province of Palermo before entering the province of Messina, Termini Imerese is an important commercial port and position along the coast, connecting Sicily to mainland Italy with regular ferries to the port of Civitavecchia near Rome. It captures the spirit of both provinces, with a stunning coastline dotted with several gracious palaces and churches.

The city gets its name from its *terme* (natural spring water spas), which have drawn visitors to the area since Roman times. Termini was also an essential part of the export of grains and wheat during the Roman empire, a history reflected in its many monuments.

GETTING HERE AND AROUND

From Palermo, take the A19 Autostrada highway connection to Palermo/Catania to the Termini Imerese exit or the S.S. 113 local road towards the exit Settentrionale Sicula. From Messina, take the A20 Messina/Palermo Autostrada highway towards Palermo and exit at Termini Imerese.

The train station in Termini Imerese is on Piazza Europa. All trains to and from Palermo and Messina stop at Termini.

VISITOR INFORMATION

CONTACT Comune di Termini Imerese. ⊠ *Piazza Duomo, Termini Imerese* ☎ *09181/28111* ⊕ *comuneterminiimerese.pa.it.*

 ## Sights

Baldassarre Romano City Museum

HISTORY MUSEUM | FAMILY | Established in 1873, this museum located directly in front of the Duomo is perfect for lovers of ancient Greek and Roman art. It houses an impressive collection of artifacts recovered from the archaeological area of Himera, including old coins, statues, and many other objects from daily life. The gallery also houses the works of Sicilian artists from the 16th and 17th centuries, some Flemish works, and even a Byzantine triptych. It is an astoundingly random collection that's a testament to the passionate dedication Sicily has always had when it comes to artists and pieces of art. ⊠ *Via Marco Aurelio Cicerone, Termini Imerese, Palermo* ☎ *091/8128550* 💶 *€2* 🕒 *Closed Mon.*

Duomo di San Nicolo di Bari

CHURCH | FAMILY | Termini's main cathedral is dedicated to St. Nicholas and, like most Sicilian churches, is filled with precious artwork. The interior chapel and altar are from the 17th century and are decorated with precious inlaid colored marble. The Duomo also has an on-site museum of sacred art, filled with silverwork, vestments, religious relics, and liturgical objects of great value. ⊠ *Piazza Duomo 2, Termini Imerese, Palermo* ☎ *091/8141291* 💶 *Free.*

★ Himera Archeological Area and Museum

RUINS | FAMILY | Not far from Termini is the hamlet of Buonfornello, a precious archaeological site that includes the remains of the ancient city of Himera, founded by Greek settlers in 648 BC. Hannibal later destroyed ancient Himera in 409 BC, and the surviving population moved to the nearby thermal springs, which later became Termini Imerese. The outdoor archaeological area houses the ruins of many Roman temples and buildings. The more precious items recovered from the excavations are housed in the on-site museum. These include artifacts like bronze and ceramic vases and intricate artworks made with other precious metals. ⊠ *Buonfornello, Palermo* ☎ *091/8140128* 💶 *€4* 🕒 *Closed Mon.*

🍴 Restaurants

Ristorante La Perla Termini

$$ | ITALIAN | FAMILY | This typical family-run Italian restaurant specializes in locally fished seafood and fine pizzas from the wood-fired oven. The staff are very accommodating and will prepare anything you require if there are specific dietary requirements, including gluten-free and vegetarian options. **Known for:** gluten-free options; family-friendly vibes; casual atmosphere. [$] *Average main: €20* ✉ *Via Vittorio Emanuele Orlando 4, Termini Imerese* ☎ *392/2837644* 🌐 *ristorante-la-perla-termini-imerese.business.site* 🕓 *Closed Mon. No lunch Tues.–Sun.*

★ **Ristorante Secondo Tempo**

$$$$ | ITALIAN | The philosophy of this contemporary restaurant is to combine modern culinary techniques with the best seasonal products, and chef Salvo Campagna creates plates that are just that: modern, elegant, and fresh. The menu is strictly seasonal and includes a fascinating percorso, a seven-course tasting menu created by the chef from the best ingredients for €60. **Known for:** excellent local seafood; great wine list; one of the coast's best fine dining experiences. [$] *Average main: €60* ✉ *Via Vittorio Amedeo 55, Termini Imerese* ☎ *091/8113775* 🌐 *www.ristorantesecondotempo.it* 🕓 *Closed Mon. No lunch Tues.–Sat.*

🛏 Hotels

Hotel Il Gabbiano

$ | HOTEL | FAMILY | This comfortable and modern hotel is a great place to stay just outside Termini, near the seaside. **Pros:** good on-site restaurant; close to the beach; free private parking. **Cons:** basic rooms; some rooms a little dark; not all rooms have balconies. [$] *Rooms from: €100* ✉ *Via Liberta 221, Termini Imerese* ☎ *091/8113262* 🌐 *www.hotelgabbiano.it* 🛏 *10 rooms* 🍴 *Free Breakfast.*

Caccamo

11 km (7 miles) south of Termini Imerese.

A stunning medieval mountain town filled with charm and character, visiting Caccamo is like taking a walk through a period drama film set. Its highlight is the one of the most well-preserved Norman castles in all of Italy, adorned with intricate stonework dating back to the 12th century.

The area immediately surrounding Caccamo is also beautiful to explore. Take a scenic drive to Caccamo Lake and the Rosamarina Dam, both part of the nearby Madonie Regional Park.

GETTING HERE AND AROUND

The quickest and most reliable way to get to Caccamo is by car. There are no regular or direct buses from Palermo to Caccamo, but you can take one from Termini Imerese.

VISITOR INFORMATION

CONTACTS Associazione Turistica Pro Loco Giorgio Ponte. ✉ *Piazza Duomo, Caccamo* ☎ *091/8122032* 🌐 *www.prolococaccamo.it.*

👁 Sights

★ **Castello di Caccamo**

CASTLE/PALACE | FAMILY | A visit to this fantastic castle, the biggest in Sicily and one of the grandest in all of Italy, is like stepping into the Middle Ages, complete with a well-stocked medieval armory, creepy dungeon prison, and elegant upper-level rooms decorated with detailed woodwork carving and majolica ceramic floors. The castle was the property of the Chiaramontes, once a powerful Sicilian aristocratic family. The views of the Rosamina lake and valley below are beyond spectacular. ✉ *Corso Umberto I, Caccamo* ☎ *091/8149252* 🌐 *www.castellodicaccamo.it* 🎟 *€4.*

One of the best-preserved Norman castles in Italy, Castello di Caccamo lords over the town of Caccamo.

Chiesa dell'Annunziata

CHURCH | The second-largest church in Caccamo, the Chiesa dell'Annunziata holds just as much precious artwork as the main cathedral and dates back to the 1700s. The rooftop frescoes are by Giambecchina while stunning stucco wall decorations are by the famous Sicilian master Giacomo Serpotta and the front altar's design of the Annunciation is by Guglielmo Borremans. ⊠ *Piazza SS. Annunziata, Caccamo* ☎ *091/8148023* ⊠ *Free.*

Chiesa dell'Oratorio

CHURCH | Located right in front of the main square at the heart of Caccamo, the Chiesa dell'Oratorio is one in a series of splendid Baroque monuments in the center of the city. Together with the Chiesa dell'Oratorio, the palace of Monte di Pietà, and the church of the Anime Sante del Purgatorio, it makes up the historic heart of the city's art and culture. The square is used as a majestic open-air stage for events and concerts, and what better backdrop than these splendid examples of Sicilian Baroque architecture. ⊠ *Piazza Duomo, Caccamo* ☎ *No phone* ⊕ *comune.caccamo.pa.it* ⊠ *Free.*

Chiesa di San Benedetto

CHURCH | **FAMILY** | As is usually the case in Sicily, this church is one of the best places in town to see some incredible art. The Chiesa di San Benedetto is decorated with an elaborate and remarkably well-preserved maiolica ceramic floor designed and crafted by 18th-century Palermo artist Nicolò Saranza. The decorative gold highlighted stucco wall decorations make the church glow in the sunlight. ⊠ *Piazza Vittorio Emanuele 4, Caccamo* ☎ *091/8103207* ⊠ *Free.*

Duomo di San Giorgio Martire

CHURCH | The main Norman cathedral of Caccamo, the original church was built in the 1400s by the Chiaramonte family and filled with artwork from many Sicilian Renaissance masters. The building was expanded and rebuilt in the 1600s in the elaborate Sicilian Baroque-style and still houses all the paintings from the previous structure and other artwork from abandoned or destroyed churches in the area. ✉ *Piazza Duomo 2, Caccamo* ☎ *091/8121808* 🎟 *Free.*

🍴 Restaurants

★ Castellana

$$ | ITALIAN | This local pizza and BBQ grill offers the usual selection of local cuisine, but with an interesting location in the old grain stores of the Castello di Caccamo. The extensive menu includes antipasti, pasta, mains, and desserts all with a focus on the preparation of local meats and grills. **Known for:** local craft beers; lots of character and charm; cool historic location. [$] *Average main: €20* ✉ *Piazza dei Caduti 4, Caccamo* ☎ *091/8148667* 🌐 *www.castellana.it* 🕓 *Closed Mon.*

Il Borgo

$$ | ITALIAN | The stone building that houses Il Borgo was built in 1942 in a style that reflects the neighboring medieval castle. The cool stone walls and wooden furnishings create a wonderfully warm atmosphere while the restaurant itself is focused on a delicious rotating seasonal menu. **Known for:** bread, pasta, and desserts all made in-house; wood-fired pizzas to-go; gorgeous setting. [$] *Average main: €20* ✉ *Via Amilcare 13, Caccamo* ☎ *091/2774401* 🌐 *www.ilborgoristorante.it* 🕓 *Closed Tues. No lunch Mon. and Wed.–Sat.*

La Spiga D'oro

$ | ITALIAN | FAMILY | For a taste of the best in local cuisine, come to this intimate, family-run spot with a nice little menu of selected pizzas, pasta dishes, and mains featuring the fresh seasonal ingredients you grow to expect in Sicilian restaurants. Service is warm, friendly, and very accommodating of children. **Known for:** wood-fire pizzas; fresh ingredients; quick meals to go. [$] *Average main: €15* ✉ *Via Margherita 74, Caccamo* ☎ *091/8148968* 🕓 *Closed Wed.*

🛏 Hotels

There really aren't that many options in Caccamo if you want to stay overnight. The only choices are small B&Bs or even smaller rental apartments.

Casa Vacanza Santa Lucia

$ | B&B/INN | This holiday home is a lovely apartment located directly across from the castle, perfectly positioned to explore the town. **Pros:** cozy decor; reasonably priced; beautiful location. **Cons:** difficult to find; very small; access via stairs only. [$] *Rooms from: €60* ✉ *Corso Umberto I, No. 10, Caccamo* ☎ *380/3484661* 🛏 *1 apartment* 🍽 *Free Breakfast.*

Casetta di Rosina

$ | B&B/INN | This B&B is located within an elegantly modern restored home in the center of town with all the comforts of a fully serviced apartment, including a kitchen and free Wi-Fi. **Pros:** beautiful decor; affordable; good location. **Cons:** difficult to find; on the small side; no elevator. [$] *Rooms from: €70* ✉ *22 Piazza Zafferana, Caccamo* ☎ *338/9243831* 🛏 *1 apartment* 🍽 *Free Breakfast.*

Cefalù

39 km (22 miles) northeast of Caccamo.

The jewel of the Tyrrhenian Coast is no doubt Cefalù, a classically appealing old Sicilian town built on a spur jutting out into the sea.

The city's medieval origins have left behind many interesting historical sites to explore. The Palazzo Maria in Piazza Duomo and the Osteria Magno in Corso Ruggero are palaces that date back to the 13th century. They were both owned by the Ventimiglia family, an influential aristocratic family that dominated and owned most of the agricultural wealth of this part of the island in the middle ages.

Another piece of history here is the medieval washhouse. Carved out of rustic

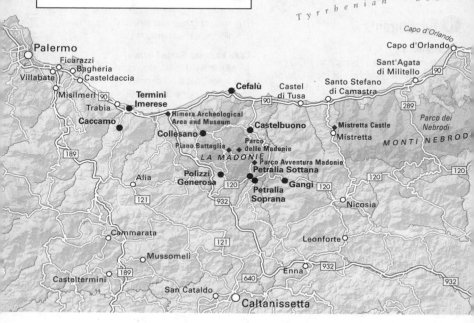

Parco delle Madonie and the Central Tyrrhenian Coast

lava stone and used until the early 20th century, the ancient bathhouse is home to a series of basins fed by the waters of the Cefalino River, which flow out from 22 iron lion-shape mouths. Here, you can get a sense of how life was in Sicily in the Middle Ages.

Cefalù's historical heritage continues with remnants of the Baroque period from the 18th century, which gave birth to the elaborate decorations and style that are quite unique to Sicily. There are the ornate facades of the church of the Monte della Pietà, which dates from 1716, and the stunning Church of Purgatory (1668). The town's historical center is dotted with endless portholes, squares, facades, and architectural details.

GETTING HERE AND AROUND

Trains and buses run between Palermo and Messina, and stop at the station about a 10-minute walk from town. Drivers can take the A20 autostrada, though the traffic going in and out of Cefalù can be heavy in summer and the 50-minute train ride from Palermo may be the better option.

VISITOR INFORMATION

CONTACT Cefalù Tourism Office. ⊠ *Corso Ruggeri 77,* ☎ *0921/421050* ⊕ *www. cefalu.it.*

 Sights

Duomo

CHURCH | Cefalù is dominated by a massive headland—*la rocca*—and a 12th-century Romanesque Duomo, which is one of the finest Norman cathedrals in Italy.

Roger II began the church in 1131 as an offering of thanks for having been saved here from a shipwreck. Its mosaics rival those of Monreale. (Whereas Monreale's Byzantine Christ figure is an austere and powerful image, emphasizing Christ's divinity, the Cefalù Christ is softer, more compassionate, and more human.)

At the Duomo you must be respectfully attired—no shorts or beachwear permitted. ⊠ *Piazza del Duomo, Cefalù* ☎ *0921/922021* ⊕ *www.cattedraledicefalu.com* 🎫 *Cloister €3* 🕐 *Cloister closed weekends.*

★ Museo Mandralisca

ART MUSEUM | This museum comprises the private collection of Baron Enrico Pirajno di Mandralisca, a member of a local aristocratic family. Throughout his life, he collected antiques, artwork, fossils, ancient ceramics, and various other geological and natural history objects to form this extensive collection. His library and other items were eventually donated to the town and became the Museo Mandaralisca. The most significant piece of art here has to be the by Antonello da Messina. Monikered as the Sicilian Mona Lisa, the mysteriously smirking man is one of the early Renaissance artist's masterpeices. ⊠ *Via Mandralisca 13, Cefalù* ☎ *092/421547* ⊕ *www.fondazionemandralisca.it* 🎫 *€6.*

🍴 Restaurants

Al Porticciolo

$$ | SICILIAN | Nicola Mendolia's seaside restaurant is comfortable, casual, and faithfully focused on food—primarily pizza, but with an extensive selection of seafood, pasta, and meat, too. Dark, heavy wooden tables create a comfortable environment filled with a mix of jovial locals and businesspeople, though you may opt to dine on the spacious terrace. **Known for:** lovely terrace overlooking the water; local seafood; high-quality pizza. 💲 *Average main: €17* ⊠ *Via C. Ortolani di Bordonaro 66, Cefalù* ☎ *0921/921981* ⊕ *www.alporticcioloristorante.com.*

Capriccio Siciliano

$$ | ITALIAN | FAMILY | This rustic little family place offers a selection of basic Sicilian antipasti and pasta dishes. It is a perfect spot to taste the local cuisine and wine and soak up the atmosphere and hospitality. **Known for:** good coffee and pastries; filling and affordable meals; nice wine list. 💲 *Average main: €20* ⊠ *Via Umberto I, Cefalù* ☎ *092/420550.*

🏨 Hotels

Kalura

$$$ | HOTEL | FAMILY | This modern hotel is on a small promontory in Caldura, 2 km (1 mile) east of Cefalù, a few minutes away by taxi or a 30-minute walk, and offers bright and cheerful rooms, many with balconies overlooking the sea. **Pros:** beautiful sea views; family-friendly environment; good swimming. **Cons:** minimum stay of two to seven nights in high season; Wi-Fi only in lobby; outside town. 💲 *Rooms from: €209* ⊠ *Via V. Cavallaro 13, Cefalù* ☎ *0921/421354* ⊕ *www.hotelkalura.com* 🕐 *Closed mid-Nov.–mid-Mar.* 🛏 *84 rooms* 🍽 *Free Breakfast.*

🍸 Nightlife

Carrè Lounge

BARS | This is a casual place to grab a beer and enjoy a light antipasto, pizza, or pasta dish at a reasonable price. They are open most of the day, so finding a late lunch when other places are closed won't be a problem here. The location is stunning, with views out toward the sea. ⊠ *Via Carlo Ortolani di Bordanaro 60, Cefalù* ☎ *0921/421210.*

Kalapinta Craft Beer

BREWPUBS | With an impressive menu of signature cocktails, wines, and beers, this is a great spot to enjoy a drink in Cefalù. They serve an excellent antipasto plate as well as casual fast food like hot

dogs, burgers, and nachos. If you love craft beer, you will find the best selection of local beers around. ⊠ *Via Carrettieri 3, Cefalù* ☎ *0921/820168* ⊕ *www.facebook. com/KalapintaCefalu.*

Lido Maljk

DANCE CLUBS | This beautiful club is located right on the beach and is open throughout the year. If you're not into clubbing, it's also a perfect spot to just sit and enjoy a cocktail or aperitif at sunset. It's especially popular in the summer when it's filled with locals and live music. They also have an alfresco restaurant. ⊠ *Lungomare Giuseppe Giardina, Cefalù* ☎ *0921/4220205* ⊕ *www.maljk.it.*

Collesano

28 km (17 miles) southwest of Cefalù.

This village deep in the Madonie Mountains is a picturesque place with ancient winding streets and charming stone houses huddled together on the mountaintop. First settled by Arab conquerors in the 10th century, it became an essential feudal town between the Roccella River and the Madonie.

Its strategic mountain location made it a perfect spot for defending the surrounding fertile lands from new invasions from the Mediterranean. The original castle fortress is still a feature of the modern city, and its scope and dimensions give you a sense of how important Collesano was for the defenses of the area. The town was also famous for its role in the Targa Florio car race.

GETTING HERE AND AROUND

The best way to get to Collesanois is by car. There are local buses available from Termini Imerese and Cefalu, too.

VISITOR INFORMATION

CONTACT Comune di Collesano. ⊠ *Corso Vittorio Emanuele 2, Collesano* ☎ *092/1664001* ⊕ *www.comune.collesano.pa.it.*

Sights

Castello Medievale Collesano

RUINS | FAMILY | Once a vital part of the city's defenses, today Collesano's medieval castle is a small but lovely part of the town's landscape. The castle's ruins can be seen rising above the northern side of the town in front of its original parish church. It was built during the 12th century by King Roger II of Sicily after he decided to move his administration to a more strategic place to head off invasions from North Africa and the Middle East. What remains of this original project are castle ruins and some imposing defensive buildings in a small medieval neighborhood, which is a fascinating place to visit. ⊠ *Via Ospedale 17, Collesano* ☎ *No phone* ⊠ *Free.*

Museo Targa Florio

OTHER MUSEUM | FAMILY | Begun in 1906, the Targa Florio car race weaved its way through the picturesque towns and villages of the Madonie Mountains every year until it was stopped in 1977 for safety reasons; today the same route is driven as part of the annual Italian Rally Championship. Collesano has been an important stage of the race since its inception, and today the city is home to a museum dedicated to the history of the car race. In a detailed exhibition, you can learn of its origins and participants, including some of the most famous drivers that Italy has ever produced. It's an excellent museum for those who love racing and cars. ⊠ *Corso Vittorio Emanuele 3, Collesano* ☎ *0921/664684* ⊕ *www.museotargaflorio.it* ⊠ *€3.*

Restaurants

La Lanterna

$ | ITALIAN | FAMILY | This family-run place cooks very rustic yet satisfying meals, including hearty pasta, filling antipasti, and wood-fire pizzas. **Known for:** wide-ranging and tasty menu; wood-fire pizzas; home-cooked and hearty meals.

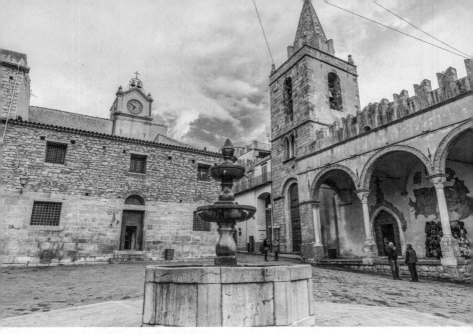

The town of Castelbuono is filled with plenty of history and charming side streets.

$ *Average main: €15* ⊠ *Via Isnello 76, Collesano* ☎ *339/8881837.*

Trattoria Carricaturi

$ | ITALIAN | FAMILY | This café, bar, restaurant, and pizzeria has a daily menu of specials to choose from, including starters, pasta dishes, meat-based mains, sides, and desserts. Your charming and helpful hosts will help you from the selection of reasonably priced dishes. **Known for:** local flavors; generous servings; early opening and late closing hours. $ *Average main: €15* ⊠ *Via Giuseppe Mazzini 1, Collesano* ☎ *0921/6613306* ✆ *Closed Mon.*

Hotels

Casale Drinzi

$ | B&B/INN | FAMILY | Located a little bit outside of Collesano, this old converted farmhouse offers visitors a farm stay experience genuinely unique to Sicily. **Pros:** excellent restaurant and pizzaria; very affordable prices; beautiful location. **Cons:** online booking only; payment only through international bank transfer; rustic farm stay not for everyone. $ *Rooms from: €30* ⊠ *Contrada Drinz, Collesano* ☎ *0921/664027* ⊕ *www.casaledrinzi.it* ⇲ *10 rooms* ⍟ *Free Breakfast.*

Castelbuono

24 km (15 miles) east of Collesano.

A beautiful mountain town, Castelbuono is filled with picturesque side streets, stunning views, and lots of small art galleries and artisan stores selling local folk art and gastronomic products to browse.

Castelbuono also has the rare privilege of being one of the few places in the world that grows a certain type of ash tree. These trees are the biblical producers of Manna, which fed the Israelites when they were in exile in the desert. Today you can buy sweet sugary manna, which is actually the sap of the trees.

GETTING HERE AND AROUND

Castelbuono is easily accessed by car from Palermo and Messina. Buses are also available from Palermo and other local towns on the coast. Trains are available from Cefalù.

VISITOR INFORMATION

CONTACT Pro Loco Castelbuono. ✉ *Piazza Margherita, Castelbuono* ☎ *389/68938* ⊕ *www.prolococastelbuono.it.*

 Sights

Castello di Ventimiglia

CASTLE/PALACE | This impressive castle fortress was built in 1316 by the Ventimiglia family. With its four imposing watchtower structures, it was once the center of Castelbuono and helped the town become the administrative and defensive capital of the Ventimiglias' vast kingdom. Later it also became the prestigious residence of the family. In 1684 its interior was renovated to accommodate the family, and a new chapel was added and filled with decorative stucco embellishments. The Ventimiglia family chapel inside the Castello was decorated by Sicilian master sculptures Giuseppe and Giacomo Serpotta and Antonello Gangini. ✉ *Piazza Castello 10, Castelbuono* ☎ *0921/671211* ⊕ *www.museocivico.eu* 🎫 *€5.*

Chiesa della Natività di Maria

CHURCH | Yet another beautiful historic church in Castelbuono that is well worth visiting, even for only a moment, Chiesa della Natività di Maria was constructed in the 14th century and is characterized by its typical Sicilian limestone stonework and elegant bell tower. Inside it is filled with delicate pieces of art, but don't miss the one above the central altar. The decorative painted altarpiece, with intricate wooden carved details and paintings of various saints, dominates the church. The images on the polyptych are from the 1500s, created by Antonio di Sabila, the nephew of the famous early Renaissance

Sicilian master Antonello da Messina. ✉ *Largo della Parrocchia 8, Castelbuono* ☎ *0921/671043* 🎫 *Free* 🕙 *Church closed during religious services.*

Chiesa Matrice SS Assunta Vecchia

CHURCH | FAMILY | Castelbuono's main cathedral, located on the central square of Piazza Margherita, is a 16th-century elegant Romanesque church filled with various religious art and paintings. The Gothic Catalan bell tower reflects a similar Andalusian style to Palermo's Duomo, and it is a prominent feature of the town's landscape. ✉ *Piazza Margherita 14, Castelbuono* ☎ *0921/671313* 🎫 *Free.*

Museo del Risorgimento

HISTORY MUSEUM | This local museum is dedicated to several significant historical periods, with the collection divided into three parts. The first and second floors focus on travel and local folk traditions, with many objects and artifacts donated from a personal collection of a local aristocrat who devoted his life to traveling the world. There is also a selection of local folk art and traditions, including Sicilian marionettes and decorative Sicilian carts from the 19th century. The other sections are dedicated to the period of Italian unification in the late 1800s. Another interesting feature of the museum is the actual building it is housed in, which features a historic bell tower and clock dating back to the 1800s; you can climb up and see the intricate clockwork beautifully maintained by the local town council. ✉ *Piazza Margherita 14, Castelbuono* ☎ *389/6893810* ⊕ *prolococastelbuono.it.*

★ Parco delle Madonie

NATIONAL PARK | FAMILY | Castelbuono is located just outside this 80,000-acre regional park of the Madonie Mountains, which means it is a perfect spot to explore the splendid natural reserve. There are walking paths, camping areas, horse-riding, mountain biking, and caving activities to experience. You can even just simply take a scenic drive out into the park for a picnic. ✉ *Corso Paolo Agliata 16, Castelbuono* ☎ *0921/684011* 🌐 *www.parcodellemadonie.it* 🎫 *Free.*

🍴 Restaurants

Ristorante Nangalarruni

$$$$ | **ITALIAN** | **FAMILY** | This Castelbuono institution has been preparing dishes with the finest local ingredients for over 30 years. Chef Giuseppe Carollo is dedicated to the products found in and around Castelbuono, including wild mushrooms, vegetables, and the sweet manna from the local ash trees. **Known for:** artisan cheeses and fresh seasonal fruits and vegetables; nice wine list; extensive tasting menu that changes with the seasons. [$] *Average main: €45* ✉ *Cortile Ventimiglia 5* ☎ *0921/671228* 🌐 *www.hostarianangalarruni.it* 🕒 *Closed Wed.*

Trattoria La Lanterna

$$ | **ITALIAN** | **FAMILY** | This rustic restaurant promises good home-cooked meals in a cozy and friendly atmosphere. It is housed in a typical Sicilian trattoria, with a very casual and relaxed ambience. **Known for:** homestyle Italian pizza and pastas; cozy setting; big servings at great prices. [$] *Average main: €15* ✉ *Salita al Monumento 11, Castelbuono* ☎ *0921/993700* 🌐 *ristorante-la-lanterna-castelbuono.business.site* 🕒 *Closed Tues.*

🛏 Hotels

Hotel Paradiso delle Madonie

$ | **MOTEL** | This small boutique hotel is an excellent spot to base yourself to explore the surrounding area and enjoy the comfortable and welcoming rooms. **Pros:** great food, including a free breakfast buffet; reasonably priced; free Wi-Fi. **Cons:** not located in town; very basic rooms; furniture is a little dated. [$] *Rooms from: €80* ✉ *Via Dante Alighieri 82* ☎ *0921/994617* 🌐 *www.paradisodellemadonie.it* 🔑 *16 rooms* 🍽 *Free Breakfast.*

Villa Levante

$$ | **HOUSE** | **FAMILY** | This agriturismo hotel housed in a beautifully restored 18th-century villa located in the countryside on the outskirts of Castelbuono makes for a great farm stay. **Pros:** nice swimming pool; excursions available into Madonie Park; free on-site parking. **Cons:** located outside of Castelbuono proper; rooms are a bit rustic; three-night minimum stay. [$] *Rooms from: €170* ✉ *Via Isnello 52, Castelbuono* ☎ *335/639474* 🌐 *www.villalevante.eu* 🔑 *8 apartments* 🍽 *Free Breakfast.*

Polizzi Generosa

52 km (32 miles) southwest of Castelbuono.

Once a critical and thriving city during the Middle Ages, Polizzi had "Generosa" added to its name to signify the generosity and richness of its agricultural territory.

During the Renaissance, Polizzi was the link between the provinces of Messina and Palermo and a focus of great trade and commerce. As a result of this importance, there are many examples of art and architecture to admire here. The intimate medieval heart of the town gives the place a mystical sense of being lost in time. The town is laid out on the top of a rocky outcrop with 360-degree views of Parco delle Madonie.

GETTING HERE AND AROUND

To get to the town via car, you need to take the Palermo-Catania Autostrada highway (A19) and exit at Scillato. Then take the SS 643 road for about 11 miles to reach the mountaintop town.

There are daily buses available from Palermo with SAIS.

VISITOR INFORMATION

CONTACTS Comune di Polizzi Generosa. ✉ *Via G. Garibaldi 13, Polizzi Generosa* ☎ *0921/551600* 🌐 *www.comune.*

Polizzi Generosa is one of several towns located within the scenic Parco delle Madonie.

polizzi.pa.it. **Ufficio Informazione Turistiche.** *⊠ Piazza Umberto I, Polizzi Generosa ☎ 0921/649187.*

 Sights

Chiesa di San Girolamo

CHURCH | This impressive church occupies an entire block of the main street in the medieval area of town, and it also houses the local library (Biblioteca Comunale) and the Civico Museo Archeologico, an archaeological museum. The church has the standard Greek cross structure. It is filled with marble vaults that host the statues of various saints and is decorated with floral embellishments typical of the extravagant Sicilian Baroque style. *⊠ Via Giuseppe Garibaldi 24, Polizzi Generosa ☎ No phone ☎ Free.*

Chiesa Madre Santa Maria Maggiore

CHURCH | Polizzi is full of churches, each one filled to the brim with fascinating artwork, but this church is probably the most gorgeous of all. Its centerpiece is an astounding Renaissance painting of the Madonna and Child, attributed to the 15th-century Flemish painter Rogier Van Der Weyden. It is astonishing to see this priceless work of art from northern Europe housed in a church in Polizzi Generosa and gives you a sense of how much wealth was brought to the town thanks to its royal patrons. *⊠ Via Roma 1, Polizzi Generosa ☎ 0921/649094 ☎ Free.*

Monastero di Santa Margherita (Badia Vecchia)

CHURCH | Even though the outside of this church seems a little run-down, taking a step inside reveals intricate details and explosions of excessive ornamentation. The old monastery dates back to 1450 and is a testament to the wealth and luxury that the church acquired from the lands and agricultural wealth of Polizzi Generosa. The church is filled with elaborate stonework, decorations, and a well-preserved and vibrant majolica ceramic floor. *⊠ Via Carlo V 46, Polizzi Generosa ☎ No phone ☎ Free.*

🍽 Restaurants

Arte Bianca
$ | **PIZZA** | **FAMILY** | This charming pizza restaurant has a fantastic array of pizza toppings, from the classic margherita to seafood. Personalize your pizza toppings and pair your meal with a selection of great antipasti for a filling and satisfying meal. **Known for:** very reasonably priced; good selection of beers and local wines; excellent pizzas. $\boxed{S}$ *Average main: €13* ✉ *Largo Zingari 1, Polizzi Generosa* 🕾 *368/7081064.*

Ristorante U Bagghiu
$$ | **ITALIAN** | **FAMILY** | This eatery's varied menu shows off the best products and ingredients from Polizzi. Some dishes feature wild asparagus and mushrooms while various antipasti and side dishes include freshly foraged vegetables and greens. **Known for:** local ingredients; authentic pizza; excellent desserts and pastries. $\boxed{S}$ *Average main: €15* ✉ *Via Gagliardo 3, Polizzi Generosa* 🕾 *0921/551111* ⊕ *www.ristoranteubagghiu.it.*

🛏 Hotels

Agriturismo Giardino Donna
$ | **B&B/INN** | This farm stay is located out in the countryside of Polizzi, and gives you a sense of tranquillity while admiring the beautiful landscape of the Madonie. **Pros:** great on-site restaurant; tranquil garden areas with restored windmills; beautiful country location. **Cons:** rooms are basic; you will need a car to get here; slightly isolated rural setting. $\boxed{S}$ *Rooms from: €80* ✉ *Contrada Donna Laura SNC, Polizzi Generosa* 🕾 *0921/551104* ⊕ *www. giardinodonnalavia.com* ⇝ *10 rooms* ⦿ *Free Breakfast.*

La Sorgente delle Madonie
$ | **B&B/INN** | **FAMILY** | In a secluded area out in the hills outside of Polizzi Generosa, this is a perfectly peaceful spot to relax and enjoy nature. **Pros:** comfortable rooms; outdoor pool; beautiful country location. **Cons:** rooms on the modest side; you will need a car to get here; not close to the sights and restaurants in town. $\boxed{S}$ *Rooms from: €80* ✉ *Contrada Chiaretta, Polizzi Generosa* 🕾 *366/7007538* ⇝ *10 rooms* ⦿ *Free Breakfast.*

★ Resort San Nicola
$$ | **HOTEL** | Located outside of Polizzi Generosa deep in the countryside, the resort offers a little luxury within the natural surroundings of an idyllic landscape. **Pros:** spa, swimming pool, and gym; spacious rooms; beautiful location. **Cons:** more expensive than other options in the area; difficult to get to without a car; rural setting not for everyone. $\boxed{S}$ *Rooms from: €130* ✉ *Contrada San Nicola, snc Statale Uscita Santa Venera, Polizzi Generosa* 🕾 *348/2101058* ⊕ *www.resortsannicola. com.*

Petralla Sottana

15 km (9 miles) east of Polizzi Generosa.

This town is in the heart of the Parco delle Madonie, and is filled with plenty of natural beauty. On the border of Palermo province and the green heartland of Caltanissetta, Petralia Sottana's rich history has blessed it with much art and culture to explore. The town is like a magical mirage in the Madonie Highlands: its cathedral appears like a castle on a hill, with the rest of the town cascading down from it.

GETTING HERE AND AROUND
Petralia Sottana is best arrived at by car, although daily buses are available from Palermo to Petralia Soprana with SAIS.

VISITOR INFORMATION
CONTACT Comune di Petralia Sottana. ✉ *Corso P Agliata 50, Petralia Sottana* 🕾 *0921/684311* ⊕ *www.comune.petralia-sottana.pa.it.*

Sights

Chiesa Madre SS. Assunta

CHURCH | In the Middle Ages, Petralia Sottana was under the dominion of the Ventimiglia family, whose immense wealth left behind many stunning public works and buildings in the town. The concentration of this architecture is focused in and around the central square of Piazza Umberto I, which is dominated by this 16th-century parish church, an impressive cathedral dedicated to the Madonna of the Assumption. The interior is filled with sculptures from the 14th, 15th, and 16th centuries, including details from Antonello Gangini, a famed Sicilian sculptor who decorated many important churches with his artwork. ✉ *Corso Paolo Agliata 91, Petralla Sottana* ☎ *0921/641031* 🎟 *Free.*

Civic Museum of Antonio Collisani

HISTORY MUSEUM | This fascinating museum consists of two sections, one dedicated to geology and another to archaeology. It's a testament to Petralia Sottana's long and fascinating human and geological history. The rocks and fossils in the locally gathered collection date back to 200 million years ago and showcase the geographical evolution of the area. The museum's archaeological collection shows a vast array of prehistoric vases, numerous ancient Greek ceramics, and items from the Bronze Age. ✉ *Corso Paolo Agaliata 100, Petralla Sottana* ☎ *0921/641811* 🌐 *www.petraliavisit.it/en/museo-civico-collisani* 🎟 *€5.*

Piano Battaglia

TOWN | **FAMILY** | Located in the geographical heart of the Parco delle Madonie about a half-hour north of Petralia Sottana, the hamlet of Piano Battaglia makes a good day trip for anyone hoping to have a true mountain experience. This is where locals, particularly from Palermo, come to enjoy the mountains, whether it's skiing in the winter or picnicking in the summer. At the town's Fun Park, you can choose from any number of summer and winter activities, including snow tubing, sleighing, skiing, mountain biking, and hiking excursions. ✉ *Piano Battaglia.*

Restaurants

Il Castello Ristorante

$$ | **ITALIAN** | **FAMILY** | This casual restaurant and B&B is located in a converted Norman castle. The restaurant offers a great menu of local Sicilian cuisine and a wood-fired pizza oven. **Known for:** beautiful castle location; excellent pizza; charming option to spend the night. [$] *Average main: €20* ✉ *Via Generale di Maria 27, Petralla Sottana* ☎ *0921/641250* 🌐 *www.il-castello.net* 🕒 *Closed Tues., Wed., and Thurs. No lunch Fri., Sat., and Mon.*

Ristoro dello Scoiattolo

$$$ | **ITALIAN** | **FAMILY** | This rustic mountain lodge is situated right near the popular winter skiing resort area of Piano Battaglia. Opened throughout the year, it offers a cozy country panorama, good hearty local fare, and friendly service at very reasonable prices. **Known for:** beautiful location; family-friendly atmosphere; classic Italian dishes. [$] *Average main: €25* ✉ *Piano Battaglia, Piano Battaglia* ☎ *349/643–9987* 🌐 *www.facebook.com/ristorodelloscoiattolo.*

Hotels

Agriturismo Monaco di Mezzo

$ | **B&B/INN** | **FAMILY** | This agriturismo offers a true taste of farm life in the Madonie with excellent food and plenty of excursions into the mountains. **Pros:** beautifully restored historic farm house; swimming pool, spa, and tennis court; excursions like horse-riding and off-roading offered. **Cons:** slightly isolated; need a car to get here; rooms a bit rustic. [$] *Rooms from: €95* ✉ *Contrada Monaco di Mezzo, Petralla Sottana* ☎ *0934/673949* 🌐 *www.monacodimezzo.com* 🔑 *11 rooms* 🍴 *Free Breakfast.*

The town of Petralia Soprana is filled with many charming old churches, including Chiesa Matrice dei Santi Pietro e Paolo.

B&B Domus Lilio

$ | B&B/INN | The little B&B is in the heart of Petralia Sottana and is an excellent spot to spend a night in the village's historic center. **Pros:** tasty breakfast; stunning views; central location. **Cons:** basic rooms; a lot of stairs to navigate; very small house. $ *Rooms from: €40* ✉ *Via Federici 14, Petralla Sottana* ☎ *327/3829840* ⊕ *www.domuslilio.com* ➴ *4 rooms* ❚◎❚ *Free Breakfast.*

Rifugio Marini

$ | B&B/INN | FAMILY | This comfortable mountain refuge is a good place to stay overnight in the area of Piano Battaglia, in the heart of Parco delle Madonie at the base of Monte Mufara. **Pros:** stunning views; beautiful mountain location; delicious on-site restaurant. **Cons:** very basic rooms; rustic setting; no Wi-Fi. $ *Rooms from: €100* ✉ *Contrada Piano della Battaglia 59, Piano Battaglia* ☎ *335/7772269* ⊕ *www.rifugiomarini.it* ⊙ *Closed Wed.* ➴ *18 rooms* ❚◎❚ *No Meals.*

Petralia Soprana

7 km (4 miles) southeast of Petralia Sottana.

The highest village in the Madonie, Petralia Soprana enjoys some of the most spectacular views of Sicily's interior, including Mount Etna. The ancient town was important during Roman times when it provided large quantities of wheat for the Roman Empire. It maintains its original medieval design, including narrow stone-paved streets, grand churches, and aristocratic palaces.

GETTING HERE AND AROUND

This town is best reached via car, although buses are available from Palermo with SAIS.

VISITOR INFORMATION

CONTACT Comune di Petralia Soprana. ☎ *0921/68411* ⊕ *www.petraliavisit.it.*

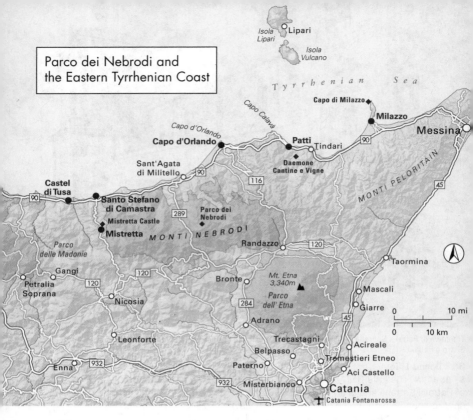

Parco dei Nebrodi and
the Eastern Tyrrhenian Coast

◉ Sights

Chiesa Matrice dei Santi Pietro e Paolo

CHURCH | On the town's Piazza Duomo, you'll find the parish church of the apostles of St. Peter and St. Paul. The church's dominating structure is in the Catalonian Gothic style, with 12 elaborate columns representing the apostles. The interior is relatively simple, but there is a remarkable life-size wooden crucifix in a side chapel. The extensively detailed carving was handmade by local monks in 1623. ✉ *Piazza Duomo, Petralia Soprana* ☎ *0921/641640* 🎟 *Free.*

★ Museo di Arte Contemporanea Sotto Sale

OTHER MUSEUM | A natural salt deposit that was once one of the largest salt mines in Europe has been converted into the town's Museum of Contemporary Art. Aside from browsing the artwork, you can also visit the underground mining caves and see how the salt has been carved into a kind of underground cathedral filled with sculptures. The museum is currently only open one day a week, so be sure to book your tickets in advance to ensure your spot. ✉ *Via del Salgemma, Petralia Soprana* ☎ *366/3878751* ⊕ *macssmuseoartecontemporanea-sottosale.business.site* 🎟 *€8* ⏰ *Closed Sun.–Fri.*

Parco Avventura Madonie

OTHER ATTRACTION | **FAMILY** | This adventure park is located inside the Parco delle Madonie and offers several activities and obstacle courses through the forest and above the trees on rope ladders. There are different levels at varying difficulties, designed for children and adults alike. You can also rent a treehouse or glamping accommodations to spend the night as well as unique tents suspended 20 feet above the ground. ✉ *Contrada Gorgonero, Petralla Sottana* ☎ *339/7655551* 🌐 *www.parcoavventuramadonie.it* 🎟 *From €28* 🕒 *Closed winter.*

Piazza del Popolo

PLAZA/SQUARE | This square is the civic center of town and is home to the local town hall, a neo-Gothic style palace that was once a Carmelite convent. Surrounding the piazza, there are two important aristocratic palaces, including the Palazzo Pottini filled with 18th-century frescoes. ✉ *Piazza del Popolo, Petralia Soprana.*

Piazza San Michele and the Fontana dei Quattro Cannoli

FOUNTAIN | This central square houses an elaborate water fountain that has been a part of the town since its origins. The Fontana dei Quattro Cannoli was once the social and commercial heart of the medieval city. ✉ *Piazza Quattro Cannoli 2, Petralia Soprana.*

🛏 Hotels

La Scaletta di Pietra

$ | **B&B/INN** | Located in the center of Petralia Soprana, a stunning, castle-esque house has been converted into a B&B with comfortable rooms and welcoming hosts. **Pros:** delicious breakfast; stunning views from balconies; unique building. **Cons:** rooms are small; a lot of stairs to navigate; steep incline into rooms. [$] *Rooms from: €70* ✉ *Piazza San Michele 9, Petralia Soprana* ☎ *328/5404500* 🛏 *5 rooms* 🍴 *Free Breakfast.*

Gangi

15 km (9 miles) east of Petralia Soprana.

Straddling the Madonie, this ancient Greek town is a fascinating place to visit. The village seems to be magically carved out of the mountains and is filled with artistic treasures and stunning mountain views from nearly any vantage point.

Gangi is indicative of the once rich agricultural heartlands of Sicily, home to economically thriving towns rich in commerce and development. This prosperity has given Gangi many precious examples of art and architecture dating back to the Middle Ages.

GETTING HERE AND AROUND

Gangi is easily reachable via car. There are also local buses from most coastal towns.

VISITOR INFORMATION

CONTACT Associazione Turistica Pro Loco Gangi. ☎ *366/2837084* 🌐 *www.gangiborgodeiborghi.it.*

👁 Sights

Museo Palazzo Sgadari

HISTORY MUSEUM | This civic museum is housed in a spectacular golden stone palace, typical of Gangi's architectural style. On the first two floors, you'll find a collection of works from the painter Gianbecchina. The upper floors hold various objects excavated from the archaeological site of Gangi and different items that reflect recent local history. ✉ *Corso Giuseppe Fedele Vitale, Gangi* ☎ *0921/689907* 🌐 *www.comune.gangi.pa.it/turismo/museo-palazzo-sgadari* 🎟 *€5* 🕒 *Closed Mon.*

Palazzo Bongiorno

CASTLE/PALACE | The best way to experience Gangi is by walking through its historical center and evocative ancient streets. Walk along the Corso Umberto I and Via G.F. Vitale until you get to the Palazzo Bongiorno, a 16th-century palace constructed by the Bongiorno family, the barons of Cacchiamo. The three-story court is filled with decorative frescoes and royally sumptuous details. ✉ *Salita Cammarate 4, Gangi* ☎ *No phone* 🎟 *€5.*

Castel di Tusa is one of the best places in Sicily to experience the Tyrrhenian Sea.

★ **Torre dei Ventimiglia**

HISTORIC SIGHT | This imposing 1337 Norman tower is attached to the facade of the church Chiesa di Saint Niccolò of Bari, with a square bell tower built upon three levels and Arabesque arched windows. It was part of the feudal kingdom of the Ventimiglia family, who left marks of their wealth and dominance all over the island. After an extensive renovation, it now houses a permanent exhibition of local artists and Christmas nativity models. The church itself is filled with artwork from the 17th and 18th centuries and its mysterious and macabre catacombs contain the mummies of 60 priests from Gangi. ✉ *Via Enea 10, Gangi* ☎ *0921/644322.*

🍴 Restaurants

Trattoria Sant'Anna

$$ | **ITALIAN** | This small restaurant is housed in a part of the Palazzo Bongiorno, making it a beautiful spot to sit and savor the tastes and sights of the town. The meals prepared here are dedicated to the best products of the area and showcase the delicious natural food of Gangi and the Madonie. **Known for:** historic setting; seasonal and local fare; location in the center of town. [$] *Average main: €20* ✉ *Via Sant'Anna 2, Gangi* ☎ *0921/602422* 🌐 *www.trattoriasantanna.it* 🕒 *Closed Wed.*

🛏 Hotels

A-MURI B&B

$ | **APARTMENT** | This intimate B&B is located in the historical center of Gangi, and has been renovated in a contemporary style while still respecting its history, including vaulted rooms and exposed stone walls. **Pros:** spectacular views; recently restored building with many modern elements; centrally located. **Cons:** a lot of stairs to navigate; apartments on the small side; a little dark. [$] *Rooms from: €90* ✉ *Via Termini F. Paolo 23, Gangi* ☎ *347/9014349* 🌐 *www.a-muri.com* 🛏 *4 apartments* 🍴 *Free Breakfast.*

Castel di Tusa

51 km (32 miles) north of Gangi, 32 km (20 miles) east of Cefalù.

This seaside town is a beautiful place to stop and admire the Tyrrhenian Sea, with local beaches that have regularly been touted as the best in Sicily. Castel di Tusa has also been given the distinguished Blue Flag designation by the FEE (Foundation for the Environmental Education), which awards seaside resorts that adhere to environmentally sustainable land management.

GETTING HERE AND AROUND

Castel di Tusa is an easy drive along the coast from both Palermo and Messina. There is a regular train service here from Palermo and Messina as well.

VISITOR INFORMATION

CONTACT Pro Loco di Tusa. ✉ *Via Popolo 45, Castel di Tusa* ☎ *347/7109049* 🌐 *www.terredidioniso.it/index.php/it/37-pro-loco-di-tusa.*

Sights

Fiumara d'Arte
PUBLIC ART | FAMILY | This outdoor sculpture park is filled with contemporary art and is especially gorgeous against the stunning Tyrrhenian coastline. One of the park's most spectacular permanent installations is the Monument for a Dead Poet by Tano Festa, a giant blue framed window that looks out towards the sea and can be seen from miles away. Other fascinating pieces include a bronze pyramid placed precisely on the 38th parallel of latitude and the labyrinth of Arianna, which recalls the ancient Greek myth of the Minotaur. ✉ *Atelier sul Mar Museo Albergo Via Cesare Battisti 4, Castel di Tusa* ☎ *0921/334295* 🌐 *www.ateliersulmare.com/it/fiumara/opere/arianna.html* 🎫 *Free.*

La Spiaggia di Castel di Tusa
BEACH | FAMILY | There's no doubt that the highlight of Castel di Tusa is its beaches, which stretch out from the beginning of the Tusa Cape in the east and end on the other side of the town at the Lungomare di Tusa. The beaches here vary from rocky, pebbly ones to golden sandy ones. Generally, Sicilian beaches are rustic with minimal facilities. Sicilians like to find a secluded spot to swim and sunbathe and might bring something for a picnic along with a simple beach umbrella. The same can be said for Tusa beaches: very basic but with crystal clear waters. **Amenities:** None. **Best for:** swimming; walking. ✉ *Via Cesare Battisti 1* 🎫 *Free.*

Restaurants

Al Punto
$$ | SEAFOOD | This little gem of a seafood restaurant right on the coast serves wonderfully fresh seafood. It is a very informal dining experience, with friendly staff and excellent prices. **Known for:** some of the town's best seafood; very reasonable prices; location close to the beach. [$] *Average main: €20* ✉ *Viale Europa Unita 50* ☎ *328/3641265* 🌐 *www.puntopunto.net* 🕒 *Closed Tues.–Thurs.*

Ristorante Le Lampare
$$ | SEAFOOD | Located near the seaside in Castel di Tusa, Le Lampare has a standard Sicilian-style menu. It specializes in seafood, with plenty of other excellent antipasti and pasta. **Known for:** fresh seafood; casual resort vibe; beachside location. [$] *Average main: €15* ✉ *Via Cesare Battisti 41/43* ☎ *0921/334294.*

Hotels

B&B Il Miglio in Piu
$ | B&B/INN | This modern and light-filled B&B is located in the heart of Tusa, just a short walk to the sea. **Pros:** large and well-lit rooms; centrally located to town; beautifully restored historical building. **Cons:** not directly on the beach; no

individual entrances to rooms so some spaces need to be shared; can get very hot in the summer. $ *Rooms from: €50* ⊠ *Via Nazionale 107, Castel di Tusa* ☏ *348/7796288* ⊕ *www.ilmiglioinpiu.com* ⇨ *6 rooms* ⦿ *Free Breakfast.*

Tus'Hotel

$$ | **HOTEL** | **FAMILY** | This beautiful seaside resort hotel and spa offers the opportunity for a family-friendly experience. **Pros:** pool and gym on-site; spa facilities; private beachfront access. **Cons:** family-friendly vibe not for everyone; rooms a bit basic; beach is rocky. $ *Rooms from: €170* ⊠ *SS 113 KM 163, Castel di Tusa* ☏ *0921/334527* ⊕ *www.tushotel.it* ⇨ *26 rooms* ⦿ *Free Breakfast.*

Santo Stefano di Camastra

11 km (7 miles) east of Castel di Tusa.

A romantic seaside town, Santo Stefano is just as well known for its ceramics as its beaches. The art of ceramics has been practiced here since Roman times and today the whole city is filled with multiple ceramic studios and factories. On the town's main street, you'll find local artisans proudly showing off their tiles, mosaics, plates, and sculptures. But be careful not to take any photos without the artist's express permission as each artist highly values their unique designs and often custom-mixed colors, and try hard not to be copied.

The town itself is also beautifully positioned, looking out over the sea and an array of hidden bays and coves.

GETTING HERE AND AROUND

Santo Stefano is easily reached via the Autostrada from both Palermo and Messina, as well as by train from both cities.

VISITOR INFORMATION

CONTACT Ufficio Turistico Comunale. ⊠ *Via Palazzo 35, Santo Stefano di Camastra* ☏ *0921/331110* ⊕ *www.comune.santostefanodicamastra.me.it.*

 Sights

Museo Civico delle Ceramiche

OTHER MUSEUM | For lovers of ceramics, this local museum is the best place to learn about the ancient art that has been practiced here since the Greeks colonized Sicily. It has a fantastic collection of ceramics from throughout this history as well as original pieces from local artisans. The museum is housed in the Palazzo Trabia, an aristocratic palace acquired by the local government and converted especially to house these extensive ceramic exhibitions. ⊠ *Via Luigi Famularo 1, Santo Stefano di Camastra* ☏ *349/2987908* ⊕ *www.museodellaceramica.com* ⊗ *Closed Mon.–Thurs.*

 Restaurants

Trattoria da Giannino

$$ | **ITALIAN** | This small, unassuming family-run restaurant is quite popular with locals. They serve traditional Sicilian cuisine with no fuss and outstanding value. **Known for:** seafood antipasto; traditional and heaty pastas; cozy and welcoming atmosphere. $ *Average main: €20* ⊠ *Via Garibaldi 14, Santo Stefano di Camastra* ☏ *0921/331748* ⊕ *www.trattoria-da-giannino1.webnode.it* ⊗ *Closed Thurs.*

 Hotels

★ B&B the Palace

$ | **B&B/INN** | In the historical center of Santo Stefano, you'll find this luxurious B&B with spacious rooms and big balconies that look out onto the town. **Pros:** elegant decor; all rooms have balconies; central location. **Cons:** can be noisy in high season; balconies are quite small; no elevators. $ *Rooms from: €80* ⊠ *Via*

Parco Regoinale dei Nebrodi offers many outdoor adventures and activities.

Borgo 62, Santo Stefano di Camastra
☎ *338/6316006* ⊕ *www.bebthepalace.it*
⤸ *3 rooms* ⦿ *Free Breakfast.*

🛍 Shopping

⭐ **Antica Fabbrica di Ceramica La Giara**

CERAMICS | One of the oldest ceramic
factories in Sicily, La Giara sells a bit of
everything from souvenirs to more substantial pieces of art. In their impressive
showroom, you will find every possible
style of Sicilian ceramics, from basic
terra-cotta to elaborate hand-painted
Baroque designs as well as large pieces
of furniture. Still run by the same family
that originally founded the factory, the
quality and artistry of the pieces are
guaranteed by many generations of
experience. They also ship worldwide.
✉ *Via Nazionale 96/102, Santo Stefano
di Camastra* ☎ *0921/331879* ⊕ *www.
ceramichelagiara.it.*

**Ceramiche d'arte Antonino
Piscitello Maioliche S. Stefano**

CERAMICS | This local ceramics factory and
producer has been around since 1683
and is still a family business. The showroom is filled with unique hand-painted
pieces that reflect the history and artistry
of the town. The owner is often at the
showroom and has been known to hand-
wrap plates, cups, and other souvenirs.
✉ *Via Nazionale 110, Santo Stefano di
Camastra* ☎ *0921/331089* ⊕ *www.ceram-
ichepiscitello.com.*

Mistretta

*17 km (23 miles) south of Santo Stefano
di Camastra.*

This beautiful town located close to
Parco Regoinale dei Nebrodi is filled
with a deep sense of history and charm
thanks to its collection of noble palaces,
churches, fountains, and archways. This
is due to the village's long and storied
history, as Mistretta has been inhabited

since paleolithic times, founded by the indigenous Sicians, the island's first inhabitants.

GETTING HERE AND AROUND

Arriving at Mistretta by car is relatively easy and quite beautiful; simply follow the Autostrada and turn off at the Santo Stefano di Camastra exit. Once you are off the Autostrada, all you need to do is follow the local road signs towards the mountains and Mistretta. The road will climb upward toward the Nebrodi highlands, so be prepared for spectacular views.

You can also catch a local bus from Santo Stefano di Camastra.

VISITOR INFORMATION

CONTACT Pro Loco Mistretta. ⊠ *Via Libertà 267, Mistretta* ☎ *328/7378884* ⊕ *www. comune.mistretta.me.it.*

 # Sights

Chiesa Madre di Santa Lucia

CHURCH | Like most small towns in Sicily, Mistretta's best artwork can be found in its local churches, which have a particularly ancient quality. The Chiesa Madre di Santa Lucia has a facade made from the characteristic golden limestone of Sicily with elegant Romanesque arches and columns. Inside, everything from the floor to the decorative altar is made of precious marble, which comes from the nearby town of San Marco D'Annunzio which has supplied marble for churches all over Messina province since the Middle Ages. The rose-color pink marble, in particular, was quite rare and the most expensive and luxurious decoration used in churches to show off a town's prosperity. ⊠ *Piazza Unità d'Italia 2, Mistretta* ☎ *0921/381136* 🎫 *Free.*

Mistretta Castle

RUINS | Located high above Mistretta are the ruins of this Arab-Norman castle. At over 3,000 feet above sea level, the location offers some spectacular views

out to the coast and the highest peaks of the mountains from Santa Croce down to Santo Stefano di Camastra. The remaining structure of the castle gives you an idea of its original dimensions, which were built to defend the city and look out all along the coast. The castle was also connected to an extended walled perimeter that encircled the original town. ⊠ *Castello di Mistrette, Mistretta* 🎫 *Free.*

Museo Civico E. Ortolani

HISTORY MUSEUM | This interesting museum housed in a beautifully restored palace of the Mastrogiovanni Tasca family has an array of local artifacts that testify to the long and complex history of Mistretta and Sicily. There is a collection of various archaeological finds from the area on the ground floor, including items from the Roman-Byzantine periods up until the Middle Ages. The local historical library's collection of rare and ancient books is located on the mezzanine level, and includes volumes recovered from the town's Franciscan convents. The building also hosts the local historical archives. In the halls of the main floor, there is a series of local religious paintings recovered from the Capuchin convent, including one attributed to the Flemish master Matthias Stom. ⊠ *Corso Umberto I 69, Mistretta* ☎ *No phone* 🎫 *Free* ⊙ *Closed weekends.*

Parco dei Nebrodi

NATIONAL PARK | One of Sicily's most stunning national parks, Parco dei Nebrodi is filled with unbelievable mountain landscapes, charming lakes, and vivid evergreen forests. The area is easy to navigate thanks to well-kept roads, multiple picnic areas, and the 24 picturesque towns that are found within the park itself. Outdoor experiences throughout the park abound, and you can drive up to Floresta, the park's highest point (and the highest town in Sicily), to see some impressive views of Mount Etna. ⊠ *Parco dei Nebrodi* ☎ *0921/333015* ⊕ *www. parcodeinebrodi.it.*

🍴 Restaurants

Di Marco Pietro

$ | **ITALIAN** | This is a good spot for a substantial lunch or dinner in Mistretta. They specialize in regional Italian cuisine with a good selection of antipasti, pasta, and mains. **Known for:** excellent pizza; reasonable prices; huge servings. [$] *Average main: €13* ✉ *Via Nazionale 13, Mistretta* ☎ *0921/38299* ⏲ *Closed Mon.*

🛏 Hotels

Heart of Sicily

$ | **APARTMENT** | This rental apartment near the center of Mistretta allows you to have a comfortable stay directly in the town. **Pros:** free breakfast; close to local cafés and sights; good views. **Cons:** small bathrooms; many stairs; a little hard to find. [$] *Rooms from: €50* ✉ *Strada Santa Caterina 63, Mistretta* ☎ *339/2106377* 🌐 *www.heartofsicily.it* 🛏 *1 apartment* 🍽 *Free Breakfast.*

Capo d'Orlando

52 km (32 miles) east of Santo Stefano di Camastra.

With a strip of sandy beaches all along the coast, this beachside resort town is a trendy holiday destination for locals in the summer. Its gorgeous beaches and buzzy partylike atmosphere even inspired a popular 1960s pop song.

GETTING HERE AND AROUND

It's an easy one-hour drive to get here from Messina and a slightly longer, but just as easy, trip from Palermo via car. There are also regular trains from both Messina and Palermo.

VISITOR INFORMATION

CONTACT Comune di Capo d'Orlando. ✉ *Via V. Emanuele, Capo d'Orlando* ☎ *0941/915280* 🌐 *www.comune.capodorlando.me.it.*

👁 Sights

Lungomare Capo d'Orlando

PROMENADE | Capo d'Orlando has a long strip of beachfront to explore, stretching out in both directions along the coast. The Lungomare is the town's main strip, with plenty to entertain tourists in the high season, including restaurants, bars, nightclubs, and kiosks where you can buy anything needed for a day on the beach. ✉ *Via Lungomare Andrea Doria, Capo d'Orlando.*

Santuario della Madonna Maria Santissima

CHURCH | This church is located high above town, reachable by walking up the zigzagging road along the Strada Provinciale 147. Once you get up the steep hill (and it will be a bit of a workout), you can admire the breathtaking views along the coast; you can even see the peak of the Madonie above Palermo in the distance. The church itself houses the statue of the town's patron saint, the Madonna Maria Santissima, taken in a procession around the streets as part of feast day celebrations in October. ✉ *SP147 25, Capo d'Orlando* 🎟 *Free.*

🍴 Restaurants

★ **Ristorante Pepe Rosa**

$$$ | **ITALIAN** | This local institution, now located in the town's trendy port area, serves gourmet Italian classics. It's a little more pricey than other places in town, but it's worth it for the fresh seafood, exceptional wine list, and beautiful location. **Known for:** charming portside setting; fresh seafood; advanced reservations recommended. [$] *Average main: €30* ✉ *Porto di Marina, Contrada Bagnoli 16, Capo d'Orlando* ☎ *0941/4260076* 🌐 *www.facebook.com/peperosacapodorlando.*

★ **Rock Brewery Marina**

$$ | **ITALIAN** | This seaside pub focuses on craft and artisan beers alongside light meals like antipasto tasting plates,

open-faced sandwiches, and gourmet panini. It's a very trendy place for a night out or a late-night drink. **Known for:** portside location; popular with locals; gourmet burgers. $ *Average main: €20* ⊠ *Porto di Marina, Contrada Bagnoli 14, Capo d'Orlando* ☎ *339/1432804* ⊕ *www. rockbrewery.it.*

Wanted Pub

$$ | **AMERICAN** | This trendy pub and steak house is a fun place to dine seaside. It serves an impressive lineup of tap beers, gourmet burgers, and hot dogs along with more traditional Sicilian options. **Known for:** charming location; excellent steaks; popularity with locals. $ *Average main: €20* ⊠ *Via XXVII Settembre 6B, Capo d'Orlando* ☎ *389/6861705* ⊕ *www. wantedpubcapodorlando.com* ⊗ *Closed Tues.*

 Coffee and Quick Bites

Bar delle Poste

$ | **ITALIAN** | **FAMILY** | Stop here to sample every Sicilian sweet imaginable from freshly made cannoli and biscotti to marzipan confections and gelato. The pastry spot also serves up great coffee. **Known for:** one-stop shop for Sicilian pastries; good coffee; excellent gelato. $ *Average main: €5* ⊠ *Via Roma 35, Capo d'Orlando* ☎ *0941/901603* ⊕ *www.bardelleposte.it* ⊗ *Closed Wed.*

Pasticceria Bar Giulio

$ | **ITALIAN** | **FAMILY** | For the best granita and gelato in town, don't miss Bar Giulio. It's also an excellent place for coffee or a traditional sweet Sicilian breakfast of granita and sweet bread brioche. **Known for:** fresh pastries made daily; very reasonable prices; best granita in town. $ *Average main: €5* ⊠ *Via Giovanni Amendola 25, Capo d'Orlando* ☎ *0941/912546* ⊕ *www.pasticceriagiulio. com.*

Hotels

Hotel Ristorante il Mulino

$ | **HOTEL** | As the most established hotel in Capo d'Orlando, located across the road from the town's main sandy beach at Capo, this is a great little place to stay in the heart of the town. **Pros:** comfortable rooms; seaside views; close to town and the sea. **Cons:** can be a bit crowded in the summer; a little more costly compared to other places in the area; some rooms do not have a balcony. $ *Rooms from: €110* ⊠ *Via Andrea Doria, Capo d'Orlando* ☎ *0941/902431* ⊕ *www.hotelilmulino.it* ⇌ *25 rooms* ⊚ *Free Breakfast.*

La Tartaruga

$ | **HOTEL** | As part of this seaside resort town since the 1960s, La Tartaruga still embodies the best of local hospitality. **Pros:** away from the crowds of the city center; great seafood restaurant; close to the beach. **Cons:** a little bit touristy; often hosts weddings; can get crowded. $ *Rooms from: €110* ⊠ *Contrada San Gregorio 41, Capo d'Orlando* ☎ *0941/955421* ⊕ *www.hoteltartaruga.it* ⇌ *30 rooms* ⊚ *Free Breakfast.*

Patti

34 km (21 miles) east of Capo d'Orlando.

This town has been a thriving port of call for religious pilgrims since the Middle Ages while its beautiful bays, sandy beaches, and natural lakes have drawn tourists since Roman times. German writer Goethe was once a guest of the religious brothers of Patti on his famous tour through Italy in the 18th century.

GETTING HERE AND AROUND

Patti is a two-hour drive from Palermo and 42 minutes from Messina. Getting here by car is relatively easy: simply take the Messina-Palermo autostrada in the direction of Patti and take the exit for the city.

Sights

★ Daemone Cantine e Vigne

WINERY | Located in the rolling hills just below Tindari, this local winery offers the chance to sample the best locally produced wines. You can also go on a tour of the historic wine press and enjoy a light meal. Wine tastings require a minimum of four people per booking. ✉ *Contrada Ronzino, Patti* ☎ *371/4947668* 🌐 *www.daemonevini.it* 🎟 *Tour and tasting €30* 🕒 *Closed Sun.*

La Villa Romana

RUINS | This late Roman villa was accidentally unearthed during construction work for the nearby Autostrada in the early 1980s, and the archaeological area has since recovered a complete Roman aristocratic home. The villa is filled with fascinating details, including mosaic tiled floors, walls, and doors. ✉ *Via Papa Giovanni XXIII 3, Patti* ☎ *0941/361593* 🌐 *www.aditusculture.com* 🎟 *€4* 🕒 *Closed Mon.*

★ Santuario di Tindari

CHURCH | A very old place of worship, the Santuario di Tindari has been an important place for religious pilgrims since the Middle Ages, after a mysterious statue of the dark-skinned Madonna was retrieved from a nearby beached ship and claimed to be a miraculous image by locals. Today Tindari is still popular with religious visitors and the clergy in general; Pope John Paul II even visited to perform mass in the 1980s. The stunning modern cathedral has been built around the original tiny medieval church, and you can access the old church from a side gate near the front altar. The newer church is filled with mosaic art, stained glass windows, an impressive church organ, and an elaborate building that still houses the famed Madonna statue.

Located high up in the mountains, Tindari has lovely views along the coast in both directions. Along a side road from the church, past a collection of tourist shops, you will find the archaeological area that includes an ancient Roman theater and several ruins of bathhouses and villas that once accommodated Roman visitors.

Below the Church of Tindari, there are also the natural lakes of Marinello and the pristine Spiaggia Mongiove, which are popular places for local beachgoers to explore. Even though the beaches are devoid of facilities, the spot is secluded and quite stunning. ✉ *Via Monsignor Pullano 12, Tindari* ☎ *0941/369003* 🌐 *www.santuariotindari.it* 🎟 *Free.*

Restaurants

Agriturismo Antica Tindari

$$$ | **ITALIAN** | **FAMILY** | This restaurant is located within a local vineyard between Patti and Tindari near the stunning Gulf of Patti, the lakes of Marinello, and Santuario di Tindari. With its extensive terrace views over the vines and olive groves, this place is a beautiful place to stop and savor good food, great wine, and local hospitality. **Known for:** beautiful countryside location; traditional Sicilian cuisine with homegrown ingredients; excellent wines. [$] *Average main: €30* ✉ *Contrada Moreri, Patti* ☎ *0941/317202* 🌐 *www.anticatindari.it.*

Hotels

Best Western Plus Hotel Terre di Eolo

$$ | **HOTEL** | **FAMILY** | This hotel located just outside of Patti is a beautiful place to stay, with comfortable beds and free Wi-Fi. **Pros:** swimming pool and spa; beautiful views; welcoming family hotel. **Cons:** not in town; can get crowded in high season; not close to the beach. [$] *Rooms from: €145* ✉ *Via Nazionale SS113, Patti* ☎ *0941/317707* 🌐 *terrediEolo.it* 🕒 *Closed Jan.–Mar.* 🛏 *67 rooms* 🍴 *Free Breakfast.*

Milazzo

41 km (25 miles) east of Patti, 39 km (24 miles) west of Messina.

Milazzo is a bustling ferry port city filled with a mixture of history and natural beauty, not to mention a vibrant array of fresh seafood markets and restaurants to enjoy. It's also the main port of entry to the Aeolian Islands.

GETTING HERE AND AROUND
Milazzo is easily reached by car via the Messina-Palermo Autostrada. There are also regular trains from both Messina and Palermo.

VISITOR INFORMATION
CONTACT Servizio Turistico Regionale di Milazzo. ⊠ *20 Piazza Caio Duilio, Milazzo* ☎ *090/9222865.*

Sights

Capo di Milazzo
SCENIC DRIVE | This rustic piece of coastline juts out from the naturally formed port of Milazzo, showing off classic Mediterranean scrub, a kind of coastal vegetation common to Sicily. The road leading to the cape is perfect for a scenic drive, and there are rustic beaches you can stop to enjoy along the way. Follow the signs from the city center to reach the cape or follow the main local road toward Palermo. ⊠ *SP72 98057, Milazzo.*

Castello di Milazzo
CASTLE/PALACE | **FAMILY** | It is common to see castles along Sicily's coastline as the Normans used them to defend the island from invaders throughout the Middle Ages. Castello di Milazzo lies high above the town and is a beautiful example of an authentic medieval castle. It's well worth the hike up for the views out to the sea.

The castle also hosts the MuMa Museum of the sea. The museum was founded by Sicilian marine biologist Carmelo Isgro who recovered the remains of a sperm whale who died after it was caught in an illegal fishing net off the nearby Aeolian Islands. Isgro reconstructed the whale's skeleton. It became the central figure of the museum with other exhibits that highlight the relationship between man and the sea and how it can be improved. ⊠ *Salita Castello, Milazzo* ☎ *090/9221291* ⊕ *www.comune.milazzo. me.it* ⊠ *€5* ⊗ *Closed Mon.*

Museum of the Sea
OTHER MUSEUM | **FAMILY** | The Castello di Milazzo is home to this museum founded by Sicilian marine biologist Carmelo Isgro who recovered the remains of a sperm whale that died after it was caught in an illegal fishing net off the Aeolian Islands. Isgro reconstructed the whale's skeleton, and it became the central figure of the museum along with other exhibits that highlight the relationship between man and the sea and how it can be improved. While the museum is free, you still have to book your ticket online at least 24 hours in advance. ⊠ *Castello di Milazzo, Bastione di Santa Maria, Complesso Monumentale, Milazzo* ☎ *380/7641409* ⊕ *www.mumamilazzo.com* ⊠ *Free* ⊗ *Closed Mon.*

Pescina di Venere
POOL | This secluded natural sea pool is located at the end of Milazzo's long wild cape. A meandering rustic path will take you on a 20-minute walk down to the unique natural rock formations that create pools of variable depths. You're able to swim in them, but there are no changing rooms, toilets, or places to buy food or drinks so be sure to bring everything you need. ⊠ *SP72, Milazzo* ⊠ *Free.*

 Restaurants

Trattoria la Casalinga
$$ | **ITALIAN** | This small family-run restaurant offers fine home cooking at reasonable prices and abundant portions. Located on a tiny side street near the seaside promenade, it provides a nice break from

the beach crowds. **Known for:** fresh local seafood; rustic garden setting; cozy and intimate atmosphere. [$] *Average main: €22* ✉ *Via Riccardo D'Amico 13, Milazzo* ☎ *090/9222697* 🕒 *Closed Mon.*

🛏 Hotels

Hotel Il Principe

$$ | HOTEL | FAMILY | Housed in an elegant 19th-century palace right in the heart of the port area, this is a beautiful place to stay if you want to explore the city or the nearby Aeolian Islands. **Pros:** spa and gym; will organize trips and tours to the islands; good location for day trips to the Aeolian Islands. **Cons:** decor is a little dated; a bit overpriced; some of the rooms are dark. [$] *Rooms from: €125* ✉ *243 Lungomare Giuseppe Garibaldi, Milazzo* ☎ *090/9224341* 🌐 *www.hotelilprincipemilazzo.com* 🛏 *6 rooms* 🍴 *Free Breakfast.*

👜 Shopping

Parco Commerciale Corolla

MALL | FAMILY | As the largest shopping mall in Messina province, Parco Corolla offers a nice selection of Italian fashion stores, including children's clothing, accessories, perfume, and jewelry. In addition, a shopping district surrounds the mall with many other diverse stores, including a food hall and a cinema. ✉ *Parco Commerciale Corolla Via Firenza, Milazzo* ☎ *090/931824* 🌐 *www.parcocorolla.it.*

THE AEOLIAN ISLANDS

Updated by
Jennifer V. Cole

 Sights
★★★★☆

 Restaurants
★★★★☆

 Hotels
★★★★☆

 Shopping
★★★☆☆

 Nightlife
★★☆☆☆

WELCOME TO THE AEOLIAN ISLANDS

TOP REASONS TO GO

★ **Food:** Sicilians live (and love) via their stomachs, and the bright flavors of the archipelago—from both land and sea—turn even the simplest meals into lunches and dinners to remember.

★ **Shopping in Panarea.** Custom sandals, hand-dyed and woven cloth, vibrant sundresses: artisans on Panarea keep visitors summer chic.

★ **Sunset-watching on Salina.** The view of the sun sinking into the sea from the Pollara Caldera is rivaled only by that same sunset experienced from a boat with an aperitivo.

★ **The Stromboli fire show.** Watching this active volcano's lava flames lick the night sky is one of the most memorable experiences of a lifetime.

★ **Filicudi Wildlife Conservation.** The natural flora and fauna of this untamed island make it a singular destination, and there's no better way to experience it than hands-on tours with marine biologists and naturalists.

1 Lipari. The largest island in the archipelago, with great trekking and a vibrant central town.

2 Vulcano. The most easily accessible island of the group, with a wide variety of beaches.

3 Salina. Lush and verdant, with luxury hotels, hillside vineyards, and strong boat culture.

4 Panarea. A chic island known for its good vibes, shopping, and nightlife.

5 Stromboli. An active and explosive volcanic island, known for fiery nighttime views.

6 Filicudi. A wild and untamed island with steep stone terraces crisscrossed by mule paths.

7 Alicudi. An off-the-beaten-path escape for peace and quiet, known for its demanding uphill climbs.

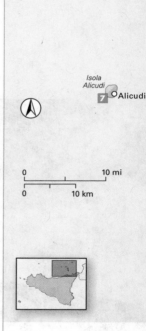

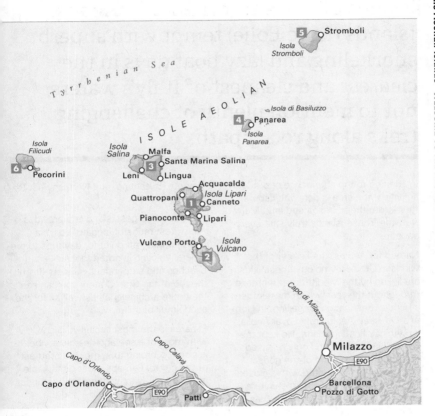

Off Sicily's northeastern coast lies an archipelago of seven spectacular islands of volcanic origin. The Aeolian Islands (Isole Eolie) tempt with superb snorkeling and lazy boat days in the clearest and cleanest of Italy's waters, not to mention plenty of challenging treks along rocky paths.

In addition to the abundance of outdoor activities, the area is rich with capers, fresh-from-the-boat seafood, and Malvasia wine. These islands truly sate every appetite.

Named for Aeolus, the keeper of the winds in Greek mythology, these isles are licked by the Mediterranean breeze throughout the year, which makes them a popular destination for sailing. In Homer's *Odyssey,* Aeolus ruled over Aeolia, a mythical, floating island. He kept the winds locked away and only released them at the command of the gods. Odysseus was entrusted with a closed bag of unfavorable winds to ensure a safe and speedy journey home. Alas, his crew opened the bag, and their ship was blown back to the shores of Aolia.

The islands emerged from the sea through a series of volcanic events nearly 700,000 years ago. On the oldest island, Panarea, researchers have found evidence of life dating back to the Neolithic period, as well as artifacts from the ancient Bronze Age. The youngest island, Stromboli, is probably close to 40,000 years old. And a litany of civilizations has inhabited this archipelago through the ages: Greek, Roman, Carthaginian, Visigoth, Byzantine, and Norman, just to name a few.

Lipari is the largest island and provides the widest range of lodging, so it's a good jumping-off point for day trips to the others. Vulcano is noted for black-sand beaches and stupendous sunsets (from the top of the Gran Cratere you can see the entire archipelago), as well as for the acrid smell of sulfur.

Panarea is the most exclusive island, with more of a see-and-be-scene vibe. It is also, according to some, the prettiest of the group. Perhaps most remarkable is Stromboli, with its constant eruptions, while the greenest island—and the one with the best hiking—is Salina. The farthest afield are Filicudi and Alicudi, where electricity was introduced only in the 1990s and where travelers can go for ultimate peace and quiet.

Planning

When to Go

Although the Aeolians are breathtakingly beautiful at any time of the year, they are decidedly a summer destination. Almost everything (that includes hotels, restaurants, shops, and some public transportation) closes from October through April. So finding a place to stay or anything to eat beyond basic bites such as sandwiches, cornetti, or *tavola calda* (cafeteria-style eats) from port bars is incredibly difficult. If you do decide to go in the off-season, you'll have the hiking paths and beaches all to yourself. Lipari (the most populated island) is your best bet for general services off-season, but you should also know that most rental homes, apartments, and hotels throughout the archipelago don't have heat, and it can sometimes get chilly at night.

Planning Your Time

The best way to reach the Aeolian islands is from the Sicilian city of Milazzo. From there, it's a veritable choose-your-own-adventure depending on how much time you have and what interests you most. Vulcano, the closest island to the Sicilian coast, can be visited as an easy day trip if you're short on time and just want to get a taste of island life. Long weekends to the isles are common among Sicilian locals, and a four-day visit to a single island provides ample opportunity for both exploration and relaxation.

If you have more time and want to delve deeper, it's convenient to choose one centrally located island, such as Salina or Lipari, as your base and take hydrofoils throughout the archipelago to visit other islands. This is especially good for visiting the more remote islands such as Filicudi and Alicudi. In fact, the Liberty Lines ferry schedule is quite conducive to this type of exploration. And if you're new to the Aeolians, it's a great way to get a sense of which island you might like to return to one day for a longer stay (repeat visitors to the Aeolians are very very common). Island hopping for a few nights each on a mix of islands is also possible, but you'll likely find that settling into a single

nightly location will help you achieve a more peaceful vacation state of mind.

Getting Here and Around

BUS

To get around Lipari, you can rely on the URSO local bus network. On Salina, use the C.I.T.I.S. buses while on Vulcano there's Scaffidi bus service.

CONTACTS C.I.T.I.S.. ☎ *090/9844150* ⊕ *www.trasportisalina.it.* **Scaffidi.** ☎ *338/6961723.* **URSO.** ☎ *090/9811026* ⊕ *www.ursobus.it.*

CAR

If you have a car and want to transport it to the islands, you can take the Siremar or NGI ferry service. Alternatively, you can leave it near the port in Milazzo. There are parking services throughout town, most of which offer shuttle service from the parking lot to the town.

On Lipari, Salina, Vulcano, and Filicudi, you can rent cars or scooters during your stay. Cars are banned on Panarea, Stromboli, and Alicudi. On Panarea and Stromboli, you can rent electric golf carts near the port. On Alicudi, you are reliant on your own two feet.

FERRIES AND HYDROFOILS

The islands are connected by an extensive network of ferries and hydrofoils. The main departure point to reach the Aeolians is Milazzo on Sicily's northeastern coast. But depending on the time of the year, there are also ferries and hydrofoils from Messina, Palermo, and Naples.

You'll find hydrofoil and ferry service from the Milazzo port, with transport times ranging from 45 minutes to 3 hours (depending on which island is your destination). Rely on Liberty Lines for hydrofoils, and Siremar or NGI for ferry service. If you have rented a car and don't want to take it to the islands, there are parking services throughout Milazzo, such as Garage Delle Isole (⊕ *www.*

garagedelleisole.it) that also offers transfer services from the Catania airport.

During the summer, Liberty Lines offers hydrofoil service from Messina and Palermo, with travel times ranging from 2½ to 5 hours. Services usually run from late June through mid-September. Liberty Lines also serves Lipari, Panarea, Salina, Stomboli, and Vulcano year-round from Reggio Calabria. Crossings take two to five hours.

Several times a week Siremar offers overnight ferry service to the islands and Milazzo from Naples. The crossing takes about 10 hours. During the summer (late May to early September), SNAV runs hydrofoils from Naples that take approximately 4½ to 6½ hours, depending on which island you're visiting.

For transportation within the islands, you'll want to rely on Liberty Lines, a high-speed hydrofoil service that offers reliable passage between all of the islands. On their website and via their app, you'll find easy tools to map out your voyage with interactive timetables and up-to-date pricing. The schedules are accurate, and delays are rare. Travel times vary, from short trips such as between Vulcano and Lipari (10 minutes) to about 1½ hours to get from Lipari to remote Alicudi. When seas are rough, hydrofoil service can be canceled. So if you're planning on doing day trips (and don't want to risk getting stranded on your return), it's advisable to download the Windfinder app on your phone and look at the wave forecasts for your travel days. If predicted wave heights are less than 2 meters, the schedule shouldn't be affected. When you buy your tickets, if you give Liberty Lines your phone number upon booking, they will send text updates to your phone about any schedule changes.

CONTACTS Liberty Lines. ☎ *0923/022022* ⊕ *www.libertylines.it.* **Siremar and NGI.** ☎ *090/5737* ⊕ *www.carontetourist.it.* **SNAV.** ⊕ *www.snav.it.*

Hotels

Just as the archipelago has an island to suit every personality, you'll find a full range of lodging options. The best luxury hotels are located on Salina. Throughout the islands, there are homes and apartments for rent through sites like VRBO and Airbnb as well as a whole swath of midlevel hotels and B&Bs where rooms are clean and usually conveniently located, but decor is pretty basic. Most hotels aren't open during the winter months. If you do find one open during that period, be sure to ask if they have heat, as the island winters can be quite chilly and damp.

Restaurants

The quintessential flavors of Sicily come through boldly and brightly in the sun-kissed Aeolian islands. You'll find lots of capers, olives, tomatoes, eggplant, anchovies, tuna, and swordfish in practically every restaurant you visit. And as befits a region dominated by fishing, most dining spots (from small cafés to pizzerias to Michelin-starred restaurants) highlight fresh seafood. Dining experiences truly run the gamut here, and you'll find great cheap bites in port bars or you can block out three hours for an immersive tasting menu. Salina, the most fertile of the seven islands, is known for their Malvasia grape production, which shows up on tables either as a dry white wine or a sweet dessert wine. Alicudi has basically no restaurants, save the odd café here and there. Instead, you'll mostly dine in private homes (reservations required). Throughout the region look for hearty *pane cunzato,* which simply means "dressed bread." Typically, a whole loaf of freshly baked bread is taken and sliced in half lengthwise, then drizzled liberally with olive oil, and everything from capers, *cucunci* (caper

Lipari's Museo Archeologico Regionale Eoliano highlights the prehistoric history of the archipelago.

berries), and tuna to tomatoes and mozzarella are added to top it.

RESTAURANT AND HOTEL PRICES
Restaurant prices in the reviews are the average cost of a main course at dinner, or if dinner is not served, at lunch. Hotel prices in the reviews are the lowest cost of a standard double room in high season. Restaurant and hotel reviews have been shortened. For full information, visit Fodors.com.

What it Costs in Euros			
$	**$$**	**$$$**	**$$$$**
RESTAURANTS			
under €15	€15–€22	€23–€30	over €30
HOTELS			
under €125	€125–€225	€226–€350	over €350

Visitor Information

CONTACTS Visit Sicily, Isole Eolie. ⊠ *Via Maurolico 47, Lipari* ☎ *090/9880095* ⊕ *www.visitsicily.info.*

Lipari

2 hours, 10 minutes from Milazzo by ferry, 1 hour by hydrofoil; 60–75 minutes from Reggio di Calabria and Messina by ferry.

The largest and most developed of the Aeolians, Lipari welcomes you with distinctive pastel-color houses. Fields of spiky agaves dot the northernmost tip of the island, Acquacalda, indented with pumice and obsidian quarries. In the west is San Calogero, where you can explore hot springs and mud baths. From the red-lava base of the island rises a plateau crowned with a 16th-century castle and a 17th-century cathedral.

GETTING HERE AND AROUND

Ferries and hydrofoils from Milazzo, which is 41 km (25 miles) west of Messina, stop here. There's also ferry service from Reggio di Calabria and Messina. On the island, if you plan to explore extensively, you should rent a car or a scooter. Lipari is the largest of the Aeolians and navigating it can be difficult without your own mode of transport.

Sights

★ Museo Archeologico Regionale Eoliano
HISTORY MUSEUM | This vast, multibuilding museum is terrific, with an intelligently arranged collection of prehistoric finds—some dating as far back as 4000 BC—from various sites in the archipelago, as well as Greek and Roman artifacts, including an outstanding collection of Greek theatrical masks, and even interesting information on volcanoes. Basic descriptions about the exhibits are provided in English and Italian, though more comprehensive information is in Italian only. That said, there is so much to see, the museum is worth at least a few hours of your time. ✉ *Via Castello 2, Lipari* ☎ *090/9880174* 🎫 *€6.*

Corso Vittorio Emanuele II
STREET | This lively street that runs the length of Lipari Town from the port blends the tourist and local worlds. You'll find the requisite souvenir shops selling trinkets and postcards, but it's also where residents go to visit their butcher, to pick up daily bread, and to buy fishing tackle. During summer evenings, it's closed to cars and becomes the primary stretch for making the evening *passeggiata* (evening stroll) past cafés that reverberate with energy late into the evenings. ✉ *Corso Vittorio Emanuele, Lipari.*

Restaurants

★ Osteria San Bartolo
$$ | **ITALIAN** | Chef Danilo Conti started with a passion for wine and subsequently grew deeper respect for the soil of his home territory. The dishes at his osteria just steps from the port in Lipari are clean and balanced—the opposite of fussy—but primarily celebrate the fishing and agricultural traditions of the island; think lime-scented carpaccio of swordfish and pasta with anchovies, wild fennel, and orange zest. **Known for:** stuffed calamari; showcasing the best of both sea and land; natural wine (chef owns a wine shop a few doors down). [$] *Average main: €16* ✉ *Via Francesco Crispi 109, Lipari* ☎ *090/8961317* 🌐 *www.sanbartolovineriaedispensa.com* 🕒 *Closed Wed.*

Ristorante da Filippino
$$ | **SICILIAN** | Founded in 1910, Filippino is rightly rated as one of the archipelago's best dining venues—and you'll understand why, when you sample the catch of the day on the gorgeous terrace. *Zuppa di pesce* (fish soup) and the antipasto platter of smoked and marinated fish are absolute musts, but be sure to leave some room for the local version of cassata siciliana, accompanied by sweet Malvasia wine from Salina. **Known for:** scrumptious local desserts; traditional Sicilian recipes; pasta, soup, and risotto with fresh seafood. [$] *Average main: €18* ✉ *Piazza Mazzini Lipari, Lipari* ☎ *090/9811002* 🌐 *www.filippino.it* 🕒 *Closed Mon. in Nov.–Jan.*

Hotels

Hotel Villa Enrica
$$ | **HOTEL** | This hotel's hillside position gives it one of the best views on the island, looking south over Marina Lunga and the castle, and it seems like nearly every part of the hotel (from rooms to

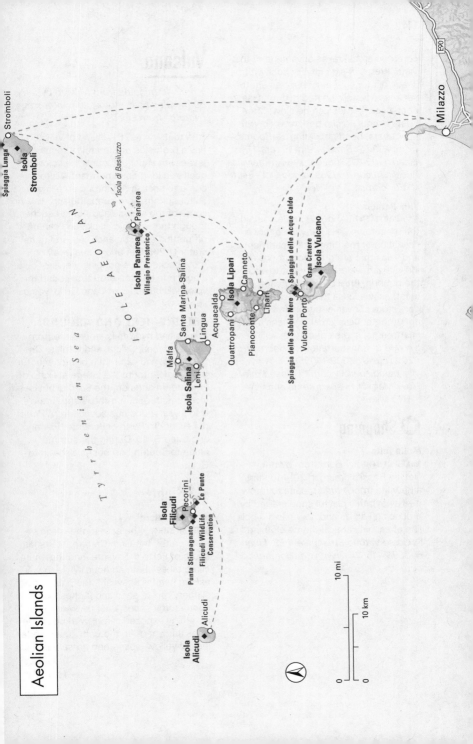

Aeolian Islands

common areas) takes advantage of that vista. **Pros:** cliff-side infinity pool with snack bar for light lunches; free shuttle service to beach; heated hydromassage pool. **Cons:** service can be slow; often hosts events so can get crowded with nonguests; needs updating. $ *Rooms from: €132* ⊠ *Strada Serra Pirrera 11, Lipari* ☎ *090/9880826* ⊕ *www.hotelvillaenricalipari.com* ⊗ *Closed mid-Oct.–Easter* ⇆ *20 rooms* ⦿ *No Meals.*

Villa Paradiso

$ | **APARTMENT** | About 2½ miles outside the main town, Villa Paradiso offers a collection of mountainside apartments and villas that are great for groups or individual travelers who want to escape the hubbub. **Pros:** complete peace and quiet; easy access to hiking trails; grocery store conveniently located near the apartments. **Cons:** small kitchens in the apartments; sparse decor; you will need a mode of transportation. $ *Rooms from: €70* ⊠ *Lipari* ☎ *339/1405583* ⊕ *www. villa-paradiso-sicily.com* ⊗ *Closed mid-Nov.–Mar.* ⇆ *14 apartments and villas* ⦿ *No Meals.*

Shopping

Mollo Tutto

MIXED CLOTHING | Born from owner Natalie Rossi's dream in 2014 to start a new life (*mollo tutto* means to throw it all away), this playful shop started by producing T-shirts and now has a whole line of casual nautical-theme clothing. ⊠ *Corso Vittorio Emanuele II 83, Lipari* ☎ *389/2416814* ⊕ *www.mollotuttoshop. com.*

Vulcano

1 hour 40 minutes from Milazzo by ferry, 50 minutes by hydrofoil; 10 minutes by hydrofoil from Lipari.

True to its name, the island of Vulcano has a profusion of fumaroles sending up jets of hot vapor, although the volcano itself has long been dormant. Visitors come to soak in the strong-smelling sulfur springs or to sunbathe and walk on some of the archipelago's best beaches, though the volcanic black sand can be off-putting at first glance. Ascend to its crater (1,266 feet above sea level) on mule-back for eye-popping views or take a boat ride into the grottoes around the volcano's base. From Capo Grillo, you can see all the Aeolians.

GETTING HERE AND AROUND

Ferries and hydrofoils arrive here from Milazzo, Lipari, Salina, and Naples. On the island, you can rent a bike or scooter from the center of the village at Porto di Levante. In addition, the Scaffidi bus service runs throughout the island. There's also a year-round bus service from Porto di Levante to Porto di Ponente, Piano, and Capo Grillo. During the summer (June to September) buses also run to Gelso.

Sights

★ Gran Cratere

NATURE SIGHT | The path to the island's main crater, the Gran Cratere, starts just south of Porto di Levante, and the entire climb takes about an hour. While the ascent itself is easy(ish), the path is a slippery mix of sand and stones, so wear good sturdy shoes. Just be aware that it's a fully exposed climb, with no shade trees anywhere on the path, just smatterings of yellow-blossomed gorse bushes, so plan to go early or late in the day to avoid the full beatdown of the sun. But the climb is truly worth it: the rim of this crater is the only place in the Aeolians where you can see the whole archipelago in one glance. ⊠ *Gran Cratere, Vulcano.*

Spiaggia delle Acque Calde

HOT SPRING | From the port of Levante, walk five minutes in the direction of Porto di Ponente, past the stone tinged yellow with sulfur that radiates constant heat. Or really just follow your nose as the natural hot springs of Vulcano have a very distinctive odor. Once you arrive at this little stretch of beach, you'll notice the water gurgling in pockets at the edges, creating natural rock-enclosed hot tubs. As of 2022, the official *fanghi* (mud bath) experience remains under construction as they work to make the pools more accessible. But you can still get in the waters along the beach to feel the hot vents pushing through the water as natural hot springs. ⊠ *Spiaggia delle Acque Calde, Vulcano.*

Spiaggia delle Sabbie Nere

BEACH | A short 15-minute walk from the port, this wide beach features soft powdery black volcanic sand that sits in sharp contrast to the clear crystalline waters. Along the strand, you'll find various beach clubs set up during the summer months with chair and umbrella rentals. During the winter you'll have the whole crescent practically to yourself. It's advised to wear a dark-colored swimsuit as the black sand has been known to discolor fabric. ⊠ *Spiaggia delle Sabbie Nere, Vulcano.*

 Restaurants

Asino Beach

$$ | PIZZA | On the southern tip of the island, the Asino Beach *lido* (beach club) is surrounded by palm trees and vegetation along a particularly beautiful stretch of volcanic sand. They offer everything from great pizzas (plus salads and *panini*) and refreshing cocktails to beach chair and umbrella service. **Known for:** wood-oven pizza; schiacciata, a sort of filled Sicilian pizza; beach-side location. $ *Average main: €15* ⊠ *Spiaggia dell'Asino, Gelso, Vulcano* ☎ *324/9845382* ⊕ *www.asinobeach.it* ⊗ *Closed Oct.–Apr. No dinner.*

Trattoria da Pina di Maniaci

$$ | SEAFOOD | Owner Franco Maniaci might be one of the most welcoming people in all of the islands, with his gentle laugh and accommodating attitude. His little restaurant (named for his parents) in the southern town of Gelso relies on the seasons and the day's fresh catch to dictate the menu. **Known for:** airy terrace with sea views; amazing fried and grilled squid; excellent use of local vegetables. $ *Average main: €18* ⊠ *Strada Provinciale 179, Gelso, Vulcano* ☎ *368/668555* ⊗ *Closed Nov.–Mar.*

 Hotels

Les Sables Noirs

$$$ | HOTEL | Named for the black sands of the beach it sits in front of, this luxury hotel is superbly sited on the beautiful Porto di Ponente and its cool modern furnishings and inviting pool and spa induce a sybaritic mood. **Pros:** stunning beachfront location; quick five-minute walk to town; delicious breakfasts. **Cons:** the spa is not included in the price; five-night minimum stay in August; no on-site restaurant. $ *Rooms from: €240* ⊠ *Porto di Ponente, Vulcano* ☎ *090/9850* ⊕ *www. lessablesnoirs.it* ⊗ *Closed mid-Oct.–Apr.* ⤴ *53 rooms* ⦿ *Free Breakfast.*

Therasia Resort Sea & Spa

$$$ | RESORT | The only five-star hotel on the island, this dramatically situated resort excels at the concept of Italian *benessere* (well-being). **Pros:** spectacular sunset views over Lipari; excellent spa; on-site vegetarian restaurant, one of very few in the region. **Cons:** Michelin-starred restaurant only open at dinner

Did You Know?

The island of Vulcano is indeed a true volcanic island, with one of Italy's four aboveground volcanos towering over the landscape. The volcano has not seen an eruption since 1890, although increased volcano activity in November 2021 did require an evacuation of the island.

As the most fertile of the Aeolian Islands, Salina has some stunningly lush views.

(no option for day-trippers); live music at sunset detracts from natural beauty; needs updating. $ *Rooms from: €300* ✉ *Therasia Resort, Vulcanello, Vulcano* ☎ *090/9852555* ⊕ *www.therasiaresort.it* ⊘ *Closed Oct.–Apr.* ⇆ *97 rooms* ⦿*Free Breakfast.*

Salina

50 minutes from Lipari by ferry, 20 minutes by hydrofoil.

The second largest of the Aeolians, Salina is also the most fertile, which accounts for its excellent Malvasia wine. Salina is the archipelago's lushest and highest island, too: Mt. Fossa delle Felci rises to more than 3,000 feet and offers a challenging two-hour hike to the summit, and the vineyards and fishing villages along its slopes add to the allure. Pollara, in the west of the island, has capitalized on its fame as one of the locations in the 1990s cult movie *Il Postino* (*The Postman*) and is an ideal location for sunset watching

and an evening passeggiata on well-maintained paths along the volcanic terrain.

GETTING HERE AND AROUND
Ferries and hydrofoils arrive here from Alicudi, Lipari, Panarea, and Stromboli. Note that there are two ports on Salina: Santa Marina Salina and Rinella. Not all ferries and hydrofoils arrive at both ports, so double-check your tickets and timetables. Once on the island, you can get around by taxi, or rent a car or a scooter. The island's bus service, C.I.T.I.S. (€1.90 one-way), runs reliably and on time between the island's towns.

TOURS
Sogno Eoliano
BOAT TOURS | Though the island's verdant hills beckon, Salina is best experienced by water. Native son Samuele, with a sparkling smile and easy charm, navigates the sea on his 21-foot boat, taking guests on excursions ranging from a two-hour aperitivo sunset cruise to Pollara Bay to full-day trips to neighboring islands. He grew up on the sea (and fishes during the off-season), so he

knows these waters intimately and that comes through in his tours, which are all customizable according to your specific interests. Prices start at €150 for up to five people. ⊠ *Salina* ☎ *331/9928032* ⊕ *www.sognoeoliano.it* ⊕ *From €150.*

🍴 Restaurants

⭐ Da Alfredo

$ | SICILIAN | Starting in 1968, the mini-empire of owner Alfredo Olivieri was built one granita and one *pane cunzato* at a time, and no summer on Salina is complete without a stop at his little shop off the Marina Garibaldi piazza in Lingua. You'll find all the classic granita flavors (almond, coffee, lemon, pistachio), but it's the seasonal fruits that shine here: mulberry, fig, wild blackberries, watermelon, and cantaloupe. **Known for:** charismatic owner; joyous atmosphere; seasonally focused granita. $ *Average main: €11* ⊠ *Via Marina Garibaldi, Santa Marina, Salina* ☎ *090/9843980* ⊗ *Closed Oct.–Apr.*

La Pinnata del Monsù

$$ | SICILIAN | Named for an historic structure that was used to store Malvasia grapes at night after sitting in the sun all day (the *pinnata*), this restaurant consistently delivers the exact flavors you want to eat on a Mediterranean island. Diners linger late into the evening over raw seafood, roasted fish, grilled octopus, and pastas dressed with wild fennel, caper pesto, fresh ricotta, or rich cuttlefish ink. **Known for:** convivial atmosphere; excellent caponata; use of local, seasonal ingredients. $ *Average main: €24* ⊠ *Comune di Malfa, Malfa, Salina* ☎ *327/7971853* ⊕ *www.lapinnatadelmonsu.it* ⊗ *Closed Oct.–Apr.*

☕ Coffee and Quick Bites

L'Oasi Snack-Bar

$ | CAFÉ | For quick and easy bites, from focaccia loaded with toppings to mixed salads, this food truck-style café (with a smattering of tables under oversize umbrellas) in the heart of Pollara is an island go-to. Stop by for a cold beer or a spritz to watch the nightly sunset from the westernmost point of the island. **Known for:** sunset drinks; quick bites; beautiful views. $ *Average main: €6* ⊠ *Via Chiesa, Pollara, Salina* ☎ *349/0059127* ⊕ *www.facebook.com/OasiPollara* ⊗ *Closed Oct.–Apr.*

🛏 Hotels

Capofaro Locanda & Malvasia

$$$$ | HOTEL | Born of the Tasca d'Almerita family's love of vineyards and the sea, this sprawling estate offers a minimalist chic environment for total relaxation that piques all the senses. **Pros:** extensive wine focus; quiet and secluded with lots of privacy; pool in the middle of vineyards. **Cons:** no full spa; no direct sea access; not within walking distance of main towns on island. $ *Rooms from: €480* ⊠ *Via Faro 3, Malfa, Salina* ☎ *090/9844330* ⊕ *www.capofaro.it* ⊗ *Closed Oct.–mid-May* ⇄ *27 rooms* ¶ *Free Breakfast.*

Hotel Signum

$$$ | HOTEL | Sun-filled and immaculately landscaped terraces and gardens, perfumed by citrus trees and honeysuckle, anchor this luxury property in Malfa. **Pros:** Michelin-starred restaurant; spa with treatments inspired by the island's flora; great bar for aperitivo. **Cons:** expensive; lower category rooms are small and lack views; entrance is down a narrow footpath, not directly on the road. $ *Rooms from: €250* ⊠ *Via Scalo 15, Malfa, Salina* ☎ *090/9844222* ⊕ *www.hotelsignum.it*

⊙ *Closed Nov.–Apr.* ⇝ *30 rooms* ⓘ◯ⓘ *Free Breakfast.*

Hotel Solemar

$ | HOTEL | In a valley between Salina's two mountains, this hotel has most of the hallmarks of Mediterranean charm—large terraces for contemplation, a location in a sleepy town, and pleasing local seafood served on summer evenings in the restaurant. **Pros:** relaxed atmosphere; terrific views; helpful staff. **Cons:** a 15-minute taxi ride from Salina's main port; very simple decor; no pool. Ⓢ *Rooms from: €100* ⊠ *Via Roma 8* ☎ *090/9809445* ⊕ *www.solemarhotel.it* ⊙ *Closed Nov.–Mar.* ⇝ *14 rooms* ⓘ◯ⓘ *Free Breakfast.*

★ Principe di Salina

$$$ | HOTEL | Awash in white with vibrant pops of color, this family-run boutique property that hugs the Malfa hillside defines barefoot chic. **Pros:** house-made breads and pastries; excellent wine and cocktail list; Ortigia bath products. **Cons:** restaurant closed to external guests; no kids under age 10; not directly on the sea. Ⓢ *Rooms from: €250* ⊠ *SP 182 3, Malfa, Salina* ☎ *090/9844415* ⊕ *www. principedisalina.it* ⊙ *Closed mid-Oct.–late Apr.* ⇝ *12 rooms* ⓘ◯ⓘ *Free Breakfast.*

 Shopping

Tacchi Dadi e Datteri

MIXED CLOTHING | For all your caftan needs—the effortlessly stylish uniform of summer—the team at Tacchi Dadi e Datteri has you covered. Breezy linen dresses form the heart of their offerings, but you'll also find breathable button-downs, men's seersucker swim trunks, and colorful alpargatas that are Sicily's chic answer to Tom's. They have a second location on Filicudi, just off the port. ⊠ *Via Risorgimento 72, Santa Marina Salina, Salina* ☎ *340/2516607.*

Panarea

2 hours from Lipari by ferry, 25–50 minutes by hydrofoil; 30 minutes from Salina by hydrofoil.

Panarea is the second smallest of the islands but has some of the most dramatic scenery, including wild caves carved out of rock and dazzling flora. The exceptionally clear water and the richness of life on the seafloor make Panarea especially suitable for underwater exploration. The outlying rocks and islets make a gorgeous sight, and you can enjoy the panorama on an easy excursion to the small Bronze Age village at Capo Milazzese.

GETTING HERE AND AROUND

Ferries and hydrofoils arrive here from Lipari, Salina, and Naples. For a splurge, you can book a helicopter flight with Air Panarea (⊕ *www.airpanarea.com*) from Milazzo, Catania, Taormina, or even Palermo. The Milazzo flight is 18 minutes and costs €1,300 for five people. Once on the island, you'll need to rely on walking, Vespas, or electric golf carts to get around—cars are banned.

 Sights

Chiesa di San Pietro Apostolo

CHURCH | This small church dedicated to Saint Peter, who was originally a fisherman in Galilee, was erected in 1881 by the island's inhabitants and took 42 years to complete. Meander the narrow streets uphill to arrive at the pale yellow church, and the first thing you'll notice is the breathtaking panoramic view from the stone terrace at the sea-facing entrance. Inside, a portrait of the saint hangs above the high altar and the small wooden pews offer respite for quiet reflection—and a break from the heat. On June 28–29, they celebrate the Festival of Saint Peter, marked by a processional through the town and traditional dances and songs. ⊠ *Chiesa di San Pietro*

Panarea is a great island to explore on foot, with one stone path that will bring you to the remains of an ancient Bronze Age village.

Apostolo, Panarea ⊹ Follow little wooden signs throughout town.

Villaggio Preistorico

HISTORIC SIGHT | A moderately easy hike across the beach at Zimmari and up a stepped stone path brings you to Punta Milazzese, the rugged headland along the southern coast. There you'll find the remnants of an ancient Bronze Age village that was inhabited between the 13th and 15th centuries BC. The outlines of the 22 stone huts, discovered in 1948, are clearly visible. During the excavation, examples of Mycenaean pottery were discovered and are now on display in Lipari's archeological museum. A set of steps lead down from the village to Cala Junco below, a rocky cove with clear water that's popular with snorkelers. ⊠ *Villaggio Preistorico, Panarea.*

 Beaches

Spiaggia Cala Zimmari

BEACH | Panarea is known more for its boat culture (and nightlife) than for an abundance of beaches. But the crescent of golden sand, gently lapping waves, and shallow waters at Zimmari make it a popular beach for sunbathing and taking a dip. From San Pietro, it's an easy 35-minute stroll as you meander south through the winding streets and continue on the path above the coastline. You'll know you've arrived when the path ultimately ends. ⊠ *Spiaggia Cala Zimmari, Panarea.*

Spiaggia della Calcara

BEACH | Only the most intrepid beachgoers will seek out Spiaggia della Calcara. Located on the northern tip of the island, it's reachable by winding through the streets of Iditella, continuing down a dirt path, and then up a steep descent through hearty shrubs. But your reward is a practically private beach of small stones with spectacular views of rocky outcroppings in the sea (not to mention a reprieve from the chaos of the vacationers who fill the island each summer). Just be sure to wear sturdy shoes to get down and back up the path; this is not a beach for flip-flops. ✉ *Spiaggia della Calcara, Panarea.*

🍴 Restaurants

Hycesia
$$$$ | SEAFOOD | Open since 1979, this family-owned restaurant is now helmed by son Gaetano Nani whose cooking relies on the offerings of the sea. There is no regular menu—instead, he works with area fishermen to select the freshest fish and *frutti di mare* from the waters of the Panarea coast, which then informs that night's dishes. **Known for:** incredible wine cellar; use of Eastern spices; relaxed atmosphere. [$] *Average main: €50* ✉ *Via San Pietro 20, San Pietro, Panarea* ☎ *090/983041* 🌐 *www.hycesia.it* 🕓 *Closed Oct.–mid-May.*

☕ Coffee and Quick Bites

Bar del Porto
$ | ITALIAN | Just off the pier where the hydrofoils dock, this modest little café serves simple pastas, sandwiches, and fresh-from-the-oven sweets. At breakfast, look for warm brioche, granita, and freshly squeezed fruit juices while in the evening, it's a gathering place for aperitivo. **Known for:** convenient location; friendly service; large seaside terrace. [$] *Average main: €10* ✉ *Via Comunale Mare, Panarea* ☎ *090/9830000* 🌐 *www.bardelportopanarea.it.*

Panarea Bakery In Forno
$ | BAKERY | If you're stocking up for a day by the sea, stop in this bakery to fill your picnic basket. In addition to the freshly baked bread (whose scent wafts into the town's narrow alleyways), look for overstuffed sandwiches, arancini, and tender focaccia. **Known for:** pistachio cannolis; wide selection of to-go items; pizza on Saturday. [$] *Average main: €8* ✉ *Via San Pietro 10, Panarea* ☎ *339/4083796* 🕓 *Closed Sun.*

🛏 Hotels

Hotel Raya
$$$$ | HOTEL | Although some visitors say it's resting on past laurels, Raya is perfectly in keeping with the elite style of Panarea—discreet and expensive, with a pool and terrace that enjoy views over the sea toward Stromboli. **Pros:** great views of Stromboli; lovely pool area; hippie-chic ambience. **Cons:** in need of renovations; uphill trudge to rooms; snooty staff. [$] *Rooms from: €500* ✉ *Via San Pietro, Panarea* ☎ *090/983013* 🌐 *www.hotelraya.it* 🕓 *Closed mid-Oct.–mid-Apr.* 🔑 *34 rooms* 🍽 *Free Breakfast* ☞ *No young children allowed.*

La Caletta
$$ | HOUSE | For a bit more privacy, space, and a live-like-a-local vibe, try this small collection of houses, villas, and apartments. **Pros:** no minimum night stay; great value; will arrange transport from the port. **Cons:** some of the bedding style is dated; not all buildings have kitchens; mostly small bathrooms. [$] *Rooms from: €162* ✉ *Panarea* ☎ *090/983338* 🌐 *www.panareatravel.com* 🕓 *Closed Oct.–Apr.* 🔑 *12 spaces* 🍽 *No Meals.*

🛍 Shopping

A'Biddikkia
WOMEN'S CLOTHING | Panarea native and stylist Giovanna Mandarano captures the vitality of the island with her women's clothing and accessories line that's known for bold prints, flowing fabrics, and lots and lots of color. Though there are now multiple locations throughout Sicily and in Rome, the original Panarea location, which opened in 2006, remains the heart of the collection. This is your go-to boutique for the effortlessly chic

Make a visit to Stromboli's beaches to experience true volcanic sands.

style that the island is known for. ✉ *Via Comunale Mare, Panarea* ☎ *333/8551318* ⊕ *www.abiddikkia.com.*

Moda Mare Sandali Artigianali

SHOES | Italians are passionate about footwear, and the summer island uniform requires a collection of sandals for that perfect *dolce far niente* look. This third-generation shoe shop specializes in bespoke hand-crafted sandals made from all-natural materials like leather and snakeskin. Choose your style (from some 20-plus designs), heel height, material, and color. They'll measure your foot, and within 30 minutes your custom sandals are ready to walk out the door. ✉ *Via San Pietro, Panarea* ☎ *339/6031571.*

Penelope

WOMEN'S CLOTHING | Artisan Barbara Calabresi hand-dyes yarns and silk with vegetable dyes from the island's flora (such as chamomile, artichokes, and pomegranates); she weaves the thread into fabric, and then designs and produces clothing and housewares (like tablecloths, bedspreads, and rugs) from

the cloth. You can shop her charming boutique or sign up for a course to learn to dye (two days; €130) where you'll forage the island to find seasonal botanicals to produce your own dye, or to weave (one day; €130) on a "nomadic" loom. Both classes are suitable for beginners. ✉ *Via San Pietro, Contrada Iditella 106, Panarea* ☎ *333/4436269* ⊕ *www.penelope-panarea.com.*

Stromboli

3 hours, 45 minutes from Lipari by ferry, 65–90 minutes by hydrofoil; 80 minutes from Salina by hydrofoil; 9 hours from Naples by ferry, 5 hours by hydrofoil.

This northernmost of the Aeolians consists entirely of the cone of an active volcano. The view from the sea—especially at night, as an endless stream of glowing red-hot lava flows into the water—is unforgettable. Stromboli is in a constant state of mild dissatisfaction, and every now and then its anger flares up, so following a devastating eruption on July 3, 2019, which killed a hiker, authorities do not allow any ascents to the principal crater. The main town has a small selection of reasonably priced hotels and restaurants, and a choice of lively clubs and cafés. In addition to the island tour, excursions might include boat trips around the sea stack of Strombolicchio, which is all that remains of the original volcano that gave rise to Stromboli. At night boats offer trips to see the Sciara del Fuoco, the lava channel that rises out of the blue waters.

GETTING HERE AND AROUND

Ferries and hydrofoils arrive here from Lipari, Salina, and Naples. Once on the island, you'll need to navigate by foot, or you can book one of the golf cart taxis located near the port.

TOURS

★ MagmaTrek

ADVENTURE TOURS | You can freely hike the volcano up to 951 feet, but for anything beyond that (up to the 1,312 foot) safe limit, you'll need an authorized guide. MagmaTrek offers five-hour hikes (€25) that get you as close as humanly possible to the volcanic activity as you ascend approximately 5 miles up the flanks of Stromboli. They provide the mandatory helmets, but you should be sure to pack sturdy walking shoes. ✉ *Via Vittorio Emanuele, Stromboli* ☎ *090/9865768* 🌐 *www.magmatrek.it* 🕓 *Closed Nov.–mid-Nov.*

Pippo Navigazione

BOAT TOURS | The best way to see Stromboli's eruptions is with a boat tour such as those run by Pippo Navigazione. Boat trips include three-hour day cruises and night tours that explore the area where the lava reaches the sea. Trips start at €25 per person for groups up to 30 people. You can also book private excursions. ✉ *Porto Scari, Stromboli* ☎ *348/0559296 Giovanni, 339/2229714 Giovanni's mother* 🎫 *From €25.*

👁 Sights

Spiaggia Lunga

BEACH | The area around Piscità and Ficogrande is full of narrow side streets that lead down to the sea, where you'll find an assortment of different coves, inlets, and lavic outcroppings. Just head downhill from the principal streets and you'll eventually hit water. The largest beach area is Spiaggia Nera on the island's northeastern coast, where the black sand and stones sit in stark contrast to the aquamarine waters. ✉ *Spiaggia Lunga, Piscità, Stromboli.*

🍴 Restaurants

Ciroristora

$$$$ | **ITALIAN** | A native of Naples, Ciro Aragione has called Stromboli home since the 1990s. From his home, he cooks lunch for visitors to the island, usually a set menu of pasta and fish he's bought straight off the boats that morning. **Known for:** literal home cooking; intimate atmosphere with an island expert; excellent sourdough bread from scratch. [$] *Average main: €40* ✉ *Via Vittorio Emanuele 67, Stromboli* ☎ *328/6477230* 🌐 *www.facebook.com/ciroristora* 💳 *No credit cards.*

★ Osservatorio

$$ | **ITALIAN** | There's no better (or easier) place on the island to watch its fiery explosions than from the terrace of Osservatorio. The diverse menu offers everything from pizza (dinner only) and locally caught fish to pastas and roasted meats. **Known for:** friendly service; great pizza; the most spectacular volcanic views. [$] *Average main: €18* ✉ *Via Salvatore di Mulattiera Salvatore di Losa, Stromboli* ☎ *090/9586991* 🌐 *www.facebook.com/osservatoriostromboli* 🕓 *Closed mid-Nov.–Feb.*

Coffee and Quick Bites

Blu Bar

$ | **CAFÉ** | Even in the off-season, this little port café serves a reliable breakfast, with flaky croissants (often filled with marmalade) and good strong coffee. In the evenings, it becomes a gathering spot for aperitivo, where locals gather for a gin and tonic, Negroni, or spritz. **Known for:** excellent coffee; good cocktails; local hangout. [$] *Average main: €5* ✉ *Via Marina, Stromboli* ☎ *348/4694646.*

Hotels

Hotel La Sciara

$$ | **HOTEL** | There's nothing much more dramatic than lying poolside here, with views of the sea in one direction and a prime view of the volcano in the other. **Pros:** welcoming environment at base of the volcano; good in-house restaurant; large pool. **Cons:** a bit old-fashioned; very simple for a luxury property; uncomfortable pool loungers. [$] *Rooms from: €195* ✉ *Via Barnao, Piscità, Stromboli* ☎ *090/9488000* 🌐 *www.hotellasciara.it* 🕒 *Closed Nov.–Apr.* 🛏 *61 rooms* 🍴 *Free Breakfast.*

Il Vulcano nel Bosco

$$$$ | **HOUSE** | Built in 1750, this expansive house embodies the local vibes of Stromboli, with its white walls, sea and volcano views, outdoor thermal soaking pools, and maiolica tile everywhere (including on the geothermal heated floors). **Pros:** full of quiet nooks both inside and out; spacious and very private; headed floors. **Cons:** really best for larger groups up to 10 people; some rooms connect without hallways; very traditional design. [$] *Rooms from: €600* ✉ *Via del Sole 3, Stromboli* ☎ *333/4248539* 📧 *ilvulcanonelbosco@gmail.com* 🛏 *5 rooms* 🍴 *No Meals.*

Nightlife

Otto a~mare

COCKTAIL LOUNGES | In a garden shrouded in bougainvillea, this cocktail lounge focuses on drinks with a botanical bent. You'll find rosemary-infused vodkas, fennel-scented gin, and cordials made from *cedro*, a pithy bitter citrus found throughout Sicily. Sit under the canopy of stars and breathe in the fragrant night air as you enjoy your drink. ✉ *Via Vittorio Emanuele, Piscità, Stromboli* 🌐 *www.otto.place.*

Filicudi

30–60 minutes from Salina and Lipari by hydrofoil; 2 hours from Cefalù and Palermo, 2 hours from Milazzo, and 10 hours from Naples by ferry.

Just a dot in the sea, Filicudi is famous for its unusual volcanic rock formations, the enchanting Grotta del Bue Marino (Grotto of the Sea Ox), and the crumbled remains of a prehistoric village at Capo Graziano. The island, which is spectacular for walking and hiking, is still a truly undiscovered, restful haven, and has a handful of hotels and *pensioni* as well as some more informal rooms with families who put up guests. Car ferries are available only in summer.

GETTING HERE AND AROUND

Ferries and hydrofoils arrive throughout the year from Salina and Lipari, and also in summer from Palermo, Cefalù, Milazzo, and Naples. Once you've arrived, you can rent a car or a scooter at the port. You can also find the minibus taxi of D&G Servizio Navetta (☎ *347/7575916*) usually waiting at the port.

TOURS

I Delfini

BOATING | Look to Nino Terrano to get you on the water in Filicudi with boat excursions, rentals, and scuba diving. Choose full or half-day options to explore the maritime side of this untamed island out of the Pecorini a Mare port. ✉ *Via Pecorini Mare, Filicudi, Filicudi Porto* ☎ *340/1484645* 🌐 *www.idelfinifilicudi.com* 🎟 *From €30 per person.*

★ Walking Eolie

WALKING TOURS | A typical excursion with guide Giusi Murabito covers about 2½ miles of easy walking to visit the highlights of the island, from prehistoric villages to spectacular look-out points. Tours usually include tastings of locally foraged treats, such as orange jam or brined wild fennel, plus lunch or dinner, a meal she prepares herself for guests in her own home cliffside home (accessible via a series of footpaths). And since she only does private groups all tours are fully customizable. ✉ *Filicudi, Filicudi Porto* ☎ *349/6419964* 🌐 *www.walkingeolie.com* 🎟 *From €120 for a ½-day tour for 2 people, including transport.*

Sights

★ Filicudi WildLife Conservation

NATURE SIGHT | This nonprofit is dedicated to research and conservation of Aeolian sea life, particularly dolphins, sperm whales, and sea turtles. You can join one of their naturalistic excursions to go snorkeling with a marine biologist, go out on a boat at dawn to watch for cetaceans and turtles, or have a guided visit to the Sea Turtles First Aid Center. If you'd like to become more involved, you can join a one-week research camp on dolphins and turtles as a volunteer. ✉ *Pecorini a Mare, Filicudi, Filicudi Porto* ☎ *320/8624917* 🌐 *www.filicudiconservation.com* 🎟 *From €40.*

Le Punte

BEACH | Near the southern tip of Filicudi, you'll find a small crescent beach of large rounded pebbles with a perfect view of nearby Alicudi. During the summer, there's a lido service that rents beach chairs and umbrellas and even offers basic concessions, such as drinks and cold salads. ✉ *Le Punte, Filicudi Porto.*

★ Punta Stimpagnato

VIEWPOINT | For the island's most panoramic views—and the best sunsets—head to the southwestern coast for the Punta Stimpagnato lookout point. Descend from the main road down a mule path with a wooden handrail to a sort of rock balcony that overlooks the sea, with Alicudi in the distance. ✉ *Punta Stimpagnata, Filicudi Porto.*

Hotels

La Canna

$$ | **HOTEL** | Set above the tiny port and commanding fabulous views of sea and sky from its flower-filled terrace, this hotel offers small but adequate guest rooms, kept clean and tidy by the family-friendly staff. **Pros:** relaxing pool and lounge area; great views; family-friendly atmosphere. **Cons:** no Wi-Fi in guest rooms; half board required in peak season; an uphill climb from the port. [$] *Rooms from: €160* ✉ *Via Rosa 43, Filicudi Porto* ☎ *090/9889956* 🌐 *www.lacannahotel.it* 🕑 *Closed mid-Oct.–mid-Apr.* 🛏 *14 rooms* 🍴 *No Meals.*

The remote island of Alicudi is only inhabited by 50 full-time residents.

Alicudi

6 hours from Milazzo by ferry; 3 hours from Lipari by ferry, 1 hour, 35 minutes by hydrofoil; 70 minutes from Salina by hydrofoil.

The most remote of the Aeolian islands, Alicudi is in an off-the-beaten-path world of its own. Inhabited full-time by 50 people (mostly aging farmers and fishermen) and 16 mules, this volcanic cone emerges from the sea like a lava buoy. Known for its rugged hiking paths laced with heather and steep stone stairways that connect small houses that hug the cliffs, it's a place that attracts visitors who want absolute peace. Electricity only arrived on the island in the 1990s, and water is preciously conserved. There's no nightlife to speak of, and to eat in a restaurant (a word used very loosely) means to break bread in a private home. Addresses are given by the number of steps from

the port. But this hard-earned isolation means you'll experience some of the most pristine landscapes and waters that Sicily has to offer.

GETTING HERE AND AROUND
Ferries arrive here from Milazzo. Ferries and hydrofoils arrive from Lipari and Salina. The only way to get around on the island is on foot or by mules, which are used by local families to carry wares up the steep paths from the port.

TOURS
★ Walking Eolie
GUIDED TOURS | There is no guide anywhere in Sicily who knows Alicudi better than Catania native Giusi Murabito of Walking Eolie. Her knowledge of plant life, culinary traditions, historical events, local customs, and the people (she knows practically every inhabitant) is without parallel. She'll set up transport, guide you on walks around the island, and organize coffee breaks and tastings

of local specialties—ultimately anything that is possible on the island, Giusi can make happen. ✉ *Alicudi* ☎ *349/6419964* 🌐 *www.walkingeolie.com* 🎟 *€160 for full-day excursion for 2 people.*

🍴 Restaurants

Dining on Alicudi requires planning. Restaurants are located in private homes and need reservations made by phone. The hosts don't speak English, and you need to pay with cash. If you don't speak Italian, your best option is to have a contact from a previous hotel on your trip make the booking for you or go through a guide, such as Giusi at Walking Eolie.

★ Da Concetta

$$$ | **ITALIAN** | Feisty Concetta serves a set menu for lunch and dinner from her long terrace, located near the Chiesa San Bartolo. You can expect a large selection of antipasti (such as wild fennel, sautéed shrimp, and roasted eggplant), a pasta course, and some variety of roasted fish. **Known for:** incredibly intimate hospitality; spectacular views; truly unique dining experience. [$] *Average main: €30* ✉ *Alicudi* ✥ *Step 200 from port toward church* ☎ *380/1775818* 💳 *No credit cards.*

Da Silvio

$$$ | **SEAFOOD** | In his humble kitchen, Silvio, a rosy-cheeked fisherman, cooks for his guests as they sit around the table. You might have a simple pasta with tomato sauce, eggplant from his garden, olives cured from his trees, simmered wild greens gathered from the hillsides, and a fish dish (roasted, fried, or sautéed). **Known for:** seasonal dining at its realest; true local flavors; freshest fish caught by Silvio that day. [$] *Average main: €25* ✉ *Alicudi* ✥ *At sea level, about 100 feet from port* ☎ *333/1994477 Gabriella* 💳 *No credit cards.*

🛏 Hotels

Casa Antico Frantoio

$$ | **HOUSE** | Located in an historic olive mill in the Tonna district, this four-bedroom house is one of the largest on the island and features an over 2,000-square-foot terrace and garden. **Pros:** spacious accommodations; hammocks perfect for afternoon naps; outdoor grill area. **Cons:** five-night minimum means it's really better for longer stays; grocery procurement can be challenging; very sparse decor. [$] *Rooms from: €180* ✉ *Via XXI Maggio, Alicudi* ✥ *Step 380* ☎ *380/7836666* 🕘 *Closed Oct.–mid-May* 🛏 *4 rooms.*

Il Giardino dei Carubi

$ | **B&B/INN** | Flooded with light and kissed by the island's winds, this bright and airy B&B brings stylish comfort to the harsh Alicudi terrain. **Pros:** abundant breakfasts; wondrously silent; accommodating host. **Cons:** getting here can be challenging with luggage; two-night minimum; limited availability in peak season. [$] *Rooms from: €120* ✉ *Via XXIV Maggio, Alicudi* ✥ *Step 365* ☎ *380/7836666* 🕘 *Closed Oct.–mid-May* 🛏 *4 rooms* 🍽 *Free Breakfast.*

🛍 Shopping

Casa 3 Archi

ART GALLERIES | French artist Elise Collet Soravito has made Alicudi her home, and in her studio, she creates chunky, colorful jewelry, pottery, and paintings inspired by the island, from lemon still-lifes to landscapes. Shopping is a very rudimentary experience (there's no storefront per se), but you can arrange a visit to see her work and pick up handcrafted souvenirs of your stay. ✉ *Casa 3 Archi, Alicudi* ☎ *345/4652578* ✉ *elisecolletsoravito@gmail.com.*

Activities

Da Simone

BOATING | To get out on the water, contact Simone to rent a traditional wooden craft or a *gommone* (a type of motorized inflatable boat). For boats with engines 40 horsepower and below, you don't need a license. The waters around this minuscule island are easy to navigate, and a half-day excursion (9 am to 1 pm) will cost approximately €60 plus the price of gas. ✉ *Alicudi Porto, Alicudi* ☎ *334/5305879* 🎫 *From €60.*

Chapter 6

MOUNT ETNA AND EASTERN SICILY

6

Updated by
Jennifer V. Cole

 Sights
★★★★☆

 Restaurants
★★★★★

 Hotels
★★★★☆

Shopping
★★★☆☆

 Nightlife
★★☆☆☆

WELCOME TO
MOUNT ETNA AND EASTERN SICILY

TOP REASONS TO GO

★ **The splendor of Mount Etna.** There's nothing like experiencing one of the world's most famous active volcanoes, with her fiery explosions, trekking adventures, and some of the world's best wineries.

★ **Taormina, Sicily's most beautiful resort.** The view of the sea and Mount Etna from its jagged, plant-covered cliffs is as close to perfection as a panorama can get.

★ **Coastal fishing villages.** Time stands still in Aci Trezza, Aci Castello, and Riposto, where the rhythm of the sea still dictates daily life.

★ **Catania's vibrant dining scene.** This Baroque city paved with lava stone bubbles over with deliciousness, from arancini street snacks to destination restaurants and wine bars.

★ **Beach life in Punta del Faro.** The island's northeastern-most point has white sand beaches and crystalline waters that form the backdrop for stunning views across the Strait of Messina.

1 Catania. The beloved anchor of the region, full of art, restaurants, bars, shops, and architecture, all against a gritty lava backdrop.

2 Aci Castello. A sweet little seaside town above ancient lava flows that's centered on an 11th-century castle and small-town life.

3 Aci Trezza. A fishing village with lava pillars emerging from the sea that inspired Homer.

4 Acireale. A reprieve from the tourist beat, along the Cyclops Riviera.

5 Mount Etna. A treasure trove of outdoor experiences on one of Mother Nature's most powerful creations.

6 Riposto. A working-class seaside village.

7 Taormina. An ultraluxe resort town from the Golden Age of Travel, with truly unforgettable views.

8 Castelmola. A hilltop town 1,800 feet above sea level, known for its sweet almond wine and a bar with a saucy reputation.

9 Savoca. The medieval town where Francis Ford Coppola filmed The Godfather.

10 Messina. A modern port city full of hidden gems.

11 Punta del Faro. Mussels, beaches, and a massive pylon on the extreme northeastern point of Sicily.

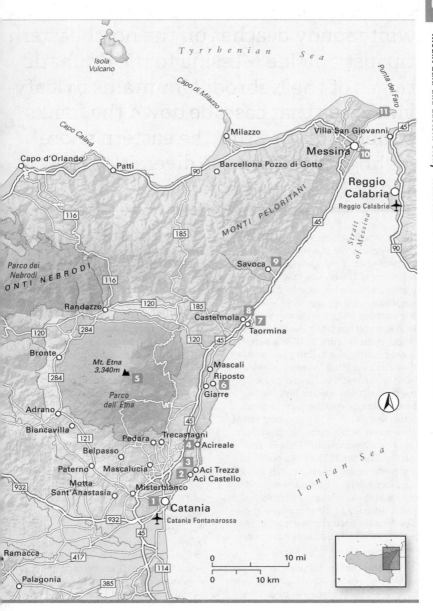

Sicily is a land of dramatic juxtapositions, and nowhere is that more evident than its eastern coast. From white sandy beaches on the northeastern tip just outside Messina to the dramatic ridges of the Nebrodi Mountains to leafy vineyards that cascade down the flanks of fiery Mount Etna, the eastern shore highlights the intense diversity of this sunny Mediterranean isle.

In this region, you see the forces of nature constantly at work, with a persistence that's only surpassed by the resilience of the human spirit. Between earthquakes, tsunamis, and volcanic eruptions, it's a wonder there's anything left standing here. Messina straddles a fault line and has been leveled multiple times, most recently in 1908 when the largest earthquake in European history (and a tsunami that followed 10 minutes later) wiped out the city and caused the shore to sink several feet overnight. Mount Etna, one of the world's most active volcanoes, is in a constant state of eruption, and in centuries past, her lava flows have covered Catania and surrounding areas. The city's buildings and roads constructed of basalt serve as daily reminders of Etna's power, and the craggy lava stone coastline reinforces the transmutability of the region's existence. Significantly, each and every time disaster has struck, these areas have been rebuilt.

It's not only Mother Nature that has tested Sicilian tenacity. All of Sicily has been conquered again and again by outside forces. With its fertile soil, mild climate, and prime location along shipping routes, it's a triangle of land that every great civilization has coveted. You can see evidence of that in the island's vastly different architectural styles. Here in the east, you'll primarily see the influence of the Romans, Greeks, Byzantines, and Normans. In Taormina, the Greek amphitheater stands as one of the best-preserved relics of the ancient world, still in use today for concerts and operas. In Aci Castello, the castle, a fortification first built by the Romans and subsequently rebuilt by the Byzantines and then the Normans, commands the shoreline of the Cyclops Riviera. In Catania, the cityscape runs from medieval to Baroque. Each town up and down the coast tells this repeated tale of persistence and rebirth.

Despite the weighty history, residents of the east have thrived, especially culturally. They have fostered great writers, such as Giovanni Verga. They have built luxury resort villages that are cemented in global memory as *the* places to be. They have turned the slopes of Etna into one of the preeminent wine destinations in the world. They have created a cuisine that highlights the island's bonanza of natural resources. And they might be some of the most adaptable people anywhere. Indeed, to visit the east is to climb into the soul of Sicily.

Planning

When to Go

There's not a bad time to visit eastern Sicily. In the spring, wildflowers explode from the hillsides and markets are full of fresh produce like asparagus, wild fennel, strawberries, and squash blossoms. During the blistering summer months (and it does get hot here), the diverse seascapes are alive with sunbathers, boaters, and open-air restaurants serving the freshest seafood imaginable. In the fall, leaves start to change on Etna, and the harvest begins in the many vineyards and olive groves. During the winter, fresh snow on Etna means you can ski during the morning and soak up the sun during a seaside *passeggiata* in the late afternoon. And the explosion of winter citrus keeps markets fragrant and colorful. If you are particularly sensitive to weather, avoid August when it can feel like an inferno (and is most crowded by other tourists), and January and February, when this area gets its most rain of the year.

Planning Your Time

Most trips to this side of the island begin in Catania, as it has a great international airport just 15 minutes outside the city with many direct flights. Though many people use Catania simply as a hub, it's worth spending a few days here. It's a city that's full of life, packed with great

architecture, museums, bars, and restaurants—plus, it's a city that people truly live in. As you stroll along the lava stone streets you'll note that the majority of the people you encounter are Catanesi. The coastal villages just north of the city center (Aci Castello, Aci Trezza, and Acireale) offer a foray into a more slow-paced way of life with small fishing ports, bustling town squares, and a craggy volcanic coastline.

No visit to eastern Sicily—or Sicily in general—is complete without experiencing Mount Etna. A couple of days (at least) is ideal for a taste of life on an active volcano. Choose among some 200 wineries to taste wines at the source, visit olive and pistachio orchards, spend a morning (or full day) trekking the volcanic craters, relax at resorts in historic palazzi, and eat at rustic osterias that draw inspiration from Etna's mineral-rich soil.

For the sheer wow factor, you don't want to miss Taormina, with its lush hillsides, perfectly framed bays, pebble beaches, and some of the best views in all of Italy. Arriving in the hillside town by car feels like entering the hanging gardens of Babylon. But note that Taormina is expensive and heavily touristed, and you might not encounter a single Italian there during the summer months if they aren't working at a shop, hotel, or restaurant. For some visitors, a week in Taormina isn't enough, but for others, it's the perfect day trip.

Messina is the most overlooked city on this side of Sicily. It tends to be frequented mostly by Italian business travelers and tourists who use it as a hub to connect with the Aeolian Islands or continental Italy via the Strait of Messina. But if you have an extra day or two on your itinerary, this easy-to-navigate town, known for granita, focaccia, and *stocco* (a local codfish specialty) is absolutely worth exploring.

Getting Here and Around

AIR

Aeroporto Internazionale di Catania (CTA) serves all of eastern Sicily, with direct flights throughout Italy and to most European hubs. You'll also find direct flights between Casablanca, Dubai, and Istanbul. The airport is conveniently located just outside the city, normally about 15 minutes from downtown.

CONTACTS Aeroporto Internazionale di Catania. ⊠ *Via Fontanarossa, Catania* ☎ *095/7239111* ⊕ *www.aeroporto. catania.it.*

BUS

Air-conditioned buses connect major and minor cities in the region and are often faster and more convenient than trains, but also slightly more expensive. Various companies serve the different routes. SAIS and FlixBus run between Catania, Palermo, and Messina, and also connect to destinations in continental Italy while Etna Trasporti connects smaller towns in the region.

CONTACTS Etna Transporti. ⊕ *www. etnatrasporti.it.* **FlixBus.** ⊕ *www.flixbus.it.* **SAIS.** ⊕ *www.saisautolinee.it.*

CAR

Driving is the ideal way to explore eastern Sicily. Modern highways and the autostrada connect the main cities, while the smaller towns are reachable by state and provincial roads. The A18, which is a toll road, connects the east from Messina down to Catania. When you get on the autostrada, take a ticket; you'll pay when you exit the highway according to how far you've driven (never more than a few Euros). Some exits have automated booths which allow you to pay with credit card, but it's best to have cash on hand.

You'll likely hear stories about the dangers of driving in Sicily. In big cities like Catania, streets can be a honking mess, with lane markings, stop signs, and traffic signals taken as mere suggestion. It's best to think of driving here as a dance with dynamic etiquette, and less as a system of hard and fast road rules. Honking is simply a way of communicating, to alert people of your presence on the road so they don't pull out in front of you. It's not always a sign of aggression. But you can avoid most of the chaos by driving through the cities at off-peak times. Once outside the urban areas, particularly on regional state highways, driving can be a motorist's dream, with winding, sparsely populated, and reasonably maintained roads and views around every corner.

In Catania, don't be surprised if people approach your car at intersections offering to clean your windshield. If you want them to clean it, a little spare change is the going rate. If you don't, simply say no and inch your car forward. If they attempt to clean it anyway, just use your car's windshield washer function to discourage them.

It's worth noting that the color of parking spaces might be different than what you're accustomed to. Here, yellow is reserved for special permits and handicap tags; blue is paid parking; and white is free. Be sure not to leave any valuables in your car, and make sure baggage is stowed out of sight.

TRAIN

There are trains from Rome to Messina (from 5½ to 9 hours) and Catania (from 8½ to 11 hours). On a direct express train, when you get to Villa San Giovanni at the tip of the boot in Calabria, the entire train is loaded onto a ferry to cross the Strait of Messina.

There are no high-speed lines within Sicily, but main lines connect Messina, Taormina, Catania, Siracusa, and Palermo. For prices and schedules, check the website of the Italian state railway, Trenitalia.

CONTACTS Trenitalia. ☎ *06/68475475* ⊕ *www.trenitalia.com.*

Hotels

You'll find high-quality hotels and resorts mostly in Catania, Taormina, and on Mount Etna. Beyond that, there are some truly destination-worthy hotels, but you'll also run into many places that, though clean and service-minded, could use some updating. There are also numerous *agriturismo* lodgings (rural country inns) throughout the region, ranging from very basic to ultraluxe.

Restaurants

Dining out in eastern Sicily is a feast for the senses. Throughout the region, you'll find a plethora of high-quality seafood, especially swordfish, mackerel, grouper, and *frutti di mare* (shrimp, sea urchin, clams, mussels, and oysters). Look for the plump, sweet local red shrimp, known as *gamberi rossi*, most often served raw with just a drizzle of oil and a spritz of lemon. And a robust agricultural scene means that fresh produce dictates the seasonal menus, specifically artichokes, squash blossoms, fava beans, melon, figs, and citrus. In Catania, eggplant is especially celebrated.

The local hero dishes are pasta alla Norma, a tomato-sauce pasta with fried eggplant and creamy salted ricotta, and *parmigiana*, the original eggplant parm. Here on the eastern side, fried rice balls are called arancini (masculine, with an i; not arancine as they call them in Palermo). And granita is said to have been invented here, with ice from the slopes of Etna. So you'll find countless iterations of the frozen treat everywhere you go; the traditional way to eat it is with fresh brioche bread. And as is befitting an area with major cities and tourist destinations, the restaurant scene has exploded in the past decade, with new additions ranging

from Michelin-starred fine dining to grab-and-go markets and seafood stalls. For sit-down restaurants, it's advised to always make a reservation, even if that just means calling the restaurant immediately before you plan to go to make sure there's availability. Unlike in the United States, restaurants don't turn tables. So if you book a table it's yours until you decide to leave; there's no hustling you out the door to seat the next party. But that's also why you might walk into a mostly empty restaurant and be told they are fully booked. They stagger seatings to give the mom-and-pop-style small kitchens room to maneuver.

RESTAURANT AND HOTEL PRICES
Restaurant prices in the reviews are the average cost of a main course at dinner, or if dinner is not served, at lunch. Hotel prices in the reviews are the lowest cost of a standard double room in high season. Restaurant and hotel reviews have been shortened. For full information, visit Fodors.com.

What it Costs in Euros			
$	$$	$$$	$$$$
RESTAURANTS			
under €15	€15–€22	€23–€30	over €30
HOTELS			
under €125	€125–€225	€226–€350	over €350

Catania

210 km (130 miles) southeast of Palermo, 60 km (37 miles) north of Siracusa.

The chief wonder of Catania, Sicily's second city, is that it's there at all. Nearly every century has seen its share of tragedy for the Catanesi: a Greek tyrant that cast the population out, another who sold the majority of the citizens into slavery, Carthaginians who drove the successive occupants away once again. Each time, the city was rebuilt, only to meet more destruction. The plague hit hard in the Middle Ages, severely decimating the population. Mt. Etna erupted in 1669, with a mile-wide stream of lava covering part of the city, and just 25 years after that, a disastrous earthquake forced Catania to begin again.

Today Catania is in the midst of yet another resurrection—this time from crime, filth, and urban decay. Although the city remains loud and full of traffic, signs of gentrification are everywhere. The elimination of vehicles from the Piazza del Duomo and the main artery of Via Etnea, and the cleaning of many of the historic buildings have added to its newfound charm. Home to what is arguably Sicily's best university, Catania is full of youthful exuberance, which comes through in its designer bistros, the chic osterias that serve wine, and the trendy boutiques that have cropped up all over town. Even more impressive is the vibrant cultural life.

GETTING HERE AND AROUND
Catania is well connected by bus and train with Messina, Taormina, Siracusa, Enna, and Palermo. The airport of Fontanarossa serves as a transportation hub for the eastern side of the island. From here you can get buses to most major destinations without going into the city center. The Alibus runs a loop from the airport through the city center (€4; *approximately every 25 minutes*).

Within the city, use the AMTS bus service (€1; ⊕ *www.amts.ct.it*), which also connects to outlying areas such as Aci Castello. The website can be difficult to use, but the AMT Catania app offers useful route suggestions, online ticket purchasing, and timetables—and it's available in English. Catania also has an underground Metro line (€1; ⊕ *www.circumetnea.it*), but with only 10 stations centered on the downtown area, it's often easier to just walk.

VISITOR INFORMATION
CONTACT Catania Tourism Office. ⊠ *Via Etnea 63/65,* ☏ *095/4014070* ⊕ *turismo.cittametropolitana.ct.it.*

Sights

Amenano River
NATURE SIGHT | This underground river flows beneath much of Catania. You can glimpse it at the Fontana dell'Amenano, but the best place to experience the river is at the bar-restaurant A Putia dell'Ostello. Here you can sit at an underground table as swirls of water rush by. If you're not planning to stay for a drink, someone from the bar will sell you a €1 ticket to walk into the cavelike seating area. Aside from the underground river, the bar area above ground is a lively, fun spot to hang out on a Monday evening when many other places are closed. ⊠ *Piazza Currò 6, Catania* ☏ *095/7233010* ⊕ *aputiadellostello.business.site.*

Cattedrale di Sant'Agata (Duomo)
CHURCH | Giovanni Vaccarini designed the contrasting black lava and white limestone facade of city's cathedral, which dominates the Piazza del Duomo and which houses the tomb of composer Vincenzo Bellini. Also of note are the three apses of lava that survive from the original Norman structure and a fresco from 1675 in the sacristy that portrays Catania's submission to Etna's eruption. Guided tours of the cathedral, which is dedicated to Catania's protector, are available in English if reserved at least a week in advance. The cathedral's treasures are on view in the Museo Diocesano Catania (www.museodiocesanocatania.com), and underneath the cathedral are the ruins of Greco-Roman baths. ⊠ *Piazza del Duomo, bottom end of Via Etnea, Catania* ☏ *095/320044, 339/4859942 for tours* ⊕ *www.cattedralecatania.it* ☞ *Museum €7, sacristy €2, baths €5; combined ticket €10.*

Centro Storico

HISTORIC DISTRICT | Black lava stone from Etna, combined with largely Baroque architecture, give Catania's historic center a very distinctive feel. After Catania's destruction by lava and earthquake at the end of the 17th century, the city was rebuilt and its informal mascot "U Liotru" (an elephant carved out of lava balancing an Egyptian obelisk) was placed outside the cathedral as a kind of talisman. This square also marks the entrance to Catania's famous *pescheria* (fish market) and is one of the few points in the city where you can see the Amenano River above ground. Another point of interest is Via Garibaldi, which runs from Piazza del Duomo up toward the impressively huge Porta Garibaldi, a black-and-white triumphal arch built in 1768 to commemorate the marriage of Ferdinando I. Also of note in the center are Castello Ursino, which is now a museum, the Greco-Roman theater off Via Vittorio Emanuele II, and the Roman amphitheater in Piazza Stesicoro. ⊠ *Catania.*

Festa di Sant'Agata

OTHER ATTRACTION | Each February 3–5, the Festa di Sant'Agata honors Catania's patron saint with one of Italy's biggest religious festivals. The saint herself was first tortured, had her breasts cut off, and then killed, when she spurned a Roman suitor in favor of keeping her religious purity. Since then, the Catanesi have honored her memory by parading her relics through the streets of Catania on an enormous silver-encrusted carriage. Throughout town, you'll see the *minne di Sant'Agata* in pastry shops. These supersugary confections (sponge cake with sweetened ricotta, candied orange, and chocolate chips, covered in fondant, and topped with a candied cherry) are meant to symbolize Agata's breasts. The entire festival is highly affecting, even for nonbelievers, and is not to be missed by February visitors. ⊠ *Catania* ⊕ *www. festadisantagata.it.*

Via Etnea

STREET | With the ever-looming volcano perfectly framed at the end of the road, this main street is lined with cafés and stores selling high-street jewelry, clothing, and shoes. At sunset, it plays host to one of Sicily's most enthusiastic passeggiatas, in which Catanesi of all ages take part. It is closed to automobile traffic (other than buses, taxis, and police) until 10 pm during the week and all day on weekends. ⊠ *Via Etnea, Catania.*

🍴 Restaurants

★ Km.0

$$ | SICILIAN | For the best of what's locally in season, look to chef Marco Cannizzaro and his 25-seat fine-dining restaurant. Harvested from Etna to the Ionian Sea, the primary ingredients of the area simply shine in his hands: Nerello mascelese grapes show up as rich sauces, wild greens harvested from the slopes of Etna make their way into risottos or stuffed into tender calamari meatballs, and donkey, an economical protein staple of the area, is transformed into flavorful and refined tartare. **Known for:** fine dining with a neighborhood feel; four-, five-, or seven-course tasting menus; Robiola-stuffed smoked onion with strawberry. Ⓢ *Average main: €22* ⊠ *Via Antonino Longo 26, Catania* ☏ *347/7327788* ⊕ *www.km0ristorante. com* ☉ *Closed Wed. yr-round and Sun. in summer.*

Me Cumpari Turiddu

$$ | SICILIAN | Following a Slow Food philosophy, this restaurant strives to be a typical Sicilian neighborhood destination in every sense. In the morning, you'll find just-from-the-oven breads, pastries, fresh-squeezed juice, and goat's milk yogurt at the front counter while the restaurant's main menu pays homage to the area's distinct culinary traditions, such as donkey steaks or donkey mortadella, pastas with anchovies and breadcrumbs, and macco soup from fava beans. **Known**

for: superb preparations of donkey; natural wines; close relationships with local producers. $ *Average main: €18* ✉ *Piazza Turi Ferro 36/38, Catania* ☎ *095/7150142* ⊕ *www.mecumparituriddu.it.*

★ Oasi Frutti di Mare da Nitto

$ | SEAFOOD | Located in the Ognina port, the little Nitto empire has exploded: what began as a mobile market in the 1960s (from the back of a Piaggio Ape) is now a standing fresh fish market and series of restaurants. Locals line up outside the little market to get their daily catch, while next door the fast-casual restaurant serves some of the best-prepared seafood in the area, including squid ink pastas, skewers of grilled fish, and raw seafood platters. **Known for:** tuna agrodolce, a sweet-and-sour tuna dish studded with pine nuts and raisins; fresh-off-the-boat seafood; vivacious atmosphere. $ *Average main: €12* ✉ *Piazza Mancini Battaglia 6, Catania* ☎ *095/491165* ⊕ *www.nittopescheria.it.*

Pamochã

$ | ITALIAN | An acronym for "Pane, Mortadella, and Champagne," Pamocha indeed specializes in bubbles, masterful salumi plates, all the bruschetta, and raw seafood towers of oysters, sweet red shrimp, tuna, and caviar. Typically the portions at this glam-meets-rustic café are small, making it perfect for aperitivo or a late-night snack (it's open until 2 am). **Known for:** Instagram-worthy meat case; French grower champagne; outside seating on a busy pedestrian street. $ *Average main: €15* ✉ *Via Gemmellaro 46, Catania* ☎ *338/8158024* ⊕ *www.pamocha.it.*

Razmataz

$ | SICILIAN | Ask for an outside table under the canopy at this charming—and always bustling—bistro, located down a pedestrian-only path in the heart of the historic district. Here, you'll find a mix of the Catanese standards (eggplant parmigiana, meatballs cooked in lemon leaves, caponata) as well as a rotation of riffs on typical Italian dishes (such as lasagna, sometimes served with radicchio, gorgonzola, and walnuts). **Known for:** vibrant atmosphere; slightly harried waitstaff; Sicilian classics done well. $ *Average main: €9* ✉ *Via Montesano 19, Catania* ☎ *095/311893* ⊕ *www.razmatazcatania.it* ⊘ *Closed Mon.*

Tantìkkia

$$ | SICILIAN | Located just off the fish market, in an alleyway covered by brightly colored parasols, Tantìkkia (which means *"a little"* in Sicilian dialect) serves little tastes of modern Sicily. Drawing on tradition, the updated twists show inspiration, yet steer far from precious. **Known for:** artichoke millefeuille with blue cheese and hazelnuts; friendly service; inspired desserts. $ *Average main: €18* ✉ *Via Gisira 28, Catania* ☎ *095/7168188* ⊕ *tantikkia-catania.business.site* ⊘ *Closed Mon. and Tues.*

★ Uzeta Bistrò Siciliano

$$ | SICILIAN | Street food meets small plates at this ode to the flavors of Sicily. Located on a foot traffic-only street below a rainbow of colored streamers, this compact bistro serves chef-style iterations of the island's greatest "fast food" hits. **Known for:** comprehensive Sicilian wine list; great cocktails; best arancini in the east. $ *Average main: €20* ✉ *Via Penninello 41, Catania* ☎ *095/2503374* ⊕ *www.uzeta.it* ⊘ *Closed Mon.*

Vite

$$ | SICILIAN | This unassuming little spot tucked on a side street between Via Umberto and Piazza Verga consistently underpromises and overdelivers. It portends to be a little neighborhood eatery, but it's a destination in its own right with chef/owner Ivan Siringo serving classics like pasta with squid ink, roulades of stuffed chicken, and red shrimp carpaccio. **Known for:** fine dining with a mom-and-pop feel; well-informed wine list; classics presented through a fresh lens. $ *Average main: €16* ✉ *Via E. A. Pantano*

61, Catania ☎ *095/16947698* 🌐 *www.viterestaurant.com* 🕒 *Closed Mon.*

Yoi

$$$ | **ASIAN** | Admittedly most visitors to Sicily aren't seeking Asian food, but when you've had your fill of caponata, Yoi is the perfect place for a palate refresher. They're known for their dim sum–style offerings (dumplings are charmingly called ravioli here), bao buns, stir-fried noodles, and classics like Peking duck or their take on Nobu's miso-marinated cod. **Known for:** tasty dim sum; top-notch wine service; intimate but lively atmosphere. [$] *Average main: €25* ✉ *Viale della Libertà 192, Catania* ☎ *096/7175110* 🌐 *www.yoifoodattitude.it* 🕒 *Closed Sun.*

Coffee and Quick Bites

Caffè del Duomo

$ | **CAFÉ** | Dive right into the hustle and bustle of Catania at Caffè del Duomo, which has handmade cookies and cakes and a great local atmosphere. The piazza-front location is the main draw, but the fantastic cannoli are another reason to stop for coffee and watch the world go by. **Known for:** typical Sicilian breakfast; handmade treats; great spot for people-watching. [$] *Average main: €5* ✉ *Piazza Duomo 11–13, Catania* ☎ *095/7150556* 🌐 *www.caffedelduomocatania.com.*

Caffè Europa

$ | **CAFÉ** | It's worth a visit for the sheer wow factor when you walk in and see the long pastry cases filled with every Sicilian delicacy you can imagine. Since 1962, they've been supplying the Catanesi with their daily *raviola fritta* (a fried pastry stuffed with sweetened ricotta) and short pulls of espresso. **Known for:** almond granita; great people-watching; perfect aperitivo. [$] *Average main: €4* ✉ *Corso Italia 302, Catania* ☎ *095/372655* 🌐 *www.caffeuropa.it* 🕒 *Closed Tues.*

Catania's Kiosks

Street corners throughout Catania are peppered with freestanding *chioschi* (kiosks), where you can stand at the counter to have a quick coffee, a glass of fresh-squeezed juice pressed from local oranges or pomegranates, or even a cocktail. Try a *seltz limone e sale*—a mix of fizzy water, fresh-squeezed Sicilian lemon juice, and salt—that's *the* classic Catanese remedy for indigestion, dehydration, and hangovers (think: Gatorade meets Alka-Seltzer).

★ **Forno Biancuccia**

$ | **BAKERY** | Lawyer-turned-baker Valeria Messina has singlehandedly revived the use of heirloom grains in Catania. At her welcoming little corner bakery, she uses tumminia, perciasacchi, maiorca, and timilia flours to create crusty sourdough loaves, focaccia, buttery biscotti, and traditional pizza marinara. **Known for:** from-the-oven tastes of ancient Sicily; rye from the slopes of Etna; schiacciata stuffed with seasonal ingredients. [$] *Average main: €3* ✉ *Via Mario Sangiorgi 12, Catania* ☎ *095/6681018* 🌐 *www.biancuccia.it* 🕒 *Closed Sun. and Mon.*

Pasticceria Savia

$ | **CAFÉ** | The lively Pasticceria Savia makes superlative arancini with ragù. Or you could choose cannoli, granita, or other snacks to munch on while you people-watch from one of the streetside tables. **Known for:** lovely outdoor seating; typical Sicilian pastries like cannoli and pasta di mandorla (almond paste); arancini with ragù. [$] *Average main: €5* ✉ *Via Etnea 302–304 and Via Umberto 2, near Villa Bellini, Catania* ☎ *095/322335* 🌐 *www.savia.it* 🕒 *Closed Mon.*

★ Scirocco Sicilian Fish Lab

$ | **SEAFOOD** | In the heart of the fish market, you'll find the best *fritto misto* in the area. Walk up to the little counter on the stone balcony overlooking the action and place your order for a paper cone of fried seafood made with the lightest and crispiest batter. **Known for:** superfresh seafood; fast service; unique seafood sandwiches called tramezzini. $ *Average main: €9* ✉ *Piazza Alonzo di Benedetto 7, Catania* ☎ *095/8365148* ⊕ *www.sciroccolab.com.*

 Hotels

Asmundo di Gisira

$$$ | **HOTEL** | Housed inside a palace built after the 1693 earthquake that destroyed Catania, this boutique property just steps from the Duomo honors historic architecture and embraces the immersive experience of modern art. **Pros:** spacious rooms; gorgeous rooftop lounge; extensive modern art collection. **Cons:** not all modern art speaks to all people; design outweighs comfort in some rooms; some street-facing rooms can be noisy. $ *Rooms from: €251* ✉ *Via Gisira 40, Catania* ☎ *095/0978894* ⊕ *www.asmundodigisira.com* ⮌ *11 rooms.*

★ Palazzo Marletta

$$$ | **HOTEL** | Baroque architecture punctuates the city, and one of the best ways to see it up close is with a stay at Palazzo Marletta, a private palace turned plush hotel. **Pros:** copious breakfast; arrangement with a local car valet service for parking; prime location just off the Duomo. **Cons:** can be difficult to navigate the historic district if arriving by car; modern rooms lack some of the charm of historic ones; some of the bathrooms have little privacy. $ *Rooms from: €252* ✉ *Via Erasmo Merletta 7, Catania* ☎ *380/2160253* ⊕ *www.palazzomarletta.it* ⮌ *7 rooms* ❍ *Free Breakfast.*

Romano House

$ | **HOTEL** | With a sleek minimalist design in a 17th-century palace and a convenient location in an increasingly trendy area not far from the train station, this boutique hotel caters to design aficionados on a budget. **Pros:** use of private beach of its sister hotel, the Romano Palace; on-site restaurant and bar; good-size rooms. **Cons:** street noise can be a problem; neighborhood won't appeal to everyone; design sometimes wins over practicality in rooms. $ *Rooms from: €119* ✉ *Via di Prima 20, Catania* ☎ *095/3520611* ⊕ *www.romanohouse.com* ⮌ *50 rooms* ❍ *No Meals.*

Una Hotel Palace

$$ | **HOTEL** | For great views of Etna, this centrally located hotel overlooking Catania's main shopping street has a rooftop terrace where you can enjoy breakfast or take in the scenery during happy hour over a cocktail and antipasti buffet. **Pros:** amazing rooftop views; eager-to-please staff; extremely central location. **Cons:** fee for parking; some noisy rooms; bit of a generic feel. $ *Rooms from: €126* ✉ *Via Etnea 218, Catania* ☎ *095/2505111* ⊕ *www.gruppouna.it/esperienze/palace-catania* ⮌ *94 rooms* ❍ *Free Breakfast.*

 Nightlife

First Lounge Bar

BEER GARDENS | Breathing new life into the San Berillo district, First is an outdoor lounge-bar with a beer garden feel, original street art, and walls covered in potted plants. Stop in for a craft beer or a cocktail in the previously forgotten back alleys a few minutes from Teatro Massimo Bellini, and you will also likely be treated to art installations or live DJ sets, depending on the constantly updated cultural calendar of events. ✉ *Via Martinez 13, Catania* ☎ *320/7633921.*

★ Oliva.co Cocktail Society

COCKTAIL LOUNGES | Tucked in an alleyway off Via Umberto, the Oliva lounge offers a bit of calm in the city's bustling center. This is where you go to geek out over the impressive selection of mezcal and rhum agricole or go deep on locally made gins and amari. The team here, a trio of hardcore bar nerds, makes all the classics perfectly (like Negronis, daiquiris, and martinis) and uses house-made bitters and tinctures to whip up inspiring drinks. ⊠ *Via delle Scale 4, Catania* ☏ *349/1732075* ⊕ *www.olivaco.it.*

★ Vermut

WINE BARS | In the heart of the city's downtown, this always-packed bar has tables that spill into the streets. With an impressive selection of vermouths and local salumi, it's a great spot to go for aperitivo or a late-night drink. But the real draw is the wine program. Don't even bother with the wine list—ask for Antonio Lombardo, a veritable expert with a mischievous smile, who consistently pulls affordable bottles to suit any mood or taste, from obscure natural wines to refined classics. It's a popular spot, so it's best to make a reservation lest you want to be among the crowds who stand in the pedestrian street, drink-in-hand. ⊠ *Via Gemmellaro 39, Catania* ☏ *347/6001978.*

Performing Arts

Teatro Massimo Bellini

OPERA | Opera season (October through June) attracts top singers and productions to the birthplace of the great composer Vincenzo Bellini. Guided tours of the theater's lavish interior, built in 1890, run Tuesday through Saturday from 9 am to noon, as theater business permits; call first to ensure you can get a tour. Enter by the box office on Piazza Bellini. ⊠ *Via Perrotta 12, Catania* ☏ *095/7306111 for info, 095/7306135 box office, 344/2249701 for guided tours* ⊕ *www.teatromassimobellini.it* ⊠ *€7 guided tours.*

Shopping

Enoteca Le 3 Botti

WINE/SPIRITS | Owners Filippo and Jelena welcome shoppers into their well-stocked enoteca as if they are inviting friends into their home. In this little spot just outside the city center, they stock one of the area's best selections of Etna and Sicilian wines as well as boutique amari, Etna-distilled gins, and a whole wall of sparkling wine. Rely on their expertise to navigate the offerings. The couple knows every bottle in the shop and never tries a gratuitous upsell. ⊠ *Via Vincenzo Giuffrida 176/D, Catania* ☏ *095/2867419* ⊕ *www.le3botti.it.*

Folk

CERAMICS | For a more pop art take on traditional Sicilian ceramics, visit Folk, a little boutique and gallery run by artist Magda Masano. You'll find iconic ceramic pinecones and *teste di Moro* (a ubiquitous pair of heads) in vibrant colors such as emerald green, lilac, or turquoise. Additionally, there are kitchenwares like plates, spoon rests, and cheese boards, all made of lava stone. ⊠ *Via San Michele 17–19, Catania* ☏ *392/2075505* ⊕ *www.magdamasano.it.*

I Dolci di Nonna Vincenza

FOOD | The selection of almond-based delights here may be small, but everything is fresh and phenomenally good. Ask for boxes of mixed cookies by weight, add in some marzipan treats dedicated to Catania's patron, Sant'Agata, and enjoy the grab-bag selection at your leisure later. International shipping is available. This is the original and most historic location, but other stores can be found on Via San Giuseppe la Rena and Piazza Mancini Battaglia. ⊠ *Palazzo Biscari, Piazza San Placido 7, Catania* ☏ *095/7151844* ⊕ *www.dolcinonnavincenza.it.*

★ Outdoor Fish and Food Market

MARKET | Beginning behind the Fontana Amenano at the corner of Piazza Duomo and spreading westward between Via Garibaldi and Via Transito, this is one of Italy's most memorable markets. It's a feast for the senses, with ricotta, fresh produce, endless varieties of meats, thousands of just-caught fish (some still wriggling), plus a symphony of vendor shouts to fill the ears. The market is at its best in early morning and finishes up around 1 pm. It's open every day except Sunday. ⊠ *Corner of Piazza Duomo, Catania.*

Uau

HANDBAGS | The brainchild and passion project of a former graphic designer, Uau sells handmade leather bags with a bit of whimsy. Look for clutches inspired by old coin purses, slim backpacks in nature-inspired prints, and bold shoulder bags—the whole line wouldn't be out of place in a Tim Burton film. ⊠ *Via San Michele 13, Catania* ☎ *342/0943867.*

Uoman

WOMEN'S CLOTHING | First opened in 2019, this Catanesi-owned shop and clothing line embraces body positivity. So much so, they abandoned all traditional sizes and instead offer five unique fits. Constucted with an eye on sustainability, the clothes are made of all natural, vegetal fabrics. And the owners work with local women artisans to highlight their hand-crafted accessory wares (like necklaces and purses) within the shop. ⊠ *Corso Italia 160, Catania* ☎ *095/7394509* ⊕ *www.uoman.it.*

Aci Castello

10 km (6 miles) north of Catania.

An ancient fishing village, this little town sits 15 meters (49.2 feet) above sea level and takes its name from the 11th-century Norman castle that dominates the edge of the central piazza, above prehistoric lava flows. Locally owned restaurants surround the square. The primary thoroughfare in town is Via Re Martino, a narrow one-way street with barely a whiff of sidewalks. Along this road you'll find butchers, bakers, fishmongers, cheesemongers, and produce stands. All of these are reminders that this town still functions very much like a village from a previous era: most of Aci Castello still shops for food by visiting individual merchants they can call by name instead of going to chain supermarkets.

GETTING HERE AND AROUND
Bus number 534 arrives from Catania, with departures roughly once an hour (€1 one-way; ⊕ *www.amts.ct.it*). You can also reach the town by walking along the sea road by way of Via Angelo Musco, which becomes Via G. Pezzana (the road is locally known as the *scogliera*, for the rocks along the coastline) from the Ognina port in Catania. It's about a one-hour walk with many beautiful vistas.

 ## Sights

Castello Normanno

CASTLE/PALACE | Built from basalt (the black lava stone of the area), this fortress sits high on a cliff jutting out into the Ionian Sea above a prehistoric lava flow. The exact construction origins are unknown, but it's generally accepted that the original fortification was built by the Romans as a spot called Castrum Jacis that was later rebuilt as a castle by the Byzantines in the 7th century, and subsequently controlled by the Arabs. The current castle was built in 1076 and is attributed to the Normans who ruled the area in the 11th century. Inside the castle there is a small museum divided into three sections: mineralogy, paleontology, and archaeology. But arguably the best reason to visit is the view from the top, from which you can see the nearby Cyclops Islands, great expanses of sea, and the craggy coastline stretching to Catania. ⊠ *Piazza*

Aci Castello's Norman castle is made out of basalt, the area's black lava stone.

Castello, Aci Castello ☎ 320/4339691 ⊕ www.comune.acicastello.ct.it ⊠ €4.

🍴 Restaurants

Pizzeria Blanca

$ | PIZZA | For a casual night out with a tremendous backdrop, stop by for a pizza at Blanca, which sits on the terrace directly under the Norman castle with views of Aci Trezza in the distance. You'll see neighborhood kids kicking soccer balls in the piazza and couples out for their evening passeggiata as you dine on excellent pizza under the stars. **Known for:** great views; good wine list; lively atmosphere. $ *Average main: €14* ⊠ *Piazza Castello 17, Aci Castello* ☎ *340/3029005.*

Ristorante Marè la Putìa Sul Mare

$$ | SEAFOOD | Linger on the sunny seaside deck as you get your fill of fresh seafood along the *scogliera* outside Aci Castello. While the pasta and *secondi* are all very well done, you could easily make a meal by ordering a shared selection of antipasti as the portions are quite ample. **Known for:** fried calamaretti (tiny fried whole squid); pasta alle vongole (clams); crudo platters. $ *Average main: €20* ⊠ *Via Antonello da Messina 46, Aci Castello* ☎ *095/274433* ⊕ *www.marè.com.*

★ Trattoria La Bettola

$$ | SEAFOOD | In a town where life still has a small town village feel, locals fill the outside tables of this trattoria in the central piazza at the base of the castle. The menu is full of seafood specialties—all excellent—but your best best is to ask the server what the chef is suggesting that day. **Known for:** plump raw gamberi rossi, dressed in olive oil and lemon; mussels pepato; frittura di paranza (a mix of fried seafood). $ *Average main: €17* ⊠ *Piazza Castello 20, Aci Castello* ☎ *095/274516* ⊕ *www.trattorialabettola. com* ☺ *Closed Tues.*

Coffee and Quick Bites

Al Castello Girarrosto-Gastronomia

$ | **SICILIAN** | Pick up lunch or dinner to go from Al Castello, perfect for a seaside picnic or a meal at your Airbnb. They roast whole chickens daily (rotisserie-style) and have an impressive line of baked pastas, roasted potatoes, sautéed or grilled vegetables, and involtini stuffed with cheese, bacon, or pistachios. **Known for:** excellent take-away options (no on-site dining at all); grilled vegetables; roast chicken. $ Average main: €12 ☒ Via Re Martino 189, Aci Castello ☎ 347/0492860.

Pasticceria Caffè & Dolcezza

$ | **CAFÉ** | In Aci Castello, your granita go-to is Caffè & Dolcezza. Their pistachio flavor is exceptionally good, creamy and studded with bits of ground pistachio. **Known for:** breakfast pastries; honey-soaked crispelle; perfect pistachio granita. $ Average main: €5 ☒ Via Re Martino 211, Aci Castello ☎ 095/16936729.

🛏 Hotels

Grand Hotel Baia Verde

$$ | **HOTEL** | This large property right on the sea feels a bit like a time capsule. **Pros:** pool and private sea access; full spa and wellness center; sea views from many rooms. **Cons:** needs considerable updating; smaller rooms tend to be dark; stuffy service. $ Rooms from: €142 ☒ Via Angelo Musco 8, Aci Castello ☎ 095/491522 ⊕ www.baiaverde.it ⇌ 147 rooms ¶O¶ Free Breakfast.

House of Palms

$$ | **APARTMENT** | Owned by a pair of artists, the House of Palms features two one-bedroom apartments that come with full kitchens, private balconies, and a stockpile of art and custom furniture (much of it created by the owners). **Pros:** rooftop terrace with BBQ grill; welcome basket that includes everything from wine and fruit to pasta and sauce; views of both the Norman castle and the Cyclops Islands. **Cons:** only two apartments means it's often booked; need a car to get here; located across busy highway from the sea. $ Rooms from: €130 ☒ Via M. Maugeri 79, Aci Castello ☎ 349/2858293 ⊕ linktr.ee/houseofpalms ⇌ 2 apartments ¶O¶ No Meals.

Aci Trezza

2 km (1 mile) north of Aci Castello.

Aci is a mythological river that is said to have flowed from the wellsprings of Etna to the sea. According to the ancient Greeks, it was created as the result of the love between Aci the shepherd and Galatea. When Aci died, he turned into the river and Galatea into the sea foam, so that they remain joined together forever, but still apart. Aci Trezza is the kind of seaside village (population 5,000) that inspires such tales. It makes appearances in Homer's *Odyssey,* and Luchino Visconti filmed *La Terra Trema* here. This hamlet of nearby Aci Castello is primarily known today for the dramatic lava stacks (*faraglioni*) that emerge from its coastal waters.

GETTING HERE AND AROUND
Bus number 534 arrives from Catania, with departures roughly once an hour (€1 one-way; ⊕ www.amts.ct.it).

Sights

★ Cyclops Islands

NATURE SIGHT | Also known as the faraglioni, these ancient volcanic islets are so dramatically stunning they have inspired writers throughout the centuries. Homer set Odysseus's battle with the cyclops here in *The Odyssey,* contending that the angered and freshly blinded cyclops Polyphemus hurled giant hunks of rock from Etna to the sea to destroy Odysseus and his ship. Sicilian writer Giovanni Verga set his most famous novel, *I*

Malavoglia, on the island of Lachea, the largest of the isles. Today the area is a protected marine preserve. You can kayak or swim the waters or take a short boat taxi to Lachea to visit the Lachea Island Museum of Sea Studies, which highlights the flora and fauna of the area in a tiny museum perched near the top. ✉ *Faraglioni, Aci Trezza* 🌐 *www.isoleciclopi.it.*

🍴 Restaurants

Arcobaleno Ristorante

$$ | ITALIAN | Located above the boat yard at the far end of the lungomare, this eatery's second floor dining room offers a unique perspective on Aci Trezza. Light permeates the room thanks to the open balcony at the front of the building, which gives an alfresco feel even though you're indoors (a nice compromise in the heat of August). **Known for:** bird's eye views; grilled seafood and pizza at night; upstairs dining room that removes you from the chaos of the lungomare. [$] *Average main: €20* ✉ *Via Provinciale 212, Aci Trezza* ☎ *380/7044749* 🌐 *www.facebook.com/arcobalenoristoacitrezza* 🕒 *Closed Wed.*

Osteria dei Marinai da Graziano

$$ | SEAFOOD | Restaurants line the Aci Trezza seafront, and you honestly can't do wrong with any of them, but Graziano's osteria is especially known for its excellent selection of fresh seafood. The pastas are quite good, as are the whole fish preparations (you can see the available catch on ice in the corner of the dining room), but the stand-out here is the mixed antipasti selections of both raw and cooked seafood. **Known for:** great people-watching; huge seafood crudo; outside terrace with view of the port. [$] *Average main: €22* ✉ *Via Lungomare Dei Ciclopi 185, Aci Trezza* ☎ *095/277921.*

☕ Coffee and Quick Bites

Anchovy Fish Bar

$ | SEAFOOD | For a quick lunch, stop by this eatery right off the port. They specialize in sandwiches, fish burgers, and five different options for fritto misto. **Known for:** fried seafood; quick sandwiches; swordfish arancini. [$] *Average main: €11* ✉ *Via Provvidenza, Aci Trezza* ☎ *095/7116047* 🕒 *Closed Mon.*

★ **Gran Cafè Solaire**

$ | CAFÉ | Even on rainy days (which admittedly there aren't many of), the sun seems to shine bright here. They serve arguably the best granita in the Catania area; the pistachio is so creamy you'll swear they added dairy. **Known for:** sublime granita; relatively fast service; shaded location off the port. [$] *Average main: €5* ✉ *Via Provinciale 81, Aci Trezza* ☎ *345/1656822.*

Sicilia's Cafe de Mar

$ | SICILIAN | Here it's all about the views. Though Etna keeps the eastern side of Sicily from having truly excellent sunsets, this southern point of Aci Trezza manages to have a pretty remarkable vista for the sun's farewell, with the Norman castle of Aci Castello visible across the Ionian inlet. **Known for:** perfect aperitivo; incredible views; good selection of wines by the glass. [$] *Average main: €9* ✉ *Via Lungomare Dei Ciclopi 119, Aci Trezza* ☎ *095/276129* 🌐 *www.siciliascafedemar.it.*

🍸 Nightlife

Jenco Cocktail Bar

BARS | Open only during the summer, this cocktail bar sits on a small wooden deck bedecked with fairy lights, overlooking the sea. At dusk, it's magical. And once night falls, in the distance to the south, you can make out the outline of the faraglioni by moonlight. They make especially good Negronis and different variations of gin-and-tonics. ✉ *Via Lachea 21, Aci Trezza* ☎ *No phone.*

In Acireale, the Belvedere di Santa Caterina gives beautiful views of the surrounding area.

Activities

Altamarea

BOATING | Throughout the summer you'll see boats of every shape and size moored all along this area of the coast, with a veritable maritime parking lot of buoys. To get on the water yourself, rent a *gommone*, a sort of reinforced inflatable motorboat from the folks at Altamarea. In Italy, you don't need a boating license for any vessels 40 horsepower and below. Cruise around the back of the Cyclops Islands, up to Santa Tecla, or even down to the Catania port, all with unparalleled views of Etna looming large over the shoreline. ✉ *Marina dei Ciclopi, Aci Trezza* ✛ *Look for the Honda Motors sign* ☎ *349/8746317* ⊕ *www.altamareanoleggio.it* 🖃 *From €100 for ½-day* ⊘ *Closed mid-Oct.–mid-May.*

Acireale

6 km (4 miles) north of Aci Trezza, 16 km (10 miles) north of Catania.

Acireale sits amid a clutter of rocky pinnacles and lush lemon groves. The craggy coast is known as the Riviera dei Ciclopi, after the legend narrated in *The Odyssey* in which the blinded Cyclops, Polyphemus, hurled boulders at the retreating Ulysses, thus creating spires of rock, or *faraglioni* (pillars of rock rising dramatically out of the sea). Tourism has barely taken off here, so it's a good destination if you feel like putting some distance between yourself and the busloads of tourists in Taormina, or if seeking an easy day trip from Catania. And though the beaches are rocky, there's good swimming here, too.

GETTING HERE AND AROUND

Buses arrive frequently from Taormina and Catania. Acireale is on the main coastal train route, though the station is a long walk south of the center. Local buses pass every 20 minutes or so.

VISITOR INFORMATION

CONTACT Acireale Tourism Office. ✉ *Via Oreste Scionti 15, Acireale* ☎ *095/891999, 095/895249.*

Sights

Belvedere di Santa Caterina
VIEWPOINT | Lord Byron (1788–1824) visited the Belvedere di Santa Caterina to look out over the Ionian Sea during his Italian wanderings. Today, the viewing point is south of the old town, near the Terme di Acireale, off SS114, and is a tranquil spot for photos or quiet reflection on one of the several benches positioned toward the water. ✉ *Off SS114, Acireale.*

Duomo
CHURCH | With its cupola and twin turrets, Acireale's Duomo is an extravagant Baroque construction dating from the 17th century. In the chapel to the right of the altar, look for the 17th-century silver statue of Santa Venera (patron saint of Acireale) by Mario D'Angelo, and the early-18th-century frescoes by Antonio Filocamo. ✉ *Piazza del Duomo, Acireale* ☎ *095/601102* 🌐 *www.diocesiacireale.it.*

Santa Maria La Scala
TOWN | A half-hour walk (or a very twisty drive) from Acireale's center, this picturesque harbor, with lava stone steps leading to the water, is filled with fishermen unloading brightly colored boats. Inexpensive lunches are served in the many restaurants along the harbor; your fresh fish dish is priced by weight. ✉ *Santa Maria La Scala, Acireale.*

Restaurants

★ **Frumento**
$ | PIZZA | FAMILY | Pizza is something Sicilians eat at least weekly, and Frumento has been the area standard-bearer of excellence since it opened in 2015. Choose from five different dough options (from a classic Neapolitan-style to rye to ancient Sicilian grains) as your base, and then pick one of the 65 different topping combos. **Known for:** locally made products for sale in the restaurant; good natural wine selection; excellent antipasti such as arancini and fried stuffed squash blossoms. [$] *Average main: €12* ✉ *Piazza Giuseppe Mazzini, Acireale* ☎ *095/601496* 🌐 *www.frumentoacireale.it.*

★ **In Un Angolo Di Mondo**
$$ | PIZZA | Walking through the gate of this little spot feels like entering a pizza speakeasy—it's located at the end of a cul-de-sac in the garden and ground floor of the owners' home (the name means "in a corner of the world"), and you'd be forgiven for thinking you've gotten the directions wrong. They use a slow, cold fermentation process to create crusts with deep flavors that they ply to turn out calzones and about 15 different pizzas each night. **Known for:** natural wines; excellent calzones; vegetarian and vegan pizza topping options. [$] *Average main: €15* ✉ *Via Nazionale per Catania 180, Acireale* ☎ *095/877724* ⏲ *Closed Mon.–Wed.*

★ **La Grotta**
$$$ | SEAFOOD | With its dining room set in a cave above the harbor of Santa Maria La Scala, this rustic trattoria specializes in seafood. Try the *insalata di mare* (a selection of delicately boiled fish served with lemon and olive oil), pasta with clams or cuttlefish ink, or fish grilled over charcoal. **Known for:** unique cave setting; superfresh seafood; the catch of the day. [$] *Average main: €26* ✉ *Via Scalo Grande 46, Acireale* ☎ *095/7648153* 🌐 *www.*

ristorantelagrotta.info ⏲ *Closed Tues. and late Oct.*

Trattoria U Puttusu

$$ | SICILIAN | Specializing in regional Sicilian cooking, this intimate little trattoria focuses on meat with a wide selection of certified Angus, Sicilian beef, donkey steaks, sausages, and rolls of involtini. You can shop the meat locker to choose your cut. **Known for:** high-quality beef; down-home atmosphere; Slow Food principles. [$] *Average main: €18* ✉ *Via Vittorio Emanuele II 175, Acireale* ☎ *388/6911548* 🌐 *www.uputtusu.com* ⏲ *Closed Wed.*

Coffee and Quick Bites

Gran Caffè Eldorado

$ | CAFÉ | The delicious ice creams and *granita di mandorla* (almond granita) at Eldorado are a must-visit when in Acireale. Just steps from the cathedral, it makes for a nice *pausa caffè* during a day of sightseeing. **Known for:** friendly staff; wonderful desserts; great ice creams. [$] *Average main: €3* ✉ *Corso Umberto 3, Acireale* ☎ *347/9717926* 🌐 *www.grancaffeeldorado.it.*

Il Rosticcere

$ | SICILIAN | Fast food has a different meaning in Sicily: in every town you'll see bars and cafés offering a selection of ready-to-eat savory pastries filled with meats and cheeses, small pizzettes, arancini, and quiches. In Acireale, *the* place to go is Il Rosticcere, where chef Puccio has some 30 years experience creating the exemplar of the genre. **Known for:** wide selection of craft beer; everything available for take-away; interesting flavor combos, such as curry chicken or brie with walnuts and honey. [$] *Average main: €5* ✉ *Corso Savoia 4, Acireale* ☎ *347/4503979* 🌐 *www.facebook.com/ilrosticcereacireale* ⏲ *Closed Tues.*

Nightlife

Moro

BARS | Throughout this bar, located in a former bank, you'll find ceramic heads (all for sale) by Catania artist Stefania Boemi. Legend has it that a Sicilian noblewoman discovered her beloved, a visiting Moor, was already married in his homeland. In a fit of rage, she cut off his head and left it on her balcony for all to see. The next morning a basil plant was sprouting from the head. And thus was born the tale of the *teste di Moro* (Moor heads). Outside, tables sit in the shadow of the Duomo where locals stop for excellent cocktails during their evening *passeggiata.* ✉ *Piazza Duomo 18, Acireale* ☎ *333/3463500* 🌐 *www.moroacireale.it.*

Performing Arts

Teatro dell'Opera dei Pupi

PUPPET SHOWS | FAMILY | Although it has died out in most other parts of the island, the puppet-theater tradition carries on in Acireale with a small but informative free exhibit at the Museo Opera dei Pupi, which recounts the history of the art and displays the puppets once used in widely beloved local performances. ✉ *Via Nazionale per Catania 195, Acireale* ☎ *095/7648035* 🌐 *www.operadeipupi.com* 🎫 *€10 for guided tours, €15 for shows.*

Mount Etna

30 km (19 miles) northwest of Acireale, 35 km (22 miles) north of Catania, 64 km (40 miles) southwest of Taormina.

The first time you see Mt. Etna, whether it's trailing clouds of smoke or emitting fiery streaks of lava, is certain to be unforgettable. The best-known symbol of Sicily and one of the world's major active volcanoes, Etna is the largest and highest volcano in Europe—the cone of the crater rises 11,014 feet above sea level. Etna is so important to locals that she's often affectionately called Mamma Etna. Although you'll get wonderful vantage points of Etna from Taormina, Castelmola, and Catania in particular, it also makes a rewarding day or overnight trip to see the mountain up close, with a hike or climb; you can find routes suitable for every fitness level. It's also become a popular destination for wine lovers thanks to the many boutique wineries on its slopes; most accept visitors with an appointment.

GETTING HERE AND AROUND
Reaching the lower slopes of Mt. Etna is easy, either by car or by bus from Catania. Getting to the more interesting, higher levels requires taking one of the stout four-wheel-drive minibuses that leave from Piano Provenzana on the north side and from Rifugio Sapienza on the south side. A cable car, called the Funivia dell'Etna, from Rifugio Sapienza takes you part of the way.

CABLE CAR Funivia dell'Etna. ⊠ *Rifugio Sapienza* ☎ *095/914141, 095/914142* ⊕ *www.funiviaetna.com.*

TOURS
Club Alpino Italiano
ADVENTURE TOURS | This is a great resource to discover Mt. Etna climbing and hiking guides for those who have some experience and don't want a lot of hand-holding. ⊠ *Via Messina 593/a, Catania* ☎ *340/2326542* ⊕ *www.caicatania.it.*

Etna Wine School
FOOD AND DRINK TOURS | For a comprehensive overview of the wine world on Mt. Etna, look to Benjamin North Spencer, an American-born wine expert, Etna resident, and author of *The New Wines of Mount Etna*. He and his team offer half-day and full-day courses suitable for professionals and casual enthusiasts alike. You'll visit a vineyard, taste wines based on Carricante and Nerello Mascalese grapes, eat local delicacies, and learn about Etna wine-making traditions

at the source. ☎ *347/3348782* ⊕ *www.etnawineschool.com* ⊠ *½-day tours €140 per person.*

★ Etna Experience
ADVENTURE TOURS | Your answer to all things outdoors in the area, Etna Experience offers sailing tours between Catania and Aci Trezza, full-day hikes to volcanic caves and the Alcantara gorges, half-day sunset hikes, and the signature Mount Etna Summit tour, which includes high-level trekking up to 10,800 feet to get you as close to the crater as humanly possible. ☎ *349/3053021* ⊕ *www.etnaexperience.com* ⊠ *From €44 per person.*

Gruppo Guide Etna Nord
ADVENTURE TOURS | This group offers more personalized (and more expensive) services than others, including excursions well suited to novice climbers. Be sure to reserve ahead of time. ⊠ *Piazza Attilio Castrogiovanni 19, Linguaglossa* ☎ *095/7774502, 348/0125167* ⊕ *www.guidetnanord.com.*

VISITOR INFORMATION
CONTACT Nicolosi Tourism Office. (*Porta dell'Etna*) ⊠ *Piazza Vittorio Emanuele,* ☎ *095/914488* ⊕ *www.nicolosietna.it.*

 ## Sights

Azienda Agricola Musa
FARM/RANCH | FAMILY | On the western side of Etna, just above the town of Bronte, Musa offers immersion into all things pistachio at their *agriturismo*. The property, with its stunning views of the volcano, is home to horses, donkeys, goats, fruit trees, and, of course, pistachio trees. You can wander the grounds (where they occasionally host small concerts) and see pistachios fruiting on the trees; the harvest happens in the early fall, every other year. On Sunday, Musa offers a set menu lunch (€30 per person; cash only) at a long wooden table under shady trees. Pistachios figure prominently on the ever-changing menu: think pistachio and artichoke lasagna; penne with pistachio

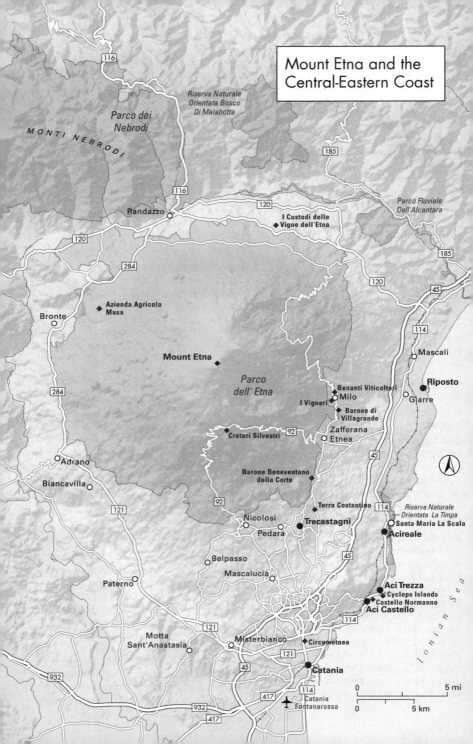

Mount Etna's Villages

The villages that surround Mount Etna make good bases for visiting nearby cities like Catania, Acireale, and Taormina. **Zafferana Etnea** is famous for orange-blossom honey and *pizza siciliana*; **Nicolosi**, at nearly 3,000 feet, is known as La Porta dell'Etna (The Door to Etna); the medieval village of **Milo** is known as the City of Wine; **Trecastagni** (The Three Chestnut Trees) has beautiful Renaissance churches; **Randazzo**, the largest of the surrounding towns, is the site of a popular wood, textile, and metalwork market; and **Bronte** is Italy's center of pistachio cultivation.

pesto, ricotta, and a veritable mountain of ground pistachios; braised pork with pistachios and porcini; pistachio cannoli; and so on. It is possible to arrange a visit to the full pistachio orchard, though it helps if you speak Italian. ⊠ *Azienda Agricola Musa, Bronte* ☎ *388/4753877 Rossella, 348/2515110 Carmelo* ⊕ *www.progetto-musa.com* ⊠ *Tour, lunch, and pistachio tasting €40* ⊗ *Closed Oct.–Apr.*

Barone Beneventano della Corte

WINERY | Located between Monte Gorna and Monte Ilice, Pierluca Beneventano guides visitors up the steep slopes of his vineyard for a tasting (featuring red, white, and rosé) among the vines. From there, you can see the other ancient craters of the southeast and all the way down to the Ionian sea. In addition to traditional Etna grapes, Pierluca is working to recultivate grape relics, varieties that were historically found on Etna, such as Moscatella dell'Etna, Muscatetuni, and Terribbile. Young and endlessly energetic, he's embracing the winemaking traditions of the volcano while forging his own path. Keep an eye on his Nubivago wine, a white made with Carricante, Catarratto, and Moscatella dell'Etna in which he freezes the grapes before pressing them. ⊠ *Via Salto del Corvo 62, Zafferana Etnea* ☎ *No phone* ⊕ *www.baronebeneventano.com* ⊠ *Free.*

★ Barone di Villagrande

WINERY | At the oldest winery on Etna, the expansive terrace shaded by oak trees looks out over vineyards and down to the sea. The staff offers friendly and informative tours (with excellent English) followed by a tasting of five wines with food pairings or a more formal lunch. Reservations are required. There are also four charming guest rooms overlooking the vineyards for overnight stays. ⊠ *Via del Bosco 25, Milo* ☎ *095/7082175* ⊕ *www.villagrande.it* ⊠ *€25 tour and tasting.*

★ Benanti Viticoltori

WINERY | At the foot of Monte Serra in Viagrande, this family-run winery is one of the most internationally significant on Etna, distributing some 170,000 bottles worldwide. And the Benanti family has been instrumental in propagating the viticulture of the volcano. As you arrive at the 19th-century estate for a tasting, you'll easily be seduced by the historic grounds and hills flanked with vines. But their wines, approximately 15 different expressions of Etna, hold the real magic. ⊠ *Via Giuseppe Garibaldi 361, Viagrande* ☎ *095/7890928* ⊕ *www.benanti.it* ⊠ *Tours and tastings from €60.*

Circumetnea

TRAIN/TRAIN STATION | Instead of climbing up Mt. Etna, you can circle it on this private railroad, which runs between Catania and Riposto, with a change at

Did You Know?

Mount Etna is not only the largest active volcano in Italy (clocking in at two-and-half times the height of Mount Vesuvius), but it's also the largest volcano in mainland Europe.

Randazzo. By following the base of the volcano, the Circumetnea stretches out a 31-km (19-mile) journey along the coastal road to 114 km (71 miles). The line was first constructed between 1889 and 1895 and remains small, slow, and single track, but it has some dramatic vistas of the volcano and goes through lava fields. The one-way trip takes about 3½ hours, with departures every 90 minutes or so. After you've made the trip, you can get back to where you started from on the much quicker, but less scenic, conventional rail service between Riposto and Catania. ⊠ *Via Caronda 352, Catania* ☎ *095/541111* ⊕ *www.circumetnea.it* 🎫 *€8 one-way* ☉ *Closed Sun.*

★ Crateri Silvestri

NATURE SIGHT | For a walk on the moonlike surface of Etna, visit the Silvestri craters on the southern side of the volcano, near Nicolosi. Located at an altitude of roughly 6,200 feet, these five extinct craters formed during the 1892 eruption. Just a few meters away, across from Rifugio Sapienza, you'll find the Funivia dell'Etna (€30 round-trip), a cable car that carries you 8,000 feet up to Monte Montagnola, where you can hike further with a guide or go skiing in winter. ⊠ *Crateri Silvestri, Nicolosi.*

I Custodi delle Vigne dell'Etna

WINERY | The name translates literally as "the custodians of the vineyards of Etna," and Mario Paoluzi and his team take their roles as guardians quite seriously. From the low-intervention management of one of the oldest producing vineyards on Etna to the use of the *alberello* trellis system, this winery specializes in producing elegant expressions of Etna wines that pay homage to the history and culture of the area. ⊠ *I Custodi, Contrada Moganazzi, Solicchiata* ☎ *393/1898430* ⊕ *www.icustodi.it* 🎫 *Tours and tastings from €40.*

I Vigneri

WINERY | Salvo Foti, the patriarch of this family-run winery, has been called the most important Sicilian agronomist and winemaker. In fact, his work cultivating native grapes is part of the reason Americans have even heard of Nerello Mascalese or Carricante. His conscientious methods, which honor both the land and cultural traditions of Etna, have been passed on to his two sons (Simone and Andrea) who now manage the winery and lead tastings in the historic Palmento Caselle (c. 1840). In the fall, they still use the palmento to stomp grapes and press wine the way it was done centuries ago on Etna. ⊠ *Via Abate 3, Milo* ☎ *333/4526403* ⊕ *www.ivigneri.it* 🎫 *Tours and tastings €15.*

★ Mt. Etna

VOLCANO | Affectionately called Idda (or "she" in Sicilian dialect), Etna is basically always active, and occasionally there are airspace closures due to the spewing ash. But for the locals who live in her shadow, Etna is not some ever-present doomsday reminder. She's a living part of the dynamic landscape, loved and revered.

In 387 BC, Plato sailed in just to catch a glimpse of it; in the 9th century AD, the first granita of all time was shaved off its snowy slopes; in 1669, it erupted continuously for four months and lava flows reached Catania; and in the 21st century, the volcano still grabs headlines on an annual basis. Significantly notable eruptions have occurred in the modern era, such as in 1971 (when lava buried the Etna Observatory), in 1981 (when the village of Randazzo narrowly missed destruction), in 2001 (when there was a large flank eruption), in 2002 (when a column of ash spewed that could be seen from space), and in 2008 (when the eruption lasted 417 days and triggered some 200 earthquakes). In February and March 2021, she erupted 11 times in a matter of three weeks, scattering windblown ash throughout the towns below, including Catania. Traveling to the proximity of the crater depends on Mt. Etna's temperament, but you can walk up and down the enormous lava dunes and wander over its moonlike surface of dead craters. The rings of vegetation change markedly as you rise, with vineyards and pine trees gradually giving way to growths of broom and lichen. ✉ *Parco dell'Etna* ☎ *095/821111* 🌐 *www.parcoetna.it.*

Terra Costantino

WINERY | This winery, in the shadow of San Nicolò, takes a decidedly biological approach to grape growing. Olive and fruit trees (kiwi, lemon, and orange) abound, and they alternate row crops between the vines to enrich the soil. Inside the winery and tasting room, you can see the stratification of Etna's lava, with flows from 50,000 years ago and 3,000 years ago, and where plant roots continue growing down into the stone. In the old palmento, you can book a private winemaking experience with barefoot grape stomping and all. ✉ *Via Giuseppe Garibaldi 417, Viagrande* ☎ *334/8946713* 🌐 *www.terracostantino.it* 🎟 *Tours and tasting €30* ⏲ *Closed weekends* ✍ *Reservations recommended.*

🍴 Restaurants

★ Cave Ox

$ | **ITALIAN** | This casual osteria is frequented by local winemakers who come for pizza dinners and rustic daily lunch specials, but most visitors are smitten with the small but amazing cellar focused on Etna natural wines. Everything's fresh, simple, and delicious—and made to pair with one of the delightful wines suggested by owner and wine enthusiast Sandro. **Known for:** local winemaker crowd; filling lunches and pizza dinners; superlative selection of natural wines from Etna. [$] *Average main: €12* ✉ *Via Nazionale Solicchiata 159* ☎ *0942/986171* 🌐 *www.caveox.it* ⏲ *Closed Tues.*

★ Gran Caffè Urna dal 1885

$ | **PIZZA** | What Americans know as Sicilian pizza quite frankly doesn't exist in Sicily, but at this historic café and pizzeria that's been around since the 1800s, you'll find the real *pizza siciliana.* Though you can find the dish throughout the area, especially in Viagrande and Zaefferana, Urna is said to be its inventor: they stuff tender calzone pastry with Tuma cheese, anchovies, and black peppercorns, and then deep fry the half-moon delicacy. **Known for:** casual, historic ambience; spacious outside courtyard; authentic pizza siciliana. [$] *Average main: €8* ✉ *Piazza Urna 36, Viagrande* ☎ *095/7894579* 🌐 *www.grancaffeurna.it.*

★ In Cucina Dai Pennisi

$$ | **STEAKHOUSE** | In the back of a butcher shop that's been operating since 1968, the Pennisi family opened this meat-focused 30-seat restaurant in December 2017. In the front, you'll find cases full of dry-aged beef; house-made sausages, guanciale, lardo, pancetta, and headcheese; whole chickens; beef liver and veal tongue; and skewers of hand-rolled *involtini.* **Known for:** salsiccia a ceppo, a hand-chopped pork sausage; excellent beef tartare; robust Etna wine selection. [$] *Average main: €16* ✉ *Via Umberto I 11, Linguaglossa* ☎ *095/643160* 🌐 *www.daipennisi.it* ⏲ *Closed Mon.*

La Tana Del Lupo

$$ | **STEAKHOUSE** | For really big plates of meat and a wine cellar full of red wine, head to this little "wolf's lair" that looks exactly how you want a Sicilian steakhouse to look (stone walls, exposed wooden rafters, and arched alcoves packed with wine). The portions are ample, so it's best to go with a group and share. **Known for:** wild boar ragù; bone-in costata steaks; after-dinner fruit service. [$] *Average main: €19* ✉ *Corso Ara di Giove 138, Pedara* ☎ *095/7800303* 🌐 *www.ristorantelatanadelupo.it* ⏲ *Closed Tues.*

★ Quattro Archi di Grasso Rosario

$$ | SICILIAN | Inside this rustic osteria, where there's not an inch of wall space spared from decor, the larger-than-life Grasso Rosario holds court as he bounces from table to table offering opinions and insight on his Slow Food–focused menu. Drawing upon the abundance of the region, the menu highlights the black hog from the Nebrodi mountains, a local cultivar of kohlrabi (in arancini and as a pasta), porcini mushrooms, and perfectly grilled and roasted meats (think pork knuckle, ribs, veal, and lamb). **Known for:** kohlrabi arancini with Ragusano cheese; wood-oven pizzas at dinner; bustling atmosphere. $ *Average main: €18* ⊠ *Via Francesco Crispi 9, Milo* ☎ *095/955566* ⊕ *www.4archi.it* ⊗ *Closed Wed. No lunch weekdays.*

★ Shalai

$$ | MODERN ITALIAN | You might not expect to find a thoroughly contemporary restaurant on the slopes of Mt. Etna, but Shalai, in the boutique hotel of the same name, is truly a modern oasis, where young chef Giovanni Santoro prepares updated and beautifully presented versions of Sicilian classics. For the full Michelin-starred experience, choose from the six-course meat or fish tasting menus; to finish, the deconstructed cannoli are a true delight. **Known for:** excellent wine list; delicious tasting menus; innovative modern Sicilian dishes. $ *Average main: €24* ⊠ *Via Marconi 25, Linguaglossa* ☎ *095/643128* ⊕ *www.shalai.it* ⊗ *No lunch weekdays.*

Terra Mia Ristorante di Campagna

$ | ITALIAN | You come upon this rustic little restaurant by navigating the small country roads between vineyards, and don't be surprised if you whip past it and have to turn around. The restaurant is divided into an interior dining room and an outside covered patio, and they're known for taking inspiration from the seasonal bounty of Etna. **Known for:** local gem in the heart of wine country; lunches that encourage lingering; expert use of seasonal produce. $ *Average main: €14* ⊠ *Terra Mia Ristorante di Campagna, SP64, Solicchiata* ☎ *393/9069704* ⊕ *terra-mia-ristorante-di-campagna.business.site* ⊗ *Closed Mon.*

☕ Coffee and Quick Bites

Caffetteria Luca

$ | DESSERTS | Bronte is the land of pistachio, and the best place to get your fix is here at Luca. You'll find perfect pistachio gelato (notably more gray than green, which means it's made with real pistachios) and every type of pastry that's possible to top with crushed pistachios or fill with pistachio cream (imagine Nutella, but made of pistachios). **Known for:** tasty cannoli; great gelato; pistachio in every form. $ *Average main: €3* ⊠ *Via Messina 273* ☎ *095/7724188* ⊕ *www.caffetterialuca.com.*

★ Pasticceria Santo Musumeci

$ | DESSERTS | In the picture-perfect medieval town of Randazzo, high on the northern side of Etna, this generations-old bakery sits at the foot of the basilica in Piazza Santa Maria. Now run by Giovanna, the daughter of Santo, the pasticceria is especially known for its exceptional gelato and granita, which are made with all natural products, with no artificial bases, colors, or flavorings. **Known for:** fried rice crispelle; seasonally driven granitas; torrone. $ *Average main: €3* ⊠ *Piazza Santa Maria 5, Randazzo* ☎ *095/921196* ⊕ *www.santomusumeci.it* ⊗ *Closed Tues.*

Putia Lab

$ | SICILIAN | In Sicily, *tavola calda* is its own food group. From arancini to filled savory pastries, this "fast food" option is the heart and soul of the Sicilian aperitivo experience (or lunch on the fly), and in Milo, your go-to is Putia Lab. **Known for:** panettone at Christmas and colombe at Easter; pizzette; show-stopping cakes.

Several charming villages, including Nicolosi, surround Mount Etna and make good bases for exploring the volcano.

[$] Average main: €5 ✉ Via Etnea 5, Milo ☎ 327/0551869 ⏲ Closed Tues.

Hotels

Hotel Villa Neri Resort & Spa
$$$ | **RESORT** | This resort on the edge of the Parco dell'Etna combines elegantly appointed guest rooms, a stunning pool, a full-service spa and wellness center, and a fine-dining restaurant to create an immersive Etna experience. **Pros:** can arrange excursions to Mount Etna; excellent service; focus on sustainability. **Cons:** slow Wi-Fi; pool can sometimes be busy; limited casual dining options. *[$] Rooms from: €300 ✉ Contrada Arrigo, Linguaglossa ☎ 095/8133002 🌐 www.nerietna.com 🛏 24 rooms 🍴 Free Breakfast.*

★ Monaci delle Terre Nere
$$$$ | **HOTEL** | This cozy boutique hotel in the foothills of Mt. Etna features spacious rustic-chic rooms on a working organic farm with vineyards, along with an elegant Slow Food–inspired restaurant. **Pros:** eco-conscious atmosphere and policies; pool with countryside views; delicious food and wine. **Cons:** bathrooms can be quite minimalist; no televisions in bedrooms; accommodations may be a little quirky for some. *[$] Rooms from: €370 ✉ Via Monaci, Zafferana Etnea ☎ 095/7083638 🌐 www.monacidelleterrenere.it ⏲ Closed Jan.–mid-Mar. 🛏 27 rooms 🍴 Free Breakfast.*

★ Shalai
$$ | **HOTEL** | In the small charming town of Linguaglossa, this boutique property located in a former palazzo offers a very tranquil retreat, with rooms awash in white and lots of natural light. **Pros:** great home base for exploring the north side of Etna; on-site spa; Michelin-starred restaurant on-site. **Cons:** no bathtubs; very simple design for a luxury hotel; very small bar. *[$] Rooms from: €136 ✉ Via Guglielmo Marconi 25, Linguaglossa ☎ 095/643128 🌐 www.shalai.it 🛏 13 rooms 🍴 Free Breakfast.*

Riposto

32 km (20 miles) east of Mount Etna, 31 km (19 miles) north of Catania.

This seaside village is said to be named for the primary business that used to dominate its shores: a depository for barrels and goods before they are shipped across the sea (*riporre* means "to store"). Through the years the port town has attracted boat builders, fishermen, recreational sailors, seafood lovers, and sunbathers who line its pebble beach. To this day the sea remains the heart of Riposto.

GETTING HERE AND AROUND

Trains arrive from Catania (*30 minutes; €3.40 one-way;* 🌐 *www.lefrecce.it*) regularly at the Giarre-Riposto station, which is about a 30-minute walk from the Porto Turistico.

👁 Sights

Riposto Fish Market

MARKET | Just across the road from the Porto Turistico, area fishermen set up stalls inside the commercial plaza every morning (even Sunday). Though it's much smaller and less chaotic than the Catania fish market, the quality of seafood is excellent, and you'll see prime examples of everything that swims or crawls in these local waters. And it has a very locals' market feel to it, with people buying fresh fish each morning for their daily meal prep (it's open until about noon); even Catanesi will make the 40-minute drive to buy fish or frutti di mare from these vendors. ✉ *Piazza del Commercio 26, Riposto.*

🍴 Restaurants

★ Zash Ristorante

$$$$ | **MODERN ITALIAN** | Though this Michelin-starred restaurant is part of the Zash Country Boutique Hotel, it's worth a visit all on its own. Chef Giuseppe Raciti highlights the traditions and flavors of the area with a repertoire of elegant riffs that delight and surprise without overwhelming you with gimmicks. **Known for:** thoughtful tasting menus; "street food" antipasti, including a mortadella mousse canolo; incredible wine list (including wines from the owner's vineyards). [$] *Average main: €35* ✉ *Strada Provinciale 2/I-II 60, Riposto* ☎ *095/7828932* 🌐 *www.zash.it* 🕒 *Closed Tues.*

🛏 Hotels

★ Zash Country Boutique Hotel

$$$ | **RESORT** | Breathe in the scent of orange blossoms as you arrive at this modern boutique hotel set among 32 acres of gardens and citrus orchards just five minutes from the sea by car. **Pros:** outdoor pool with views of Mount Etna; Michelin-starred restaurant and top wine program; full service spa with a lava stone pool, hammam, and sauna. **Cons:** only a few rooms so books up fast; best if you have a car; no casual dining options on-site. [$] *Rooms from: €282* ✉ *Strada Provinciale 2/I-II 60, Riposto* ☎ *095/7828932* 🌐 *www.zash.it* 🕒 *Closed Jan. and Feb.* 🛏 *17 rooms* 🍽 *Free Breakfast.*

🏃 Activities

★ Mario Casu Cooking School

FOOD AND DRINK TOURS | In eastern Sicily, there's no better person to teach you how to cook Sicilian classics than chef Mario Casu. Born locally, he cooked in the U.K. for many years (his English is excellent) before returning home to open his own namesake restaurant, Casu Osteria Contemporanea. On Monday through Thursday, he opens his kitchen to guests (reservations required) to teach how to make dishes such as caponata, eggplant parmigiana, swordfish involtini, pasta alle sarde, and cannoli. You'll start your class with a morning visit to the Riposto fish market, just down the

Taormina's Villa Comunale is one of Sicily's most beautiful public gardens.

street; the day's finds inform the menu. Chef Casu can customize the class to be as hands-on as you like. During the prep work you'll snack on aperitivi and then afterward sit down to a lavish lunch (with wine) of all the things prepared during class. ⊠ *Corso Italia 294, Riposto* 🕾 *380/8622848* ⊕ *www.mariocasu.it* ⧆ *From €70 per person.*

Taormina

35 km (22 miles) north of Riposto, 54 km (34 miles) northeast of Catania.

The view of the sea and Mt. Etna from Taormina's jagged, cactus-covered cliffs is as close to perfection as a panorama can get—especially on clear days, when the snowcapped volcano's white puffs of smoke rise against the blue sky. Even when overrun with tourists, its natural beauty is hard to dispute. Writers have extolled Taormina's charms almost since it was founded in the 6th century BC by Greeks from nearby Naxos; Goethe

and D.H. Lawrence were among its well-known enthusiasts. The town's boutique-lined main streets get old pretty quickly, but the many hiking paths that wind through the beautiful hills surrounding Taormina promise a timeless alternative. A trip up to stunning Castelmola (whether on foot or by car) should also be on your itinerary. It should be noted that in general, Taormina becomes a ghost town in January and February, with almost every hotel and restaurant closed.

GETTING HERE AND AROUND

Buses from Messina or Catania arrive near the center of Taormina, while trains from these towns pull in at the station at the bottom of the hill. Local buses bring you the rest of the way. A cable car takes passengers up the hill from a parking lot about 2 km (1 mile) north of the train station.

VISITOR INFORMATION
CONTACT Taormina Tourism Office.
⊠ *Piazza Santa Caterina,* 🕾 *0942/23243* ⊕ *www.comune.taormina.me.it.*

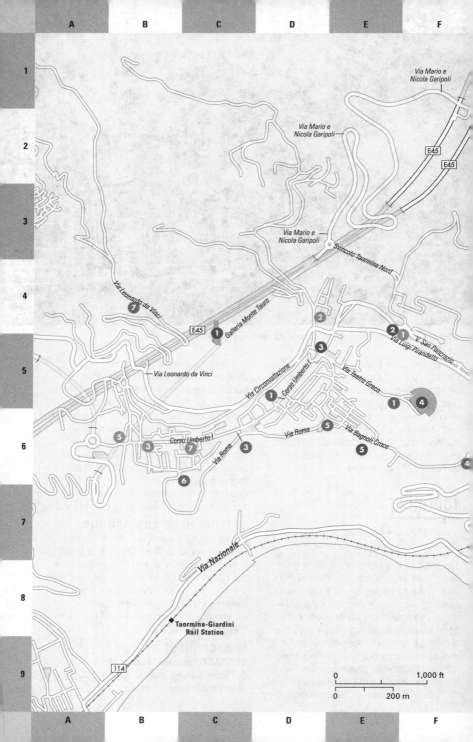

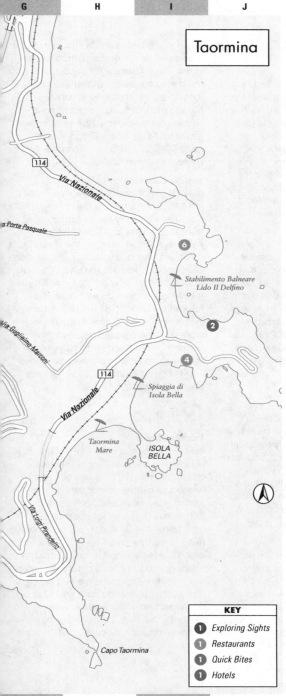

Taormina

Sights ▼

1. Castello Saraceno...................C5
2. Funivia E5
3. Palazzo Corvaja....................D5
4. Teatro Greco F5
5. Villa Comunale E6

Restaurants ▼

1. Bella Blu............................F5
2. L'Arco dei Cappuccini.............D4
3. Osteria RossoDiVino B6
4. Pizzichella I5
5. Ristorante Cuti Lu Dissi B6
6. Trattoria Il Barcaiolo I4
7. Trattoria Tischi Toschi.............C6

Quick Bites ▼

1. Pasticceria Etna D5

Hotels ▼

1. Belmond Grand Hotel Timeo E5
2. Belmond Villa Sant'Andrea........J5
3. Hotel Metropole Taormina.........C6
4. Hotel Villa Carlotta.................F6
5. Hotel Villa Paradiso................D6
6. San Domenico Palace,
   A Four Seasons Hotel C6
7. Villa Ducale.........................B4

6

Mount Etna and Eastern Sicily TAORMINA

KEY

- ① Exploring Sights
- ① Restaurants
- ① Quick Bites
- ① Hotels

Sights

Castello Saraceno

VIEWPOINT | An unrelenting 20-minute walk up the Via Crucis footpath takes you to the church of the Madonna della Rocca, hollowed out of the limestone rock. Above it towers the 1,000-year-old stone walls of Castello Saraceno, which is built on the site of earlier Greek and Roman fortifications. Although the gate to the castle has been locked for decades, it's worth the climb just for the panoramic views. ⊠ *Monte Tauro, Taormina.*

Funivia

OTHER ATTRACTION | Taormina Mare and the Bay of Mazzarò are accessible by a funivia, or suspended cable car, that glides past incredible views on its way down to the beach at Mazzarò. It departs every 15 minutes, until 8 pm. In June, July, and August, the normal hours are extended until 1 am. ⊠ *Via L. Pirandello, downhill from town center toward bus station, Taormina* ☎ *0942/23906* ⊕ *www. taorminaservizipubblici.it* 🎫 *€3 one-way, €10 day ticket.*

Palazzo Corvaja

NOTABLE BUILDING | Many of Taormina's 14th- and 15th-century palaces have been carefully preserved. Especially beautiful is the Palazzo Corvaja, with characteristic black-lava and white-limestone inlays. Today it houses the tourist office and a museum dedicated to Sicilian art and traditions. ⊠ *Largo Santa Caterina, Taormina* ☎ *0942/620198.*

★ Teatro Greco

RUINS | The Greeks put a premium on finding impressive locations to stage their dramas, such as Taormina's hillside Teatro Greco. Beyond the columns, you can see the town's rooftops spilling down the hillside, the arc of the coastline, and Mt. Etna in the distance. The theater was built during the 3rd century BC and rebuilt by the Romans during the 2nd century AD. Its acoustics are exceptional: even today a stage whisper can be heard in the last rows. In summer, many music and dance performances are held in the Teatro Greco after sunset, when the marvelous vistas of the sparkling Ionian Sea are shrouded in darkness, but the glow of Sicily's most famous volcano can sometimes be seen in the distance. ⊠ *Via Teatro Greco, Taormina* ☎ *0942/23220* ⊕ *www.parconaxostaormina.com* 🎫 *€10.*

★ Villa Comunale

GARDEN | Stroll down Via Bagnoli Croce from the main Corso Umberto to the Villa Comunale to enjoy the stunning views from the seaside city's best terrace walkways. Also known as the Parco Duca di Cesarò, the lovely public gardens were designed by Florence Trevelyan Cacciola, a Scottish lady "invited" to leave England following a romantic liaison with the future Edward VII (1841–1910). Arriving in Taormina in 1889, she married a local professor and devoted herself to the gardens, filling them with native Mediterranean and exotic plants, ornamental pavilions, and fountains. ⊠ *Via Bagnoli Croce, Taormina.*

Beaches

Taormina Mare

BEACH | Below the main city of Taormina is Taormina Mare, where summertime beachgoers jostle for space on a pebble beach against the scenic backdrop of the aptly named Isolabella. The first section of beach is reserved for expensive resorts but the far end, next to Isolabella, has a large free area. The tiny "beautiful island" of Isolabella was once a private residence, but is now a nature preserve reached by walking along a narrow rocky path and visited for a small fee of €4. **Amenities:** none. **Best for:** walking. ⊠ *Taormina Mare, Taormina* ⊕ *www. parconaxostaormina.com* 🎫 *€4 for Isola Bella.*

Taormina offers some of the most gorgeous views in all of Sicily.

🍴 Restaurants

Bella Blu

$ | **SICILIAN** | **FAMILY** | If you fancy a meal with a view but don't want to spend a lot, this casual and convivial seafood and pizza restaurant caters to an international crowd with multilingual staff and decent prices. Try the spaghetti with fresh clams and mussels or the pizza alla Norma (with ricotta, eggplant, and tomatoes) while you watch the funivia fly up and down from the beach, with the coastline in the distance. **Known for:** moderate prices; tasty pizza; lovely views of the funivia and coast. [$] *Average main: €14* ✉ *Via Pirandello 28, Taormina* ☎ *0942/24239* 🌐 *www.bellablutaormina.com* 🕒 *Closed Jan.–Mar.*

L'Arco dei Cappuccini

$$ | **SEAFOOD** | Just off Via Costantino Patricio, by the far side of the Cappuccini arch, lies this diminutive restaurant. Outdoor seating and an upstairs kitchen help make room for a few extra tables—a necessity, as locals are well aware that neither the price nor the quality is equaled elsewhere in town. **Known for:** a great wine list; authentic local cooking; fine inexpensive dining. [$] *Average main: €16* ✉ *Via Cappuccini 7, off Via Costantino Patricio, Taormina* ☎ *392/2442484* 🌐 *www.arcodeicappuccini.com* 🕒 *Closed Feb.*

Osteria RossoDiVino

$$ | **SICILIAN** | Run by two sisters, this intimate restaurant in a cobblestone courtyard just before the old city gate is one of the friendliest in town, with creative daily menus highlighting house-made pastas, seasonal produce from the market, and freshly caught fish; seating is primarily outdoors on the patio (bug spray is provided, if mosquitoes become an issue). As the name suggests, wine is a specialty, so let them recommend a glass or bottle. **Known for:** delicious modern Sicilian food; excellent wine choices; daily-changing menus. [$] *Average main: €18* ✉ *Vico de Spuches 8, Taormina* ☎ *0942/628653* 🕒 *Closed Jan. and Feb and Tues.*

Pizzichella

$$ | **SEAFOOD** | Dine right on the water's edge at this local seafood favorite on the Isola Bella beach. Seafood reigns supreme, and in early mornings you might even see fishermen pulling their boats directly up to the restaurant to make fresh deliveries. **Known for:** linguine with Mediterranean lobster; very casual beach vibes; grouper ravioli. [$] *Average main: €18* ✉ *Via Spiaggia Isola Bella, Taormina* ☎ *338/6581525* 🌐 *www.ristorantepizzichella.it.*

Ristorante Cutì Lu Dissi

$$ | **SICILIAN** | Family-owned for generations, Cutì Lu Dissi (which means "who told you" in Sicilian) specializes in excellent renditions of Sicilian food. From their lofty open-air terrace just beyond the Porta Catania, you can see the sea below and Etna in the distance. **Known for:** excellent caponata; meatballs cooked in lemon leaves; pasta with gamberi rossi and truffles from Etna. [$] *Average main: €18* ✉ *Via Ospedale 9, Taormina* ☎ *0942/615306* 🌐 *ristorante-cutiludissi.business.site* 🕒 *Closed Jan.–Mar.*

★ **Trattoria Il Barcaiolo**

$$$ | **SEAFOOD** | Just behind the public beach in Mazzarò Bay, this intimate little terrace restaurant is shrouded by an enormous old grapevine and looks out onto postcard-perfect views of paradise. Since 1981, the family-owned trattoria has been serving pristine seafood to discerning locals and in-the-know tourists. **Known for:** swordfish carpaccio with citrus and capers; cassata and cannoli for dessert; extensive wine list. [$] *Average main: €25* ✉ *Via Castelluccio 43, Taormina* ☎ *379/2089564* 🌐 *www.barcaiolo.altervista.org* 🕒 *Closed Tues.*

Trattoria Tischi Toschi

$$ | **SICILIAN** | Chef Luca Casablanca is like a character out of a Sicilian storybook. Full of personality and endlessly dedicated to the showcasing the food of his native land, he adheres to the Slow Food philosophy more than anyone else in Taormina. **Known for:** fish meatballs; small space so be sure to reserve ahead; all vegetables, especially caponata. [$] *Average main: €20* ✉ *Vico Cuscona-Paladini, Taormina* ☎ *339/3642088* 🌐 *www.tischitoschitaormina.com.*

Coffee and Quick Bites

Pasticceria Etna

$ | **BAKERY** | Fans of marzipan will delight at the range of almond sweets on offer here in the shape of the ubiquitous *fico d'India* (prickly pear) and other fruit. A block of almond paste makes a good souvenir—you can bring it home to make an almond latte or granita. **Known for:** housemade granita; fresh cannoli; almond sweets. [$] *Average main: €2* ✉ *Corso Umberto I 112, Taormina* ☎ *0942/24735* 🌐 *www.pasticceriaetna.com.*

Hotels

★ **Belmond Grand Hotel Timeo**

$$$$ | **HOTEL** | On a princely perch overlooking the town, the Greek theater, and the bay, this truly grand hotel, Taormina's oldest, wears a graceful patina that suggests la dolce vita, with a splash of Baroque and a dash of Mediterranean design in the lobby, which has tile- and brickwork walls and vaulted ceilings. **Pros:** feeling of indulgence; exemplary service; amazing location with fantastic views. **Cons:** spa is on the small side; lower category rooms only have partial views; very expensive. [$] *Rooms from: €900* ✉ *Via Teatro Greco 59, Taormina* ☎ *0942/6270200* 🌐 *www.belmond.com/grand-hotel-timeo-taormina* 🕒 *Closed Jan.–mid-Mar.* 🛏 *70 rooms* 🍴 *Free Breakfast.*

★ **Belmond Villa Sant'Andrea**

$$$$ | **HOTEL** | **FAMILY** | In a prime location on its own private beach at Taormina Mare, this elegant hotel in a late-1800s villa offers phenomenal views of the water, attentive service, and luxurious and comfortable guest rooms. **Pros:**

glorious private beach; free shuttle service to Taormina town; flawless service. **Cons:** pricey food and drinks; spa is small; limited on-site parking. $ *Rooms from: €900 ⊠ Via Nazionale 137, Taormina ☏ 0942/6271200 ⊕ www.belmond.com/villa-sant-andrea-taormina-mare ⊗ Closed Nov.–mid-Apr. ⇄ 70 rooms ⦿ Free Breakfast.*

Hotel Metropole Taormina
$$$$ | HOTEL | This trendy boutique hotel boasts a prime location, with the main shopping street of Corso Umberto on one side and sea views on the other. **Pros:** most rooms are suites; amazing views from restaurant and pool; lovely spa and public areas. **Cons:** not all rooms have good views; expensive overall, with high prices particularly in the bar; bathrooms can be small and dark. $ *Rooms from: €432 ⊠ Corso Umberto 154, Taormina ☏ 0942/24013 ⊕ www.hotelmetropoletaormina.it ⊗ Closed Jan.–Mar. ⇄ 23 rooms ⦿ Free Breakfast.*

Hotel Villa Carlotta
$$$$ | HOTEL | This small luxury hotel, in a former noble home a short walk from the center of town, has contemporary accommodations with calming neutral tones and a seamless mix of modern and period furniture, but the true allure of the property is in its incredible rooftop terrace and the attentive staff. **Pros:** most rooms have sea views; relaxing pool and garden area; fabulous breakfast on beautiful rooftop terrace. **Cons:** no free parking; some rooms are a bit dark; not all rooms have balconies. $ *Rooms from: €419 ⊠ Via Luigi Pirandello 81, Taormina ☏ 0942/626058 ⊕ www.hotelvillacarlottataormina.com ⊗ Closed mid-Nov.–mid-Mar. ⇄ 29 rooms ⦿ No Meals.*

Hotel Villa Paradiso
$$$ | HOTEL | On the edge of the town's historic center, overlooking lovely public gardens and facing the sea, this under-the-radar family-run hotel was renovated in 2021, but still maintains its antique furnishings, paintings, and Persian rugs, as well as its delightful service, good rooftop restaurant, and Etna views from many guest rooms. **Pros:** good value; great rooftop views; free shuttle bus to beach. **Cons:** beach club fee is extra; only three free parking spaces (paid parking nearby); not all rooms have views. $ *Rooms from: €259 ⊠ Via Roma 2, Taormina ☏ 0942/23921 ⊕ www.hotelvillaparadisotaormina.com ⇄ 37 rooms ⦿ Free Breakfast.*

★ San Domenico Palace, A Four Seasons Hotel
$$$$ | HOTEL | The sweeping views of the castle, the sea, and Mt. Etna from this converted 14th-century Dominican monastery will linger in your mind, along with the equally memorable levels of luxury and wonderful food in the hotel's highly lauded restaurant, Principe Cerami. **Pros:** strong sense of history and grandeur; quiet and restful; gorgeous infinity pool with amazing views. **Cons:** beach access through partner affiliates; parking €50 per day; very expensive. $ *Rooms from: €1200 ⊠ Piazza San Domenico 5, Taormina ☏ 0942/613111 ⊕ www.fourseasons.com/taormina ⊗ Closed early Jan.–mid-Mar. ⇄ 111 rooms ⦿ Free Breakfast.*

Villa Ducale
$$$$ | HOTEL | The former summer residence of a local aristocrat has been converted into a luxurious hotel in which each individually styled guest room is furnished with antiques and has a balcony with a view. **Pros:** away from the hubbub; personalized service; camera-ready views. **Cons:** some rooms are a bit dark; the restaurant menu can be limited; a 10- to 15-minute walk to the center of Taormina. $ *Rooms from: €399 ⊠ Via Leonardo da Vinci 60, Taormina ☏ 0942/28153 ⊕ www.villaducale.com ⊗ Closed mid-Nov.–Mar. ⇄ 17 rooms ⦿ Free Breakfast.*

 Performing Arts

Taormina Arte

ARTS FESTIVALS | The Teatro Greco and the Palazzo dei Congressi, near the entrance to the theater, are the main venues for the summer festival dubbed TaoArte, held each year between June and August. Performances encompass classical music, ballet, and theater. ⊠ *Taormina* ☎ *391/7462146* ⊕ *www.taoarte.it.*

Shopping

Corso Umberto

NEIGHBORHOODS | The primary passage between Taormina's two imposing gates (Porta Messina and Porta Catania) is a pedestrian-only thoroughfare lined with both locally owned boutiques and massive international chains. During the height of summer, it can be an untenable traffic jam of foot traffic, but in the shoulder seasons, it's a lovely quick stroll for shopping and stops for coffee at area cafés. ⊠ *Corso Umberto, Taormina.*

Il Sandalo Caprese

SHOES | The classic Capri sandal has been part of the Italian summer uniform since the 1960s, and icons like Audrey Hepburn, Brigitte Bardot, Sophia Loren, and Anita Ekberg ensured its enduring legacy. Stop into the Taormina outpost to have a pair custom-made. ⊠ *Corso Umberto 173, Taormina* ☎ *094/2626360* ⊕ *www.caprihandmade.com.*

Castelmola

5 km (3 miles) west of Taormina.

Although many believe that Taormina has the most spectacular views, tiny Castelmola—floating 1,800 feet above sea level—takes the word "scenic" to a whole new level. Along the cobblestone streets within the ancient walls, 360-degree panoramas of mountain, sea, and sky are so ubiquitous that you almost

get used to them (but not quite). Collect yourself with a sip of the sweet almond wine (best served cold) made in local bars, or with lunch at one of the humble pizzerias or panino shops.

A 10-minute drive on a winding but well-paved road leads from Taormina to Castelmola; you must park in one of the public lots below the village and walk up to the center, only a few minutes away. On a nice day, hikers are in for a treat if they make the trip from Taormina on foot instead. It's a serious uphill climb, but the 1½-km (¾-mile) path offers breathtaking views, which compensate for the somewhat poor maintenance of the path itself. You'll begin at Porta Catania in Taormina, with a walk along Via Apollo Arcageta past the Chiesa di San Francesco di Paola on the left. The Strada Comunale della Chiusa then leads past Piazza Andromaco, revealing good views of the jagged promontory of Cocolonazzo di Mola to the north. Allow around an hour for the ascent, a half hour for the descent. There's another, slightly longer (2-km [1-mile]) path that heads up from Porta Messina past the Roman aqueduct, Convento dei Cappuccini, and the northeastern side of Monte Tauro. You could take one up and the other down. In any case, avoid the midday sun, wear comfortable shoes, and carry plenty of water with you.

GETTING HERE AND AROUND
Regular buses bound for Castelmola leave from Taormina's bus station on Via Pirandello.

Sights

★ Castello Normanno

RUINS | In all of Sicily there may be no spot more scenic than atop Castello Normanno, reached by a set of steep staircases rising out of the town center. From here you can gaze upon two coastlines, smoking Mt. Etna, and the town spilling down the mountainside. The area was fortified by the Byzantines in the 9th century and was later rebuilt by the Normans, but all that stands today are the remains of the 16th-century castle walls. Come during daylight hours to take full advantage of the vista. ✉ *Castello Normanno, Castelmola* 🌐 *www.comune-castelmola.it.*

🍴 Restaurants

Il Vicolo

$ | **SICILIAN** | Located on a side street, this trattoria is one of the simpler dining choices in town, and also one of the better ones—what it lacks in views it makes up for with a pleasant rustic ambience plus a great selection of handmade pasta and, in the evening, *forno a legna* (from a wood-fired oven). In winter, pizzas are served weekends only. **Known for:** signature squid ragù; pasta and pizza; cozy environs. [$] *Average main: €12* ✉ *Via Papa Pio IX 26, Castelmola* ☎ *0942/28481* ⏲ *Closed Tues. Sept.–June and 2 wks late Jan.–early Feb.*

🛏 Hotels

Villa Sonia

$$ | **HOTEL** | Many guest rooms at this well-situated hotel have private terraces with gorgeous grab-the-camera views of Etna without the crowds (or high prices) of nearby Taormina. **Pros:** bus stop to Taormina outside door; friendly service; on-site sauna and pool. **Cons:** iffy Wi-Fi; not much to do in the evening; some rooms are quite small. [$] *Rooms from: €139* ✉ *Via Porta Mola 9, Castelmola* ☎ *0942/28082* 🌐 *www.hotelvillasonia.com* ⏲ *Closed Nov.–mid-Dec. and early Jan.–mid-Mar* 🛏 *44 rooms* 🍴 *Free Breakfast.*

🍸 Nightlife

Antico Caffè San Giorgio

BARS | This knickknack-filled bar has lorded over Castelmola's town square since 1907, and if you manage to resist the pull of the enchanting view on the terrace, you can explore the historic interior to learn more about the village's past. Try the *vino alle mandorle* (almond wine) from a recipe produced by the original owner more than a century ago, then follow luminaries such as Guglielmo Marconi, Winston Churchill, John D. Rockefeller, and John Steinbeck by signing the visitors' book. ✉ *Piazza Sant'Antonino, Castelmola* ☎ *0942/28228* 🌐 *www.barsangiorgio.com.*

Bar Turrisi

BARS | Truly one of the most infamous places to have a drink in all of Italy, this humorous bar has cozy nooks and crannies on three levels—all decked out with phallic images of every size, shape, and color imaginable, from bathroom wall murals inspired by the brothels of ancient Greece to giant wooden carvings honoring Dionysus. If you can get past the design choices, the roof terrace has extraordinary views of Taormina and the coast, while a limited selection of hearty pasta dishes are served inside. ✉ *Piazza del Duomo 19, Castelmola* ☎ *0942/28181* 🌐 *www.turrisibar.it.*

Savoca

25 km (15 miles) north of Castelmola, 71 km (44 miles) northeast of Catania, 20 km (12 miles) north of Taormina.

Located on a ridge amid a pair of tremendous hills, Savoca sits at the end of a 2-mile stretch of road that serpentines up from the coast. With views galore (from practically every point in town), this little medieval village also offers excellent examples of architecture from the 13th and 15th centuries and many lovingly restored houses. While approximately 1,500 residents call the town home, only 65 live in the central historic *borgo,* and you can easily walk the whole town in a half-hour.

But these days, most visitors to Savoca are there on a pilgrimage to see where Francis Ford Coppola filmed the Sicilian scenes of *The Godfather.* Coppola found the real Corleone (in western Sicily near Palermo) to be too modern and lacking the charm needed for his cinematic masterpiece. So instead, he chose the picturesque town of Savoca and nearby Forza D'Agrò. In the central piazza you'll find a steel sculpture made by local artist Nino Ucchino in honor of Coppola's filmmaking.

GETTING HERE AND AROUND
The best way to get to Savoca is by car. Without one, getting here can be a bit complicated. You can take the train to Santa Teresa di Riva (the coastal town below Savoca) from Messina or Catania, but from there you'll need to take a taxi, about a 15-minute ride. In town, everything is accessible by foot.

⊙ Sights

★ Bar Vitelli
RESTAURANT | FAMILY | Though the bar first opened in 1962—and the building has been around since the 1400s—this little café didn't gain worldwide popularity until Francis Ford Coppola chose it as the setting of significant scenes in *The Godfather.* In fact, prior to Coppola, the bar didn't even have an official name. He chose "Bar Vitelli" for his fictional café, had the name painted on the exterior wall, and the name has stuck for decades. Here, Michael Corleone famously asked Apollonia to marry him. And most street scenes where Michael is seen walking up the road were filmed on the building's side. The interior of the café functions as a small museum of the filming that happened in Savoca,

with film stills and photos throughout. Outside, small tables sit under fairy lights and an arbor of vines. Be sure to order a lemon granita with a splash of Zibbibo, a sweet dessert wine. And though the rest of Sicily serves granita with brioche, here you'll find lightly sweetened "zuccarata" cookies. ⊠ *Piazza Fossia 7, Savoca* ☎ *334/9227227* ⊕ *www.barvitelli.it.*

Catacombs
CEMETERY | Nobles of the 17th and 18th centuries in this area opted to have their corpses mummified. You can visit the somewhat creepy crypt, located beneath a 17th-century Capuchin monastery, to see their preserved remains and hand-woven silk garments. The catacombs are technically open daily (from 9:30 am to 7:30 pm), but it's advised to call ahead to be sure that someone is actually on-site to let you in. ⊠ *Via Cappuccini 10, Savoca* ☎ *328/7958098* 🖭 *Free.*

Chiesa di San Nicolò
CHURCH | Built in the 13th century, this church was renovated at the end of the 15th century, the beginning of the 18th century (perhaps due to damage from an earthquake), and most recently in 1981. From the Middle Ages up through the 19th century, it offered a final resting place to common citizens of Savoca. It's also known as the Chiesa di Santa Lucia, because of the silver statue of St. Lucia it houses, in addition to other sculptures and paintings from the nearby 15th-century church of St. Lucia that collapsed in a landslide in 1880. In popular culture, it's best known as the church where Michael Corleone wed Apollonia in *The Godfather.* ⊠ *Via San Nicolò 4, Savoca* 🖭 *Free.*

Nino Ucchino Steel Art Gallery
ART GALLERY | Throughout Savoca you'll see works by steel artist Nino Ucchino, such as the now-iconic sculpture of Francis Ford Coppola behind his camera and an amusing talking donkey. You can visit his studio, perched on the hillside on the road into town, to see the master at

work or buy some of his creations. He's there in his studio most afternoons, but it's smart to call ahead to be sure he's available. ✉ *Via Provinciale s/n, Savoca* ☎ *393/9793886* 🎫 *Free.*

🍴 Restaurants

Ristorante Gelso Nero

$$ | **SICILIAN** | This restaurant claims to be located between heaven and earth, and its hillside perch with sweeping vistas certainly helps make its case. Go for classic Sicilian dishes, such as spaghetti with pistachio pesto or a many-layered slice of eggplant parmigiana. **Known for:** grilled meats; panoramic views; spritzes on the patio. [$] *Average main: €20* ✉ *Via Provinciale, Savoca* ☎ *327/2015466* 🌐 *ristorante-gelso-nero.business.site* ⏲ *Closed Jan. and Feb.*

🛏 Hotels

Bar Vitelli Charming Suites

$$$$ | **HOTEL** | This boutique property is housed in a structure dating to the 1400s, but has been fully updated with all the modern amenities, including luxury marble bathrooms, complete with Acqua di Parma toiletries, hydromassage showers, and soaking tubs. **Pros:** spacious, quiet rooms; luxe furnishings and draperies throughout; rooftop terrace with views of the valley and Mount Etna. **Cons:** one of the top floor rooms has very low ceilings; bedspreads feel dated; expensive. [$] *Rooms from: €466* ✉ *Piazza Fossia 7, Savoca* ☎ *334/9227227* 🌐 *www.barvitelli.it* 🛏 *6 rooms* 🍴 *Free Breakfast.*

Messina

42 km (26 miles) north of Savoca, 94 km (59 miles) northeast of Catania, 237 km (149 miles) east of Palermo.

Messina's ancient history recounts a series of disasters, but the city once vied with Palermo in a bid to become the island's capital, developing a fine university, a bustling commercial center, and a thriving cultural environment. At 5:20 am on December 28, 1908, Messina was reduced from a flourishing metropolis of 120,000 to a heap of rubble, shaken to pieces by an earthquake that turned into a tidal wave; 80,000 people died as a result, and the city was almost completely leveled. As you approach by ferry, you won't notice any outward indication of the disaster, just the modern countenance of a 3,000-year-old city. The somewhat flat look is a precaution of seismic planning: tall buildings are not permitted.

GETTING HERE AND AROUND

Frequent hydrofoils and ferries carry passengers, cars, and trains across the Strait of Messina from Villa San Giovanni, from just below the train station. There are also regular hydrofoil departures for foot passengers from Reggio Calabria. Cruise ships also stop in Messina's port.

From within Sicily, Messina is easily reachable by car, as it sits just off the E45 autostrada from Catania and the E90 autostrada from Palermo. There are regular train and bus services from both cities as well.

VISITOR INFORMATION

CONTACT Messina Tourism Office. ✉ *Via dei Mille 270, Messina* ☎ *090/7761048, 090/776146* 🌐 *turismoecultura.cittametropolitana.me.it.*

👁 Sights

Duomo

CHURCH | The reconstruction of Messina's Norman and Romanesque cathedral, originally built by the Norman king Roger II and consecrated in 1197, has retained much of the original plan—including a handsome crown of Norman battlements, an enormous apse, and a splendid wood-beamed ceiling. The adjoining bell tower contains one of the largest and most complex mechanical clocks in the

The Northeast Coast

world: constructed in 1933, it has a host of gilded automatons (a roaring lion and crowing rooster among them) that spring into action every day at the stroke of noon, lasting for 12 minutes.

Don't miss the chance to climb the bell tower itself. As you head up the internal stairs, you'll see the system of levers and counterweights that operates the movements of the gilded bronze statues that parade through the open facade high over the Duomo's square. At the top, an open-air terrace offers 360-degree views of Messina and the Strait. ✉ *Piazza del Duomo 29, Messina* ☎ *090/66841* 🌐 *www.diocesimessina.it* 🎫 *Clock tower €4.*

Museo Regionale di Messina

ART MUSEUM | One of Italy's most celebrated Renaissance painters, Caravaggio spent a good deal of time in Sicily toward the end of his life, while on the run after committing a murder in Rome. The artwork he left behind includes two on display at this regional museum. The scandal-prone artist is best known for his religious works, which utilize dramatic shadows and heavenly lighting. The two here are the highlight of the collection, though there are also some interesting archaeological pieces salvaged from shipwrecks and several works by Antonello da Messina. ✉ *Viale della Libertà 465, Messina* ☎ *090/361292* 🌐 *www.mume.in* 🎫 *€8* 🕒 *Closed Mon.*

Sky Wheel Ruota Panoramica

AMUSEMENT RIDE | This modern oversize Ferris wheel is very much a tourist attraction, but the views from the top, especially at sunset, are magnificent. You can see across the Strait to Calabria and on clear days all the way to Etna. At night, it puts on a multicolor light show that's made its way into many an Instagram story. ✉ *Piazza Cairoli, Messina* ☎ *380/4705490* 🌐 *www.ruotapanoramica.net* 🎫 *€8.*

Museo Archeologico Nazionale di Reggio Calabria

HISTORY MUSEUM | Though it's located across the Strait in Reggio Calabria, this fantastic museum delves into the shared archeological and geological history of these sister regions and is worth a visit. You'll find incredible examples of fossils from the Paleolithic and Mesolithic periods (including the fossilized bones of a Neanderthal child), tools from the Bronze Age, insight into the military organization of the Iron Age, and details of Greek settlements on both sides of the Strait. Don't miss the bronze Riace warriors, a pair of impressive statues that were cast about 460 BC and found in the sea in 1972. To get there, take a 30-minute hydrofoil from the Messina port (*€6.50 round-trip,* 🌐 *www.blujetlines.it*). ✉ *Piazza Giuseppe De Nava 26, Reggio Calabria* ☎ *0965/898272* 🌐 *www.beniculturali.it* 🎫 *€8* 🕒 *Closed Mon.*

🍴 Restaurants

★ A Cucchiara

$$ | **MODERN ITALIAN** | A light nautical theme permeates this stone-walled restaurant, where the open kitchen provides theater and owner Peppe Giamboi takes the stage as a gustatory storyteller, roaming from table to table. The menu is constantly changing, but you'll find excellent work with vegetables (a rarity in Sicily) and really lovely preparations of local cod. **Known for:** locally, sustainably sourced seafood; robust wine program; elegant food in a relaxed, welcoming atmosphere. [$] *Average main: €18* ✉ *Strada San Giacomo 19, Messina* ☎ *090/711023* 🌐 *www.ristoranti.messina.it* 🕒 *Closed Sun.*

I Ruggeri

$$ | **ITALIAN** | An intimate little spot a block from the port, I Ruggeri prides itself on a mix of tradition and experimentation. For example, you might find a savory Babà (typically a dessert pastry soaked in rum) made of pecorino romano. **Known for:** fine

Messina's Duomo contains one of the largest and most complex mechanical clocks in the world.

dining at reasonable prices; neighborhood vibe with lots of local regulars; thoughtful wine suggestions. $ *Average main: €18* ✉ *Via Pozzo Leone 23, Messina* ☏ *090/343938* ⊕ *www.iruggeri.it* ⊙ *Closed Sun.*

Casa & Putia

$$ | ITALIAN | Dedicated to the Slow Food movement, Casa & Putia puts the emphasis on their raw materials, with the idea that excellent ingredients need little fuss. The emphasis is on letting those ingredients shine through, such as with a flan made of artichokes and caciocavallo cheese. **Known for:** responsibly sourced ingredients; olive oil gelato; Sicilian products for sale on-site. $ *Average main: €18* ✉ *Via San Camillo 14, Messina* ☏ *090/2402887* ⊕ *www.casaeputiaristorante.it.*

☕ Coffee and Quick Bites

Bar del Sud

$ | ICE CREAM | Throughout Sicily there are fierce arguments about who makes the best granita, and everyone has an opinion. But for many Messinese, the end of the discussion is Bar del Sud, a neighborhood favorite since 1968; their dairy-free granita is spectacularly creamy and resembles gelato in its consistency. **Known for:** delicious granita; strong coffee; Gianduia gelato. $ *Average main: €3* ✉ *Via Garibaldi 85, Messina* ☏ *090/675212.*

★ Francesco Arena

$ | BAKERY | You'll smell this panificio and focacceria before you arrive, as the scent of baking bread wafts down the street. The 45-year-old Francesco Arena works with ancient grains (like tumminia, perciasacchi, and rusello) and a hearty mother yeast to produce tender focaccia topped with everything from sun-sweetened tomatoes to escarole, crusty loaves, ham-and-cheese filled *pidone*, and the flakiest croissants. **Known for:** detour-worthy focaccia; barchette, a pizza "boat" loaded with toppings; official master baker. $ *Average main: €4* ⊠ *Via T. Cannizzaro 137, Messina* ☎ *090/9218792* ⊘ *Closed Sun.*

Pasticceria Irrera 1910

$ | **CAFÉ** | A local favorite for over a century, Irrera is known for its cassata, *pignolata* (little balls of sweet fried dough held together by honey or chocolate), and filled-to-order cannoli. Grab a spot on the outside terrace to sate your sweet tooth and do a little people-watching. **Known for:** excellent versions of historic sweets; marzipan fruits; breakfast on the terrace. $ *Average main: €4* ⊠ *Piazza Cairoli 12, Messina* ☎ *090/712148* ⊕ *www. irrera1910.it.*

Hotels

Hotel Messenion

$$ | **HOTEL** | This independent hotel provides tidy accommodations in the style you might expect in a chain aimed at business travelers, but the name and ambience of the hotel are much more connected to the town's local spirit. **Pros:** balconies in half the rooms; clean and spacious rooms; good location for exploring Messina by foot. **Cons:** paid parking; more of a business hotel feel; small showers. $ *Rooms from: €140* ⊠ *Via Francesco Faranda 7, Messina* ☎ *090/712674* ⊕ *www.hotelmessenion.it* ⤴ *18 rooms* ❏ *Free Breakfast.*

Re Vittorio De Luxe

$$ | **HOTEL** | This updated historic palazzo maintains elements of its early 1900s grandeur: parquet floors, 13-foot ceilings, and porcelain stoneware tiles. **Pros:** a balcony in almost every room; incredibly pastry selection for breakfast; conveniently located near the Duomo and great area restaurants. **Cons:** street parking or in a nearby garage; a couple of the rooms are a little dark; the entrance of

the hotel is actually on the second floor of a residential building. $ *Rooms from: €129* ⊠ *Via Attilio Gasparro 7, Messina* ☎ *090/9012726* ⊕ *www.revittoriodeluxe.it* ⤴ *10 rooms* ❏ *Free Breakfast.*

★ V Maison

$$ | **HOTEL** | Hardwood floors, vibrant wallpaper, extensive original artwork, and spacious rooms are the hallmarks of this charming boutique property. **Pros:** good soundproofing in rooms; stylish, updated accommodations; beautiful rooftop terrace for breakfast. **Cons:** no counter space in bathrooms; no bathtubs; bar open only for private events. $ *Rooms from: €126* ⊠ *Viale Europa 59, Messina* ☎ *090/2938901* ⊕ *www.vmaison.it* ⤴ *7 rooms* ❏ *Free Breakfast.*

Nightlife

Le Roi Emotional Drinks

COCKTAIL LOUNGES | When you're ready to upgrade your spritz or Negroni, look to Le Roi. They sling drinks from within the 1929 Vittorio Emanuele III galleria, where the mosaic tile floors and electric Liberty style (an Italian version of Art Nouveau) give historic heft to the inventive cocktails. ⊠ *Piazza Antonello, Galleria Vittorio Emanuele III 18, Messina* ☎ *348/5524536* ⊕ *www.leroiemotionaldrinks.it.*

Punta del Faro

15 km (9 miles) north of Messina.

Located on the extreme northeastern tip of Sicily, Punta del Faro looks across the Strait of Messina to Calabria where you can see the hillside beach town of Scilla in the distance. This lighthouse point *(faro* means "lighthouse" in Italian) is where the Ionian and Tyrrhenian seas meet, and beneath the shimmering aquamarine waters, the strait runs deep and is famous for its strong currents and whirlpools. In Ancient Greek mythology, those dangerous waters were attributed to the powerful and deadly sea creatures Charybdis (on the Sicilian side) and Scylla (on the Calabrian side) who were known to swallow entire ships. These days Punta del Faro is known as the local seaside beach escape of the Messinese, and its white-sand beaches, excellent seafood, and clear blue waters are as alluring to visitors as the ancient sirens— though with much better consequences.

GETTING HERE AND AROUND

From Messina, take the number 1 or number 32 bus to Ganzirri or Torre Faro (*about 30 minutes; €1.50, €2 if bought on board*). During the summer, ATM runs a shuttle bus around the Punta del Faro area.

Sights

Bonavita Azienda Agricola

WINERY | Based in an ancient borgo, on a hillside overlooking the Tyrrhenian Sea, this 74-acre winery and vineyard specializes in natural reds and rosés made from Nerello Mascalese and Nocera grapes. From the vine-covered hilltop, you can see all the way to the island of Stromboli in the Aeolian Islands, and the wind whips through the oak, olive, and citrus trees and wild fennel and rosemary brushes. The ground here is a lesson in Earth's ancient history: throughout the white sand-clay mix, you can find sea fossils in the soil. Tastings (for up to six people) can take place in the vineyard or in the winery itself, and upon request include local cured meats and cheeses. ⊠ *Bonavita Azienda Agricola, Faro Superiore, Punta del Faro* ☎ *347/1754683* ⊕ *www.bonavitafaro.com* ⟟ *Tastings from €15 per person.*

Lake Ganzirri

BODY OF WATER | A little bigger than a square mile, this lake, along with the nearby Lake Faro, is fed by groundwater mixed with seawater that flows in from a pair of canals built by the British around 1830. As a result, the waters are particularly great for growing mussels, one of the most iconic foods of the area. You'll see little sticks poking up from the water to indicate various aquaculture plots. And on sunny days, it's common to see people rowing crew in the lake. ⊠ *Lake Ganzirri, Punta del Faro.*

Lido Punta Faro

BEACH | At the base of the pylon at Capo Peloro, where the Ionian and Tyrrhenian seas meet, this little beach club stays open year-round. From the white-sand beaches you can see the Calabrian town of Scilla just across the strait. Because of the convergence of the seas, the waters are known for strong currents and whirlpools, which the ancient Greeks referred to as the sea monster Charybdis who would swallow ships whole. But the clear waters immediately hugging the coast are shallow and perfect for a dip. At the lido, you can rent chairs and umbrellas for the day or just pop in for a quick bite of lunch, a coffee, or a sunset aperitivo. ⊠ *Via Fortino, Capo Peloro, Punta del Faro.*

Pylon of Torre Faro

OTHER ATTRACTION | One of a pair of pylons (the other is across the strait in Villa San Giovanni, Calabria) that carried electricity across the strait from 1955 to 1994, this steel tower stands 761 feet over the most northeastern point of Sicily. Though the pylons are no longer officially in use, they do have protected historic monument status and are used to gather meteorological data. Access to the 1,000-odd steps to the top is closed to the public, but there's always some daredevil who decides to try. ⊠ *Pilone di Torre Faro, Punta del Faro.*

 Restaurants

Bellavista Ristorante

$$$ | SEAFOOD | With views of the sea and Calabria in the distance, this bright dining room framed by plate glass windows serves picture-perfect plates

of composed antipasti, fresh pastas dressed with every sea creature possible, and showstopping secondi, such as lobster from the Messina Strait and fish cooked to perfection. During the summer season, they often set up alfresco tables directly along the water. **Known for:** excellent wine list; fine dining presentation; beautiful sea views. [$] *Average main: €30* ✉ *Via Circuito, Torre Faro, Punta del Faro* ☎ *090/326682* 🌐 *www.bellavistaristorante.info* ⏲ *Closed Mon.*

Nonna Lilla Trattoria Marinara

$$ | SEAFOOD | Located on the spit of land between Ganzirri Lake and the sea, this earnest little trattoria serves the freshest fish possible. A young chef, Gaetano Borgosano, has taken over the 60-year-old restaurant and has smartly kept its iconic dishes, such as fried mussels (stuffed with breadcrumbs and fried on the half shell) and fish meatballs in a Messinese *ghiotto* (sauce of tomatoes, capers, and celery) while introducing his own updates such as swordfish agrodolce. **Known for:** fried mussels; off-the-boat seafood; gracious old-fashioned service. [$] *Average main: €18* ✉ *Via Verso Lido, Punta del Faro* ☎ *320/3749409.*

Coffee and Quick Bites

★ Pasticceria-Gelateria Giuseppe Arena

$ | ICE CREAM | In the Sicilian food world, the name Giuseppe Arena is synonymous with sweets. He's a *maestro gelatiere* (master gelato maker) who specializes in artisanal gelato, sorbet, and granita, working with fresh fruits of the season and products from the region, such as hazelnuts from the nearby Nebrodi mountains. **Known for:** fantastic experimental flavors, such as clam gelato; granita made with fruits the owner harvests himself; citrus sorbets. [$] *Average main: €3* ✉ *Via Consolare Pompea 1773, Punta del Faro* ☎ *090/9214738* ⏲ *Closed Mon.*

Hotels

Casa di Ale

$$ | HOUSE | Here the gracious hostess, Ale, has turned two rooms outside her seaside home into a private casetta for guests. **Pros:** expansive terrace directly on the sea; full kitchen; outside shower at entrance from beach. **Cons:** very basic accommodations; three-night minimum; only two rooms available in shared space. [$] *Rooms from: €134* ✉ *Via Adolfo Romano 17, Punta del Faro* ☎ *392/5492099* 💳 *No credit cards* 🛏 *2 rooms* 🍴 *No Meals.*

Chapter 7

SIRACUSA AND THE SOUTHEAST

7

Updated by
Craig McKnight

👁 Sights	🍴 Restaurants	🛏 Hotels	🛍 Shopping	🍸 Nightlife
★★★☆☆	★★★☆☆	★★★☆☆	★★☆☆☆	★☆☆☆☆

WELCOME TO SIRACUSA AND THE SOUTHEAST

TOP REASONS TO GO

★ **Siracusa's Parco Archeologico della Neapolis:** Step back in time and take at least a day to explore one of the greatest Greek and Roman archaeological sites in Italy.

★ **Ortigia Island:** On this small island off Siracusa, you'll find everything you might need for a true Sicilian experience: delicious rustic dishes at a myriad of restaurants, picture-postcard bars perfect for people-watching, and Greek architecture that will make your head spin.

★ **Architecture of the Val di Noto:** This entire region was rebuilt after a devastating earthquake in 1693, with towns like Noto rebuilt to reflect the late Baroque style, which UNESCO has described as "the final flowering of Baroque art in Europe."

★ **Chocolate in Modica:** Unique to the town of Modica, this method of chocolate-making prevents the sugar crystals from melting, giving the chocolate a grainy yet delicious texture in a variety of flavors.

1 Siracusa. The center of southeastern Sicily and one of the great capitals of the ancient Western world.

2 Noto. A small city filled with architecture from Sicily's Baroque heyday.

3 Scicli. One of the island's hidden gems, filled with Baroque architecture and village charm.

4 Modica. Home to world-famous chocolate along with impressive cuisine, architecture, and views to match.

5 Ragusa. A small yet spectacular town with 14 UNESCO World Heritage buildings and to-die-for views of the surrounding valley.

6 Palazzolo Acreide. An off-the-beaten path town with some great architecture and interesting Greek ruins.

7 Sortino. The gateway to Necropoli di Pantalica, one of Sicily's earliest settlements and a bastion of the island's history.

Grammichele

Francofonte

Augusta

124

194

E45

Melilli

Priolo Gargallo

Vizzini

10

124

Fiume Anapo

7 ◆ Necropoli
di Pantalica

Floridia

25

1

Granieri

194

124

Siracusa

Palazzolo Acreide

6

287

74

Roccazzo

Giarratana

14

E45

MONTI IBLEI

12

Comiso

10

287

Cassibile

Ragusa

Fiume Tellaro

Avola-Gallina

Gallina

E45

5

Noto

2

Avola

60

Modica

115

4

E45

Gulf
of Noto

Marina
di Ragusa

Rosolini

Ionian Sea

3

Scicli

E45

19

nnalucata

Ispica

Irminio

Marina di
Modica

49

Marzamemi

Cava d'Aliga

65

Pozzallo

Pachino

Marina di Modica

Portopalo di
Capo Passero

Capo Passero

Mediterranean   Sea

If you want to experience Sicily at its most beautiful then head to the southeastern portion of the island, where you can explore stunning baroque-style towns that seem to glow in the evening sun, unspoiled beaches where you can swim almost all year round, and hidden hillsides full of olive groves and wild herbs. And you'll be taking in all of these while indulging in world-class Sicilian food and wine.

The cities of Siracusa (Syracuse to non-Italians) and Modica are the most popular stops for travelers to this region. Siracusa has the charming island of Ortigia attached to it, where you can wander around the relatively traffic-free streets, bar-hopping and taking in the sights and an obligatory gelato along the way. Head into the main part of Siracusa for an afternoon wandering around its remarkably well-preserved Siracusa Archeological Park, which includes the stunning Greek theater (the most complete still in existence).

Surrounding Siracusa, you'll find the Val di Noto, one of the three *valli*, or administrative regions, that historically made up Sicily. The towns in this region have all been declared UNESCO World Heritage Sites, due to their stunning Baroque architecture.

On the opposite side of the region from Siracusa, the UNESCO World Heritage town of Modica is famous for its chocolate, made with a special cold-working process. But it's also a charming, historical stop on its own, partly due to it being "split" into high and low parts. You can indulge in chocolate-tasting in the lower half and then walk it off by hiking up to the upper part of the city to glimpse some beautiful architecture and stunning views over the local valley.

Beyond these two hubs, there are more hidden delights to discover in the region. Travel a short distance from Siracusa to the less frequently visited Noto, filled with many picture-postcard examples of Baroque architecture; you might even feel like you're walking around a film set. A city of a similar name has existed in this area since records began, but the "modern" city was rebuilt in the 18th century after the earthquake of 1683 devastated the area.

From Noto, move onto Scicli, where you will experience the most relaxed of the towns in the southeast. Its main street is a UNESCO World Heritage site, and around every corner you'll find breathtaking architecture and tempting bars; just outside the town, ruined churches dot the hillside. If the weather is nice, make a visit out to the churches by taking a small trek on the well-worn steps that lead up to them. The churches themselves might not be much to behold, but the accompanying views will make your head spin.

Head next to Ragusa, where a labyrinth of cobblestone streets houses a collection of Baroque palazzi and churches. Also separated into two sections, Ragusa Ibla, or lower Ragusa, is only slightly larger than one square kilometer, but is home to no less than 14 UNESCO World Heritage buildings. If you're staying in the more modern section (Upper Ragusa), don't miss the chance to climb the steps to Church of Santa Lucia at sunset; at the top, you'll be awed by the scene of tiled rooftops, domes, and other architectural delights lit by the evening sun. The final part of your tour of this fabulous area should be the small town of Palazzolo Acreide, home to the fascinating archaeological park of Akrai. Further north is the just as underrated Necropoli di Pantalica, where more than 5,000 tombs of various shapes and sizes line the limestone cliffs. The site is said to date back to the 13th century BC, but was updated and built up by the Romans.

Whether you hit up all the major sites in southeastern Sicily or just a few, a trip here is bound to be filled with all the highlights you expect from Sicily (quaint countryside, magnificent architecture, and fascinating history) and none of the crowds.

Planning

When to Go

Sicily's southeast is best avoided in July and August when the temperatures and the crowds ramp up, but the region is a pleasure to visit any other time of the year. March through June and September through November are warm enough to enjoy alfresco dining without the summer crowds. Bring a coat if you visit in December, but the Christmas festivities are bound to help warm you up. Sicilians take Christmas very seriously, so anywhere you visit from December 8 onward will be transformed into a winter wonderland of Christmas-related street markets and theme street parades.

Festivals are part of life here, as there are elsewhere in Sicily, and normally take place during religious holidays. Every Easter Saturday at 9 pm in Siracusa, all the city's churches are illuminated, fireworks explode in the sky, and a statue of Christ is carried around the town in a torchlight vigil. Modica's Easter celebration is a more somber affair, where a statue of the Virgin Mary is paraded around the town before meeting for an embrace with Jesus Christ.

If you visit in May or June, you can combine a visit to the Archeological Park in Siracusa with a performance at the Greek Theatre on-site, when performances take place daily. In July, the island of Ortigia comes alive with the lights, sounds, and colors of the city's annual film festival. There are several alfresco screenings around town, along with more traditional indoor ones.

In October, Ragusa plays host to the Scale de Gusto, a festival devoted to the wine, olives, almonds, and cheeses of the area. Also in October, Modica is transformed into ChocoModica, which celebrates the town's great contribution to the world of chocolate with tastings, music, workshops, cultural events, exhibitions, and much more.

Planning Your Time

Most visitors to this region will start in Siracusa (although you can also fly into the Comisa Airport, closer to Ragusa). Indeed, some may come only for Siracusa, and at least two full days is necessary to truly get a sense of what the city entails. A full week will be enough time to visit three of the region's towns, but it's better to devote at least two weeks to soak in this area's beauty at a more sedate pace. Siracusa can also serve as a good base if you're renting a car and driving out to towns like Noto, Ragusta, and Modica for day trips.

Getting Here and Around

AIR

The nearest major international airport is Catania-Fontanarossa Airport, located about 40 miles north of Siracusa. If you take the Autostrada, you can be in Siracusa in less than an hour by car or taxi; taking the scenic coastal road is only an additional 10 minutes.

If you don't have a car, most towns in the area are served by buses outside the Arrivals terminal. The fast Flixbus service will get you to Siracusa in two hours; the average price of a ticket of €12, or even cheaper if you buy in advance during one of their many promotional events. There is also a local direct train service from Catania Airport to Siracusa, which takes around 90 minutes and costs €7.60.

The much smaller Comiso Airport is about 15 miles from Ragusa, and mostly sees flights from other Italian destinations as well as a few select European cities. As this is in the west of the region, you can drive to Modica in 40 minutes. This airport is not served by any public transport, so you would need to get around by car.

If you would like to rent a car upon arrival, all the major rental companies can be found at the Arrivals terminal at Catania Airport. Comiso Airport is only served by Hertz and Avis.

CONTACTS Catania-Fontanarossa Airport. ⊠ Via Fontanarossa, Catania ☎ 095/7239111 ⊕ www.aeroporto. catania.it/en. **Comiso Airport.** ⊠ SP5, Comiso ☎ 0932/961467 ⊕ aeroportodicomiso. eu/en. **Flixbus.** ⊕ www.flixbus.com.

BUS

Traveling via bus here is actually quite cheap and quick. The main companies Interbus and SAIS Autolinee will get you nearly anywhere in the region from the other major cities and towns in Sicily. You can also use Flixbus to get to the main towns of Siracusa and Modica.

CONTACTS Interbus. ⊕ www.interbus.it. **SAIS Autolinee.** ☎ 091/2776999 ⊕ www. saisautolinee.it.

CAR

As train service in Sicily can be unreliable, most locals use a car to get around and while visitors could get by using just the local bus service, renting a car can be the most time-effective way to explore the region. You will definitely need a car, or need to hire a guide with a car, to visit the Necropoli di Pantalica.

The road network is very modern, but roadwork, even on the Autostrada, can sometimes slow you down. An extra section of the highway, which will extend the A18 Autostrada from Ispica to Modica, is due to open toward the end of 2022. Ignore the stereotypes of Italian drivers. If you keep a steady speed, use your GPS, and don't make any sudden moves, you will be perfectly fine.

TRAIN

A direct Intercity train is available from Rome to Siracusa, but just keep in mind that this takes 11 hours and an individual ticket costs around €80. This is a little more comfortable and quicker than the old regional trains, but still not as fast and luxurious as the Frecciarossa trains that link major towns and cities on mainland Italy. However, you will have the unique experience of all the train carriages being loaded onto a ferry for the journey across the Straits of Messina.

All the major towns and cities in this region are served by Trenitalia, but services are unreliable at best due to one track serving the area, and there are frequent cancellations, or at best, trains are rescheduled.

You can reach Siracusa from Catania in 90 minutes by direct regional train for €8. However, even connections to and from other major cities in Sicily are served only by the quite old *regionale voloce* (fast regional) trains. This means that a journey from Siracusa to Palermo can take between five and seven hours depending on the train that you catch, with tickets starting at €17. A coach journey between these two towns will cost no more than €12, and will get you there in approximately four hours.

CONTACTS Trenitalia. ☎ 892021 *in Italy, 06/68475475 outside Italy* ⊕ *www. trenitalia.com.*

Hotels

In most towns in this region (and especially Siracusa), you will be able to find a range of accommodations to suit your needs, from high-end hotels to quaint B&Bs. Just keep in mind that Scicli and Palazzolo Acreide are less visited by tourists, so you won't find too many proper (or recommendable) hotels there, but there are some quality apartments and rentals available for travelers.

Restaurants

Like the rest of Sicily, this region has been invaded numerous times, so southeastern Sicilian cuisine tends to have various culinary influences, particularly from North Africa. Expect stunning seafood and meats and plenty of seasonal vegetables, like asparagus and artichokes in the spring, eggplants and chilies in summer, and chestnuts, hazelnuts, and wild mushrooms in the winter. As a major city, Siracusa has the biggest selection of restaurants, but there has been a mini-explosion of new-wave gourmet restaurants in the Baroque towns of Ragusa, Modica, and especially Noto.

The majority of restaurants here tend to be casual and relaxed, but if you prefer to dress up for the occasion and spend a little more, options like Don Camillo in Siracusa or Duomo restaurant in Ragusa are good places for a celebration.

RESTAURANT AND HOTEL PRICES
Restaurant prices in the reviews are the average cost of a main course at dinner, or if dinner is not served, at lunch. Hotel prices in the reviews are the lowest cost of a standard double room in high season. Restaurant and hotel reviews have been shortened. For full information, visit Fodors.com.

What it Costs in Euros			
$	**$$**	**$$$**	**$$$$**
RESTAURANTS			
under €15	€15–€22	€23–€30	over €30
HOTELS			
under €125	€125–€225	€226–€350	over €350

Visitor Information

Each town or city has its own tourist information office that will be more than happy to give you advice and travel leaflets to help you make the most of your time in the region.

Siracusa

Siracusa, known to English speakers as Syracuse, is a wonder to behold. One of the great ancient capitals of Western civilization, the city was founded in 734 BC by Greek colonists from Corinth and soon grew to rival—and even surpass—Athens in splendor and power. It became the largest, wealthiest city-state in the West and a bulwark of Greek civilization. Although Siracusa lived under tyranny, rulers such as Dionysius filled their courts with Greeks of the highest cultural stature—among them the playwrights Aeschylus and Euripides and the philosopher Plato. The Athenians, who didn't welcome Siracusa's rise, set out to conquer Sicily, but the natives outsmarted them in what was one of the greatest military campaigns in ancient history (413 BC). The city continued to prosper until it was conquered two centuries later by the Romans.

Present-day Siracusa still has some of the finest examples of Baroque art and architecture; dramatic Greek and Roman ruins; and a Duomo that's the stuff of legend—a microcosm of the city's entire history in one building. The modern city also has a wonderful, lively Baroque old town worthy of extensive exploration, as well as pleasant piazzas, outdoor cafés and bars, and a wide assortment of excellent seafood. There are essentially two areas to explore in Siracusa: the Parco Archeologico (Archaeological Zone) on the mainland, and the island of Ortigia (spelled Ortygia by English speakers), the ancient city first inhabited by the Greeks, which juts out into the Ionian Sea and is connected to the mainland by two small bridges. Ortigia has become increasingly popular with tourists, and although it's filled with lots of modern boutiques (and tourist shops), it still retains its charm despite the crowds.

GETTING HERE AND AROUND

On the main train line from Messina and Catania, Siracusa is also linked to Catania and the nearby Val di Noto by frequent buses.

Although Ortigia is a compact area and a pleasure to amble around without getting unduly tired, mainland Siracusa is a grid of wide modern avenues. At the northern end of Corso Gelone, above Viale Paolo Orsi, the orderly grid gives way to the ancient quarter of Neapolis, where the sprawling Parco Archeologico is accessible from Viale Teracati (an extension of Corso Gelone). East of Viale Teracati, about a 10-minute walk from the Parco Archeologico, the district of Tyche holds the archaeological museum and the church and catacombs of San Giovanni, both off Viale Teocrito (drive or take a taxi or city bus from Ortigia). Coming from the train station, it's a 15-minute trudge to Ortigia along Via Francesco Crispi and Corso Umberto. If you're not up for that, take one of the free electric buses leaving every 10 minutes from the station around the corner.

VISITOR INFORMATION

CONTACT Siracusa Tourism Office. ✉ *Via Roma 31, Ortygia* ☎ *800931/055500* ⊕ *www.siracusaturismo.net.*

Archaeological Zone

Sights

Catacomba di San Giovanni

RUINS | Not far from the Archaeological Park, off Viale Teocrito, the catacombs below the church of San Giovanni are one of the earliest known Christian sites

Walk inside the Ear of Dionysius, the Greek god of wine, fertility, ritual madness, and religious ecstasy.

in the city. Inside the crypt of San Marciano is an altar where St. Paul preached on his way through Sicily to Rome. The frescoes in this small chapel are mostly bright and fresh, though some dating from the 4th century AD show their age. To visit the catacombs, you must take a 45-minute guided tour (included with the admission price), which leaves about every half hour and is conducted in Italian and English. ⊠ *Piazza San Giovanni, Tyche* ☎ *0931/64694* ⊕ *www.kairos-web.com* 🖼 *€8* ⊗ *Closed daily 12:30–2:30 and Mon. in winter.*

Museo Archeologico Regionale Paolo Orsi
HISTORY MUSEUM | The impressive collection of Siracusa's splendid archaeological museum is organized by region and time period around a central atrium and ranges from Neolithic pottery to fine Greek statues and vases. Compare the Landolina Venus—a headless goddess of love who rises out of the sea in measured modesty (a 1st-century-AD Roman copy of the Greek original)—with the much earlier (300 BC) elegant Greek

statue of Hercules in Section C. Of a completely different style is a marvelous fanged Gorgon, its tongue sticking out, that once adorned the cornice of the Temple of Athena to ward off evildoers. ⊠ *Viale Teocrito 66, Tyche* ☎ *0931/489514* ⊕ *www.regione.sicilia.it/beniculturali/ museopaoloorsi* 🖼 *€10; combined ticket with Parco Archeologico della Neapolis €22; additional fees for special exhibitions* ⊗ *Closed Mon.*

★ Parco Archeologico della Neapolis
RUINS | Siracusa is most famous for its dramatic set of Greek and Roman ruins, which are considered to be some of the best archaeological sites in all of Italy and should be combined with a stop at the Museo Archeologico. If the park is closed, go up Viale G. Rizzo from Viale Teracati to the belvedere overlooking the ruins, which are floodlit at night.

Before the park's ticket booth is the gigantic Ara di Ierone (Altar of Hieron), which was once used by the Greeks for spectacular sacrifices involving hundreds of animals. The first attraction in the

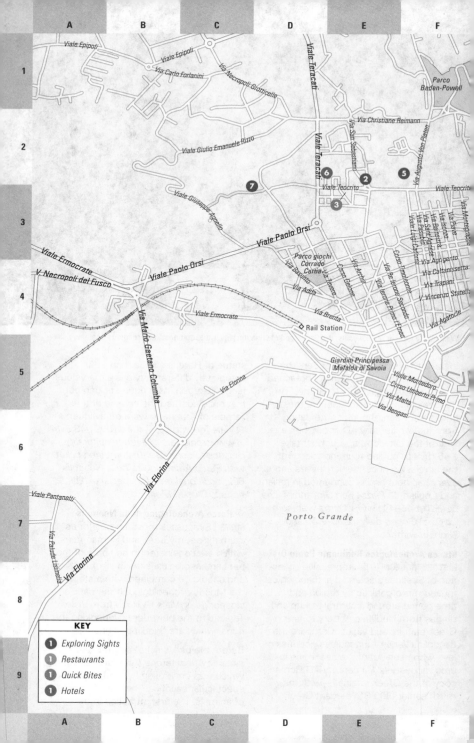

Siracusa

Ionian Sea

Porto Piccolo

7

Siracusa and the Southeast SIRACUSA

0 ────── 1,000 ft
0 ──┴──── 200 m

park is the Latomia del Paradiso (Quarry of Paradise), a lush tropical garden full of palm and citrus trees. This series of quarries served as prisons for the defeated Athenians, who were enslaved; the quarries once rang with the sound of their chisels and hammers. At one end is the famous **Orecchio di Dionisio (Ear of Dionysius)**, with an ear-shape entrance and unusual acoustics inside, as you'll hear if you clap your hands. The legend is that Dionysius used to listen in at the top of the quarry to hear what the enslaved people were plotting below.

The **Teatro Greco** is the chief monument in the Archaeological Park. Indeed it's one of Sicily's greatest classical sites and the most complete Greek theater surviving from antiquity. Climb to the top of the seating area (which could accommodate 15,000) for a fine view: all the seats converge upon a single point—the stage—which has the natural scenery and the sky as its backdrop. Hewn out of the hillside rock in the 5th century BC, the theater saw the premieres of the plays of Aeschylus, and Greek tragedies are still performed here every year in May and June. Above and behind the theater runs the Via dei Sepulcri, in which streams of running water flow through a series of Greek sepulchers.

The well-preserved and striking Anfiteatro Romano (Roman Amphitheater) reveals much about the differences between the Greek and Roman personalities. Where drama in the Greek theater was a kind of religious ritual, the Roman amphitheater emphasized the spectacle of combative sports and the circus. This arena is one of the largest of its kind and was built around the 2nd century AD. The corridor where gladiators and beasts entered the ring is still intact, and the seats (some of which still bear the occupants' names) were hauled in and constructed on the site from huge slabs of limestone. ✉ *Viale Teocrito, entrance on Via Agnello, Archaeological Zone* ☎ *0931/66206* 🌐 *www.regione.sicilia.it/beniculturali/museopaoloorsi* 🎫 *€17, combined ticket with Museo Archeologico €22; free 1st Sun. of month.*

☕ Coffee and Quick Bites

Leonardi

$ | BAKERY | For some great Sicilian cakes and ice cream on your way to the Archaeological Park, visit this bar-cum-pasticceria. It's popular with locals, so you may have to line up for your cakes during holiday times. **Known for:** handy location near the Archaeological Park; a favorite of locals; great coffee and cakes. [$] *Average main: €3* ✉ *Viale Teocrito 123, Siracusa* ☎ *0931/61411* 🌐 *www.pasticcerialeonardi.com.*

🛏 Hotels

★ **Algilà Ortigia Charme Hotel**

$$$$ | HOTEL | It's hard to say what's more charming about this boutique hotel: its location overlooking the sea on the edge of the old town, or its delightful interiors, including guest rooms done up in country-chic style, with a mix of modern amenities (Bulgari toiletries, free minibar) and antique touches (wood-beamed ceilings, hand-painted tiles in the bathroom). **Pros:** wonderfully central location; eager-to-please service with valet parking (fee); prime water views. **Cons:** not all rooms have sea views; lots of stairs could be an issue for some; no spa, pool, or gym. [$] *Rooms from: €328* ✉ *Via Vittorio Veneto 93, Ortygia* ☎ *0931/465186* 🌐 *www.algila.it* 🔑 *54 rooms* 🍴 *Free Breakfast.*

Grand Hotel Villa Politi

$$ | HOTEL | Winston Churchill, European royalty, and other VIPs have frequented the grand 18th-century Villa Politi, and although it's now a little faded, it retains a sense of charm and elegance with rococo furnishings alongside modern luxuries like comfy beds. **Pros:** excellent service; expansive outdoor pool and nearby private beach; free parking in the hotel

The Parco Archeologico della Neapolis is home to a vast collection of Greek and Roman ruins.

lot. **Cons:** not as sparkling and fresh as in the past; not many restaurants in the neighborhood; a fair distance from the sights of Ortigia. [$] *Rooms from: €180* ✉ *Via M. Politi 2, Archaeological Zone* ☎ *0931/412121* 🌐 *www.villapoliti.com* 🛏 *100 rooms* 🍴 *Free Breakfast.*

Mercure Siracusa Prometeo
$$ | HOTEL | This spot occupies a glass-fronted building along the busy Viale Teracati and, like most other hotels in the same chain, it's a slick operation with first-rate amenities. **Pros:** two-minute walk from the archaeological site of Neapolis; good parking; swimming pool on the roof. **Cons:** €10 breakfast; a long way from the island of Ortigia; chain hotel with little character. [$] *Rooms from: €150* ✉ *Viale Teracati 20, Tyche* ☎ *0931/464646* 🌐 *www.hotelmercuresiracusa.com* 🛏 *93 rooms* 🍴 *No Meals.*

🍸 Nightlife

Red Moon
BARS | Located on the waterfront that divides the mainland from Ortigia, Red Moon is hidden in plain sight and can be easy to miss. But once you find it, it's the perfect setting for a nightcap and snack at the end of the night. More substantial meals are available too. Ignore the official closing time of 10:30 pm; it actually closes whenever the last customer leaves. ✉ *Riva Porto Lachio 36, Santa Lucia* ☎ *0931/60356.*

🎟 Performing Arts

Teatro Greco (*Greek Theater*)
THEATER | From early May to mid-July, Siracusa's ancient Teatro Greco stages performances of classical tragedy and comedy. Tickets range €36–€73, with a small discount if you buy the ticket in person. ✉ *Via del Teatro Greco, Archaeological Zone* ☎ *0931/487248 ticket office* 🌐 *www.indafondazione.org.*

Ortigia

Sights

Castello Maniace

CASTLE/PALACE | The southern tip of Ortigia island is occupied by this castle built by Frederick II (1194–1250), from which there are fine sea views (until recently, it was an army barracks). There's also a small museum with information about the castle's history and artifacts found during excavations, though English translations are limited. ⊠ *Via del Castello Maniace 51, Ortygia* ☎ *0931/4508211* ⊕ *aditusculture.com/biglietti/sicilia/siracu-sa/castello-maniace-siracusa* ⊠ *€7.*

★ Duomo

RELIGIOUS BUILDING | Siracusa's Duomo is an archive of more than 2,000 years of island history, and has creatively incorporated ruins through the many time periods it has survived, starting with the bottommost, where excavations have unearthed remnants of Sicily's distant past, when the Siculi inhabitants worshipped their deities here. During the 5th century BC (the same time Agrigento's Temple of Concord was built), the Greeks erected a temple to Athena over it, and in the 7th century, Siracusa's first Christian cathedral was built on top of the Greek structure. The massive columns of the original Greek temple were incorporated into the present structure and are clearly visible, embedded in the exterior wall along Via Minerva. The Greek columns were also used to dramatic advantage inside, where on one side they form chapels connected by elegant wrought-iron gates. The Baroque facade, added in the 18th century, displays a harmonious rhythm of concaves and convexes. In front, the sun-kissed stone piazza is encircled by pink and white oleanders and elegant buildings ornamented with filigree grillwork, and is typically filled with frolicking children and street musicians. Check with the tourist office for guided tours of its underground tunnels, which are located to the right when you stand facing the cathedral. ⊠ *Piazza del Duomo, Ortygia* ☎ *0931/65328* ⊕ *arcidi-ocesi.siracusa.it/chiesa-cattedrale* ⊠ *€2.*

Fonte Aretusa

FOUNTAIN | A freshwater spring, the Fountain of Arethusa, sits next to the sea, studded with Egyptian papyrus that's reportedly natural. This anomaly is explained by a Greek legend that tells how the nymph Arethusa was changed into a fountain by the goddess Artemis (Diana) when she tried to escape the advances of the river god Alpheus. She fled from Greece, into the sea, with Alpheus in close pursuit, and emerged in Sicily at this spring. It's said if you throw a cup into the Alpheus River in Greece, it will emerge here at this fountain, which is home to a few tired ducks and some faded carp—but no cups. If you want to stand right by the fountain, you need to gain admission through the aquarium; otherwise look down on it from Largo Aretusa. ⊠ *Largo Aretusa, Ortygia* ⊹ *Off promenade along harbor* ☎ *0931/65861* ⊕ *www.fontearetusasiracusa.it* ⊠ *€5* ⊘ *Closed Tues.*

Museo del Papiro

OTHER MUSEUM | Housed in the 16th-century former convent of Sant'Agostino, the small but intriguing Papyrus Museum uses informative exhibits and videos to demonstrate how papyri are prepared from reeds and then painted—an ancient tradition in the city. Siracusa, it seems, has the only climate outside the Nile Valley in which the papyrus plant—from which the word "paper" comes—thrives. ⊠ *Via Nizza 14, Ortygia* ☎ *0931/22100* ⊕ *www.museodelpapiro.it* ⊠ *€5* ⊘ *Closed Mon.*

Piazza Archimede

PLAZA/SQUARE | The center of this piazza has a Baroque fountain, the Fontana di Diana, festooned with fainting sea nymphs and dancing jets of water. Look for the Chiaramonte-style **Palazzo**

Montalto, an arched-window gem just off the piazza on Via Montalto. ✉ *Piazza Archimede, Ortygia.*

Tempio di Apollo

RUINS | Scattered through the piazza just across the bridge to Ortigia are the ruins of a temple dedicated to Apollo, which dates back to the 6th century BC. A model of this is in the Museo Archeologico. In fact, little of this noble Doric temple remains except for some crumbled walls and shattered columns; the window in the south wall belongs to a Norman church that was built much later on the same spot. ✉ *Largo XXV Luglio, Ortygia* ☞ *Free.*

 Restaurants

Archimede

$$ | **PIZZA** | Although the restaurant gets decidedly mixed reviews, the Archimede pizzeria offers well-made pizzas with classical names, such as the Teocrite, topped with fresh tomato, mozzarella, garlic, onion, and basil. For those who can't face the full-size offerings, minipizzas are also available (albeit at the same price), and everyone should find enough space to sample one of the many bottled beers on the menu. **Known for:** good beer selection; reasonable prices; satisfying pizzas. ⓢ *Average main: €15* ✉ *Via Gemmellaro 8, Ortygia* ☎ *0931/69701.*

★ Don Camillo

$$ | **SICILIAN** | A gracious series of delicately arched rooms at this beloved local eatery are lined with wine bottles and sepia-tone images of the old town. À la carte preparations bring together fresh seafood and inspired creativity: sample, for instance, the sublime spaghetti *delle Sirene* (with sea urchin and shrimp in butter) or *gamberoni* (prawns) prepared, unexpectedly (and wonderfully), in pork fat. If you want, you can put yourself in the hands of the chef and opt for one of the exquisite tasting menus, which start at €70 excluding wine. **Known for:**

fantastic wine list; helpful service; fish, meat, and vegetarian tasting menus. ⓢ *Average main: €20* ✉ *Via Maestranza 96, Ortygia* ☎ *0931/67133* ⊕ *www. ristorantedoncamillosiracusa.it* ☾ *Closed Sun., 2 wks in Jan., and 2 wks in July.*

Il Pesce Azzurro Osteria

$$$ | **SICILIAN** | As the name suggests, this is a temple to everything from the sea, caught fresh and prepared simply. Choose from local clams, prawns anointed with lime, calamari, or whatever else that has been recently caught. Just prepared to book ahead as this is very popular with locals, and a table may be hard to find if you just walk in. **Known for:** lively restaurant packed with locals; extensive menu of fresh seafood; very popular so booking ahead is smart. ⓢ *Average main: €30* ✉ *Via Cavour 53, Ortygia* ☎ *366/2445056* ⊕ *www.facebook.com/ osteriailpesceazzurro.*

Le Vin de l'Assassin

$$ | **MODERN ITALIAN** | A short walk from the Fontana di Diana, this restaurant prepares traditional Sicilian dishes with a French influence, such as the savory cannoli starters. One of the mainstays on the menu is tuna lasagne, which is quite popular with locals. **Known for:** always changing seasonal menu; cozy and intimate atmosphere; interesting interpretations of traditional Sicilian dishes. ⓢ *Average main: €20* ✉ *Via Roma 115, Ortygia* ☎ *0931/66159* ⊕ *levindelassassin.eatbu.com* ☾ *Closed Mon. No lunch Tues.–Sat.*

Osteria Sveva

$$ | **SICILIAN** | At this slow-food tavern, conveniently located right behind the Castello Maniace, you can sit back and enjoy both surf and turf dishes in the studiously modern but minimalist surroundings. One major plus is that you can order half portions of several pasta dishes or opt for a secondo, like the unusual *pesce in crosta di patate* (grilled fish in a potato crust)—all served on hand-painted ceramic ware. **Known for:** charming

setting on a square; good-value meals; authentic Sicilian dishes. [$] *Average main: €15* ✉ *Piazza Federico di Svevia 1, Ortygia* ☎ *0931/24663* 🕓 *Closed Jan., Nov., and Wed. mid-Sept.–June. No lunch June–Sept.*

Coffee and Quick Bites

Caseificio Borderi

$ | **SICILIAN** | If you are visiting the local historic market nearby, this is an essential place to stop and refuel. The owner can usually be found outside tempting people with paninis that will keep you full until dinner. **Known for:** substantial and varied panini; freshly prepared food from the local market; friendly atmosphere. [$] *Average main: €7* ✉ *Via Emmanuele De Benedectis 6, Ortygia* ☎ *329/9852500* 🌐 *www.caseificioborderi.eu* 🕓 *Closed Sun. No dinner.*

★ **Fratelli Burgio**

$ | **SICILIAN** | This small bar and deli is another must-visit spot on the fringes of Ortigia's historic market. You can choose from a generously stuffed panini, a plate of the local antipasti, or a small plate of whatever is in season from the sea. **Known for:** great location next to local market; generously sized dishes using local produce; shop for wine and food-based souvenirs. [$] *Average main: €7* ✉ *Piazza Cesare Battisti 4, Ortygia* ☎ *0931/60069* 🌐 *www.fratelliburgio.com/en* 🕓 *Closed Sun. No dinner.*

Hotels

★ **Anime a Sud–Casa Sabir**

$$ | **APARTMENT** | A stylish, luxurious, and modernized apartment originally built in the early 19th century, Casa Sabir faces the historic open market of Ortigia, with balconies that open up onto the market and views of the Ionian Sea. The apartment has been tastefully restored using original materials and handmade bespoke furniture, and also has a huge kitchen with a steel island for those who want to cook using local produce from the market. **Pros:** ideal location for exploring Ortigia; full kitchen and on-site wine cellar; fabulous sea views. **Cons:** no on-site parking; only fits four guests total; self-catering although restaurants are within walking distance. [$] *Rooms from: €150* ✉ *Via Giaracà 7, Ortygia* 🌐 *www.animeasud.it/en* 🛏 *1 apartment with 2 bedrooms* 🍴 *No Meals.*

★ **Domus Mariae**

$$ | **HOTEL** | On Ortigia's eastern shore, this hotel, in an unusual twist, is owned by Ursuline nuns, who help to make the mood placid and peaceful, but the elegant accommodations are far from monastic. **Pros:** nice breakfast; enthusiastic staff; gorgeous sea views and rooftop terrace. **Cons:** small rooms and not all rooms have sea views; not much street parking near the hotel; stairs to climb. [$] *Rooms from: €149* ✉ *Via Vittorio Veneto 76, Ortygia* ☎ *0931/60087* 🌐 *www.domusmariaebenessere.com* 🛏 *12 rooms* 🍴 *Free Breakfast.*

Grand Hotel Ortigia

$$$ | **HOTEL** | An elegant though somewhat old-fashioned design of inlaid wood furniture and stained-glass windows prevails in the guest rooms at this venerable institution, which has enjoyed a prime position on the Porto Grande at the base of Ortigia since 1890. **Pros:** wonderful seafront views from the restaurant; convenient location; private parking (a rarity on Ortigia). **Cons:** Wi-Fi weak in some rooms; small bathrooms; back rooms have no view. [$] *Rooms from: €247* ✉ *Viale Mazzini 12, Ortygia* ☎ *0931/464611* 🌐 *www.grandhotelortigia.it* 🛏 *57 rooms* 🍴 *Free Breakfast.*

Nightlife

Vecchio Pub 1979

PUBS | If you want to escape from the noise and bustle of Ortigia during high tourist season, this well-hidden courtyard pub in one of the island's back streets

One of Noto's many architectural gems is the gorgeous Cattedrale di San Nicolò.

will feel like an oasis of calm. Sit in the secluded garden and finish off your night with a drink and a bruschetta or something more substantial from the reasonably priced menu. ⊠ *Via delle Vergini 9, Ortygia* ☎ *0931/1960430* ⊕ *www.facebook.com/vecchiopub.siracusa.*

🛍 Shopping

★ Ortygia Street Market

MARKET | This historic food market is still the daily shopping center for residents of Ortigia and mainland Siracusa. Seafood stalls display the catch of the day, ranging from local clams that you'll find in most restaurants to sea urchins that normally only appear on the more expensive menus. Even in the colder months, the vegetable and fruit stalls are still vibrant and inviting. One thing to look out for is the local Pachino tomato. It has protected status and can be found fresh, dried, or reduced to a gloriously intense thick paste used in pasta. Intertwined within the stalls are several local bars where you can rest and take in the hustle and bustle

of local Italian food culture. The market is open every day except for Sunday, from 7 am to 1:45 pm. ⊠ *Vicolo Bagnara, Ortygia* ☎ *No phone.*

Noto

38 km (23 miles) southwest of Siracusa.

If Siracusa's Baroque beauties whet your appetite for that over-the-top style, head to Noto, a UNESCO World Heritage site. Lying about 40 minutes away on the A18, the compact and easy-to-navigate city is doable as a day trip—though staying overnight lets you see the lovely buildings glow in the setting sun after the tourist hordes have departed. Despite being decimated by an earthquake in 1693 and rebuilt in the prevailing fashion of the day, Noto has remarkable architectural integrity. A prime example of design from the island's Baroque heyday, it presents a pleasing ensemble of honey-color buildings, strikingly uniform in style but never dull. Simply walking

Corso Vittorio Emanuele, the pedestrianized main street, qualifies as an aesthetic experience.

GETTING HERE AND AROUND

Trains leave from Siracusa at least eight times daily (fewer trains on Sunday); there are also four trains a day from Ragusa, though the station is a bit outside of town. Buses depart numerous times a day from Siracusa, Catania, and Ragusa.

VISITOR INFORMATION

CONTACT Noto Tourism Office. ⊠ *Corso Vittorio Emanuele 135,* ☎ *339/4816218* ⊕ *www.notoinforma.it.*

Sights

★ Cattedrale di San Nicolò

CHURCH | Noto's domed cathedral (divine in more ways than one) is an undisputed highlight of the extraordinary Baroque architecture for which the town is world-famous. Climb the monumental staircase to get a glimpse of the interior—restored over a 10-year period after the dome collapsed in 1996—which is simple compared to the magnificent exterior, but still worth a look. ⊠ *Corso Vittorio Emanuele,* ☎ *0931/835286* ⊕ *www.diocesinoto.it.*

Palazzo Castelluccio

CASTLE/PALACE | This long-abandoned palazzo (originally built in the 18th century) has recently been restored by French journalist and filmmaker Jean-Louis Remileux. If you want an idea of what life was like for the nobility of Noto in days long gone by, call ahead to book a guided tour. ⊠ *Via Camillo Benso Conte di Cavour 10, Noto* ☎ *0931/838881* ⊕ *palazzocastelluccio.it* ⤢ *€12.*

Palazzo Ducezio

CASTLE/PALACE | **FAMILY** | Designed by architect Vincenzo Sinatra in the 17th century, Palazzo Ducezio is still a sight to behold. You can visit both of its two floors, with the top floor offering panoramic views of the surrounding area. The best time to visit is in the afternoon or evening when the local buildings take on a golden hue in the fading light. ⊠ *Piazza Municipio, Noto* ☎ *0931/836462* ⊕ *www.comune.noto.sr.it* ⤢ *€4.*

Palazzo Nicolaci di Villadorata

CASTLE/PALACE | For a rare insight into the lifestyle of social climbers in the 18th century, this palace is a must-see. It contains about 90 rooms belonging to the noble Nicolaci family, and although only some are on view to the public, they include a splendid frescoed ballroom. Outside the palace, note the gorgeous balconies featuring mythical creatures. ⊠ *Via Corrado Nicolaci, Noto* ☎ *338/7427022* ⊕ *www.palazzonicolaci. it* ⤢ *€4.*

Piazza Municipio

PLAZA/SQUARE | While the whole of Noto can make you feel that you are on a film set, its central plaza will really do it. The Palazzo Municipo is home to three of the grandest buildings in Noto, including Palazzo Ducezio, now home to the local town hall, that forms the plaza's main part. If you climb to the top of the ornate staircase to the north you will find Basilica Cattedrale di San Nicolo while on the western side of the palazzo is Palazzo Landolina, which was once home to one of the most powerful families in Noto, the Sant'Alfano family. ⊠ *Piazza del Municipio, Noto.*

Teatro Tina Di Lorenzo

PERFORMANCE VENUE | This still working theater from the 19th century offers guided tours of its small, ornate interior. Check ahead as it often presents programs of classic and contemporary theater in Italian. It was named for silent film actress Tina Di Lorenzo. ⊠ *Piazza XVI Maggio 1, Noto* ☎ *0931/896659* ⊕ *www. fondazioneteatrodinoto.it* ⤢ *€3.*

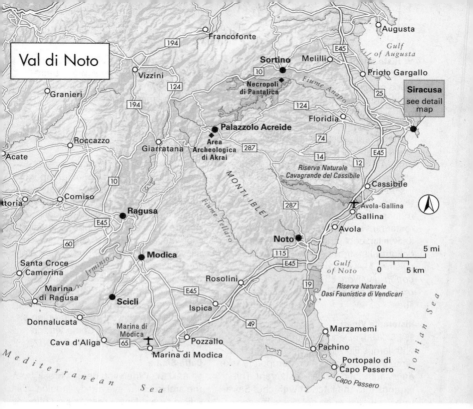

🍽 Restaurants

Anche gli Angeli

$$ | ITALIAN | Part concept store, part bar, and part fine gourmet dining experience, this unique eatery is built into a grotto underneath the Chiesa di San Carlo and specializes in deceptively simple grilled dishes and contemporary cocktails. There's live music on the weekends, but it's quite laid-back and unobtrusive. **Known for:** high-end takes on local meat dishes; excellent drinks; beautiful design under historic arched ceiling. $ *Average main: €18* ✉ *Via Arnaldo da Brescia 2, Noto* 🕾 *0931/576023* ⊕ *www.anchegli-angeli.it.*

★ Ristorante Crocifisso

$$ | SICILIAN | Considered by many as one of Noto's best restaurants, getting to Crocifisso is a bit of a hike as it's away from Noto's tourist area and up a hill only accessible by many steps. However, intrepid diners will be rewarded with one of the Baroque town's finest restaurants, serving traditional dishes presented in a contemporary style in a beautiful modern dining room. **Known for:** fantastic wine selection with a focus on Sicilian and natural wines; superlative house-made pastas; new takes on classic Sicilian dishes. $ *Average main: €18* ✉ *Via Principe Umberto 48, Noto* 🕾 *0931/968608* ⊕ *www.ristorantecrocifisso.it* ⊘ *Closed mid-Jan.–late Feb. and Wed. No lunch Thurs.*

★ Ristorante Manna

$$ | SICILIAN | The plain exterior here gives no hint of the sleek, cool design inside this welcoming restaurant just off of Noto's main street where all of the dishes—from fresh pastas to creative seafood and exceptional daily specials—shine a light on local premium ingredients. Although the small outdoor patio allows for great people-watching, it's inside that the restaurant really shines; the chic multilevel dining area highlights modern art, a stylish complement to the restaurant's thoroughly modern food. **Known for:** cool, contemporary setting; delightful staff; modern, creative Sicilian cuisine. $ *Average main: €18* ⊠ *Via Rocco Pirri 19, Noto* ☎ *0931/836051* ⊕ *www.mannanoto.it* ⊘ *Closed Nov., Jan., and Tues.*

Ristorante Vicari

$$ | SICILIAN | Decorated in a modern style with lamps illuminating each table, Ristorante Vicari provides a contemporary take on an authentic Sicilian restaurant. This extends into the kitchen with chef Salvatore Vicari delivering delicious, modern, and humorous versions of classic dishes, like octopus, potato millefeuille, and red onion in sweet and sour cream or roast chicken with cream of carrots, lemon, and spinach. **Known for:** clever interpretations of classic dishes; intimate atmosphere; the best cannoli in southeastern Sicily. $ *Average main: €18* ⊠ *Ronco Bernardo Leanti 9, Noto* ☎ *0931/839322* ⊕ *www.ristorantevicari.it/en/home* ⊘ *No lunch Sun. and Mon.*

Trattoria del Carmine

$ | SICILIAN | This family-run eatery in the center of town is known for low-key but reliable local dishes and a pleasant atmosphere. If you're not tempted by the fish of the day, you can choose between the various land-based dishes offered, such as ravioli with pork ragù, roasted veal, and rabbit with olives and mint. **Known for:** affordable prices; generous portions; traditional Sicilian dishes.

$ *Average main: €8* ⊠ *Via Ducezio 1/a, Noto* ☎ *0931/838705* ⊕ *www.trattoriadelcarmine.it* ⊘ *Closed Mon. and mid-Jan.–mid-Mar.*

☕ Coffee and Quick Bites

Amuri

$ | SICILIAN | Ideally located for people-watching on Noto's main thoroughfare, this place serves up jam-packed panini, with most of the ingredients (including meats) supplied by local producers, who also subscribe to the slow food movement. Once you've had your fill, you can head next door to their store to stock up on high-quality Sicilian gifts. **Known for:** prime people-watching spot; unusual gift shop next door run by the same company; huge sandwiches using ethical and locally sourced ingredients. $ *Average main: €7* ⊠ *Corso Vittorio Emanuele 80, Noto* ☎ *0931/1620070.*

Caffè Sicilia

$ | BAKERY | When you need a break from the architectural eye candy, indulge in an edible sweet (and a restorative coffee or granita) at this wondrous cake shop. Their cannoli and gelato are particularly highly rated and considered some of the best in the country. **Known for:** house-made ice cream; delicious cannoli; perfect almond granita. $ *Average main: €5* ⊠ *Corso Vittorio Emanuele 125, Noto* ☎ *0931/835013* ⊕ *www.caffesicilia.it* ⊘ *Closed mid-Jan.–mid-Mar.*

Hotels

Gagliardi Boutique Hotel

$$$ | HOTEL | For an unbeatable location only a block from the main pedestrian street, visitors to Noto can't do better than this hotel with an industrial vibe and spacious minimalist rooms accented with chandeliers—all inside a former 18th-century palace. **Pros:** extremely central location; large rooms and good public spaces; friendly service. **Cons:** short on amenities (no restaurant, spa, or pool);

iffy Wi-Fi connection; only one room has a bathtub. [$] *Rooms from: €228* ✉ *Via Silvio Spaventa 41, Noto* ☎ *0931/839730* 🌐 *www.gagliardihotel.com* 🛏 *11 rooms* 🍴 *Free Breakfast.*

Masseria degli Ulivi
$$ | B&B/INN | FAMILY | Up on the Hyblean plateau, a good 15-minute drive north of Noto, this rural *masseria* (farm) is surrounded by tastefully designed two-story lodging and immersed in olive groves. **Pros:** excellent restaurant; courteous staff; airy breakfast room with patio. **Cons:** rooms are sparsely decorated; breakfast could be better; really need your own transport. [$] *Rooms from: €144* ✉ *Contrada Porcari SS287, Noto* ☎ *0931/813019* 🌐 *www.masseriadegliulivi.com* 🕒 *Closed Nov.–Mar.* 🛏 *34 rooms* 🍴 *Free Breakfast.*

★ Seven Rooms Villadorata
$$$ | HOTEL | Once the residence of the illustrious Villadorata princely family, this luxury hotel now offers guests a taste of the real Sicilian aristocracy. **Pros:** luxurious toiletries provided; parking on-site; good restaurant. **Cons:** some rooms only have views of the courtyard; can be pricey if not booked far in advance; restaurant a bit expensive. [$] *Rooms from: €300* ✉ *Via Camillo Benso Conte di Cavour 53, Noto* ☎ *0931/835575* 🌐 *www.7roomsvilladorata.it* 🛏 *7 rooms* 🍴 *Free Breakfast.*

Scicli

44 km (27 miles) west of Noto.

Overshadowed by its larger neighbors, Modica and Ragusa, Scicli is a Baroque beauty in its own right and one of the eight villages designated by UNESCO in the Val di Noto. In recent years, it has entered Italian popular culture as the filming location of the hugely popular Montalbano series, but its decorated stone palaces and unique Madonna delle Milizie (Virgin Mary of Militias) will delight visitors who may not yet know the Sicilian detective show.

GETTING HERE AND AROUND

Buses from Siracusa, Ragusa (by way of Modica), and Noto stop in Scicli on a regular basis.

Sights

Chiesa di San Bartolomeo
CHURCH | An enchanting fusion of the Baroque and rococo lies behind the lace grate doors of this church on the edge of the town's historic center. Inside the single-nave church is a wooden nativity scene that dates back to the 16th century. ✉ *Via S. Bartolomeo, Scicli* 🎫 *Free.*

Chiesa di San Matteo
VIEWPOINT | Scicli is a city of honey-hued churches, all built after the devastating earthquake in the 17th century. The church of San Matteo is abandoned, but it's well worth climbing the shallow stairs up the steep hillside to take in the panoramic views of Scicli's old town from the terrace in front of the church. ✉ *Via San Matteo 9, Scicli.*

Chiesa di Sant'Ignazio
CHURCH | Founded in the 17th century as a Jesuit church, this was rebuilt following the 1693 earthquake. Housing the remains of Scicli's patron saint Guglielmo the hermit, a side chapel also hosts the life-size papier-mâché statue of the Madonna *su cavallo* (on a horse), the Madonna delle Milizie. This is paraded through the streets on the last Saturday in May to celebrate her feast day. ✉ *Piazza Italia, Scicli* ☎ *0932/931278.*

Palazzo Beneventano
HISTORIC SIGHT | If the other palazzoli in Scicli simply hint at the luxury of the town's golden age, then this is a full-on assault on the senses. The exterior is covered by stone-carved statues, including representations of mythical creatures and enslaved people that serve as an essential reminder of the town's

role in the region's slave trade. ✉ *Via Beneventano 17, Scicli.*

Palazzo Bonelli Patanè

CASTLE/PALACE | Quite plain on the outside, it's easy to walk straight past this gem. But if you venture inside, you'll be overwhelmed by the opulence of the antique furniture, silk wallpapers, and frescoes that adorn the interiors. If you want to see how the high society of Scicli once lived, then this is the place. ✉ *Via Francesco Mormino Penna 1, Scicli* ☎ *338/8614973* ⊕ *sistemamusealescicli. it/sites/palazzo-bonelli-patane* ✉ *€3.*

Restaurants

★ **My Name is Tannino**

$$ | SICILIAN | In a fantastic spot by the now-drained river in Scicli, you'll need to book ahead here to enjoy a meal since it's quite popular with locals. That's thanks to the menu and the fact that you can enjoy a variety of dining options, from a simple aperitivo to a full-blown meal from the ever-changing seasonal menu. **Known for:** prime riverfront location, with outdoor and indoor seating; locally grown and ethically sourced ingredients; small store at the back selling ingredients and gifts. $ *Average main: €18* ✉ *Via Aleardi 36/38, Noto* ☎ *338/9261431* ⊕ *www. facebook.com/mynameistanninovinieali-menti* ⊗ *No lunch.*

Ristorante Non Lo So

$$ | SICILIAN | A must-visit for seafood lovers, here you'll find various fish-only tasting menus ranging from €25 for six appetizers to the full experience of 10 courses (six appetizers, one first course, two mains, and one dessert) for €45. If you are here on a Sunday, book ahead and enjoy a set price menu of an appetizer, first course, main course, dessert, and wine for only €30. **Known for:** some of the region's best fish; reasonably priced tasting menus; intimate ambience. $ *Average main: €20* ✉ *Via Caneva 8, Noto* ☎ *331/4967801* ⊕ *www.*

ristorantenonloso.it ⊗ *Closed Mon., Tues., and Wed. No lunch Thurs.*

🛏 Hotels

★ **Scicli Albergo Diffuso**

$ | HOTEL | Since it's a bit off-the-beaten-path, Scicli doesn't have too many hotels, but a good choice to rest your head is Albergo Diffuso, which can best be described as a "horizontal hotel" where rooms are located in different historic homes throughout the town. **Pros:** good breakfast provided; free parking; fabulous decor. **Cons:** no restaurant on-site; might not know your exact room or location until check-in (especially in high season); some apartments substantially smaller than others. $ *Rooms from: €75* ✉ *Via Francesco Mormino Penna 15, Noto* ☎ *0932/1855555* ⊕ *sciclialbergodiffuso. it* 🛏 *24 rooms, 5 apartments* ❙❀❙ *Free Breakfast.*

Modica

37 km (23 miles) west of Noto.

Modica and Ragusa are the two chief cities in Sicily's smallest province (also called Ragusa), and the centers of a region known as Iblea. The dry, rocky, and gentle countryside filled with canyons and grassy knolls is a unique landscape for Sicily. In Modica, the main artery—Corso Umberto I—is lined with shops and restaurants and is in the valley at the bottom of the town (called Modica Bassa), while the old town of Modica Alta is built atop a ridge. That's part of this UNESCO-listed area's charm; it's a joy to wander its steep 14th-century lanes traversed by endless staircases and lined with Baroque architecture. Modica is also famed for its chocolate—don't miss trying it at one of the many stores on Corso Umberto I.

GETTING HERE AND AROUND

Trains leave from Siracusa six times a day, while buses from Catania, Siracusa, Ragusa, and Noto also stop in Modica on a regular basis.

VISITOR INFORMATION

CONTACT Modica Tourism Office. ✉ *Corso Umberto I 141,* ☎ *346/6558227.*

Sights

Cattedrale di San Pietro

CHURCH | Statues of the apostles line the staircase of Modica's cathedral, which was originally constructed in the 14th century, then rebuilt in an impressive Baroque style following its destruction in the 1693 earthquake. ✉ *Corso Umberto I 120,* ☎ *0932/941074* 🌐 *www.scoprimodica.it/cosa-vedere/le-chiese/san-pietro* 🎫 *Free.*

★ **Chiesa di San Giorgio**

CHURCH | This lovely Baroque church in Modica Alta, dating from after the 1693 earthquake, is reached by climbing 250 steps that crisscross in a monumental staircase leading up to the main doors. It's worth the effort for the amazing views over the old town. ✉ *Corso San Giorgio, Modica* ☎ *0932/941279* 🌐 *www.scoprimodica.it/cosa-vedere/le-chiese/san-giorgio* 🎫 *Free.*

Museo del Cioccolato di Modica

OTHER MUSEUM | There is an abundance of choice when it comes to indulgent desserts in Sicily, but the chocolate of Modica—cooked at a low temperature and possessed of a distinctive granular texture—is prized above all others. It feels only natural, then, to find a museum in the center of the old town dedicated to the local sweet. The small exhibits (with English translations) follow the history of chocolate in general, before describing the way cacao beans first arrived in Modica, and how they were traditionally processed by being ground on a board made of volcanic stone. There is also an eccentric collection of sculptures and celebrity portraits made entirely of chocolate. ✉ *Corso Umberto I 149, 1st fl., behind Museo Civico, Modica* ☎ *347/4612771* 🌐 *museocioccolatomodica.business.site* 🎫 *€3* 🕒 *Closed Mon.*

Restaurants

★ **Accursio Ristorante**

$$$$ | **SICILIAN** | This intimate Michelin-starred restaurant is a fantastic option if you are staying in Modica overnight. Forget the usual starchy tablecloths and formal service, this place is all about the food, with the chef cooking his own personal takes on classic Sicilian dishes, including options like Trucioli pasta with cheese fondue, lemon, and capers; grilled lettuce with pork cheek, caviar, and walnuts; and cannoli with ricotta cheese and cotton candy for dessert. **Known for:** equally extensive and more affordable lunch menu; Michelin-starred food at reasonable prices; relaxed atmosphere. [$] *Average main: €120* ✉ *Via Grimaldi 41, Modica* ☎ *0932/941689* 🌐 *www.accursioristorante.it* 🕒 *Closed Mon. No dinner Sun.*

★ **Singola Ristorante Naturale**

$$ | **VEGETARIAN** | Vegetarians and vegans will find their options can be somewhat limited when dining in Sicily, so they will be delighted to find Singola, a restaurant that focuses on organic vegetarian and vegan food with Sicilian flare. It's a little outside of town, but it's set within a lovely garden. **Known for:** locally sourced vegetarian and vegan food; extensive choice of organic wines; eco-friendly wood cabin setting. [$] *Average main: €18* ✉ *Via Risorgimento 88, Modica* ☎ *0932/904807* 🌐 *www.singolaristorantenaturale.com* 🕒 *No lunch.*

The Upper Town of Ragusa, known as Ragusa Ibla, is a historic collection of buildings perched on a hilltop.

Coffee and Quick Bites

Caffè dell'Arte

$ | **ITALIAN** | **FAMILY** | Across the street from the Museo del Cioccolato, this small coffee bar makes excellent granita. The shaved ice is often eaten for breakfast in the summer months with a soft brioche, and the toasted almond flavor here is particularly good. **Known for:** casual outdoor seating; great almond granita; best hot chocolate in town. [$] *Average main: €5* ✉ *Corso Umberto I 114* ☎ *0932/943257* 🌐 *caffedellarte.it* 🕒 *Closed Tues.*

Pasticceria Di Lorenzo

$ | **BAKERY** | **FAMILY** | Wood lined and unadorned, this family-run pastry shop is one of the best places to try Modica's signature crescent-shape cookies, the *'mpanatigghi*. These soft cookies are filled with a mixture of chocolate, almonds, and veal, a combination that works surprisingly well. The meat was added to the cookies as a way of making the snacks more nutritious on long voyages. **Known for:** specialty cookies; family run; chocolate squares that resemble the city's cobblestones. [$] *Average main: €5* ✉ *Corso Umberto I 225, Modica* ☎ *0932/945324* 🌐 *www.pasticceriadilorenzo.it* 🕒 *Closed Wed.*

Shopping

Modica is famous for its chocolate, which uses an ancient Aztec technique. Made at a low heat, it has a grainier consistency than most. It's actually more difficult to find a shop here that doesn't sell the local chocolate, usually in a wide variety of flavors.

★ Antica Dolceria Bonajuto

CHOCOLATE | Bonajuto is the oldest chocolate producer in town, dating from 1880. This busy shop on Modica Bassa's main street lets you sample many varieties of their delightful product before you buy, and also makes renowned cannoli and candied orange peel. ✉ *Corso Umberto I 159, Modica* ☎ *0932/941225* 🌐 *www.bonajuto.it.*

Ragusa

21 km (13 miles) northwest of Modica.

Ragusa, a modern city with a beautiful historic core, is known for some great local red wines and wonderful cheese—a creamy, doughy, flavorful version of *caciocavallo,* made by hand every step of the way. It also has some wonderful Baroque buildings with fabulous vantage points throughout its narrow, twisty, and steep old town.

GETTING HERE AND AROUND

Trains and buses leave from Siracusa four or five times daily.

VISITOR INFORMATION

CONTACT Ragusa Tourism Office. ⊠ *Piazza della Repubblica,* ☎ *0932/684780.*

Sights

Basilica di San Giorgio

CHURCH | Designed by Rosario Gagliardi in 1738, the duomo is a fine example of the Sicilian Baroque. ⊠ *Salita Duomo 15, Ragusa* ☎ *0932/220085* ⊕ *www.diocesidiragusa.it.*

Giardino Ibleo

GARDEN | Set on the edge of the old town, Giardino Ibleo is a tranquil public garden lined with palm trees and dotted with fountains and churches along stone paths. The ambling walkways skirt the cliff side and offer dramatic views of the valley below. ⊠ *Via Giardino, Ragusa* ☎ *0932/652374.*

Ragusa Ibla

HISTORIC DISTRICT | The lovely historic center of Ragusa, known as Ibla, was completely rebuilt after the devastating earthquake of 1693. Its tumble of buildings are perched on a hilltop and suspended between a deep ravine and a sloping valley. The tiny squares and narrow lanes make for pleasant meandering, but expect plenty of stairs. ⊠ *Ragusa.*

Restaurants

Duomo

$$$$ | **SICILIAN** | In an understated palazzo on a cobblestone street near the Duomo, star chef Ciccio Sultano prepares imaginative and beautifully plated splurge-worthy dinners and a four-course set lunch menu (a terrific value) that include unforgettable variations on classic Sicilian cuisine. Although dishes can be ordered à la carte, tasting menus convey a fuller sense of the chef's signature style, which uses the finest ingredients from around the island in subtly extravagant combinations. **Known for:** intimate and elegant setting; imaginative wine pairings; spaghettone with yellowtail tuna and carrot sauce. $ *Average main: €45* ⊠ *Via Capitano Bocchieri 31, Ragusa* ☎ *0932/651265* ⊕ *www.cicciosultano.it* ⊗ *Closed early Jan.–late Feb. and Sun. No lunch Mon., except in Aug. and Dec. 26–Jan. 6.*

Locanda Gulfi

$$ | **SICILIAN** | On the grounds of the expansive Gulfi winery, which produces well-regarded organic wines, you'll find a unique place for a sophisticated lunch or dinner, with sweeping views of the Chiaramonte hills and vineyards (about a half-hour drive north of Ragusa). The chef skillfully uses local ingredients to prepare Sicilian dishes with a twist in the modern dining room which features handblown chandeliers and a design-focused black-and-red color scheme; in warmer months, enjoy your meal on the lovely terrace. **Known for:** vineyard views and an inn to stay the night; renowned Gulfi wine; seasonal, local Sicilian dishes. $ *Average main: €18* ⊠ *C. da. Patria, Chiaramonte Gulfi* ☎ *0932/928081 reservations, 0932/921654 winery* ⊕ *www.locandagulfi.it.*

Hotels

★ Eremo della Giubiliana

$$ | **B&B/INN** | Set in the countryside, a 20-minute drive from Ragusa, this charming family-run monastery-turned-hotel features friendly service and a relaxed but luxurious vibe, with unique rooms in former monks' chambers that vary in size and lay-out but are all quiet and well-appointed. **Pros:** peaceful atmosphere; top-notch service; rooms filled with character. **Cons:** no other nearby eateries due to remote location; restaurant food could be better for the price; grounds, while lovely, could use better upkeep. [$] *Rooms from: €200* ✉ *Contrada Giubiliana, Marina di Ragusa* ☎ *0932/669119* 🌐 *www.eremodellagiubiliana.it* 🛏 *24 rooms* 🍴 *Free Breakfast.*

La Moresca

$$ | **HOTEL** | If you plan on visiting Ragusa and Modica but want to stay by the water, you can't do better than this artsy boutique hotel on Sicily's southeastern coast—it's two blocks from the beach and a pleasant half-hour drive from either town. **Pros:** modern, large bedrooms; beautiful courtyard garden; artsy vibe. **Cons:** parking can be an issue; no hotel restaurant other than breakfast; town itself not so charming. [$] *Rooms from: €200* ✉ *Via Dandolo 63, Marina di Ragusa* ☎ *0932/1915535* 🌐 *www.lamorescahotel.eu* 🛏 *15 rooms* 🍴 *Free Breakfast.*

★ Locanda Don Serafino

$$ | **HOTEL** | This small boutique hotel offers contemporary rooms and excellent service inside a historic manor house in the heart of Ragusa Ibla. **Pros:** modern design in a historic setting; valet parking service; incredibly attentive staff. **Cons:** steep stairs limit the accessibility of some rooms; some rooms are a few doors down from the main building; bathrooms can be small or quirky. [$] *Rooms from: €160* ✉ *Via XI Febbraio 15, Ragusa* ☎ *0932/220065 hotel, 0932/248778 restaurant* 🌐 *www.locandadonserafino.it* 🛏 *11 rooms* 🍴 *Free Breakfast.*

★ Tenuta Cammarana

$$ | **HOTEL** | Set on its own private farm, Tenuta Cammarana offers a full package of authentic Sicilian cooking, sumptuous accommodations, and a spa and pool on-site to relax in away from the sometimes packed streets of Ragusa. **Pros:** beautiful accomodations; impeccably prepared local food; spectacular surroundings and views. **Cons:** car is necessary to get here and tour the area; cell phone reception can be spotty; half-hour drive from Ragusa. [$] *Rooms from: €200* ✉ *S.da Consortile Carcarazzo Iaconello Salomone, Ragusa* ☎ *0932/616158* 🌐 *www.tenutacammarana.it* 🕒 *Closed Nov.–Mar.* 🛏 *9 rooms* 🍴 *Free Breakfast.*

Palazzolo Arceide

36 km (22 miles) northeast of Ragusa.

Hidden away in the mountains and often overlooked by visitors, Palazzolo Arceide is part of the UNESCO World Heritage Site of the Val di Noto, and its main street (Corso Vittorio Emanuele) is filled with grand buildings. You could easily spend a night or two here escaping the crowds and enjoying the calm.A short walk from the center of Palazzolo Acreide is one of the region's best-kept secrets, the archaeological park of Akrai. This hillside town was originally built to help defend the overland trading route to Greece. The most substantial of the ruins is the Greek theater, but there is enough up here to keep you busy for an afternoon.

GETTING HERE AND AROUND

Given its elevated location, it is easier to drive to Palazzolo Acreide. It can be reached in just over an hour from Catania and a pleasant 45-minute countryside drive from Siracusa. Buses also drive the same route from Siracusa seven times a day; the journey time can vary from 45 minutes to over two hours depending on

Necropoli di Pantalica, with its 5,000 prehistoric tombs, is one of the more off-the-beaten-path archaeological sites in Sicily.

the route of that service. Always check before booking that you are taking the most direct service. Tickets start at €5 one way.

Sights

★ Area Archeologica di Akrai

RUINS | One of Sicily's best-kept secrets, the archaeological park of Akrai is home to what is said to be Siracusa's first inland settlement, built to defend its overland trading route from other Greek colonies. You can access the site by a steep but steady 20-minute walk or a five-minute drive. Today, the site contains mainly ruins, but it is well worth visiting simply to see the Teatro Greco, originally constructed in the 3rd century BC to seat 600. Around the site, you'll also find two old stone quarries used to build the settlement, then converted into burial chambers as well as a remarkably well-preserved portion of the stone road into the area. On a clear day, you can also see Mount Etna rising majestically in the

distance. ⊠ *Area Archeologica di Akrai, Palazzolo Arceide* ☎ *0931/876602* 💳 *€6.*

Basilica di San Sebastiano

CHURCH | This church and UNESCO World Heritage site dominates the main square in Palazzolo Acreide. The interior is worth a visit not only for its ornate decorations but also for the interesting information on the town's annual procession in celebration of the local saint. ⊠ *Piazza del Popolo, Palazzolo Arceide* ☎ *095/601313* ⊕ *www.sansebastianoacireale.it/basilica/basilica.htm* 💳 *Free.*

★ Basilica di San Paolo

CHURCH | Locals consider this the most important church in Palazzolo Acreide, rebuilt and repaired after an earthquake ravaged the majority of the region in the 17th century. When you enter, usually a volunteer will be available to take you on a brief tour. The main focal points are the relics and the statue of St. Paul paraded through the town's streets between June 26 and June 29 each year. Entry is technically free, but be prepared to make a modest contribution toward the church's upkeep at the end of your tour. ✉ *Piazza San Paolo 4, Palazzolo Arceide* 🎫 *Free; donation encouraged after tour.*

Casa Museo Antonino Uccello

HISTORY MUSEUM | Prior to his untimely death in 1979, poet Antonino Uccello made it his life's work to collect artifacts to re-create 18th-century rural Sicilian life, resulting in this small museum. The collection is interesting, but the majority of the information boards are in Italian. Sometimes the guides can also be a little too enthusiastic in making sure you don't linger during your visit. ✉ *Via Niccolo' Machiavelli 19, Palazzolo Arceide* ☎ *0931/881499* 🌐 *www.regione.sicilia.it/beniculturali/casamuseouccello* 🎫 *€5.*

Castello di Palazzolo Acreide o Rocca di Castelmezzano

CASTLE/PALACE | Originally from the early 800s, today this castle is mostly in ruins, but if you follow the well-constructed paths that wind through it, you can still pass through some rooms and doorways and get a sense of what the castle once looked like. The views are lovely near the castle walls that extend above the cliffs, and you can see how castle defenders watched for enemies here. Access to the ruins is wheelchair-friendly, but some climbing of stairs is required to complete the tour of the entire site. ✉ *Via Calendoli 22, Palazzolo Arceide* 🌐 *www.palazzolo-acreide.it/il_centro_storico_di_palazzolo_acreide/quartieri_medioevali_a_palazzolo_acreide.htm* 🎫 *Free.*

🍴 Restaurants

★ Quel Che C'e

$$$ | **SICILIAN** | Palazzolo Acreide has become a bit of a food town in recent years, and this blink-and-you-miss-it spot, housed in an ancient grotto off the main street, is a big part of that. The family-run restaurant offers house antipasti big enough to share (like the unique Mortadella mousse) and a short menu of high-quality entrées including a black lentil risotto. **Known for:** prime location just off the main street; great value; delicious grape granita for dessert. [$] *Average main: €25* ✉ *Via Ortocotogno 5, Palazzolo Arceide* ☎ *328/7773015.*

Scrigno dei Sapori

$$ | **SICILIAN** | Following the slow food approach, this restaurant is known for showcasing high-quality, local ingredients, thanks to a chef who captures the essence of classic Sicilian dishes while still upgrading them to the level of fine dining. The menu changes daily depending on what's in season and available at the local market, but there's always the award-winning sausage and an excellent rabbit pasta dish. **Known for:** always changing seasonal menu; local peasant dishes upgraded to a fine dining standard; famous sausages. [$] *Average main: €20* ✉ *Via Maddalena 50, Palazzolo Arceide* ☎ *0931/882941* 🌐 *www.scrigno-deisapori.eu.*

🛏 Hotels

★ B&B del Corso

$ | **B&B/INN** | Situated a stone's throw from Palazzolo Acreide's main street, this recently restored B&B offers a charming selection of rooms with all the modern essentials. **Pros:** all rooms have air-conditioning; central location; tastefully restored decor. **Cons:** can get booked up quickly in high season; no restaurant on-site; only three apartments to choose from. [$] *Rooms from: €60* ✉ *Via Ortocotogno 11, Palazzolo Arceide* ☎ *339/7328523* 🌐 *www.bebdelcorsopalazzolo.it* 🛏 *4 rooms* 🍽 *Free Breakfast.*

Sortino

25 km (15 miles) northeast of Palazzolo Arceide.

The gateway to Necropoli di Pantalica, the town of Sortino has all the hallmarks of the Baroque-era architecture seen in other parts of this region. It is also well known for its locally produced honey, and also for its unusual bread stuffed with figs. Although there is an interesting beekeeping and puppet museum in the town, the main attraction is the Necropoli, and, therefore, it is not worth planning an overnight stay here.

GETTING HERE AND AROUND

Sortino is served four times a day by buses from Siracusa; tickets start at €5 one-way and the journey takes just over an hour. However, it is infinitely quicker and easier to take the direct route by car, and the same journey will take no more than 35 minutes.

TOURS

The Necropoli is best seen via a guided tour, and several local companies provide full- or half-day tours of the site. It is worth getting quotes from several, as prices vary depending on the time of year, and if the tour is not fully booked. Good options include Hermes Sicily (⊕ *www.hermes-sicily.com/en*), with prices starting at €75 per person; Sicily Unearthed (⊕ *www.sicilyunearthed.com*), with tours starting at €90 per person; and Lemon Tour (⊕ *www.lemontour.it*), with prices from €90 per person for a private tour, including transport from surrounding towns and cities if you do not have your own car.

Sights

★ Necropoli di Pantalica

CEMETERY | It's best to hire a guide to explore the over 5,000 tombs covering limestone cliffs that make up this Iron and Bronze Age burial site. Located on a huge plateau over the Anapo River, the necropolis dates back to between the 13th and 8th centuries BC. If you decide not to hire a guide, be prepared to drive to get here. There are two main entrances: one near the town of Sortino, and the other from the town of Ferla. The entrance by Sortino involves a good walk down the sides of the gorge while the Ferla entrance is more of a gentle stroll along a well-beaten path. Set aside a minimum of two hours for your visit, but it is better to allocate at least half a day; be sure to wear a good pair of walking shoes and bring plenty of water. ⊠ *Necropoli di Pantalica* ☎ *0931/67450* ⊕ *www.pantalica.org* ⊠ *Free.*

CENTRAL SICILY AND THE MEDITERRANEAN COAST

Updated by
Ros Belford

👁 **Sights**	🍴 **Restaurants**	🛏 **Hotels**	🛍 **Shopping**	🍸 **Nightlife**
★★★★★	★★★☆☆	★★★☆☆	★☆☆☆☆	★☆☆☆☆

WELCOME TO CENTRAL SICILY AND THE MEDITERRANEAN COAST

TOP REASONS TO GO

★ **The Valley of the Temples:** In Agrigento, you'll find three of the best-preserved ancient Greek temples in the world, dating back to the time the town was one of the wealthiest—and most extravagant—cities in the Mediterranean.

★ **Villa Romana del Casale:** This Roman country villa in Piazza Armerina has perhaps the most lavish mosaic pavements in existence anywhere.

★ **Pantelleria:** Sicily's most remote volcanic island has everything except crowds, including a dramatic coastline, hot springs, mountain walks, and wineries producing a much-prized dessert wine.

★ **Scala dei Turchi:** This astonishing cliff of pure white marble is eroded into a natural "staircase" with a sandy beach below.

1 Mazara del Vallo. Sicily's most North African town, with a medieval Kasbah and a museum housing an astonishing ancient Greek bronze of a dancing satyr.

2 Selinunte. Ruins of ancient Greek temples in a stunning setting by the sea, with good beaches nearby.

3 Sciacca. An off-the-beaten-path but authentic south coast town famous for its ceramics.

4 Caltabellotta. A high, craggy village worth a detour for its breathtaking views.

5 Eraclea Minoa, Torre Salsa, and Sant'Angelo Muxara. A small stretch of the coast with an ancient Greek port and pristine beaches that culminate in the most famous—and most photographed—cliff in Sicily.

6 Porto Empedocle. A down-to-earth port and hometown to author Andrea Camilleri and his fictional detective, Inspector Montalbano.

7 Agrigento. The bustling provincial capital home to the world-famous Valley of the Temples and a fabulous archaeological museum.

Isola di Pantelleria
← **9**

8 Licata. A seaside town that was at the forefront of the Allied invasion of Sicily in World War II, now home to a remarkable fine dining restaurant.

9 Pantelleria. A fascinating volcanic island great for swimming, hiking, and wine-tasting.

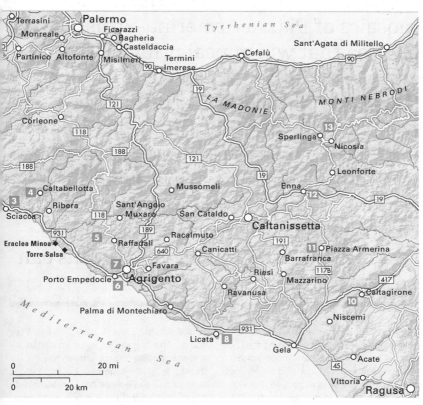

10 Caltagirone. An inland hill town worth a visit for its famous hand-painted ceramics.

11 Piazza Armerina. The gateway to Villa Romana del Casale, the most extravagantly mosaic-ed Roman villa in existence,

12 Enna. A lively provincial capital perched high above sea level and crowned by a medieval castle.

13 Sperlinga. Home to mysterious houses carved out of the mountainside above the town.

Despite being home to two of the most famous sights in Sicily—the Greek temples of Agrigento and the Roman mosaics of Piazza Armerina—this is an area that will appeal primarily to travelers who are already in love with Sicily and curious to find out more. Along the coast are fantastic sandy beaches protected by nature reserves while in the unspoiled interior, rural traditions ranging from snow-harvesting and ice-cream-making to bread-baking, cheese-making, and foraging for wild greens can be experienced firsthand.

Although most towns here have moments of architectural beauty, their historic centers can be in various states of preservation and decay and are almost inevitably ringed by unattractive modern outskirts. Most smaller villages and towns have little in the way of quality tourist infrastructure; in-town accommodations tend to be functional rather than fashionable and aimed at the business traveler. Thankfully, there are several truly outstanding places to stay in the countryside. Indeed, the ideal way of experiencing this part of Sicily would be to select two or three lovely country hotels with restaurants as your bases and explore the surrounding areas through day trips.

Few other areas of Sicily will give you such an intense sense of being off-the-beaten tourist track. Come in early spring or late autumn and you may well find that you are the only visitor to an immense ancient site like Morgantina, to the Byzantine cave village near Calascibetta, or to one of the even more undiscovered sites like the Cava di Casa quarry, strewn with column discs that broke before they could be transported to build the temples in nearby Selinunte. The port town of Mazara del Vallo is the only place in Sicily where, every evening, you can hear the call of the muezzin in its medieval Kasbah, while up in the hills above Cammarata, you can see how until the last century, Sicilians used techniques introduced by the Arabs to preserve snow throughout the summer. There are acute reminders of harsher episodes of history, too, from the fiendish defenses of hill towns fearing attack and museums recording rural poverty to the horrendous conditions of sulfur mines and the reminders of World War II around the town of Licata.

There is also plenty to appeal to the hedonist, like the unspoiled beaches of the Torre Salsa nature reserve, the remote and magical island of Pantelleria, any number of simple yet excellent seafood restaurants, and innovative wineries both on the mainland and on the island of Pantelleria.

Planning

When to Go

Facing straight across to Africa, this is a hot region of Sicily and in summer it can be blasted by the warm southwestern libeccio winds from Libya. Although there are some wooded areas, there is usually little shade here, which should be a major consideration when visiting ancient sites like Agrigento, Selinunte, and Morgantina. As with everywhere in Sicily, it can take some time to warm up after the winter, but it cools down slowly during autumn. Late spring and fall (right through to the beginning of November) are usually the best times to visit. In early spring, the weather can be unpredictable; one day you'll be in short sleeves, the next bundled up in a winter coat and a hat to protect you from chill mistral winds. Easter sees celebrations all over the region, most spectacularly in the village of San Biagio Platani where huge arches of elaborately woven reeds and agave are decorated with citrus fruit, curlicues, and twists of bread. High summer is best avoided as inland it becomes unbearably hot and the coast gets extremely crowded.

Planning Your Time

Easily accessible from Palermo and its airport, Mazara del Vallo is a good place to start a trip in this region as it's not only a convenient base for seeing the ancient site of Selinunte, but it's a fascinating introduction to the North African influence in this part of Sicily. Following the coast south, you could pause at one of several country hotels to explore the coastal nature reserves of Foce del Belice, Foce del Platani, and Torre Salsa before heading to the Agrigento area. Here, choose between a country or city base, and give yourself a couple of days to explore the incredible Valley of the Temples, not forgetting the Gardens of Kolymbetra and the archaeological museum. Fans of Sicilian author Andrea Camilleri's fictional detective, Inspector Montalbano, should take a guided tour of Porto Empedocle, Agrigento's town center, and other sites that appear in the books. More rural pursuits include guided walks in the Sant'Angelo Muxara area or following the Via del Ghiaccio to discover how ice was "farmed" and preserved here (and how ice cream and granita were made) in the days before electricity.

Anyone interested in the American landings during World War II should head to Licata (easily done on a day trip from Agrigento). Turning inland, the ceramics city of Caltagirone is slightly run-down but worth a daytime stop to see its incredible ceramic-tile staircase and ceramics museum, perhaps taking in a visit to the Tenuta Valle delle Ferle winery as well.

In the center of the island, give yourself a day to see the magnificent Roman mosaics of Piazza Armerina, and another to explore the ancient site of Morgantina and the ancient goddess sculptures in the museum of tiny Aidone, returned to Sicily by the Getty, Malibu after a long legal battle. From here you could either immerse yourself deeper in

Did You Know?

This part of Sicily is famous for its colorful Easter celebrations, especially in the village of San Biagio Platani, where huge arches and other constructions are made of reeds and agave, and decorated with citrus fruits and twisted bread.

Sicily's ancient past at the sanctuary of Cozze Matrice (and the so-called Cave of Hades) above the lake of Pergusa or get a taste of its more harrowing recent history in the museum of sulfur mining in the town of Valguarnera Caropepe. Spend your last night near Enna, the so-called navel of Sicily, visiting the Byzantine cave-village and seeing how ricotta and the local specialty of Piacentino Ennese (saffron-infused and peppercorn-studded cheese) is made, then take the autostrada back to Palermo.

Getting Here and Around

AIR

There are no airports in the region. Palermo, the island's main international airport, is 102 km (63 miles) from Mazara del Vallo and 157 km (96 miles) from Agrigento, while Catania airport is 158 km (198 miles) from Agrigento (with better bus connections than Palermo). The E90 Austrostrada runs from Palermo airport to Mazara del Vallo, with a journey time of around an hour. Travel onward down the main SS115 coast road to Agrigento is slower, with an entire journey time of just over two hours. There are just four direct buses per day from Palermo airport to Agrigento (run by Autolinee SAL) with a journey time of three hours, while Sais Trasporti has a far more regular service from Catania Airport to Agrigento.

AIRPORTS Catania Airport. ☎ 095/7239111 ⊕ www.aeroporto.catania.it. **Palermo Airport.** ☎ 800/541880 ⊕ www.aeroporto-dipalermo.it.

BUS

In Sicily, traveling by bus is quicker than by train, but even so, advance planning is essential, and getting off the beaten track requires true dedication, with many villages accessible just once a day (after lunch) with no return service until early the following morning.

Agrigento has direct bus connections with Palermo (and its airport), Catania (and its airport), Trapani, and Mazara del Vallo. Mazara del Vallo has good links to Palermo, Trapani, and Marsala while Enna has good links to Catania, Palermo, Piazza Armerina, Calascibetta, and Aidone.

CONTACTS Autolinee SAL. ⊕ www.autolineesal.it. **Autoservizi Salemi.** ☎ 0923/981120 ⊕ www.autoservizisalemi.it. **Cuffaro.** ☎ 091/6161510 ⊕ www.cuffaro.info. **SAIS.** ☎ 800/211020 toll-free ⊕ www.saisautolinee.it.

CAR

To get the most out of the region, you really do need your own transport, unless you are content to travel by bus and limit yourself to the main cities. Rental cars are widely available right at Sicily's major airports.

In Agrigento province, the main SS115 coast road is a divided highway in places, but can be very slow when it is not. Two good and particularly scenic roads are the SS189 from Agrigento to Cammarata, and the SS118 from Agrigento to Corleone.

Side roads heading down into the Torre Salsa reserve and Eraclea Minoa are prone to flooding in spring and autumn, though warning signage is generally good. Roads into the hills can be twisty and very slow, but the sense of being off-the-beaten-track amid magnificent scenery is ample reward. Several areas (especially in the clay uplands around Caltanisetta) are prone to landslides, but these usually reliably signposted, with diversions in place. Enna is just off the A19 autostrada that runs from Palermo to Catania (with wonderful views of the Madonie to boot), and thus very easy to reach and a good place to begin or finish a tour.

TRAIN

This area is very poorly served by train. The rail network is scant and train service skeletal. Agrigento, Mazara del Vallo, and Enna do have train service, but once again, these are very unreliable and those committed to train travel can consequently find a journey involving several changes and some very roundabout routes. There is no line at all between Mazara del Vallo and Agrigento, and no direct connections between Enna and Agrigento.

CONTACTS Trenitalia. ☎ 892021 in Italy, 06/68475475 outside Italy ⊕ www. trenitalia.com.

Hotels

The real jewels in this part of Sicily are the country hotels—most of them recent additions to the lodging scene that have embraced the aesthetics and ethos of a typical boutique hotel. Most have restaurants and swimming pools, some are attached to wineries or olive oil farms, and all are run with a personal touch. They make excellent and comfortable bases, and the staff is usually full of information about things to see and do locally. More typical hotels found in towns and by the seaside can be rather dated in style and service, and tend to lag behind those of Palermo and the southeast of Sicily, although there are exceptions.

Restaurants

Along the coast, fish and seafood inevitably dominate, and generally there is very little invention or variation on menus. However, as the produce is almost always incredibly fresh, little intervention is honestly even needed. Expect to find fish and seafood combined with traditional Sicilian ingredients such as capers, tomatoes, almonds, citrus fruits, anchovies, and breadcrumbs in pasta dishes. Secondi usually consists of fish or other seafood grilled, roasted, or deep-fried. Look out as well for fish couscous on menus around Mazara.

Inland, you will tend to find more meat featured—pork and beef are common while lamb is occasionally offered (you almost never see chicken on menus). Awareness of vegetarian and vegan diets is increasing but not universal, and in out-of-the-way places, vegetarians should explain clearly what they don't eat as many meat products tend to be viewed as flavorings rather than ingredients.

Some of the best food here is found in country hotels, often with a daily changing fixed menu that is open to adaptation for people with special dietary requirements.

RESTAURANT AND HOTEL PRICES
Restaurant prices in the reviews are the average cost of a main course at dinner, or if dinner is not served, at lunch. Hotel prices in the reviews are the lowest cost of a standard double room in high season. Restaurant and hotel reviews have been shortened. For full information, visit Fodors.com.

What it Costs in Euros			
$	$$	$$$	$$$$
RESTAURANTS			
under €15	€15–€22	€23–€30	over €30
HOTELS			
under €125	€125–€225	€226–€350	over €350

Tours

This is a part of the island where having a guide can truly transform your experience, as the idea of hidden treasures really isn't a cliché here. Plagued for centuries by poverty, exploitation, and, as a consequence, emigration and depopulation, the area is just beginning to come into its own. An increasing sensibility toward intangible heritage like ancient traditions and ways of life as well as new archaeological explorations are changing the understanding of an entire culture, and a good guide with deep insider knowledge and a gift for storytelling will add new layers of insight for a visitor.

Esplora Travel

CULTURAL TOURS | Check out this company's small-group Hidden Sicily tour for the chance to transverse the interior of the island in a journey that starts at Gangi in the Madonie, and heads through Mussomeli, Sant'Angelo Muxaro, Corleone, and Piana degli Albanesi to arrive at the Tyrrhenian Coast at Scopello. The focus is on the unusual and unexpected, and along the way it visits a Byzantine village near Calascibetta and incorporates a village-experience day with Val di Kam in Sant'Angelo Muxaro. Departures are in May, when the profusion of wildflowers in the Sicilian countryside is most abundant. Accommodation is in countryside hotels and rural retreats and the menus are exclusively home-produced fare and local specialties. ☎ 01223/328446 ⊕ www.esplora.co.uk ✉ From £1,795.

★ La RosaWorks

CULTURAL TOURS | FAMILY | This boutique travel company arranges custom tours and small group tours exclusively to Sicily that are designed to highlight the island's history, cultural heritage, traditions, wine, and food. There's a refreshing focus on taking visitors off-the-beaten path as well as on. The company has exceptional contacts throughout Sicily, but their knowledge of southern and western Sicily is truly unique. The western Sicily tour starts at Palermo and takes in Selinunte, Agrigento, Mazara del Vallo, and the islands of Favignana and Mozia and includes visits to wineries, olive oil producers, and a torrone (nougat) maker. ☎ 646/3974175 in U.S. ⊕ www.larosa-works.com ✉ From $3,925 for 8 nights.

Sicily Travel Net

SPECIAL-INTEREST TOURS | Michele Gallo is an outstanding English-speaking Agrigento-based guide whose passion for Sicily and curiosity about finding out

new things is unabated after 30 years. As well as wonderfully lively tours of the Valley of the Temples and Archeological Museum, he has an entire portfolio of theme-day and half-day tours throughout the region, and taking your pick of these is the perfect way of getting under the skin of this fascinating area of Sicily. Tours range from literary journeys exploring the Agrigento and Porto Empedocle of Camilleri and the Sicily of Tomasi di Lampedusa's The Leopard, to tours of the sites of the 8th Army's 1943 landings and a gastronomic tour into the world of ice and ice-cream making. For anyone wanting to find out more about their Sicilian ancestry, there are made-to-measure genealogical journeys. ✉ Agrigento ⊕ www.sicilytravel.net.

Mazara del Vallo

131 km (81 miles) southwest of Palermo.

Until recently few travelers visited Mazara, but in the late 1990s local fishermen caught in their nets an extraordinary ancient Greek bronze of a dancing satyr. Larger than life and attributed to Praxiteles, the most famous Greek sculptor of all, it is now displayed in a beautifully converted former church and has made Mazara an irresistible stop for travelers visiting the nearby temples of Selinunte and Segesta.

And if you're here, it would be a shame to visit without seeing more of the town's historic center. Of all the towns in Sicily, it is in Mazara del Vallo that the island's ancient Islamic heritage remains most tangible. Several Sicilian towns might retain an old Arabic quarter of twisting labyrinthine streets and dead-end courtyards, but only in Mazara is the so-called Kasbah a thriving North African neighborhood. Mazara's present-day Islamic community has its origins in the 1960s when the town's fishing fleet was the biggest in Italy, but short on labor.

Mazara del Vallo has one of Sicily's most interesting historic centers.

A call was put out to North Africa, and sailors, fishermen, and eventually their families began to move back into the largely abandoned Kasbah. However, the town's links with North Africa are far more ancient, perhaps inevitably so given that it is the closest point on mainland Sicily to the coast of Africa. Under the ancient Greeks of Selinunte, it became a thriving trade center, and in the 9th century AD, it was here that an Islamic army of over 10,000 landed and began the conquest of Sicily.

GETTING HERE AND AROUND
Mazara is the final destination of the A29 (E90) motorway from Palermo. Buses connect Mazara with Palermo, Palermo Airport, Trapani, Agrigento, and Marsala, and there is a reasonable train service to Marsala and Trapani. Trains to Palermo may involve a change elsewhere.

TOURS
Kasbah Tours
CULTURAL TOURS | These rather rough-and-ready tours (in Arabic, Italian, and admittedly eccentric English) are led by Italian-Tunisian Paolo Ayed, who was born and raised in the Kasbah and knows absolutely everyone. It's not a formal historical tour, but a chance to walk around the Kasbah with a local, and meet whoever you chance to meet. ⊠ *Mazara del Vallo* ☎ *339/4030780* ⌨ *€10.*

★ Regina Hundemer Tours
CULTURAL TOURS | An English-speaking German guide who has lived in western Sicily for 30 years, Regina has a wonderful flair for storytelling and making history come to life. She specializes in Mazara del Vallo, taking you around the town's main sights and the Kasbah, as well as Segesta, Selinunte, and the entire northwest of Sicily. ⊠ *Mazara del Vallo* ☎ *348/3868505* ⊕ *www.guidetrapani.it/staff-member/regina-hundemer* ⌨ *From €150.*

👁 Sights

Benedictine Monastery of San Michele Arcangelo

CHURCH | FAMILY | There is no general access to the 17th-century Benedictine convent of San Michele, currently inhabited by just four nuns, but if you ring the doorbell, the nuns will invite you into the lobby to buy the traditional cookies they make, including nutty *muconetti,* made of candied pumpkin and almonds. You place your money—and the nuns place your cookies—in a small revolving hatch originally designed so that unwanted babies could be left to the care of the nuns while maintaining the anonymity of the mother. ✉ *Via Sant'Agostino 21, Mazara del Vallo* ☎ *0923/906565.*

Collegio dei Gesuiti

CHURCH | Opposite the Museo del Satiro Danzante, the exuberant Baroque Jesuit College, with its portal framed by hefty male caryatids, was once the center of the Catholic Inquisition in town during the 18th century, charged with rooting out and punishing anything they deemed to be heresy. In 1824, the Jesuits clashed with Sicily's Bourbon rulers, and were kicked out (probably missed by few). The damaged church of Sant'Ignazio next door is sometimes open; it's an evocative elliptical space, framed by red-gold sandstone and marble columns, and open to the sky. It is occasionally used for open-air concerts and exhibitions. ✉ *Piazza Plebiscito, Mazara del Vallo* ⊕ *www.westofsicily.com/punti-interesse/collegio-dei-gesuiti* ▦ *Free.*

Duomo

CHURCH | The city's Duomo was founded in 1093 by Sicily's first Norman ruler, Roger I, who is depicted in relief above the main entrance on horseback trampling a turbanned Arab. It has an interior dominated by the huge marble tableau of the Transfiguration above the altar, revealed as if behind stucco curtains held back by cherubs, designed by the Palermitan Renaissance sculptor Antonello Gagini who is thought to have worked with Michelangelo in Rome. In the right transept is the fragment of a fresco of Christ Pantokrator dating back to the original Norman church and created by Greek Byzantine artists. ✉ *Piazza della Repubblica, Mazara del Vallo* ☎ *0923/941919* ▦ *Free.*

★ Kasbah

HISTORIC DISTRICT | The twisted maze of narrow streets and tiny courtyards at the core of Mazara's historical center is most interesting if you visit with a local guide. There is no danger, but as the distinction between what is a private courtyard and a public thoroughfare is blurred, it is far more comfortable, as a stranger, to be accompanied by a local (in addition, you will probably get to meet a few of the 4,000-strong Tunisian community who live here). Throughout the Kasbah (and indeed scattered all over the historic center) are a series of ceramic statues, some commissioned from local artists, others by schoolchildren, as an appealing initiative by the local administration. On Via Porta Palermo, students from the local art school were given free rein to decorate the metal doors of abandoned lock-ups. Tours are at their most evocative just before sunset, when men gather after a day's work in little social clubs, children play in the street or go to the community play center, and the sound of a recorded muezzin calls the faithful to prayer. ✉ *Mazara del Vallo.*

★ Museo del Satiro Danzante

ART MUSEUM | In 2005, after four years of painstaking restoration in Rome (and several attempts to keep it there in the capital), the Dancing Satyr, the ancient Greek statue found by fishermen off the town's coast, found its permanent home here in the deconsecrated church of Sant'Egidio. Exquisitely lit and larger than life, it is a truly extraordinary work (despite missing both arms and a leg) caught mid-air, mid-dance in the throes of ecstasy, with the musculature and grace of movement associated nowadays with contemporary ballet. Scholars think it probably formed part of a group with other dancing Maenads, lost when the ship carrying them capsized in the Sicilian Channel. Ancient Greek bronze statues are extremely rare—only five have survived—as bronze was precious, and most were melted down. The satyr was created using the lost wax process, a technology designed to use as little bronze as possible: a clay model of the statue was made and fired, and when it cooled, it was covered with a layer of wax, followed by another layer of clay, this time with several holes. Then liquid bronze (heated to something like 1800°F) was poured through the holes. The melted wax then ran out, and the clay core turned to sand, leaving a bronze shell that would then have been polished. Other finds from under the sea are displayed in the museum, the most intriguing of which is the bronze foot of an elephant. ✉ *Chiesa di San Egidio, Piazza Plebiscito, Mazara del Vallo* ☎ *0923/933917* 🕒 *Closed Mon.*

🍴 Restaurants

La Bettola

$$ | SICILIAN | A quite subdued place, La Bettola has walls with wooden shelves full of Sicilian wine, white linen tablecloths, elegant cutlery, and service imbued with the ease of tradition. The focus, inevitably, is on fish, with seafood pasta and fish mains, several featuring the red prawns for which Mazara is known throughout Italy. **Known for:** excellent seafood dishes; interesting wine selection; charming outdoor terraces. [$] *Average main: €17* ✉ *Via Franco Maccagnone 32, Mazara del Vallo* ☎ *0923/946422* 🕒 *Closed Wed.*

★ **Mare a Viva**

$ | SEAFOOD | FAMILY | This wholesaler specializes in oysters, mollusks, and crustaceans, and offers a tasting room that has become an obligatory stop for seafood aficionados in town. There are 24 kinds of oysters, all manner of clams (including Galician percebes), local red prawns in several sizes, and a tank of lobsters and crabs as well as fresh seasonal tuna. **Known for:** incredible selection of oysters from all over Europe; absolute favorite with locals; delicious fish couscous. [$] *Average main: €12* ✉ *S.S. 115 Km 50, Mazara del Vallo* ☎ *0923/934151* 🌐 *www.mareaviva.it* 🕒 *No dinner Thurs.–Sat. in winter.*

Osteria Scopari

$ | SICILIAN | FAMILY | A cozy place tucked up a narrow alley behind the Duomo, Osteria Scopari is relaxed and buzzy, with good scorched wood-fired pizza, often with inventive and original toppings, and delicious fish and seafood pasta and risotto. Mains, as ever, are grilled fish and seafood. **Known for:** friendly atmosphere good for families; busiate pasta with Mazara's red prawns, cherry tomatos, almonds, and bottarga; inexpensive pizza with interesting toppings and uncommon ingredients. [$] *Average main: €13* ✉ *Via Scopari 3, Mazara del Vallo* ☎ *349/2316328* 🕒 *Closed Tues. in winter.*

🛏 Hotels

★ **Casa Melia**

$ | B&B/INN | Set on the fringe of the Kasbah and built within the Norman fortifications, this quirky, unconventional little hotel is ideal for anyone who wants to inhabit a piece of Mazara's multilayer history. **Pros:** quirky and unique decor and history; lovely courtyard for evening drinks and breakfast; within earshot of the evening call of the muezzin. **Cons:** on the shabby side of shabby chic; not much natural light inside; solo women may feel unsafe walking in the neighborhood at night. [$] *Rooms from: €120* ✉ *Via Bagno 2, Mazara del Vallo* ☎ *335/1250100* 🌐 *www.meliaresortmazaradelvallo.com* 🛏 *10 rooms* 🍴 *Free Breakfast.*

Mahara Hotel & Spa

$ | **HOTEL** | This functional and reliable hotel is set around two courtyards, with uniform rooms opening off long corridors with no surprises in decor or character. **Pros:** open all year long; close to beach and town center; great breakfast. **Cons:** not much atmosphere or Sicilian character; rather perfunctory service; decor is lackluster. [$] *Rooms from: €85* ✉ *Lungomare S. Vito 3, Mazara del Vallo* ☎ *0923/673800* 🌐 *www.maharahotel.it* 🛏 *81 rooms* 🍴 *Free Breakfast.*

🍸 Nightlife

Da Luigi

BARS | Don't expect too much from the nightlife scene here, but this decent café comes with plenty of tables outside on the main (and pedestrianized) shopping street, so it's a good place to sit and watch Mazara life pass by. Stop for a coffee or an evening aperitivo, when Aperols or Campari Spritzs come accompanied by tasters of *panelle* (chickpea flour fritters), arancini, and *crocchè* (potato croquettes). ✉ *Corso Umberto I 50, Mazara del Vallo* ☎ *340/8910525.*

Selinunte

35 km (22 miles) southeast of Mazara del Vallo, 114 km (71 miles) southwest of Palermo.

Numerous ruined Greek temples perch on a high, undulating plateau overlooking the Mediterranean at Selinunte (or Selinus). The town is named after a local variety of wild celery (*Apium graveolens* or *petroselinum*) that in spring grows in profusion among the ruined columns and overturned capitals. Although the nearest village of Marinella di Selinunte is a rather unremarkable seaside resort, there are some very nice places to stay just inland as well as some good beaches, including Porto Palo and the wild dunes of the Foce del Belice nature reserve. Although many travelers treat Selinunte as a quick stop between the temples of Segesta and Agrigento, the area makes a very pleasant holiday base.

GETTING HERE AND AROUND

Selinunte is a half-hour drive from Mazara del Vallo, and an 85-minute drive from Agrigento, which means it can be easily visited via car as a day trip from any of the towns south along the coast. Getting here by public transport is trickier. There are five buses daily to Selinunte from the town of Castelvetrano, 11 km (7 miles) north, which is itself accessible from Palermo by bus and train.

TOURS

Elisabeth Kutschke

CULTURAL TOURS | An English-speaking guide who lives in Selinunte and works throughout the province of Trapani, Elizabeth works closely with archeologists from the German Archeological Institute who oversee the excavations at Selinunte every summer. She's always a font of exciting information on all the latest discoveries. ✉ *Marinella Selinunte* ☎ *338/6514595 WhatsApp* ✉ *tanitselinunte@libero.it* 🌐 *www.guidetrapani.it/staff-member/elisabeth-kutschke* 🎟 *From €130.*

VISITOR INFORMATION

CONTACT Selinunte Tourism Office. ✉ *Via Cantone 21,* ☎ *0924/46117* 🌐 *en.visitselinunte.com.*

👁 Sights

Cava di Cusa

RUINS | The sandy limestone from this quarry was much prized by ancient Greek builders. Lacking the fossilized shells abundant in much local stone, it was a stronger and more resistant construction material, and consequently a natural choice for the temples of Selinunte. Nevertheless, quarrying the stone in the huge discs required for temple columns was clearly no easy task, and as you wander through and above the gorge,

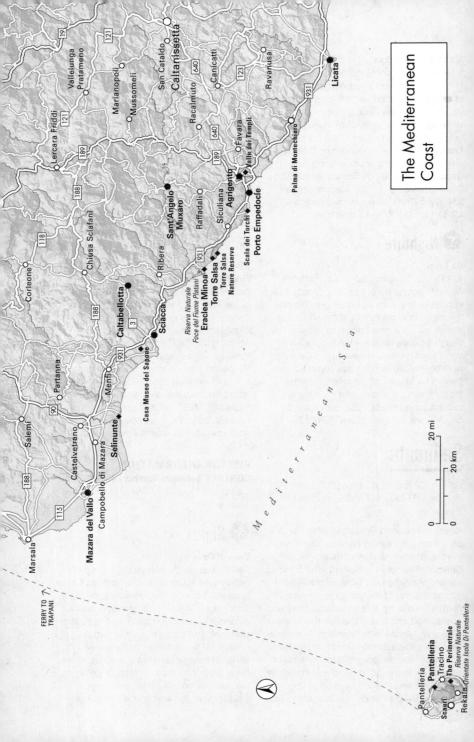

The Mediterranean Coast

Caltanissetta
San Cataldo
Marianopoli
Mussomeli
Vallelunga Pratameno
Lercara Friddi
Racalmuto
Canicattì
Ravanusa
Licata
Favara
Valle dei Templi
Agrigento
Siculiana
Palma di Montechiaro
Raffadali
Sant'Angelo Muxaro
Scala dei Turchi
Porto Empedocle
Ribera
Eraclea Minoa
Torre Salsa
Torre Salsa Nature Reserve
Riserva Naturale Foce del Fiume Platani
Chiusa Sclafani
Corleone
Sciacca
Caltabellotta
Casa Museo del Sapone
Menfi
Partanna
Salemi
Castelvetrano
Selinunte
Campobello di Mazara
Mazara del Vallo
Marsala

FERRY TO TRAPANI

Mediterranean Sea

20 mi
20 km

Pantelleria
Pantelleria
Tracino
The Perimetrale
Scauri
Rekale
Riserva Naturale Orientata Isola Di Pantelleria

you come across several broken discs, including one that was abandoned, split, before it had been fully removed from the bare rock. Even without the historical interest, this is a lovely place for a quiet stroll through olives, asphodel, and wildflowers, although in low season the site is unmanned and used by goatherds, so keep an eye out for untethered dogs. ✉ *Marinella Selinunte* 🎟 *Free.*

★ Greek Temple Ruins

RUINS | Selinunte was one of the most important colonies of ancient Greece, recently discovered to have been home to the largest industrial quarter found in any ancient European city. Founded in the 7th century BCE, the city became the rich and prosperous rival of Segesta, making its money on trade and manufacturing ceramics. When in 409 BCE Segesta turned to the Carthaginians for help in vanquishing their rival, the Carthaginians sent an army to destroy Selinunte. The temples were demolished, the city was razed, and 16,000 of Selinunte's inhabitants were slaughtered. Archaeologists recently discovered pots with the remains of food inside, proof that some were in the middle of eating when the attackers arrived. The remains of Selinunte are in many ways unchanged from the day of its sacking—burn marks still scar the Greek columns, and much of the site still lies in rubble at its exact position of collapse. The original complex held seven temples scattered over two sites separated by a harbor. Of the seven, only one—reconstructed in 1958—is whole. ■ **TIP→ This is a large archaeological site, so you might make use of the private navetta (shuttle) to save a bit of walking. Alternatively, if you have a car, you can visit the first temples close to the ticket office on foot and then drive westward to the farther site. Be prepared to show your ticket at various stages.** ✉ *SS115, Marinella Selinunte* ✣ *13 km (8 miles) southeast of Castelvetrano* ☎ *0924/46277* 🎟 *€6.*

🍴 Restaurants

★ Da Vittorio

$$ | **SEAFOOD** | Located right on the beach at Porto Palo, Da Vittorio is something of a local legend, highly regarded and much loved by everyone from wine and olive oil makers to celebrating families. The focus is on fresh fish and seafood, with pasta for the first course, and grilled fish for a second, all enhanced with traditional Sicilian flavors such as capers, almonds, and wild fennel. **Known for:** open all year long; creative seafood on the beach; neighborhood institution since the 1960s. [$] *Average main: €16* ✉ *Via Friuli Venezia Giulia 9, Marinella Selinunte* ☎ *0925/78381* 🌐 *www.ristorantevittorio.it* 🕒 *Closed mid-Dec.–mid-Jan.*

Lido Zabbara

$ | **SICILIAN** | This eatery right on the beach at Selinunte is really no more than a glorified salad bar, although it also serves a nice selection of grilled fish and seafood (often sardines). Serve yourself from the delicacies on the center spread; the lunch buffet is very affordable, while dinner doesn't cost much more, often served by the owner whose constant back-and-forth to look after customers has earned this place the nickname "Da Yoyo". **Known for:** beachside dining; great value; buffet of appetizers and salads. [$] *Average main: €12* ✉ *Via Pigafetta, Marinella Selinunte* ☎ *0924/46194* 🌐 *www.facebook.com/lidozabbara* 🕒 *Closed Nov.–Mar.*

Tukè

$ | **SICILIAN** | **FAMILY** | An amicable beach bar-restaurant right on the harbor at Marinella di Selinunte, Tukè is ideal for a simple hearty lunch after seeing the temples. They have two daily fixed menus, comprising pasta (they do an excellent Norma), a main of grilled meat or fish, a salad, water, and coffee. **Known for:** delicious shared aperitivo platter; great value fixed-price menus; fabulous sea views. [$] *Average main: €9* ✉ *Via Usodimare,*

Marinella Selinunte ☎ *320/5398785* 🕒 *Closed Thurs.*

Hotels

★ Baglio Villa Sicilia

$$$ | **HOUSE** | You'll experience refined upscale living on a landed aristocratic estate when you stay at this stylishly renovated villa surrounded by vineyards and olive groves. **Pros:** aristocratic ambience with refined decor; peaceful location among vines and olives; excellent salt water swimming pool. **Cons:** no self-catering facilities (on-site chef will prepare all your meals); works better as a fully rented villa than rented individual rooms; no restaurants or bars nearby. [$] *Rooms from: €330* ✉ *Contrada Latomie, SP 13, Zangara dei Prefetti Amari 1, Marinella Selinunte* ☎ *335/6022825* 🌐 *www.villasicilia.com* 🛏 *3 rooms* 🍴 *Free Breakfast.*

★ Case di Latomie

$ | **HOTEL** | **FAMILY** | This authentic rural accommodation on the Centonze olive oil estate rings is a short drive from the coast and from the temples of Selinunte. **Pros:** olive oil tastings can be arranged; two big pools and little farm on-site; unpretentious and welcoming. **Cons:** not directly on the sea; nearest village of Castelvetrano isn't much to see; rustic rather than chic. [$] *Rooms from: €85* ✉ *SS 115 103, Marinella Selinunte* ☎ *0924/907727* 🌐 *www.casedilatomie.com* 🕒 *Closed Nov.–Easter* 🛏 *29 rooms* 🍴 *Free Breakfast.*

★ La Foresteria Planeta Estate

$$$ | **HOTEL** | Belonging to the Planeta family of winemakers, La Foresteria is a truly gorgeous contemporary hotel with exceptional food and views from herb-scented terraces over the vineyards to the sea. **Pros:** location away from it all; gorgeous decor in an intimate small designer hotel; excellent food and wine pairings. **Cons:** a car is essential; no villages or towns in walking distance; can be a bit too wine-focused for those who don't drink. [$] *Rooms from: €330* ✉ *Contrada Passo di Gurra, SP79 Km 91, Menfi, Agrigento* ☎ *0925/1955460* 🌐 *www.planetaestate.it* 🛏 *12 rooms* 🍴 *Free Breakfast.*

Sciacca

38 km (24 miles) southeast of Selinunte.

Many seasoned travelers in Sicily cite the fishing port of Sciacca as one of their favorite destinations on the island—precisely because it goes so often unmentioned in the tourist literature. Its low profile is largely due to the town's lack of both major sights and the glamour attached to other must-see places. However, Sciacca makes up for its lack of pull with its sheer authenticity as a working town. True, it's somewhat unpolished and often ill-equipped to cater to foreign tourists, but visitors to Sciacca will appreciate its grand terrace high above the port, Piazza Scandaliato, the focus of promenading and a great vantage point for sea and harbor views. Sciacca can also boast a great range of moderately priced eateries specializing in seafood that is freshly caught here every morning.

Sciacca does stand out for two things: its ceramics—it is one of the island's three great ceramics centers—and its coral, and visitors will find ample examples of both in the numerous ceramics and jewelry stores in town. A little more niche is the charming soap museum you can visit on the outskirts of town.

GETTING HERE AND AROUND

Drivers to and from Sciacca can use SS115, which links up to the A29 autostrada at Castelvetrano for onward travel to Palermo and Mazara del Vallo.

Lumia operates bus services between Sciacca and Agrigento, Caltabellotta, Castelvetrano, and Trapani. Autolinee Gallo buses connect Sciacca with Palermo.

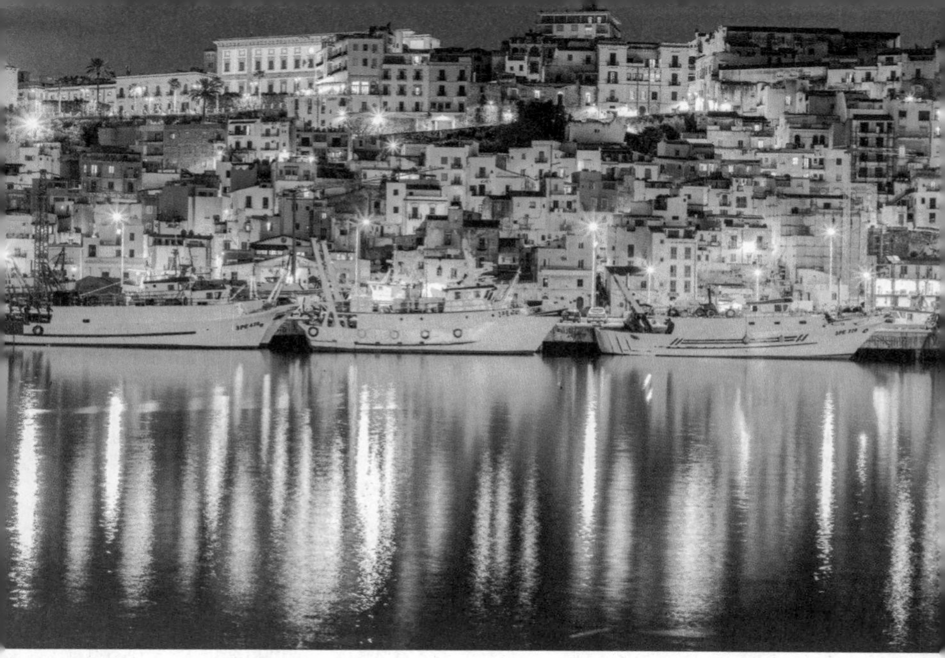

Mostly known as a working-class fishing port, Sciacca is a great place to go for low-key but excellent seafood.

CONTACTS Autolinee Gallo. ☎ *091/6171141* 🌐 *www.autolineegallo.it.* **Lumia.** ☎ *0925/21135* 🌐 *www.autolineelumia.com.*

Sights

Casa Museo del Sapone

OTHER MUSEUM | A 15-minute drive out of town will bring you to an olive plantation where soap is made from olive oil, continuing a tradition that stretches back for millennia. The fascinating, 50-minute tours in good English take you through the process of creating soap in this way and sketch out the history of soap manufacture. Following an introduction outside in the olive grove, the tour moves indoors where you can examine examples of different kinds of soap and even try your hand at making it. Afterward, there are opportunities to purchase the soap as well as other products made here. Call to book at least a day ahead. ✉ *Via Cartabubbo 30, Sciacca* ☎ *349/6087713* 🌐 *www.casamuseodelsapone.it* 🎫 *€6.*

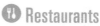

🍴 Restaurants

Ristorante Otto

$$ | **SICILIAN** | **FAMILY** | Inconspicuously located near Piazza Scandaliato in the upper town, Otto serves top-class dishes in a quiet setting that is refined but lacking any airs. The carefully selected modern art on the walls is reflected in the visual care with which the dishes are presented, while the menu shows a penchant for creatively combining disparate elements, such as cod cooked in Marsala wine with dried figs, almonds, and walnuts. **Known for:** quality cuisine; small space so reserve ahead; refined but unpretentious atmosphere. [$] *Average main: €20* ✉ *Corso Vittorio Emanuele 107, Sciacca* ☎ *388/6916517.*

Trattoria Il Faro

$ | **SEAFOOD** | Locals flock to this elegant, modern restaurant down by the port, whose white walls are embellished with the colorful ceramics for which Sciacca is renowned. Seafood is the top choice (you'll see what's available as you enter), served in basically every form, from *zuppa di cozze* (mussel soup) to squid ink pasta, grilled calamari, and red prawns from Mazara served on the skewer. **Known for:** fresh seafood dishes; moderate prices; varied menu, including fixed-price options. $ *Average main: €13* ⊠ *Via al Porto 25, Sciacca* ☎ *0925/25349* ⊙ *Closed Sun.*

Hotels

Hotel Aliai
$ | **HOTEL** | Right by the port, the small and modern Hotel Aliai is Sciacca's best choice for anyone wishing to lodge in the lower town. **Pros:** good position for the port; friendly staff; easy parking. **Cons:** low ceilings in top-floor bathrooms; three stories and no elevator; needs refurbishment. $ *Rooms from: €80* ⊠ *Via Gaie di Garaffe 60, Sciacca* ☎ *349/0507942, 0925/905388* ⊕ *www.aliai.com* ⇜ *15 rooms* ⦿ *Free Breakfast.*

Vittorio Emanuele Boutique Hotel
$ | **HOTEL** | This hotel on the main drag is housed within one of Sciacca's few palazzi that have been renovated to showcase their period finery. **Pros:** low rates; good for families; central location. **Cons:** difficult to negotiate one-way traffic system to arrive; busy road outside; one-week minimum stay in August. $ *Rooms from: €100* ⊠ *Corso Vittorio Emanuele 210, Sciacca* ☎ *328/4044836, 0925/28321* ⊕ *www.hotelvittorioemanuele.com* ⊙ *Closed Feb. and Mar.* ⇜ *7 rooms* ⦿ *Free Breakfast.*

Nightlife

Murphy's
PUBS | In the back streets of the upper town, this pub offers a warm and welcoming atmosphere, energetic jazz music (sometimes live), and a range of international draught and bottled beers as well as aperitifs and cocktails. Service is fast

and cheerful, and there's seating indoors and out. Snacks are available, too. ⊠ *Piazza Inveges 4, Sciacca* ☎ *347/6969353.*

Shopping

Cristiana
JEWELRY & WATCHES | Exquisitely hand-crafted jewelry is available at this shop on the main Corso, much of it using the coral for which Sciacca is famous. Buy from the examples on display here or work together with the exciting young designer Cristiana Turano Campello to create something to your exact tastes. ⊠ *Corso Vittorio Emanuele 175, Sciacca* ☎ *329/6817596* ⊕ *www.cristianacreatricedigioielli.com.*

Xacca Maioliche
CERAMICS | As you would expect from a town renowned for its ceramic products, ceramics stores are ubiquitous in Sciacca, mostly filled to the rafters with attention-grabbing displays of exuberant plates, spoons, pine cones, moor's heads, jugs, and birds. In this store, though, you will find these same designs but imbued with the singular artistic vision of the young craftsman Giovanni Muscarnera. ⊠ *Corso Vittorio Emanuele 192/B, Sciacca* ☎ *327/9228482.*

Caltabellotta

21 km (13 miles) northeast of Sciacca.

Dramatically sited on a high rocky elevation, the inland village of Caltabellotta was where the Angevins and Aragonese signed the peace treaty that ended the Wars of the Vespers in 1302. Its lofty position makes it a great diversion from the monotony of the coastal SS115 and a worthwhile excursion from Sciacca, with its striking 360-degree views over the village's gray roofs and the distant mountain landscape. The panorama is best appreciated from Caltabellotta's low-lying and fortress-like Chiesa Madre ("Mother Church"), situated at the top of the village and hunkered down against the fierce winds that frequently sweep across.

Nearby on a yet higher pinnacle stand the ruins of the Norman castle where the famous peace treaty was signed, accessible via steep, rock-cut steps when it's open for visits (it frequently isn't). There's not much else to view in Caltabellotta, and little in the way of eating or sleeping options.

GETTING HERE AND AROUND

It's a half-hour drive to Caltabellotta from Sciacca using SP37. Lumia buses run direct to the village from Sciacca's Via Agatocle, taking 45 minutes.

CONTACTS Lumia. ☎ *0925/21135* 🌐 *www.autolineelumia.com.*

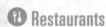

🍴 Restaurants

Lu Saracinu

$ | **SICILIAN** | Perched on the edge of the Arab quarter of the beautifully preserved village of Sambuca di Sicilia (14 miles northwest of Caltabellotta), this pizzeria/restaurant is the perfect stop for a lunchtime sightseeing break. The menu offers a range of local dishes, including *busiate* pasta with shrimps and fresh tomatoes; sausages; escalopes with mushrooms; and grilled fish—particularly noteworthy is the fine selection of antipasti. **Known for:** brilliant views; low prices; great antipasti. [$] *Average main: €9* ✉ *Via Fantasma, Sambuca di Sicilia, Caltabellotta* ☎ *333/8276821* 🕒 *Closed Mon.*

Eraclea Minoa, Torre Salsa, and Sant'Angelo Muxara

38 km (24 miles) southeast of Caltabellotta.

A really wonderful coastline with long golden sands—most of it protected by the Torre Salsa nature reserve—stretches from the ancient Greek site of Eraclea Minoa to the mighty natural stairway of Scala dei Turchi. In the rural hinterland, the well-kept hill village of Sant'Angelo Muxara is dedicated to keeping rural traditions alive and allowing travelers to experience them at first hand. There are a couple of good places to stay, making the area a base well worth considering for anyone who wants to alternate sightseeing and exploring with days on the beach.

GETTING HERE AND AROUND

This area is only possible to explore by car. Roads along the coast can get very busy in summer, in particular between Scala dei Turchi and Agrigento, so if you are visiting in the high season, try to get an early start. In winter, the coastal road below Eraclea Minoa and the tracks of the Torre Salsa nature reserve are prone to flooding.

👁 Sights

Area Archeologica di Eraclea Minoa

RUINS | Splendidly set on a promontory above a long stretch of cliff-backed sandy beach that runs right down to Scala Dei Turchi, Eraclea Minoa was once an ancient Greek city. Today, it's worth a visit to follow the path along the mostly buried circuit of its walls to get a sense of its strategic position above a fertile river valley that so appealed to the west coast Greeks. Located approximately halfway between Selinunte and Agrigento, it

was founded by the former but fought over by both for most of the 5th century BC. Its fortune barely improved over the following centuries: Eraclea's position on the west coast made it a desirable target for the armies of Carthage. Warfare, landslides, and a propensity to use ancient sites as quarries for ready-cut stone mean that little is left of the city today, and mistakes have been made in attempts to preserve what does remain.

The perspex roof added to the theater in the 1960s created warm, damp conditions perfect for the growth of abundant weeds that further damaged the stone, and a "temporary" roof erected in the early 2000s is still in place, but severely damaged. That said, the site is atmospheric, especially in spring when covered with wildflowers. There is also a small museum, with lots of finds relating to everyday life and death in the town, including a broken pot with the fragment of someone's name written on the side, several votive statuettes, and some beautifully decorated lidded pots (pyxis) for jewels or cosmetics found in graves. ✉ *Contrada Minoa, Cattolica Minoa, Agrigento* ☎ *0922/846005* 🎟 *€4.*

★ Sant'Angelo Muxara and the Val di Kam Experience

TOWN | FAMILY | A beautifully kept hill village of neat stone houses and cobbled streets, Sant'Angelo Muxara is where locals have collaborated to give travelers a firsthand look at rural traditions. Programs can be adapted to meet individual needs and interests, but highlights include cheese-making and tasting with a local shepherd, making bread or pizza in the wood-fired oven of the village's ancient bakery, and visiting a herbalist in his remote cabin and learning how to gather edible wild greens. Guided walks can also be organized, led by an archaeological and nature guide, that take in ancient cave dwellings and tombs and the town's small but very well-presented archaeological museum. Mindful walks

with yoga and meditation are also on offer and highly recommended. ✉ *Piazza Umberto I 31, Sant'Angelo Muxara, Agrigento* ☎ *338/6762491 WhatsApp* ⊕ *www.valdikam.it* 🎟 *€140 per person for 2 people.*

★ Scala dei Turchi

NATURE SIGHT | After the active volcanoes of Mount Etna and Stromboli, the tilted white "staircase" of the Scala dei Turchi cliff is the most stunning geological site in Sicily. Formed by eroded strata of pure white marl, with a silken gold sandy beach below, the cliff was allegedly named after the so-called Turkish (actually Saracen) pirates who plagued the Sicilian coast in the 16th century. The Scala and its beach are extraordinarily popular, so try if you can to visit in low season. The best access is from the signposted paid car park just to the south of the cliff (follow the sign to Majata Beach/Ingresso Scala dei Turchi). ✉ *Contrada Punta Grande, Realmonte, Agrigento* 🎟 *Free.*

★ Torre Salsa Nature Reserve

NATURE PRESERVE | The seemingly endless pristine sands of Torre Salsa, overlooked by cliffs of crystal selenite, are one of the best-kept secrets of coastal Sicily. This is in part because they are easily reached only in summer. The rest of the year underground springs make the several dirt tracks to the sands inaccessible, not only by car but also on foot except for those intrepid enough not to be put off by knee-deep mud. If the sea is calm, those prepared to paddle can usually walk along the sands from the beaches at either end: Bovo Marina to the north and Siciliana Marina to the south. Bring plenty to eat and drink, as there are no facilities. If approaching by car in the dry months, the easiest access is via the Pantano entrance towards the northern end of the reserve. ✉ *Siciliana, Agrigento* ⊕ *From SS115 follow signs for Torre Salsa, then for the Ingresso Pantano* ☎ *0922/818220* ⊕ *www.wwftorresalsa. com* 🎟 *Free.*

Beaches

Spiaggia Bovo Marina

BEACH | **FAMILY** | This good sandy beach lies between the nature reserves of Foce del Platani and Torre Salsa and is easily reached by car. It comes with a handful of lidos where you can eat and drink well and rent sunloungers in season. **Amenities:** food and drink. **Best for:** swimming; walking. ✉ *Bovo Marina, Montallegro, Agrigento* ✣ *Follow signs from SS115 to Bovo Marina.*

Spiaggia Foce del Belice

BEACH | **FAMILY** | This beach of sandy red-gold dunes offers lots of fascinating sea plants and flowers growing straight out of the sand. There are no facilities, so bring provisions and sun protection. It's lovely for beach walks and birdwatching (look out for kingfishers, egrets, and herons) as well as swimming. **Amenities:** none. **Best for:** swimming; walking. ✉ *Riserva Natural Foce del Fiume Belice, Contrada Cavallaro, Via Trenta Salme, Castelvetrano, Agrigento* 🌐 *www.parks.it/riserva.foce.fiume.belice.*

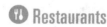

Restaurants

★ Capitolo Primo

$$ | **SICILIAN** | Simply one of the finest restaurants in Sicily, Capitolo Primo offers an utterly unique dining experience in the graceful winter garden of Relais Briuccia's Art Nouveau town house. Chef-owner Damiano Ferraro is an endlessly creative chef, spinning his magic daily with the freshest of local Sicilian produce. **Known for:** sophisticated cuisine by a master chef; impressive tasting menus at great prices; intimate Art Nouveau town house. [$] *Average main: €16* ✉ *Relais Briuccia, Via Trieste 1, Montallegro, Agrigento* ☎ *0922/847755* 🌐 *www.relaisbriuccia.com* 🕒 *Closed Mon. No lunch.*

Il Canaima

$ | **ASIAN FUSION** | **FAMILY** | This beach bar and restaurant comes with a chef who trained with Rick Stein and Giorgio Locatelli and spends his winters in Thailand and Indonesia, adding a Southeast Asian flair to the spanking fresh fish, seafood, and vegetables of his native Sicily. Il Canaima is far more in touch with contemporary eating trends than many Sicilians, so you'll be happy to find dedicated gluten-free and vegan/vegetarian menus. **Known for:** Southeast Asian twists on fresh Sicilian seafood and vegetables; late hours in the summer; relaxed dining on the beach. [$] *Average main: €13* ✉ *Spiaggia di Frazione Bovo Marina, Montallegro, Agrigento* ☎ *334/9849640* 🌐 *www.facebook.com/ilcanaima* 🕒 *Closed Nov.–Easter.*

Lustru di Luna

$ | **SICILIAN** | **FAMILY** | The village of Siculiana is nothing special, but its idyllic location above a golden beach backed by glinting white cliffs is best appreciated from a table at this inexpensive restaurant-bar right on the seafront. Along with the usual seafood pasta and grilled and deep-fried fish mains, there are several more inventive dishes, including some tempting vegetarian pastas and a daily fish soup. **Known for:** unique fish soups; reasonably priced pasta and seafood; beachside location. [$] *Average main: €10* ✉ *Via Principe di Piemonte SNC, Siculiana Marina, Agrigento* ☎ *0922/815179* 🌐 *www.lustrudiluna.it* 🕒 *Closed Tues. and Nov.–mid-Feb.*

Hotels

Baglio Caruana

$$ | **HOTEL** | Here you'll find tasteful contemporary rooms within a small organic winery set among 50 acres of vineyards a short drive from the unspoiled beaches of the Torre Salsa nature reserve. **Pros:** utterly peaceful; contemporary lodging on a wine estate with spa and pool; short drive to beach. **Cons:** no town or beach in walking distance; wine tastings and tours only available three days a week; no restaurant on-site (but can arrange wine tastings with food in advance). $ *Rooms from: €135* ⊠ *Contrada Torre Salsa, Montallegro, Agrigento* ☎ *0922/847739* ⊕ *www.bagliocaruana.it* ⊗ *Closed Nov.–Easter* ⇆ *12 rooms* ⦿ *Free Breakfast.*

★ Feudo Muxarello

$ | B&B/INN | FAMILY | A working farm producing almonds, olives, and wine (all of which feature in abundance at evening meals), Feudo Muxarello offers huge vistas toward the Sicani mountains and a to-die-for night sky. **Pros:** welcoming family atmosphere; genuine and authentic home-cooked cuisine; comfortable and spacious rooms. **Cons:** no reduced rate for single-occupancy rooms so can be pricey for solo travelers; a long way from essential services; only accessible by car. $ *Rooms from: €120* ⊠ *Contrada Muxarello, Sant'Angelo Muxaro, Agrigento* ☎ *338/5298724* ⊕ *www.feudomuxarello. it* ⇆ *7 rooms* ⦿ *Free Breakfast.*

★ Relais Briuccia

$$ | HOTEL | This exquisitely restored and furnished Art Nouveau palazzo is perhaps the most improbable hotel on the entire island of Sicily: it sits in the heart of Montallegro, a shabby agricultural town that lacks both charm and beauty, yet the Briuccia and its fine dining restaurant are special enough to deserve consideration as your main base for exploring this part of the island. **Pros:** intimate and individual service; gorgeously decorated Art Nouveau town house; fantastic and creative cuisine. **Cons:** town is not particularly attractive or appealing; romantic ambience not for everyone; not the most modern hotel. $ *Rooms from: €140* ⊠ *Via Trieste 1, Montallegro, Agrigento* ☎ *0922/847755* ⊕ *www.relaisbriuccia. com* ⇆ *5 rooms* ⦿ *Free Breakfast.*

🏃 Activities

Foce del Platani

BIRD WATCHING | FAMILY | This pale sandy dune beach to the north of Eraclea Minoa, at the mouth of the Platani river, is a fantastic spot for bird-watching in spring, with many birds making it their first stop as they migrate back to Sicily from Africa. The area directly below the ancient site, known as Pineta, can get busy in the high season as there are campsites and bars. ⊠ *Riserva Naturale Orientata Foce del Platani, Sciacca* ⊹ *From SS115, take SP57 marked Ribera/Borgo Bonsignore* ☎ *0925/561111* ⊕ *www.parks.it/riserva.foce.fiume. platani/pun.php* ⊟ *Free.*

Porto Empedocle

28 km (17 miles) southeast of Torre Salsa.

The birthplace of writer Andrea Camilleri, who wrote the incredibly popular Inspector Montalbano series that became an equally popular television series, Porto Empedocle is a salty old port that will appeal mainly to fans of the best-selling detective novels (the TV series was filmed in the far more glamorous and scenographic Baroque towns of the Val di Noto). Porto Empedocle is fictionalized in the books as the town of Vigàta, with certain locations clearly recognizable, from crime scenes to the beach-side home and favorite restaurant of Montalbano.

Main sites include La Mannara, the abandoned factory used as a base by affable rogue Gigi (located in real-life behind the ENI plant on the road to Agrigento); the flat rock at the end of the dock where Montalbano lies down after lunch to mull over his latest case; and Marinella, the beach where Montalbano has his house. Fans may also wish to pay homage to the statue of Montalbano half-way down the main street, Via Roma.

GETTING HERE AND AROUND

A short drive from Agrigento, Porto Empedocle is also connected by frequent SAL buses from Agrigento's joint bus and train station.

TOURS

Inspector Montalbano Tour

CULTURAL TOURS | Michele Gallo's tours of the sights of Agrigento and Porto Empedocle that feature in both Andrea Camilleri's detective novels are not merely of interest to fans of the books. Visiting sights that few would feel worth a second glance reveals stories that resonate with Sicily's complex, and often extraordinary, past. ⊠ *Via Dante Alighieri 49, Agrigento* ⊕ *www.lavalledeitempli. it/en/itineraries/agrigento/literary-tours/ montalbano* 🖾 *€170 for 3-hour tour.*

 Restaurants

Il Timone da Enzo

$$$ | **SICILIAN** | This family-run fish restaurant shaped like a fishing boat was made famous by its frequent appearances in the Inspector Montalbano novels. There is a daily fixed menu (€30) comprising mixed Sicilian antipasti, three "tastes" of pasta, and then a choice among deep-fried calamari, roast prawns, or grilled seabass or bream. **Known for:** one of Montalbano's favorite restaurants; gelato a pezzo for dessert; selfie-friendly papier-mâché figure of writer Camilleri. 🖫 *Average main: €30* ⊠ *Via Nino Bixio 9, Porto Empedocle, Agrigento* ☎ *320/2828057.*

Hotels

★ Borgo delle Pietre

$$ | **RESORT** | Although it lies just a five-minute drive from Porto Empedocle, and less from Marinella beach, Borgo delle Pietre feels as if it is in a world apart, set among olives and vineyards, with the only sounds those of birdsong and goat-bells. **Pros:** peaceful rural location; relaxing outdoor spaces and good food; beautiful architecture and interior

design. **Cons:** better as a retreat than as a touring base; not the most interesting stretch of coast; car essential. 🖫 *Rooms from: €190* ⊠ *Via delle Madonie, Porto Empedocle, Agrigento* ⊕ *www.borgo-dellepietre.com* 🕙 *Closed Nov.–Easter* 🖙 *8 rooms* |◎| *Free Breakfast.*

Palazzo Melluso

$$ | **B&B/INN** | This is an exceptional B&B with five rooms, occupying an Art Nouveau town house overlooking the main drag, Via Roma. **Pros:** perfect for Camilleri fans; outstanding breakfasts; period charm and personal service. **Cons:** no restaurant; quite expensive for a hotel in a shabby provincial port; only really of interest for Camilleri fans. 🖫 *Rooms from: €149* ⊠ *Piazza Chiesa Vecchia 6, Porto Empedocle, Agrigento* ⊕ *www. palazzomelluso.com* 🖙 *5 rooms* |◎| *Free Breakfast.*

Agrigento

8 km (5 miles) northeast of Porto Empedocle, 128 km (80 miles) south of Palermo.

Agrigento owes its fame almost exclusively to its stunning ancient Greek temples—though it was also the birthplace of playwright Luigi Pirandello (1867–1936) and the setting for the Montelusa scenes of Andrea Camilleri's Inspector Montalbano books. For fans of the books in particular, the old town is an evocative place for a wander, culminating in a visit to nuns for an almond pastry and the fascinating Museo di Santo Spirito. There is much to fascinate and intrigue in the area around Agrigento, too, both in the rural hinterland and along the coast south to Licata, scene of the Allied landings of 1943.

GETTING HERE AND AROUND

If you're driving, take the A19 autostrada to Caltanissetta, follow the SS640 to Agrigento. Motorists can also access the town easily via the coastal SS115 and, from Palermo, by the SS189. Buses and trains run from Enna, Palermo, and Catania; both bus and train stations are centrally located.

VISITOR INFORMATION

CONTACT Agrigento Tourism Office. ⊠ *Via Empedocle 73,* ☎ *0922/20391* ⊕ *www. visitsicily.info.*

Sights

Giardino della Kolymbetra

GARDEN | Easy to miss behind the Temple dei Dioscuri, the Giardino della Kolymbetra is a sunken garden created within what was once a huge "tank" excavated in the stone on the orders of the Tyrant Theron in 480 BC. In time, it was transformed into a lush garden, irrigated by a series of little channels, a technique brought to Sicily by the Arabs, who had learned this craft in the deserts of North Africa. Now planted with citrus, olive, almond, pistachio, pomegranate, and even banana trees, it forms a true oasis, where often the only sound is that of running water. ⊠ *Viale Caduti di Marzabotto, Agrigento* ☎ *335/1229042* ⊕ *www. fondoambiente.it/luoghi/giardino-della-kolymbethra* 🎟 *€7.*

Monastero di Santo Spirito

RELIGIOUS BUILDING | First built in 1299, these cloisters and courtyard, up the hill above the Valle dei Templi near the modern city, are open to the public. However, most visitors stop by the adjacent abbey for a treat and tour of the church, so be sure to ring the doorbell and try the chewy almond cookies. On special occasions, there may be *kus-kus dolce*—a sweet dessert dish made from pistachio nuts, almonds, and chocolate—that the Cistercian nuns learned from Tunisian servants back in the 13th century. ⊠ *Cortile Santo Spirito 9, off Via Porcello, Agrigento* ☎ *0922/1552737, 349/4792401* ⊕ *www.monasterosspirito.wixsite.com/ agrigento.*

Museo Civico di Santo Spirito

HISTORY MUSEUM | FAMILY | Housed in a restored palace that originally belonged to the Chiaramonte, one of the most powerful noble families in Sicily, this museum's architecture is a wonderful testimony to Sicily's complex history, an appealing fusion of Romanesque, Byzantine, Norman, Gothic, and Spanish. Highlights are the Gothic chapterhouse and the old defensive tower; the holes in the faded Byzantine frescoes of saints were created by American soldiers billeted here during World War II, who needed pegs to hang their kits on. Best of all is the Ethnographic collection on the top floor. Formed entirely of bits and pieces donated by locals at the end of the 20th century, it offers fascinating and often funny insights into everyday life, with exhibits ranging from recipe books to an ammunition belt modified for school exams so that cheat notes could be rolled up and stored in the bullet pockets. ⊠ *Via Santo Spirito 1, Agrigento* ☎ *0922/590371* 🎟 *Free, but donations appreciated* ⊘ *Closed Sun.*

★ Museo Regionale Archeologico

HISTORY MUSEUM | Ancient Akragas (the Greek name for Agrigento) was synonymous with decadence and excess, a lifestyle perfectly summed up by the philosopher Plato who remarked that its people "built as if they are going to live forever, and eat as if they will never eat again." This museum is testimony to the fact that the people of Akragas had the means to buy the very best, from the high quality of the red-figured Greek banqueting ware to scenes on some of the magnificent kraters (used for mixing wine and water) that evoke life at an ancient dinner party in vivid detail. Look out as well for the double-walled wine jar, with space between its two walls for snow to chill the wine. ⊠ *Contrada San Nicola, Agrigento* ☎ *0922/401565* ⊕ *www.coopculture.it/it/poi/museo-archeologico-regionale-pietro-griffo* 🎟 *€8, €14 with Valle dei Templi.*

The Temple of Juno is perhaps the most beautiful of the temples at Agrigento's Valle dei Templi.

Palma di Montechiaro

TOWN | Donnafugata, the country seat of the Salina family in Giuseppe Tomasi di Lampedusa's novel *The Leopard*, is a fictional place, but it's a fusion of Santa Margherita del Belice (where the Tomasi di Lampedusa palace was until destroyed by a 1968 earthquake) and the Chiesa Madre and Benedictine Convent in Palma di Montecchiaro. The town was founded in the 17th century by Tomasi di Lampedusa's ancestors, at a time when Spain, who ruled Sicily, needed the island to be its main source of wheat. As rural Sicily was beset with banditry, and considered far too dangerous for individual families to live in isolated farmhouses, the Crown encouraged landowners to found new towns, where peasants could live in relative safety, heading out to the fields each day and returning at night, to live cheek-to-cheek with their animals in one story houses. These days it is a rather grim, dilapidated-looking place, but for fans of *The Leopard,* a visit to the convent to buy almond cookies from one of the four remaining nuns is an eerie

experience, offering a brief glimpse of the hidden lives that have changed little in centuries. ✉ *Palma di Montechiaro, Agrigento* ☎ *338/7333323*.

★ Valle dei Templi

RUINS | The temples of Agrigento, a UNESCO World Heritage site, are considered to be some of the finest and best-preserved Greek temples in the world. Whether you first come upon the valley in the early morning light, bathed by golden floodlights after sunset, or in January and February when the valley is awash in the fragrant blossoms of thousands of almond trees, it's easy to see why Akragas (Agrigento's Greek name) was celebrated by the poet Pindar as "the most beautiful city built by mortals." The temples were originally erected as a showpiece to flaunt the Greek victory over Carthage, and they have since withstood a later sack by the Carthaginians, mishandling by the Romans, and neglect by Christians and Muslims.

Although getting to, from, and around the dusty ruins of the Valle dei Templi is pretty easy, this important archaeological zone still deserves several hours. The temples are a bit spread out, but the valley is all completely walkable and usually toured on foot. However, since there's only one hotel (Villa Athena) that's close enough to walk to the ruins, you'll most likely have to drive to reach the site. The best place to park is at the entrance to the temple area. The site, which opens at 8:30 am, is divided into western and eastern sections, linked by a bridge. The best way to see them both is to park at the Temple of Juno entrance and walk downhill through the eastern zone, across the footbridge into the western zone, and then return back uphill, so that you see everything again but from a different angle and in a different light. The best time to go is a couple of hours before sunset, although if you are in Agrigento in high summer you might want to consider a night visit; the gates open a short while before sunset, with the temples floodlit as night falls.

You'll want to spend time seeing the eight pillars of the Tempio di Ercole (Temple of Hercules) that make up Agrigento's oldest temple complex, dating from the 6th century BC. The Tempio di Giunone (Temple of Juno) at the top of the hill is perhaps the most beautiful of all the temples, partly in ruins and commanding an exquisite view of the valley (especially at sunset). The low wall of mighty stone blocks in front of it was an altar on which animals were sacrificed as an offering to the goddess. Next down the hill is the almost perfectly complete Tempio della Concordia (Temple of Concord), perhaps the best-preserved Greek temple currently in existence, thanks to having been converted into a Christian church in the 6th century, and restored back to being a temple in the 18th century. Below it is the valley's oldest surviving temple, the Temple of Hercules, with nine of its original 38 columns standing, the rest tumbled around like a child's upended bag of building bricks.

Continuing over the pedestrian bridge, you reach the Tempio di Giove (Temple of Jupiter). Meant to be the largest temple in the complex, it was never completed, but it would have occupied approximately the site of a soccer field. It was an unusual temple, with half columns backing into a continuous wall, and 25-foot-high telamon, or male figures, inserted in the gaps in between. A couple of the telamon have been roughly reassembled horizontally on the ground near the temple. Beyond is the so-called Temple of Castor and Pollux, prettily picturesque, but actually a folly created in the 19th century from various columns and architectural fragments. ✉ *Zona Archeologica, Via dei Templi, Agrigento* ☎ *0922/1839996* ⊕ *www.parcovalledeitempli.it* ✆ *€10, €14 with museum (free 1st Sun. of month).*

★ Via del Ghiaccio

OTHER ATTRACTION | FAMILY | In the 19th and 20th centuries, the twin hill towns of Cammerata and San Giovanni Gemini were famous throughout Sicily for their traveling ice cream and granita makers. The key to this ice-cream industry was the collection and preservation of snow, and a local family of ice-cream makers has restored several of the *neviere*, circular buildings resembling stone igloos, strewn over the forested slopes above the towns. Snow was shoveled into the neviere, trodden down until it turned to a thick layer of ice, then covered with a mat of rushes and straw before another layer of snow was added on top. Stored like this, the snow would keep frozen for months, and with the giant blocks of ice fetching the equivalent of €3,000, it had to be carefully guarded. The best way to see the neviere, learn how to make Sicilian granita, and visit a small private ice museum, is on a guided tour, which can include a lunch of cold cuts, local cheeses, and grilled meat and vegetables in a pretty family-run café. ✉ *Via Dante Alighieri 49, Agrigento* ☎ *360/397930* ⊕ *www. lavalledeitempli.it/en/itineraries/agrigento/ gastronomy/guided-tour-via-del-ghiaccio*

🎟 *€130 for 2 people including guided tour, lunch, and tastings.*

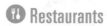

🍴 Restaurants

★ Il Re di Girgenti
$$ | **SICILIAN** | You might not expect to find an ultramodern—even hip—place to dine within a few minutes' drive of Agrigento's ancient temples, yet Il Re di Girgenti offers up pleasing versions of Sicilian classics in a trendy, country-chic atmosphere (think funky black-and-white tile floors mixed with shelves lined with old-fashioned crockery) popular with young locals. The thoughtful wine list offers good prices on both local wines and those from throughout Sicily. **Known for:** delightful wine selections; contemporary setting with lovely views; Sicilian dishes with a twist. [$] *Average main: €22* ✉ *Via Panoramica dei Templi 51, Agrigento* ☎ *0922/401388* 🌐 *www.ilredigirgenti.it* 🕒 *Closed Tues.*

Osteria Ex Panificio
$$ | **SEAFOOD** | One of Agrigento's most popular restaurants, Osteria Ex Panificio is housed in a former bakery on the main street of the old town. Typical Sicilian fish and seafood dishes dominate, and there is a terrace for outside dining in summer, and a cozy interior decorated with bakery equipment and hand-written bread recipes. **Known for:** delicious seafood risotto; outside dining with views of some splendid Baroque palace facades; year-round popularity with locals. [$] *Average main: €15* ✉ *Piazza G Sinatra, Agrigento* ☎ *0922/595399* 🌐 *www.osteriaexpanificio.it.*

Trattoria dei Templi
$$ | **SICILIAN** | Along a road on the way up to Agrigento proper from the temple area, this vaulted family-run restaurant serves up tasty traditional food, namely daily house-made pasta specials and plenty of fresh fish dishes, all prepared with Sicilian flair. Your best bet is to ask the advice of brothers Giuseppe and Simone, the owners and chief orchestrators in the restaurant, who can also help select a Sicilian wine to pair with your meal. **Known for:** good choice of local wines; fresh fish; exceptional antipasti, like carpaccio of cernia (grouper). [$] *Average main: €18* ✉ *Via Panoramica dei Templi 15, Agrigento* ☎ *0922/403110* 🕒 *Closed Sun.*

☕ Coffee and Quick Bites

Antica Panelleria Musicò
$ | **SICILIAN** | **FAMILY** | This food van, parked at the start of the main boulevard Viale della Vittoria, has been selling pane e panelle (soft bread rolls stuffed with deep-fried chickpea flour fritters) since 1954. If you are interested in other traditional street food, look out for the Grattatella van (ice shaved to order and served in cups with fruit syrups) and U Panuzzu Ca Meusa (soft rolls with spleen, lemon, and ricotta), both of which have no fixed place, but the Grattatella is often in the resort of San Leone in the summer, while U Panuzzo can be found at lots of local summer events. **Known for:** old-fashioned Sicilian street food; a taste of local life; authentic eat-as-you-walk sandwiches of chickpea flour fritters. [$] *Average main: €5* ✉ *Viale della Vittoria SNC, Agrigento* ☎ *No phone* 💳 *No credit cards.*

★ Gelateria Le Cuspidi
$ | **ICE CREAM** | **FAMILY** | Agrigento's finest ice-cream parlor creates memorable versions of key Sicilian favorites such as pistachio, almond, and cassata, along with a superb "pecorino" made with fresh sheep's milk ricotta. The pastries are excellent, too. **Known for:** tasty breakfast pastries; the hub of life in Agrigento on summer evenings; ice cream made from riccotta. [$] *Average main: €3* ✉ *Piazza Cavour 19, Agrigento* ☎ *0922/39101* 🌐 *www.lecuspidi.com* 🕒 *Closed Tues.*

Hotels

Doric Bed Boutique Hotel

$$ | **RESORT** | Ideal for sophisticated urbanites who want to combine a poolside holiday with sightseeing, this stylish contemporary hotel on a hilltop is an innovative addition to Agrigento's lodging scene. **Pros:** some rooms have private plunge pools and hot tubs; homegrown produce served in the restaurant; shady pool perfect for relaxing in summer. **Cons:** a bit far from Agrigento proper; nearby Villagio Mosè is unattractive; more suited to couples than families. [$] *Rooms from: €180* ✉ *Strada E.S.A. Mosé, San Biagio 20, Agrigento* ☎ *0922/1808509* 🌐 *www.doric.it* ⏲ *Closed Nov.–Easter* 🛏 *27 rooms.*

Fontes Episcopi

$$ | **RESORT** | Fontes Episcopi is a country mansion full of art and warm Sicilian hospitality. **Pros:** genuine country family atmosphere; hands-on cooking lessons; lovely garden and pool. **Cons:** the Macalube nature reserve (with its erupting mud volcanoes) next to the hotel is permanently closed following an accident; the nearest town, Aragona, is not very appealing; quite remote—car essential. [$] *Rooms from: €220* ✉ *Agrigento* ⏲ *Closed Nov.–Mar.* 🛏 *7 rooms, with 4 new suites under construction.*

Foresteria Baglio della Luna

$$ | **HOTEL** | In the valley below the temples, fiery sunsets and moonlight cast a glow over the ancient 12th-century watchtower at the center of this farmhouse-hotel complex, which is composed of stone buildings surrounding a peaceful geranium- and ivy-filled courtyard and the garden beyond. **Pros:** quiet setting; top-notch restaurant; pretty gardens. **Cons:** location a bit remote; no pool; hotel a little dark inside. [$] *Rooms from: €145* ✉ *Via Serafino Amabile Guastella 1, Agrigento* ☎ *0922/511061* 🌐 *www.bagliodellaluna.com* ⏲ *Closed Dec.–Feb.* 🛏 *23 rooms* 🍴 *Free Breakfast.*

★ **Mandranova**

$$ | **HOTEL** | Set amid a vast olive grove, this tranquil rural retreat feels as if it's in the middle of nowhere yet is just a 20-minute drive from the UNESCO-listed temples of Agrigento. **Pros:** cooking classes and olive oil tastings with owner; peaceful and rural; romantic swimming pool. **Cons:** might be too off-the-beaten-track for some; no room service; car is essential. [$] *Rooms from: €178* ✉ *SS115, KM 217, Palma di Montechiaro, Agrigento* ☎ *393/9862169* 🌐 *www.mandranova.com* 🛏 *15 rooms* 🍴 *Free Breakfast.*

★ **Villa Athena**

$$$$ | **HOTEL** | The 18th-century Villa Athena, updated into a sleek, luxurious place to stay, complete with gorgeous manicured gardens and swimming pool, holds a privileged position directly overlooking the Temple of Concordia, a 10-minute walk away—an amazing sight both during the day and when it's lit up at night. **Pros:** unbeatable location for the Valle dei Templi, with phenomenal temple views; plenty of free parking; good restaurant and spa. **Cons:** lack of information on local attractions; very expensive compared to other area options; lobby on the small side. [$] *Rooms from: €420* ✉ *Via Passeggiata Archeologica 33, Agrigento* ☎ *0922/596288* 🌐 *www.hotelvillaathena.it* 🛏 *27 rooms* 🍴 *Free Breakfast.*

Licata

44 km (27 miles) southeast of Agrigento.

Although its outskirts are unappealing, Licata retains a small and lively historic center, and anyone interested in history of the American landings in Sicily during World War II may well wish to pay the town a visit. A more recent claim to fame is its famous restaurant, one of only two in Sicily to be awarded two Michelin stars.

GETTING HERE AND AROUND

Licata is fairly well connected by bus to Agrigento, Palermo, and Catania's airport. By train, the main destinations are Caltanissetta and the oil refinery town of Gela. By car, it lies on the SS115 coastal road.

TOURS

The Seventh Army Landings of 1943

SPECIAL-INTEREST TOURS | These fascinating tours of southwest Sicily focus on Licata and bring the extraordinary strategies and struggles of the Allied invasion and its main characters—ranging from Patton and Montgomery to Lucky Luciano and Göring—vividly to life. The English-speaking guide is both extremely well-informed and a brilliant storyteller. ✉ *Via Dante Alighieri 49, Agrigento* ☎ *360/397930* 🌐 *www.sicilytravel.net/st_tour/wwii-sicily-landing* 🎫 *€270 for full day tour.*

Sights

The Museum of World War II and the Air Raid Shelter

HISTORY MUSEUM | On the morning of July 10, 1943, the port of Licata became the first town in Sicily to be taken by American soldiers of the 7th Army under General Patton. Anyone interested in this history should visit the small museum of memorabilia within the tourism office, where the finds include a Coca-Cola bottle found in a shipwreck, ammunition boxes, huge mobile food containers, and even a packet of American razor blades. The staff can also help you get access to the town's former air raid shelter. ✉ *Largo San Salvatore, Licata* ☎ *389/6367251* 🌐 *www.prolocolicata.it* 🎫 *Free.*

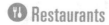

Restaurants

★ La Madia

$$$$ | **SICILIAN** | One of the most famous restaurants in Sicily, and one of only two on the island to have been awarded a second Michelin star, La Madia is a must-visit when you're here. Chef Pino Cuttaio is a legend within Sicily and beyond thanks to his incredible talent for creating unique dishes that fuse tradition and innovation, without ever losing sight of the kind of simplicity that allows the brilliance and flavors of first-rate Sicilian produce to shine. **Known for:** once-in-a-lifetime special occasion dining; one of the best restaurants in Italy; world-class dishes with Sicilian produce. [$] *Average main: €35* ✉ *Corso F. ReCapriata 22, Licata* ☎ *0922/771443* 🌐 *www.ristorantelamadia.it* 🕒 *Closed Tues. No dinner Sun. in winter. No lunch Sun. mid-June–mid-Sept.*

★ Uovo di Seppia

$$ | **SICILIAN** | The brainchild of La Madia chef Pino Cuttaio, Uovo di Seppia is a combination kitchen, cooking school, shop, and bar where you can buy exquisite fresh and stuffed pasta, hand-made bottled sauces, biscuits, cakes, and other gastronomic goodies to take away. Saturday night is arancino and champagne night, kicking off at 6 pm. **Known for:** take-home gourmet pasta and sauces; Saturday night arancini with sparkling wine; learning to cook with a Michelin-starred chef. [$] *Average main: €20* ✉ *Corso Filippo Re Capriata 31, Licata* ☎ *0922/894250* 🌐 *www.uovodiseppia.it.*

Hotels

Relais Villa Giuliana

$ | **HOTEL** | This 19th-century villa with a restaurant and 12 rooms is set on a hill above Licata. **Pros:** great restaurant; quiet location above Licata; country house atmosphere. **Cons:** pool is small; a car is essential; weddings and other events often hosted in conservatory restaurant. [$] *Rooms from: €110* ✉ *Via Oreto Grata Trav. B n. 14, Licata* ☎ *0922/894424* 🌐 *www.villagiulianarelais.it* 🛏 *12 rooms* 🍴 *Free Breakfast.*

Pantelleria

177 km (110 miles) off the coast of Trapani.

Closer to Africa than Sicily, this remote volcanic island is an extraordinary place, with its forbiddingly craggy black coastline encircling an interior of mountains and meticulously terraced valleys peppered with tiny lava-stone domed houses, miniature walled gardens, and neat vineyards of zibbibo grapes. Indeed, the island remains agricultural at its heart, with an economy based on producing much-prized dessert wines and almost equally-prized capers. This is just as well, as Pantelleria is notorious for its strong winds and the tourism season is short, with many hotels and restaurants opening only from late April or May to September.

Over the centuries, the people of Pantelleria have evolved unique ways of cultivation and architecture to overcome the challenges of living on a remote stony island plagued with fierce winds, and these traditions have earned the island an UNESCO World Heritage status. The lava-stone terraces, drystone walls, *dammusi* (single-story domed houses), and circular or elliptical walled gardens that define the island all evolved as ways of clearing and adapting the land of stone so that crops could be planted. Vines and olive and citrus trees were trained to grow low to escape the winds—a practice that continues today, with knee-high vines and waist-high olive and citrus trees. It is still common to find a single citrus or other fruit tree surrounded by a *giardino pantesco* (a walled garden) to protect it from the winds.

For anyone seeking tranquility, beauty, and fantastic walking, Pantelleria in spring or autumn is heavenly. There is a vast network of clearly marked paths and tracks (highlights include a natural volcanic sauna) and on days when the sea is too rough or cold for swimming, there are natural hot tubs to wallow in at Gadir and Scauri.

Accommodations on the island include high-end dammusi with pools as well as exclusive boutique hotels and country retreats. Those on a tighter budget will find some excellent privately owned places to rent. Just keep in mind that the island's main town and port, Pantelleria, is pretty ugly and strictly functional, so it's best avoided except for practicalities like grocery shopping and gas (it has the island's only gas station). The long straggly settlement of Khamma-Tracino is not immediately appealing, but has some very picturesque corners and fabulous views of the coast as well as a handful of small grocery stores. East coast villages like Gadir, Cala Levante, Cala Tramontana, and Martingana are all extremely gorgeous and desirable, but the best all-round base is Scauri in the southwest of the island, an attractive and lively village with lots of good places to eat and rocky coves to swim.

Walking maps are essential (for drivers as well as walkers) and are available online or from the Parco Nazionale Isola di Pantelleria tourism office. There is some stunning swimming to be experienced among the dramatic volcanic rock formations, but swimming shoes are essential. Jellyfish are common, so swimming without a mask and snorkel is not advisable.

GETTING HERE AND AROUND

There are flights to Pantelleria year-round from Palermo and Trapani, and seasonal flights from several mainland Italian airports. Ferries operate year-round from Trapani, and in high season, there are hydrofoils as well (which are much faster but more expensive).

The island's local bus service is scant, so renting a car is almost essential if you want to explore. Driving is exciting or challenging, depending on your point of

The remote volcanic island of Pantelleria has a stunning craggy black coastline.

view (and skills at reversing) with some very steep and narrow inland roads. Although it is possible to stick to asphalted roads, more adventurous drivers can enjoy exploring the numerous rough tracks that criss-cross the mountainous interior. A vehicle with four-wheel drive is not essential, but one with a high carriage is, and do not even consider renting a car here without full insurance.

AIRPORTS Aeroporto di Pantelleria.
☎ *0923/911172* ⊕ *www.aeroportodipan-telleria.it.*

CAR RENTALS Pantelrent. ✉ *Pantelleria Airport, Pantelleria* ☎ *338/3054229 WhatsApp* ⊕ *www.noleggioautopantel-leria.it.*

TOURS

Gaspare Busetta
BOAT TOURS | Hop on a 60-foot traditional fishing boat captained by Gaspare Busetta, who knows all there is to know about the waters surrounding Pantelleria, and frequently works with fashion brand Armani on photoshoots. Specific itineraries

for trips depend on the weather, but this is a man who knows every rock, cranny, and current, and if anyone can find a calm cove for a swim on a windy day, it's him. ✉ *Pantelleria* ☎ *339/3984810* 🖥 *€600 per day.*

Giuseppe d'Aietti
WALKING TOURS | A former lawyer, Giuseppe d'Aietti gave up the humdrum and stress of legal life in Sicily to become a walking and nature guide on Pantelleria, where he was born. Peppe knows the routes of the island literally stone by stone and plant by plant, and also takes walkers to secret, wild places on excursions known as adventure trekking. He has also written several books about Pantelleria, and his stories bring the island and its unique culture to life as you walk. ✉ *Pantelleria* ☎ *328/4165598* ⊕ *www. pantelleriaculturaenatura.it* 🖥 *From €25 per person for a two-hour hike.*

◉ Sights

Azienda Agricola Almanza

FARM/RANCH | Denny Almanza took over his grandfather's beekeeping farm just outside the little village of Madonna delle Grazie at the age of 15. Now he has hives in three zones—by the sea, above the Lago di Venere, and on Montagne Grande—and his bees produce five or six different kinds of honey, including prickly pear, clover, rosemary, heather, and mountain strawberry, that tend to sell out very quickly as he is the only person on the island to produce honey at any scale.

Along with honey-making, Denny makes two dry white zibbibo wines and a passito, and produces truly excellent capers and oregano. Contact him beforehand to organize a wine tasting accompanied by local snacks such as caper and almond pesto and primosale cheese. ✉ *Contrada Madonna delle Grazie 137, Pantelleria* ☎ *366/8253519* ✍ *dennysalvatore16@ gmail.com* ☕ *Tastings €10.*

Cantina Basile

WINERY | An exuberant welcome awaits you at Cantina Basile from winemaker Fabrizio and his English-speaking wife, Simona. Fabrizio is something of a wine rebel and innovator, and if anyone can convince you that sweet passito dessert wine works its magic better with well-chosen savory dishes than sweet, he will be the one to do it. Along with dry and sweet zibbibo wines, Fabrizio has planted cabernet franc, merlot, and syrah vines, and tastings give an opportunity to try some of his red wines. His whites include Sora Luna, 100% zibbibo grown in volcanic sandy soil where Fabrizio trains the vine leaves to grow big and act as shade to the grapes, and Trequartidiluna, where the wine must is left in oak for a month then aged in stainless steel for 10 years. Tasting include four or five wines, and are accompanied by foods chosen to demonstrate how differently the same wines can react to various different foods. ✉ *Via San Michele 65, Bukkuram, Pantelleria* ☎ *333/6592553* ⊕ *www.cantinabasile.it* ☕ *Tastings €30.*

★ Emanuela Bonomo

WINERY | The island's first female winemaker, Emanuela Bonomo not only makes a fantastic *passito* dessert wine, but also had the vision to see that Pantelleria's traditional gastronomic preserves made of capers, olives, fruits, vegetables, herbs, and oil that many islanders took for granted could find an international market. Her beautifully packaged preserves, pestos, and condiments inspired many islanders to revisit their own family's traditions. Book ahead for a tour of the vineyard that includes visiting the Bonomo's caper fields on Monte Gibele. ✉ *Via Ziton di Rekale 43, Rekale, Pantelleria* ☎ *0923/916489* ⊕ *www. aziendabonomopantelleria.it* ☕ *Tastings from €15.*

Favare Grande

NATURE SIGHT | Park in the car park (waymarked 974 Favare Grande) just off the main inland road that leads from Tracino to Rekale. From here a really lovely path leads up to lush upland meadows (carpeted with wildflowers in spring) where *favare,* natural emissions of sulphurous steam, billow through crevices in the rock. If you want a longer walk, a path continues from here to the Grotta del Bagno Asciutto. Alternatively you could continue and climb one of Pantelleria's two main peaks, Montagne Grande (1 hour, 40 minutes) or Monte Gibele (50 minutes). ✉ *Pantelleria.*

★ The Perimetrale

SCENIC DRIVE | An excellent road with some fabulous coastal views, the Perimetrale encircles the entire island, although its most interesting stretch is along the east and south coasts between Cala Cinque Dente and Scauri. Although you could drive the entire stretch in far less than an hour, exploring all the little coves and villages and taking a few walks could easily keep you busy for several days.

Cala Cinque Denti may literally mean "Bay of the Five Teeth", but opinions vary over which of the fearsome jagged rock formations inspired the name. The bay is most dramatically approached on foot from the signed car park at Punta Spadillo, from where a well-marked 30-minute path crosses a lunar landscape of black lava formations, scattered among which are doughnut-shaped gun emplacements dating back to World War II. A rocky branch of the path clambers down to the Laghetto Ondine, a natural pool fed by the sea, where you can swim under fabulous formations of lava. The main path continues along the clifftop, with more fantastic views, before climbing up to the top of Cala dei Cinque Denti.

The next stop along the Perimetrale is the picturesque village of Gadir, set around a sheltered inlet. The harborside has been smartly decked for sunbathing, and there are ladders into the inlet, from which you can swim out into the cove. Right by the water are three tomb-shaped pits enclosing hot water springs. Be warned that the temperature in one of them is dangerously hot so check before choosing which one to dunk yourself in. Following the path around the headland brings you to another (cool but protected) natural swimming pool, with two hot water springs behind it.

Driving on, you come to photogenic Cala Levante and Cala Tramontana, twin bays divided by a small peninsula. There is good swimming and sunbathing from each, and a narrow road continues south along the coast to the island's most famous rock formation, the Arco dell'Elefante, which is said to resemble an elephant dipping its trunk into the sea. Little paths across the rocks lead to the best places to access the sea for a swim.

Returning to the Perimetrale, carry on south until the sign to Martingana, where a very steep but asphalted road curves down to a pretty settlement of lava stone and white-domed dammusi. The road then becomes a track (drivable even in an ordinary car) leading to a small car park where a path leads to a cove (with more good swimming) and where you can sunbathe atop a solidified river of lava. The next bay, Balata dei Turchi, can be reached by several clearly marked footpaths or along a rough and steep road, best attempted only by an adventurous driver. The bay is jaw-droppingly beautiful on a calm sunny day, backed by cliffs stained ochre, china blue, and rose by volcanic minerals, but can be quite inhospitable and forbidding in strong winds. Punta Nikà, reached by a steep track a little farther along the Perimetrale, has similar polychrome cliff formations and offshore hot springs accessible only in calm seas. The path to them is not signposted, but they're fairly easy to find. Instead of going downhill to the main bay, look for a narrow path after the first house on the left (with contemporary metal gates). Follow this downhill and along the perimeter of the house's garden. At the bottom of the garden, follow the white arrows (a bit faded) which will guide you down to a place where you can get into the sea. Don't attempt this track unless you are a fit and experienced hiker. ⌧ *Pantelleria*.

Piana di Ghirlanda

SCENIC DRIVE | Starting at the town of Tracino, follow signs to the idyllic valley of Mueggen where immaculate vineyards and an intricate network of drystone walls and terraces are scattered with pepper-pot dammusi, some exquisitely restored as holiday homes, others picturesquely crumbling. From here, a narrow unpaved but drivable track leads down into the island's most fertile valley, the Piana di Ghirlanda, before winding uphill and over into the next valley and the village of Rekale. Just beyond Rekale a narrow paved road leads steeply uphill (marked Zighidi) then runs past the Byzantine tombs and along a spectacular ridge with views down to the sea and into the Valle di Monastero. Follow signs to Sibà, to discover what may be the island's most charming village, nestled among lush greenery on the lower slopes of the Montagna Grande, then continue to the village of Bugeber, perched high above the Lago di Venere (Lake of Venus), with its green-turquoise waters filling a spent volcanic crater. There are swimming spots from the lake's beaches, and smearing oneself with lake mud, and then lying in the sun until it is baked hard, is considered beneficial. ✉ *Pantelleria.*

★ Scauri

TOWN | An appealing village in two parts, Scauri's upper part is set around a church with a clock tower high above the sea and has a couple of good places to eat, a fishmonger, and a small grocery store as well as gorgeous views down to the sea from the wiggly maze of tiny streets behind the church. You could drive straight down to Scauri Porto, but if you like walking, leave the car in the car park and follow the main road down hill past La Nicchia restaurant, until you reach a minor side road called Via Sopra La Scala. This becomes a track that leads downhill through meadows to the intriguing remains of a Roman or Byzantine settlement with the ruins of lava-stone buildings scattered among prickly pears, wild grains, and capers. The path continues along the coast, passing a tiny rocky bay with a natural hot pool, before arriving at a tiny quayside where you'll find the La Vela restaurant-bar and usually some kayaks to rent. From here a small road crosses a low headland to the rest of Scauri, with a handful of picturesque places to eat or rent boats set around a well-protected harbor. The wind-lashed west coast is not alluring, and in places has been marred with shoddy beach villas and hideous hotels, though anyone interested in archeology may want to see the Sesi Grande, a huge dammuso-like structure, with 11 spooky tunnels leading to 12 oval cells, created as a burial mound by the island's prehistoric inhabitants. ✉ *Scauri, Pantelleria.*

Zighidi and the Grotta del Bagno Asciutto

CAVE | From Scauri, steep and narrow Contrada Zighidi climbs up to a small roadside parking lot (marked track 971 Grotta del Bagno Asciutto). Take a look first at the Byzantine tombs cut into the rock, then head downhill along a narrow track into broad, flat Valle di Monastero, planted with miniature olive trees and neat vineyards. The path then leads up through a charming crumbling and semi-abandoned village of dammusi before arriving at a car park with information boards, from where a clearly marked path leads to the Bagno Asciutto, a natural cave with hot steam emissions where you can lie and sweat before cooling off from a small courtyard surrounded by stone benches and fantastic views. ✉ *Grotta del Bagno Asciutto, Pantelleria* 🎫 *Free.*

🍴 Restaurants

Emporio del Gusto

$ | **SICILIAN** | This gourmet delicatessen and bistro-café makes a trip to the island's scruffy main town worth your while (and helpfully happens to be close to the gas station). The Emporio is a showcase for the many artisan pestos, pates, sauces, preserved vegetables, and jams produced and beautifully bottled by islanders, and also has a very good selection of local wines. **Known for:** encyclopedic selection of gourmet products and wines from the island; aperitivi on the terrace; ability to ship products worldwide. [$] *Average main: €10* ✉ *Via Napoli 97, Pantelleria* ☎ *336/7556620* 🌐 *www.emporiodelgusto.net* 🕒 *No on-site dining Nov.–Apr.*

★ La Nicchia

$ | **SICILIAN** | Open since 1987, La Nicchia is a Pantelleria institution, occupying an old dammuso and serving typical island dishes made with carefully sourced island ingredients: typically potatoes, cherry tomatoes, capers, almonds, and fresh herbs married with seasonal

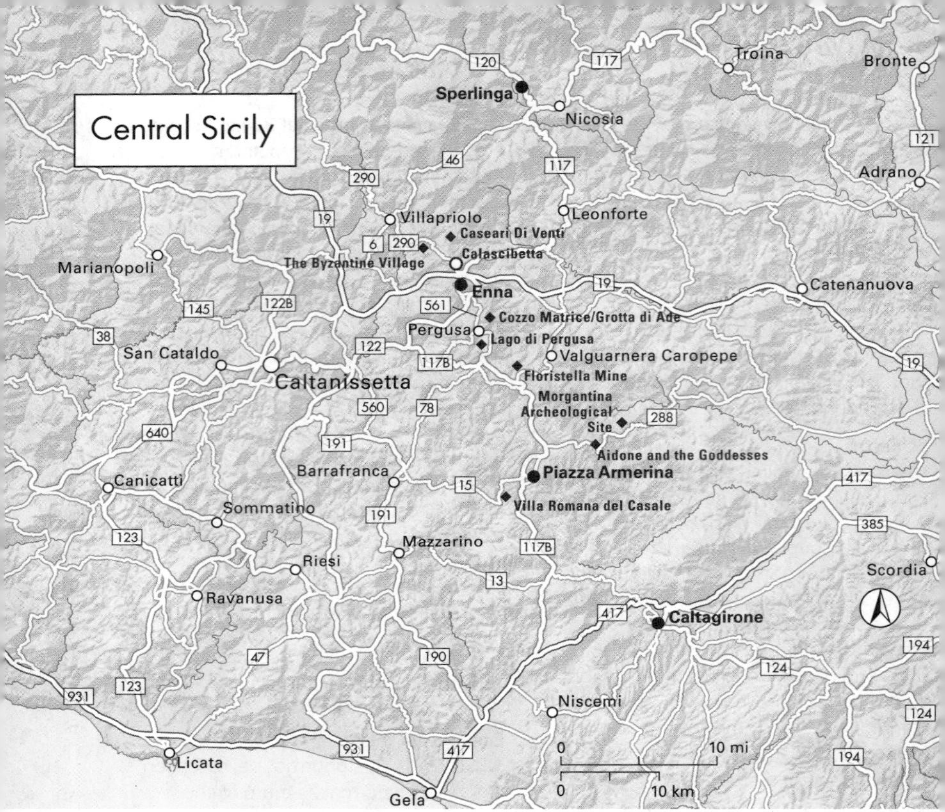

vegetables, fresh fish, and other seafood. In summer there are tables under the lemon trees in a traditional walled Pantescan garden. **Known for:** ravioli stuffed with ricotta and mint; sunset views; perfect taste of Pantelleria cuisine. [$] *Average main: €14* ✉ *Contrada Scauri Basso 11, Pantelleria* ☎ *345/9616763* 🌐 *www.lanicchia.it* ⏲ *Closed late Sept.–late Apr.*

U Friscu

$ | **SICILIAN** | This cool, relaxed café-bar-restaurant is the hub of Scauri life, and has very loyal local following since it stays open all year long. The menu—written on a chalkboard—is strictly seasonal, featuring a nice mixture of traditional Sicilian dishes and more creative dishes, all focusing on island and mainland Sicilian produce and served on blue-rimmed white enamel plates. **Known for:** simple interior and charming outdoor terrace; natural cloudy island wine from island producer Abbazia San Giorgio; platters of mixed cold cuts and cheeses or smoked fish to accompany evening aperitivi. [$] *Average main: €8* ✉ *Via S. Gaetano SNC, Pantelleria* ☎ *0923/1570070* ⏲ *Closed Tues. Oct.–Mar.*

Hotels

Le Ballute

$$ | **B&B/INN** | An instantly beguiling and intimate country resort with just four sensitively restored dammusi, Le Ballute is set among the utter peace and quiet of the village of Mueggen. **Pros:** intimate atmosphere that feels more like staying with friends than being in a hotel; nearly everything served is grown on the land; completely in harmony with the island and its landscape. **Cons:** a long drive from anywhere else; dinner is not served every night; not for guests used to a more traditional hotel. $ *Rooms from: €192* ✉ *Strada per Randazzo, Località Mueggen 8, Pantelleria* ☎ *339/3343975* 🌐 *www.pantellerialeballute.com* 🛏 *4 suites* 🍴 *Free Breakfast.*

Pantelleria Dream

$$ | HOTEL | Home to several individual, purpose-built dammusi, Pantelleria Dream is set in its own grounds above Cala Levante and the Arco dell'Elefante. **Pros:** wonderful sea views; each room has its own terrace; excellent prices, especially in low season. **Cons:** restaurant a little inconsistent; the road below can be busy in high season; no good bars or restaurants in easy walking distance. $ *Rooms from: €200* ✉ *Contrada Tracinio SNC, Pantelleria* ☎ *375/5768541* 🌐 *www.pantelleriadreamresort.it* 🕒 *Closed Nov.–Mar.* 🛏 *46 rooms* 🍴 *Free Breakfast.*

Sicily Luxury Villas

$$ | APARTMENT | This Sicilian villa specialist has good links to Pantelleria, exacting standards, and a choice selection of outstandingly restored dammusi on the island, including the dammuso where Luca Guadagnino's film, *A Bigger Splash,* starring Tilda Swinton and Ralph Fiennes, was filmed. **Pros:** fully catered villas with privacy; all have pools; local flavor in authentic dammusi. **Cons:** car is essential for all; need to make own meals or hire an on-site cook for extra; need to book far in advance. $ *Rooms from: €175* ✉ *Pantelleria* ☎ *335/8228993* 🌐 *www.sicilyluxuryvillas.com* 🛏 *6 villas* 🍴 *No Meals.*

★ **Sikelia**

$$$$ | HOTEL | Walking through the heavy bronze sculpted door of the Sikelia is a step into an utterly luxurious retreat, where time stands still and the stresses and cares of the world evaporate. **Pros:** utter peace and quiet; curated personal service; luxurious rooms and grounds. **Cons:** detached from the rest of the island; no bathtubs; restaurant not up to the same quality of the hotel itself. $ *Rooms from: €500* ✉ *Via Monastero SNC, Pantelleria* ☎ *0923/408120* 🌐 *www.sikeliapantelleria.com* 🕒 *Closed late Sept.–mid-Apr.* 🛏 *20 suites* 🍴 *Free Breakfast.*

U Loco Vecchio

$ | HOUSE | A tastefully restored dammuso with wonderful sea views, U Loco dates back to the 18th century, and is ideal for anyone who wants a comfortable place to stay, cook, eat, and relax, without requiring the luxuries of a hotel or designer villa. **Pros:** comfortable yet stylish; lovely outdoor spaces with sea views; in walking distance of food shops. **Cons:** nearby village is not the most charming; requires a drive to reach the sea; parking can be tricky. $ *Rooms from: €150* ✉ *Via del Garofano 9, Tracino, Pantelleria* ☎ *335/5786450* 🛏 *1 villa* 🍴 *No Meals.*

🍸 Nightlife

Birreria Pantesca

BREWPUBS | Founded in 2017 by a Pantescan jazz pianist and his brother-in-law, Birreria Pantesca is the island's first and only craft brewery. They make five beers, including a summery blond lager, a German-style weiss beer, and Pantipa, an America IPA. More unexpected is the Perla Nera, an Irish stout and—even more interesting—La Zibirra, beer made with a percentage of dried zibibbo grapes. The latest plan is a hemp beer made with legally-grown hemp from Bugeber. Look out for Birreria Pantesca beers in island bars and restaurants or book ahead for tastings in their Pantelleria town brewery (€10). ✉ *Via Francesco Crispi 52, Pantelleria* ☎ *327/8319458* 🌐 *lapanteska.it.*

Did You Know?

Caltagirone's best example of its long ceramic tradition is the 142 individually decorated tiled steps that lead up to Scala Santa Maria del Monte.

Caltagirone

72 km (41 miles) northeast of Licata.

Built over three hills, Caltagirone's functional modern periphery gives way to an imposing, if slightly run-down, Baroque town center. The town is one of the main centers of Sicily's ceramics industry, evidenced by churches and palazzi featuring majolica decorations on their balustrades, domes, windowsills, and facades. The best-known sight is the monumental Scala Santa Maria del Monte.

GETTING HERE AND AROUND
Driving is the best way to get to Caltagirone. Regular buses from Catania stop in the lower town, which is a pleasant stroll from the center. Connections by bus with other towns in Sicily are infrequent, and train connections are even worse.

VISITOR INFORMATION
CONTACT Caltagirone Tourism Office. ⊠ *Via Volta Libertini 3,* ☎ *0933/53809* ⊕ *www. cittadicaltagirone.it.*

Sights

Museo della Ceramica
OTHER MUSEUM | Caltagirone was declared a UNESCO World Heritage site for its ceramics as well as for its numerous Baroque churches. Although the museum offers little information in English about the beautiful items displayed in its many glass cases, you can still see one of Sicily's most extensive ceramics collections, ranging from Neolithic finds to red-figure pottery from 5th-century BC Athens and 18th-century terra-cotta Nativity figures. ⊠ *Via Roma, inside Giardini Pubblici, Caltagirone* ☎ *0933/58418, 0933/58423* ⊕ *www. poloregionalecatania.net/home/caltagirone_museo_it* ⊠ *€4.*

★ Scala Santa Maria del Monte
VIEWPOINT | While you can see examples of Caltagirone's long ceramic tradition throughout the city, the most impressive display can be found in the 142 individually decorated tiled steps of this monumental staircase leading up to the neglected Santa Maria del Monte church. On July 24 (the feast of San Giacomo, the city's patron saint) and again on August 15 (the feast of the Assumption), the stairs are illuminated with candles that form a tapestry design. Months of work go into preparing the 4,000 *coppi,* or cylinders of colored paper, that hold oil lamps—then, at 9:30 pm on the nights of July 24, July 25, August 14, and August 15, a squad of hundreds of youngsters (tourists are welcome to participate) spring into action to light the lamps, so that the staircase flares up all at once. ⊠ *Begins at Piazza Municipio, Caltagirone.*

★ Tenuta Valle delle Ferle
WINERY | This wonderful little winery is run with passion and energy by three young locals. Many wineries run tours, but few make the experience as personal and interesting as the Valle delle Ferle. Call ahead to book a personal tour of the vineyards, where Nero d'Avola and Frappato—the two grapes used to create Cerasuolo di Vittoria wine—are planted together, a traditional practice that has died out as newer joint plantings are not permitted. Guests are encouraged to taste blind, in order to demonstrate how the wines produced in these heavy clay hills are characterized by a far longer life and softer palette than those produced at lower elevations in the sandier soils closer to the sea. Tastings are accompanied by carefully selected local cheeses and salamis, so guests can experience the way the wines work with a salty or fresh cheese, or a fattier or chill-spiked salami. Tours also take in the cantina, where there is often a chance to taste immature wines straight from the tanks. ⊠ *Contrada Valle delle Ferle SNC, Caltagirone* ☎ *328/8359712* ⊕ *www.valledelleferle.it* ⊠ *Tastings from €40.*

 Restaurants

Ristorante Il Dasa

$ | SICILIAN | With a clean white interior and an outdoor terrace in summer, Il Dasa is a popular choice for locals, with something to please everyone. They serve pizzas and gourmet hamburgers alongside delicious and inventive twists on Sicilian favorites. **Known for:** spicy caponata with Sichuan pepper; family-friendly atmosphere; tasty gourmet hamburgers. $ *Average main: €10* ⊠ *Via d'Antona 1, Caltagirone* ☎ *0933/350099* ⊕ *dasaristorante.webnode.it* ◷ *Closed Tues.*

Hotels

⭐ La Vecchia Masseria

$ | RESORT | FAMILY | Set in a pretty stone-built masseria (Sicilian farmstead), you'll find La Vecchia in a beautiful, secluded location that feels as if it is miles from anywhere yet is within easy driving distance of most of central Sicily's points of interest, including Caltagirone, Piazza Armerina, and Enna. **Pros:** beautiful rural location good for exploring central Sicily; excellent and reasonably priced food; spacious rooms and big pool. **Cons:** comfortable and welcoming rather than chic; car is essential; prix-fixe menu for dinner may not suit everyone. $ *Rooms from: €120* ⊠ *CDA Cutuminello KM 68, SS117 bis, San Michele Ganzaria* ⊕ *www.vecchiamasseria.com* ⥲ *33 rooms* ⦿ *Free Breakfast.*

Shopping

Improntibarre Handcraft & Design Laboratory

CERAMICS | Of the numerous ceramics shops in Caltagirone's old center, this one 13 steps up Caltagirone's fabled ceramic staircase is one of the best, selling eye-catching work with a modern aesthetic that is inspired by the town's long artisan tradition. ⊠ *Scala Santa Maria del Monte 5, Caltagirone* ☎ *0933/24427* ⊕ *www.improntabarre.it.*

Piazza Armerina

30 km (18 miles) northwest of Caltagirone.

Crowned by a mighty cathedral, the medieval hill town of Piazza Armerina is a magnificent sight from afar. Up close, the historic center's crumbling yellow-stone architecture with Sicily's trademark bulbous balconies creates quite an effect despite a feeling of dilapidation and abandonment (most locals have moved to the modern suburbs). It is a place to visit rather than stay, with the most appealing lodging options in the surrounding countryside.

Piazza Armerina is most famous for the ancient Roman mosaics down the road at Villa Romana del Casale, but lovers of ancient history may be even more entranced by the huge and rarely visited Greek town of Morgantina and the incredible finds from the site, which once graced the galleries of the Getty museum in Malibu, California.

GETTING HERE AND AROUND

Piazza Armerina is linked to Catania, Enna, and Palermo by regular buses, with less frequent buses also connecting to Caltagirone. There's no train station.

VISITOR INFORMATION

CONTACT Piazza Armerina Tourism Office. ⊠ *Via Monsignore Sturzo 3,* ☎ *338/8524872.*

Sights

⭐ Aidone and the Goddesses

ART MUSEUM | A vast archaeological site in a remote location, Morgantina long provided rich pickings for illegal excavators: when Italian detectives raided an 18th-century villa in Enna belonging to a Sicilian art dealer, they discovered

The Villa Romana del Casale is quite well-preserved and gives a good glimpse into the Roman history of Sicily.

more than 30,000 ancient artifacts, most of them plundered from Morgantina. In 1986, American archaeologist Malcolm Bell, director of the University of Princeton's excavations at Morgantina, established that the heads, hands, and feet of 6th-century BC Greek statues of goddesses from a private collection exhibited at the Getty museum outside of Los Angeles also derived from Morgantina. Identified as Demeter and Persephone, the statues were acroliths, with wooden bodies (long rotted away) and marble extremities. Returned to Sicily in 2009 after a lengthy legal battle, they are currently displayed at a small museum in the village of Aidone, beautifully lit and hauntingly "dressed" by Sicilian fashion designer Marella Ferrara.

Equally powerful is the so-called Aphrodite Getty, or Venus of Malibu, bought by the Getty in 1987 for $18 million on the basis of provenance documents that were later proved to have been forgeries. Returned to Sicily in 2011, the hefty maturity of her body, revealed by wind-blown drapery, has led most scholars to identify her as the Mother Goddess Demeter. Other objects returned from the Getty include the Eupolmos Silver, a set of ritual dining ware, and a head of Hades, identified as belonging to Morgantina when a student working in the site archives discovered a terra-cotta curl of blue-tinted "hair" and suspected that it belonged to a head on display in the Getty. When the curl was sent to the museum, it was found to be a perfect fit, and in 2016 the head was returned to Sicily. ✉ *Largo Torres, Aidone, Piazza Armerina* ☎ *0935/87955* ⊕ *www. prolocoaidone.it* 🎟 *€6.*

★ Morgantina Archeological Site

RUINS | A remote and atmospheric archaeological site, Morgantina is quite beautiful, especially in spring when carpeted with wildflowers. In addition, it attracts few tourists, despite the fact that it hit the international headlines in the 1980s when it was discovered that several priceless but illegally excavated finds from the site had ended up in the

Getty Museum in California. These have now been returned to Sicily and are on permanent exhibition in the small museum in nearby Aidone.

Here, Greeks and indigenous Sikels seem to have lived together in relative peace on a hill named Cittadella until 459 BC, when the Sikel leader Ducetius, determined to free Central Sicily of Greek influence, drove the Greeks out. By the following century, the Greeks had regained control of Sicily, and Syracuse, in the southeast, had become the most powerful city in the Mediterranean. Lying roughly halfway along the road that led from the east to the north coast of Sicily, Morgantina was rebuilt, this time on the hill now known as Serra Orlando. The ancient economy of Morgantina was founded on the cultivation of wheat, so it is little surprise that the dominant cults were those of Demeter, goddess of harvest and fertility, and her daughter Persephone. Even today, the site is surrounded by an ocean of wheat and cereal fields, and asphodels, the flower sacred to Persephone, are abundant.

In 211 BCE, the city was sacked by the Romans and handed as a war prize to Spanish mercenaries, who seem to have paid it little attention; according to the geographer Strabo, by the end of the following century, the city was nowhere to be seen. Excavations began in 1955, led by Princeton University with funding from the King and Queen of Sweden (who became regular summer visitors to the site).

Today you enter the site through what was once a well-to-do residential area where several fine mosaic floors, made with tiny tesserae, can be spotted in the foundations of large houses. Beyond, Plateia A, once the main shopping street, leads into the Agora, or official center of town, with a public fountain, several abandoned lava grain mills, an Archive office (where you can still see holes where documents were pegged to the wall), and a very ingenious system of interlocking terra-cotta water pipes, each with an inspection panel that could be easily lifted to clear blockages. Overlooking the Agora is a small but beautifully preserved theater (where performances are still held in summer), and the stepped benches of the Ekklesiaterion, the meeting place of the town rulers. On the far side of the Agora, you can walk up through ancient kilns to the foundations of what was once the public granary—under Siracusan rule, all citizens had to surrender a quota of the grain they grew as tax. Above are the remains of two elegant private houses, each with a courtyard and mosaic floors. ⌧ *Contrada Morgantina, Aidone, Piazza Armerina* ☎ *0935/87955* ⊕ *www.prolocoaidone.it/ morgantina* ⌸ *€6.*

★ **Villa Romana del Casale** (*Imperial Roman Villa*)

HISTORIC HOME | The exceptionally well-preserved Imperial Roman Villa is thought to have been a hunting lodge of the emperor Maximian (3rd–4th century AD) and offers some of the best mosaics of the Roman world, artfully covering more than 12,000 square feet. The excavations were not begun until 1950, and most of the wall decorations and vaulting have been lost, but the shelter over the site hints at the layout of the original building. The mosaics were probably made by North African artisans; they're similar to those in the Tunis Bardo Museum, in Tunisia. The entrance was through a triumphal arch that led into an atrium surrounded by a portico of columns, which line the way to the *thermae,* or bathhouse. It's colorfully decorated with mosaic nymphs, a Neptune, and enslaved people massaging bathers. The peristyle leads to the main villa, where in the Salone del Circo you look down on mosaics illustrating scenes from the Circus Maximus in Rome. A theme running through many of the mosaics—especially the long hall flanking one entire side of the peristyle courtyard—is the capturing and shipping of wild animals, which may have been a major source of the owner's wealth. Yet the most famous mosaic is the floor depicting 10 girls wearing the ancient equivalent of bikinis, going through what looks like a fairly rigorous set of training exercises. ✉ *SP15, Contrada Casale, 4 km (2½ miles) southwest of Piazza Armerina,* ☎ *0935/680036 ticket office, 0935/687667 office* 🌐 *www.piazzaarmerina.org* 🎫 *€10 (free 1st Sun. of month).*

🍴 Restaurants

★ Al Fogher

$$ | MODERN ITALIAN | This culinary beacon in Sicily's interior features ambitious—and successful—dishes with the creative flair of chef Angelo Treno, whose unforgettable pastas topped with truffles or caviar, for example, offer a decidedly different expression of traditional regional ingredients. The unassuming and elegant dining room is inside an old railway house and is the perfect place to enjoy a bottle from the 500-label wine list; in cold weather, you can cozy up to a fireplace, but the terrace is the place to be in summer. **Known for:** well-thought-out wine list; local ingredients; sophisticated preparations. [$] *Average main: €18* ✉ *Contrada Bellia, near SS117 bis, Aidone exit, about 1 km (½ mile) north of Piazza Cascino, Piazza Armerina* ☎ *0935/684123* 🌐 *alfogher.sicilia.restaurant* 🕒 *No dinner Sun. No lunch Mon.*

★ Trattoria al Goloso

$ | SICILIAN | FAMILY | People from all walks of life, from winemakers and hotel owners to local families, all speak with affection about this comfortable trattoria and its delicious Sicilian dishes. The menu is filled with wonderful pasta dishes with generous use of local ingredients like ricotta, pistachios, and fresh vegetables. **Known for:** probably the best popular trattoria in Piazza Armerina; hearty main dishes of local lamb; pasta dishes featuring local cheeses and fresh vegetables. [$] *Average main: €12* ✉ *Via Garao 4, Piazza Armerina* ☎ *0935/684325* 🕒 *Closed Wed.*

☕ Coffee and Quick Bites

Pasticceria Agora

$ | CAFÉ | FAMILY | One of the very few places to eat in Aidone, this is a simple bar just down the hill from the museum. The welcoming owner makes great coffee and fills cornetti to order with chocolate, custard cream, jam, or ricotta. **Known for:** no-frills but friendly atmosphere; cornetti filled to order; only bar in town open all year. [$] *Average main: €3* ✉ *Via Gianfilippo Calcagno 42, Aïdone, Piazza Armerina* ☎ *0935/87888* 🕒 *Closed Mon.*

★ Pasticceria Diana

$ | BAKERY | Set on a big square in Piazza Armerina that hosts the town's weekly market, this is one of the very few pasticcerias that continue to make their own cornetti—light, delicious, and filled to order with custard cream, ricotta, jam, or chocolate. Other delights include iris (a deep-fried doughnut ball filled with chocolate) and krapfen (a doughnut ring filled with custard cream). **Known for:** great selection of traditional Sicilian cookies; indulgent doughnut-like pastries; cornetti made from scratch straight from the oven. [$] *Average main: €3* ✉ *Piazza Generale Cascino 34, Piazza Armerina* ☎ *0935/682224* 🕒 *Closed Mon.*

Enna

33 km (21 miles) northwest of Piazza Armerina.

Deep in Sicily's interior, the fortress city of Enna (altitude 2,844 feet) commands exceptional views of the surrounding rolling plains, and, in the distance, Mt. Etna. It's the highest provincial capital in Italy and, thanks to its central location, is nicknamed the "Navel of

Head up the tower of Enna's Castello di Lombardia for great views of the surrounding countryside.

Sicily." Virtually unknown by tourists and relatively untouched by industrialization, this lively town charms and prospers in a distinctly old-fashioned Sicilian way. Its surrounding towns and areas are also well worth exploring, and will take you even further off the beaten track.

Due to its historic lack of tourists, the most appealing lodgings are outside town. Those short on time will discover that Enna makes a good stopover for a touch of sightseeing with lunch, as it is right along the autostrada about halfway between Palermo and Catania.

GETTING HERE AND AROUND

Just off the A19 autostrada, Enna is easily accessible by car. With the train station 5 km (3 miles) below the upper town, the most practical public transportation is by the efficient bus service from Palermo or Catania.

TOURS

Terre Rare

ECOTOURISM | FAMILY | Based in Calascibetta, Terre Rare (Rare Lands) is the brainchild of Siculo-American Matteo Platania and Calascibettan herbalist Giorgio Sciocolone. Both are committed to enabling travelers to experience the beauty, tranquility, and culture of the still largely unknown interior that they call home. The emphasis is on life-enhancing experiences rather than history lessons, with the stories and myths of the ancient places that dot the landscape just part of the fabric of everyday life. Experiences include learning to make hyper-local cuisine, foraging for wild greens and medicinal herbs, donkey-led hiking excursions, and even guided mediation. ✉ *Contrada San Leonardo 1, Calascibetta, Enna* ☎ *202/5369609 Matteo Platania, 389/3482944 Giorgio Sciocolone.*

VISITOR INFORMATION

CONTACT Enna Tourism Office. ✉ *Via Roma 413,* ☎ *0932/521243* ⊕ *www.provincia. enna.it.*

👁 Sights

★ Calascibetta and the Byzantine Village

TOWN | FAMILY | Just a 20-minute drive from Enna, occupying a similarly dramatic crag-top, the town of Calascibetta is built atop a honeycomb of caves, most of them hidden from sight as they form the cellars of simple houses. Look closely, however, and you'll spot some houses built straight into the rock, and keep an eye open if anyone opens a garage door as there may well be a cave inside. An entire network of these caves has been uncovered—and is evocatively floodlit at night—on Via Carcere. Head up to Piazza San Pietro, where there are the ruins of a Norman tower and panoramic views. Follow signs from Calascibetta to the "Villaggio Bizantino" and you'll come to a stunning complex of caves overlooking a magnificent valley inhabited (and used as a cemetery) from ancient times until the Byzantine period, when some of the caves were turned into tiny churches. The caves continued to be used by shepherds as shelter for themselves and their flocks until relatively recently. Today, the villaggio is run by volunteers, who will organize guided tours and walks in English, and introduce you to some of the local shepherds and cheesemakers. It's always open Friday and Saturday, but reach out in advance if you want to visit another day. Not far from the villagio (and clearly signposted from Calascibetta), there is another series of caves (not guarded) at Realmese which you can scramble into and explore alone (but be careful as the rock is slippy). From here, a clearly marked track leads back to the village, a walk of just over 3 miles. ✉ *Casa del Maestro, Calascibetta, Enna* ☎ *328/3748553* ⊕ *www.villaggiobizanti-no.it* 🎟 *€8.*

Castello di Lombardia

CASTLE/PALACE | Enna's narrow, winding streets are dominated at one end by the impressive cliff-hanging Castello di Lombardia, rebuilt by Frederick II to create an expansive summer residence on the foundations of an ancient Sicani fort raised more than 2,000 years ago. While there is little to see inside the castle, climb up the tower for great views from the dead center of the island—on a very clear day, you can see to all three coasts. Immediately to the south you see Lake Pergusa (dry, in late summer), now almost swallowed by Enna's sprawling suburbs and the racetrack around its perimeter. According to Greek mythology, this was where Persephone was abducted by Hades. While a prisoner in his underworld realm she ate six pomegranate seeds, and was therefore doomed to spend half of each year there. For the ancients, she emerged at springtime, triggering a display of wildflowers that can still be admired all over Sicily. ✉ *Piazza di Castello di Lombardia, Enna* ⊕ *www.icastelli.it/it/sicilia/enna/enna/ castello-di-lombardia-a-enna* 🎟 *From €3 combined ticket with Torre di Federico II.*

★ Caseari Di Venti

FARM/RANCH | FAMILY | This husband-and-wife team makes artisanal cheese from the rare breed sheep that graze on their fields, and also grows and collects their own saffron to make a distinctive local cheese, Piacentino Ennese, flavored with saffron and studded with black peppercorns. If you want to watch the whole cheese-making process, you will need to book several days ahead and be prepared to rise well before dawn. Otherwise, give them a ring and pop by for a morning bowl of hot ricotta curds with fresh bread. Groups of nine or more can book a lunch or an aperitif. ✉ *Caseari di Venti, Contrada Tresaudo, Calascibetta, Enna* ☎ *338/8454255* ⊕ *www.facebook.com/ CaseariDiVenti* 🎟 *From €10.*

Floristella Mine

MINE | Central Sicily is peppered with sulfur mines, most abandoned since the 1980s, and testaments to one of the most horrific aspects of Sicily's history. Many children ended up working in the mines, most of them orphans, and if they died at work, no time was wasted in burying them. Conditions for men were hardly better—they worked naked underground in 98°F temperatures, and thousands died of respiratory diseases. The Floristella Mine near the town of Valguarnera Caropepe is overlooked by a splendid villa, built, with chilling insensitivity, as a summer residence by the mine's noble owners, and later used as offices. A path leads down to the minehead where a winching mechanism lowered the lift to nine different levels, giving access to tunnels that stretched for over 3 miles. The small ovens where the extracted rock was heated for a week until liquid sulfur emerged are still evident, as are the tracks along which small trains hauled the rock to the surface.

The best way to explore the haunting history of Valguarnera is with local guide Paolo Bellone, who has interviewed many of the miners and their families. He will meet you at the mine, then take you to see the town's powerful and moving private museum collections, which include documentary footage of the sulfur miners at work in the 1960s and rooms furnished to demonstrate everyday living conditions for the poor and the better-off in the 19th and early 20th centuries. Tours culminate with a visit to the Casa Museo, where one woman lived for her entire life, from her birth in 1911 until her death at the age of 89 in 2000, rarely throwing anything away, including her father's Fascist party membership card and a 1922 water bill. The house has been kept as it was found, down to the garlic, herbs, and sugar in the ancient kitchen, cigarette butts in an ashtray, and a packet of American Black Jack chewing gum. ⊠ *Contrada Floristella,*
Enna ☎ *329/7781138* ⊕ *www.enteparco-floristella.it.*

★ Lago di Pergusa, Cozzo Matrice, and the Grotta di Ade

CAVE | FAMILY | According to legend, it was at the huge natural lake of Pergusa that the Greek goddess Persephone was abducted by Hades and taken to live with him in hell. Ringed these days by a motor-racing track and overlooked by modern villas, a less evocative setting for the myth would be hard to imagine. Far more inspiring is the nearby hilltop known as Cozzo Matrice, riddled with caves that have niches carved into their walls for tombs, votive objects, and candles, with 360-degree views stretching as far as Mount Etna and the coast. One of the caves is known as the Grotta di Ade, or Cave of Hades, and would indeed be a far more resonant spot for his abduction of Persephone to the Underworld than the over-exploited lake. ⊠ *Str. Vicinale Monte Salerno 289, Enna* ⊕ *www.ilcampanileenna.it/cozzo-matrice.html.*

Piazza Vittorio Emanuele

PLAZA/SQUARE | In town, head straight for Via Roma, which leads to Piazza Vittorio Emanuele—the center of Enna's shopping scene and evening passeggiata. The attached **Piazza Crispi,** dominated by what used to be the grand old Hotel Belvedere, affords breathtaking panoramas of the hillside and smoking Etna looming in the distance. The bronze fountain in the middle of the piazza is a reproduction of Gian Lorenzo Bernini's famous 17th-century sculpture *The Rape of Persephone,* a depiction of Hades abducting Persephone. ⊠ *Piazza Vittorio Emanuele, Enna.*

Rocca di Cerere (*Rock of Demeter*)

VIEWPOINT | The Greek cult of Demeter, goddess of the harvest, was said to have centered on Enna, where its adherents built a temple atop the Rocca di Cerere, protruding out on one end of town next to the Castello di Lombardia. The spot enjoys spectacular views of the expansive countryside and windswept Sicilian interior. ✉ *Enna* ☎ *93/5504717* 🌐 *www.roccadicereregeopark.it.*

Torre di Federico II

VIEWPOINT | This mysterious octagonal tower stands above the lower part of town and has been celebrated for millennia as marking the exact geometric center of the island—thus the tower's (and the city's) nickname, Umbilicus Siciliae (Navel of Sicily). Climb the 97 steps of the spiral staircase for views over the city and beyond. ✉ *Enna* 🌐 *www.torredienna.it* 🎫 *From €2, combined ticket with Castello di Lombardia.*

🍴 Restaurants

Centrale

$ | **SICILIAN** | Housed in an old palazzo, this casual place has served meals since 1889 and famously keeps a medieval specialty, *controfiletto all'Ennese* (a veal fillet with onions, artichokes, guanciale, and white wine), on the menu, in addition to a range of slightly more modern seasonal dishes. Choose from a decent selection of Sicilian wines to accompany your meal while you take in the large mirrored wall and local pottery. **Known for:** atmospheric outdoor terrace in summer; classic Sicilian dishes and local wines; antipasti buffet. [$] *Average main: €13* ✉ *Piazza VI Dicembre 9, Enna* ☎ *0935/500963* 🌐 *www.ristorantecentrale.net* 🕒 *No lunch Sat. in Sept.–Mar.*

★ **Giovane Hostaria San Marco**

$ | **SICILIAN** | This eatery has minimalist decor and young owners who are committed to local produce—right down to listing all producers on their website—without being scared to experiment. The wine list is really interesting, focusing mainly on small Sicilian bottles, and there is also a good selection of artisan beer. **Known for:** excellent wine list; inventive food; cool atmosphere. [$] *Average main: €12* ✉ *Via Roma 353, Enna* ☎ *0935/1960029* 🌐 *www.hostariasanmarco.it* 🕒 *Closed Tues.*

★ **Umbriaco**

$ | **SICILIAN** | **FAMILY** | This refreshingly atypical spot raises simple Sicilian street food to new gastronomic heights. The exuberant owner, Rosario Umbriaco, has won national prizes for his arancini; try the version with two strata of rice and melted saffron Piacentino Ennese cheese to find out why. **Known for:** unique gourmet arancini using local produce; outside seating in summer; maybe the best cannoli in Sicily. [$] *Average main: €3* ✉ *Viale IV Novembre 11–13, Enna* ☎ *0935/37467* 🕒 *Closed Mon. No lunch.*

🍸 Nightlife

Al Kenisa

GATHERING PLACES | Atmospherically housed in a deconsecrated medieval church with an underground crypt, this self-styled literary café is one of the hubs of Enna's cultural scene, open evenings only for glasses of good wine and artisan spirits while you enjoy its live music and DJ sets. ✉ *Via Roma 481, Enna* ☎ *0935/500972* 🌐 *alkenisa.blogspot.com.*

Sperlinga

44 km (27 miles) north of Enna.

Sperlinga is wedged between the Nebrodi and Madonie mountains and is a fascinating slice of Sicily's interior and one of the island's oldest inhabited areas. The name of the town comes from the Greek word "speloca," which means cavern or cave. A fitting moniker thanks to the town's mysterious cave dwellings carved out of the mountains, a reminder of the area's first inhabitants who chose to live in these stone-carved houses. No one knows the origins of these strange houses, but they are a truly amazing sight to behold.

GETTING HERE AND AROUND

The best way to get to this out-of-the-way town is by car.

Sights

Castello di Sperlinga

CASTLE/PALACE | Sperlinga's Norman castle is built from the foundations of a rocky outcrop. This kind of construction is rare, and since no one can quite figure out its exact origins, it gives the castle an aura of mystery. The castle was used as a cemetery by ancient Sicilians and later became a strategic defense point during the Byzantine period. The castle is at the highest part of the town and offers the best views of the rugged landscape and the rest of Sperlinga. ✉ *Via Castello, Sperlinga* ☎ *0935/643221* 🎟 *€5.*

★ **Le Grotte Bizantine di Sperlinga**

CAVE | Thought to be originally from the Byzantine period (although their exact history is still unknown), these caves carved out of stone can be found in and around town. They were originally used as burial sites, but then eventually became homes, although how or why is still a mystery. They were actually still inhabited up until the 1960s. Today the curious tiny houses are open to the public, and those closest to town have been turned into a museum by the local government. ✉ *Via Principe Amedeo 51, Sperlinga* ☎ *0935/643221* 🌐 *grotte-di-sperlinga.business.site* 🎟 *Free.*

Coffee and Quick Bites

Bar al Castello

$ | **ITALIAN** | This tiny café is located right in the square just below Castello di Sperlinga, and is an excellent place to grab a quick drink, panino, or light meal. **Known for:** convenient location; affordable quick bites; friendly owner. [$] *Average main: €7* ✉ *Largo Castello, Sperlinga* ☎ *338/5483324* 🌐 *www.facebook.com/bar.alcastello.*

Index

Photo Credits

Front Cover: Findlay / Alamy Stock Photo [Description: Taormina village from the Greek Roman amphitheatre ruins, Taormina, Messina district, Sicily, Italy]. **Back cover, from left to right:** Master2/ iStockphoto. Emicristea/Dreamstime. Canbedone/ iStock. **Spine:** Ellesi/ Dreamstime.**Interior, from left to right:** IgorZh/Shutterstock (1). Maurizio De Mattei/ Shutterstock (2-3). **Chapter 1: Experience Sicily:** Master2 (6-7). Nataliia Gr/Dreamstime (8-9). ENIT India (Italian National Tourist Board) (9). Cge2010/Shutterstock (9). Paolo Barone (10). Ivansmuk/ Dreamstime (10). Stefano Termanini/Shutterstock (10). Rolf52/Dreamstime (10). Di Giovanna Winery (11). ENIT India(Italian National Tourist Board) (11). Vvoevale/Dreamstime (11). Lebasi0601/Shutterstock (11). Paolo Barone (12). Dorinmarius/Dreamstime (12). Leoks/Shutterstock (12). Andiz275/Dreamstime (13). Marco mayer/Shutterstock (18). Paolo Barone (18). Julie208/Shutterstock (18). Paolo Barone (19). Angelo Giampiccolo/Shutterstock (19). Marco Ossino/Shutterstock (20). Medvedeva Oxana/Shutterstock (21). Serge Yatunin/ Shutterstock (22). Silky/Shutterstock (22). Frog Dares/Shutterstock (22). Eddy Galeotti/ Shutterstock (22). Fabio Michele Capelli/Shutterstock (23). **Chapter 2: Travel Smart:** Pawel Kowalczyk/Shutterstock (43). **Chapter 3: Palermo and Western Sicily:** Font83/ iStockphoto (45). Altrendo Images/Shutterstock (53). Wojtkowskicezary/Dreamstime (57). Gap di gitto antonino/iStockphoto (61). Vvoevale/Dreamstime (68). Lucarista/Shutterstock (71). Dorinmarius/ Dreamstime (77). Michal Hlavica/Shutterstock (80). Davidedamicoph/ Dreamstime (86). Eug Png/Shutterstock (90). Barmalini/Shutterstock (92). Roman Babakin/Shutterstock (94-95). Lucamato/Shutterstock (97). **Chapter 4: The Tyrrhenian Coast:** Eva Pruchova/Shutterstock (99). Tito Slack/Shutterstock (105). DaLiu/Shutterstock (108). Bloodua/iStockphoto (112-113). EmilyMWilson/iStockphoto (115). Nicola Pulham/Shutterstock (118). Marco Crupi/Shutterstock (121). Marco Crupi/Shutterstock (124). Ol/irg/ Dreamstime (127). Andrew Mayovskyy/ Shutterstock (132). **Chapter 5: The Aeolian Islands:** Andrey Bayda(Bayda127)/Dreamstime (135). Simon Lane / Alamy Stock Photo (141). Peste65/iStockphoto (146-147). Marco Crupi/Shutterstock (148). Cristian Puscasu/Shutterstock (151). Alessio Tricani/Shutterstock (153). Paolo Tralli/Shutterstock (156). Eugenia Struk/Shutterstock (158). **Chapter 6: Mount Etna and Eastern Sicily:** Wiesdie/Shutterstock (161). Aliaksandr Antanovich/Shutterstock (175). Robypangy/Shutterstock (178). Steveblandino/Dreamstime (184-185). Agefotostock / Alamy Stock Photo (189). Rpulham/ Dreamstime (191). ENIT India(Italian National Tourist Board) (195). ENIT India(Italian National Tourist Board) (204). Clara Leonardi/iStockphoto (207**). Chapter 7: Siracusa and the Southeast:** SergeYatunin/ iStockphoto (209). Sbellott/ Shutterstock (217). SergeYatunin/ iStockphoto (221). DarioGiannobile//iStockphoto (224-225). Marcociannarel/ Dreamstime (227). Elifranssens/Dreamstime (232). Andrew Mayovskyy/ Shutterstock (235). S.Leggio/Shutterstock (238). **Chapter 8: Central Sicily and the Mediterranean Coast:** Matteo Bignotti/Shutterstock (241). Pecold/Shutterstock (246). Stefanovalerigm/Dreamstime (250). Emilymwilson/Dreamstime (257). Myzbika/Dreamstime (260). Roberto Lo Savio/Shutterstock (266). Bepsphoto/ Dreamstime (272). Marius Dobilas/ Shutterstock (278). Fabiomichelecapelli/1145452943 (281). Aappp/Shutterstock (284). **About Our Writers:** All photos are courtesy of the writers.

Every effort has been made to trace the copyright holders, and we apologize in advance for any accidental errors. We would be happy to apply the corrections in the following edition of this publication.

Notes

Notes

Notes

Notes

Notes

Notes

Notes

Notes

Fodor's SICILY

Publisher: Stephen Horowitz, *General Manager*

Editorial: Douglas Stallings, *Editorial Director;* Jill Fergus, Amanda Sadlowski, *Senior Editors;* Kayla Becker, Brian Eschrich, Alexis Kelly, *Editors;* Angelique Kennedy-Chavannes, *Assistant Editor*

Design: Tina Malaney, *Director of Design and Production;* Jessica Gonzalez, *Senior Graphic Designer;* Erin Caceres, *Graphic Design Associate*

Production: Jennifer DePrima, *Editorial Production Manager;* Elyse Rozelle, *Senior Production Editor;* Monica White, *Production Editor*

Maps: Rebecca Baer, *Senior Map Editor;* Mark Stroud (Moon Street Cartography), *Cartographer*

Photography: Viviane Teles, *Senior Photo Editor;* Namrata Aggarwal, Neha Gupta, Payal Gupta, Ashok Kumar, *Photo Editors;* Eddie Aldrete, *Photo Production Intern;* Kadeem McPherson, *Photo Production Associate Intern*

Business and Operations: Chuck Hoover, *Chief Marketing Officer;* Robert Ames, *Group General Manager;* Devin Duckworth, *Director of Print Publishing*

Public Relations and Marketing: Joe Ewaskiw, *Senior Director of Communications and Public Relations*

Fodors.com: Jeremy Tarr, *Editorial Director;* Rachael Levitt, *Managing Editor*

Technology: Jon Atkinson, *Director of Technology;* Rudresh Teotia, *Lead Developer*

Writers: Robert Andrews, Ros Belford, Jennifer V. Cole, Rochelle Del Borrello, Craig McKnight

Editor: Amanda Sadlowski

Production Editor: Elyse Rozelle

1st Edition

ISBN 978-1-64097-527-9

ISSN 2833-1117

All details in this book are based on information supplied to us at press time. Always confirm information when it matters, especially if you're making a detour to visit a specific place. Fodor's expressly disclaims any liability, loss, or risk, personal or otherwise, that is incurred as a consequence of the use of any of the contents of this book.

SPECIAL SALES
This book is available at special discounts for bulk purchases for sales promotions or premiums. For more information, e-mail SpecialMarkets@fodors.com.

PRINTED IN CANADA

10 9 8 7 6 5 4 3 2 1

About Our Writers

Born of Sicilian stock, **Robert Andrews** has been living and working in various parts of Italy for most of his adult life. He has written articles and guidebooks on this multifaceted peninsula, and provides travel consultancy services as well as leading individual and small-group tours in Sicily and Sardinia. For this edition, Robert wrote the Experience, Travel Smart, and Palermo and Western Sicily chapters.

Ros Belford lived full-time in Sicily for twelve years, raising her daughters on the Aeolian island of Salina. She now spends her time between Sicily, Florence, and her home in Cambridge, England, and is the author of several guidebooks to Italy, Mediterranean Europe, and Cornwall—several of which have won prizes. Ros lectures on the gastronomic culture of Sicily and has written articles and created radio programs on travel and food for the BBC, *Vogue, Conde Nast Traveller,* and *National Geographic Traveler;* she's also the *Telegraph's* luxury hotel expert for Cornwall and Sicily. She wrote the Central Sicily and the Mediterranean Coast chapter this guide, and is currently trying to find a way to spend more of her life on the island of Pantelleria.

Mississippi-born **Jennifer V. Cole** is a freelance writer and editor. Her work appears in *Food & Wine, Garden & Gun,* Eater, *Fast Company, Coastal Living, Travel + Leisure, Esquire, Punch, Modern Farmer,* and more. She was formerly Deputy Editor of *Southern Living,* where she covered the South for nearly a decade. After going freelance, she circumnavigated the globe for about two years, and these days she calls Sicily home. Jennifer wrote the Aeolian Islands and Mount Etna and Eastern Sicily chapters.

Rochelle Del Borrello is an Italian-Australian writer from Perth, Western Australia. Rochelle has lived in Sicily since 2002 and has written extensively about the island. She is currently working on a travel memoir entitled *Sicilian Descent* that explores her journey as an expat in Sicily and her own family's connection to this unique part of Italy. Rochelle regularly publishes her thoughts and musings about life and travels on her blog Sicily Inside and Out (⊕ *www.sicilyinsideandout.com*). She wrote the Tyrrhenian Coast chapter of this book.

Craig McKnight was originally born in northeast England, and has had a love of Italy since childhood, when he spent many happy holidays there. After a change of career, he is now based as a teacher in Reggio Calabria, which gives him the time to explore Sicily and Calabria, and to write and blog about both. Craig wrote the Siracusa and the Southeast chapter for this edition.